Asian American Women

Asian American Women
The *Frontiers* Reader

EDITED BY
LINDA TRINH VÕ AND
MARIAN SCIACHITANO
WITH SUSAN H. ARMITAGE
PATRICIA HART, AND
KAREN WEATHERMON

University of Nebraska Press, Lincoln and London

Library of Congress Catalog-
ing-in-Publication Data
Asian American women : the
Frontiers reader / edited by
Linda Trinh Vo and Marian
Sciachitano with Susan H.
Armitage, Patricia Hart, and
Karen Weathermon. p. cm.
Essays originally published in
Frontiers : a journal of
women's studies. Includes
bibliographical references
and index.
ISBN 0-8032-9627-4
(pbk. : alk. paper)
1. Asian American women –
History.   2. Asian American
women – Social conditions.
3. Asian Americans – Ethnic
identity.   4. Women
immigrants – United States –
Social conditions.
5. Transnationalism.
6. United States – Relations –
Asia.   7. Asia – Relations –
United States.
I. Vo, Linda Trinh, 1964–
II. Sciachitano, Marian, 1962–
III. Frontiers (Boulder,
Colo.) E184.A75A8425 2004
305.48'895073–dc22
2003056523

We dedicate this collection to our students, who over the years have inspired, challenged, and educated us with their creativity, energy, and courage – you remind all of us that there are no boundaries.

Contents

Introduction

Reimagining Asian American Women's Experiences

Asian American Women: The "Frontiers" Reader brings together a sampling of landmark scholarship about Asian American women that originally appeared in *Frontiers: A Journal of Women Studies.* The collection originated from our role as guest coeditors of a special issue on Asian American women for this journal.[1] We chose six essays from that issue and selected nine more essays previously published in the journal to complement the collection. Our selections were made based on the important impact the essays made across disciplinary fields of study and their relevancy today. For over twenty-five years, *Frontiers* has continually sought to publish pieces on Asian American women by established and emerging scholars, and as a result has played an instrumental role in contributing to the literature in Asian American studies, women's studies, American studies, and ethnic studies.

Since its inception in 1975, *Frontiers* has served, as its mission statement explains, as a critical site for interdisciplinary, feminist, and multicultural scholarship that crosses and reexamines boundaries, and explores the diversity of women's lives as shaped by race, ethnicity, class, sexual orientation, and region. As early as 1977 and long before it was academically in vogue to talk about transnational feminism, let alone address the dynamics of globalization and its impact on women, *Frontiers* published such pieces as Matsui Yayori's "Sexual Slavery in Korea" and Diana E. H. Russell's "Report on the International Tribunal on Crimes against Women."[2] In the spirit of the intent of the journal, the chapters in this collection reveal the lived experiences and struggles of Asian American women within a geopolitical, economic, cultural, and historical context. Crucial to this endeavor is broadening our critical understanding of Asian American women's resistance to the forces of racism, patriarchy, militarism, cultural imperialism, neocolonialism, and narrow forms of nationalism. Our cover photograph, titled *Make Me* (1989) by Yong Soon Min, a Korean American artist who emigrated to the United States in 1960, features four provocative photographic self images that are somewhat reminiscent of today's passport photos; that is, with the exception of the words "assimilated alien," "exotic emigrant," "model minority," and "objectified other" superimposed on the artist's face.[3] Min's four-part photo ensemble critically captures, in nuanced form, the cultural and political significance of disconnections, invisibilities, memories, marginalizations, migrations, objectifications, oppositions, and silences that resonate with the themes interwoven in this collection.

Elaine Kim and Lisa Lowe so clearly state, "As the formation of Asian Americans within the United States is placed in dialectical relation to international histories and locations, the objects and methods of neither Asian American studies nor Asian studies can remain the same."[4] This colliding or connecting of Asian area studies and American ethnic studies is reconfiguring these fields; however, these engagements are still uneven and inconsistent, given that the political and philosophical trajectories of the fields differ significantly. We are connected to Asia for personal, economic, political, and sociohistorical reasons.[5] For example, our families or relatives may still live in Asia; transnational corporate capitalism participates in the ongoing racialization and feminization of Asian and Asian American women and girls, treating them as interchangeable, low-wage laborers throughout the Pacific; and others remind us we "belong" over "there" without regard to how many generations we have been "here." In fact, the race, gender, class, and sexual boundaries, or "frontiers" of our lives, have always been transnational, originally forced on us when Asian American families were divided by racist, sexist, and orientalist U.S. immigration policies and when first-generation immigrants were categorized as "aliens ineligible for U.S. citizenship."[6]

This anthology reflects the changing immigration patterns and ethnic demographics of the Asian American population over the decades, as well as transformative regional concentrations. In our early history, Asian American female immigrants were rare, and those who were admitted were classified as prostitutes, merchant's wives, or picture brides, and perceived as secondary to the men who immigrated. Since the passing of the 1965 Immigration Act there has been a feminization of Asian immigration; Asian women are now entering this country on their own or as the primary immigrant sponsor of their relatives.[7] As this collection reveals, Asian immigrant women come to this country as mothers, wives, daughters, and sisters to reunite with family members, as sweatshop and domestic workers to fulfill labor needs, and as students, war brides, and refugees. Asian immigrant women have also emerged over the decades as "sweatshop warriors," student activists, artists, writers, grassroots organizers, researchers, and public intellectuals. These trajectories create substantially different lived experiences and struggles, and differ according to each woman's ethnic and racial background, sexual orientation, class and occupational position, generational experience, cultural practices, religious values, and political ideologies.

HISTORICAL MOMENTS AND (RE)COLLECTIONS

Inspired by the courageous and perilous journeys of Asian immigrant women, scholars have challenged our absence from both the American and Asian American historical imagination. For example, while there has been acknowledgment of the thousands of Chinese "paper sons" who at the turn of the nineteenth century purchased a paper identity so that they could transgress the various racial exclusion acts that would detain them at the Angel Island immigration center, there has been very limited recognition to date of the many Chinese "paper daughters" who also struggled to transgress those same racial exclusion acts. With the notable exception of Genny Lim's *Paper Angels,* a play that specifically addresses the daily struggles of both Chinese immigrant men and women detained at Angel Island; a coedited collection of Angel Island poetry; and, more recently, M. Elaine Mar's memoir, *Paper Daughter,* which was inspired by her grandfather who lived and died as a "paper son" in the United States, Asian American studies has been slow to critically understand the ways in which Asian immigrant women have historically resisted the intersections of racism, patriarchy, and imperialism.[8]

We begin our collection with two chapters by Judy Yung that disrupt these masculinist frames and that span twenty years of her historical scholarship on the lived struggles of nineteenth-century Chinese immigrant women. The first, originally published in 1977, is about the experiences of Chinese immigrant women who came through Angel Island, and the second, published in 1997, is the reconstruction of the life of a fiercely independent and unconventional Chinese American woman, Flora Belle Jan, who struggled to define her own identity and goals. These chapters are representative of Yung's groundbreaking books, *Unbound Feet: A Social History of Chinese Women in San Francisco,* and the companion volume, *Unbound Voices: A*

Documentary History of Chinese Women in San Francisco, which have established her as a preeminent historical scholar on Chinese women in America, the wives of Chinese American men who remained in China, and their second-generation Chinese American daughters.[9] In the first chapter, Yung conveys the physical conditions the women faced, as well as their emotional state, while being detained for processing and interrogation at the Immigration Station at Angel Island, a historical site for Asian immigration history. The second chapter reveals the dreams and hopes of a second-generation Chinese American woman who refused to accept the limiting cultural, political, and economic conventions imposed on her. Rather than reading her narrative as a tragic story of a woman eventually overcome by traditional gender roles and racism, Yung reconstructs the life of a complex woman who was "a noteworthy social critic, a talented writer, and a feminist ahead of her time."

We follow with two pioneering chapters by another historian, Valerie Matsumoto, who documents the lives of the Nisei, or second-generation Japanese Americans, in the prewar and World War II eras. The first is considered a classic work on Japanese American women's experiences in the internment camps during World War II, which was originally published in 1984. At the time, Matsumoto was writing her dissertation on the lives of three generations of women and men in a Japanese American farming community in California, a project that became the basis for her book *Framing the Home Place: A Japanese American Community in California, 1919–1982* and established her as a leading scholar in the field.[10] Matsumoto's first chapter presents the physical and "spiritual" hardships that Japanese American women faced during this trying period as well as the unexpected ways in which the experience altered gender roles, family life, and occupational opportunities. Matsumoto's second chapter, originally published in 1991, examines how Nisei women writers of the 1930s, particularly columnist Mary Oyama, who wrote under the name Deirdre, attempted to create their own sense of ethnic culture, to find role models, and to contend with the gender roles defined for them against a backdrop of racial discrimination. As Matsumoto states, Deirdre's responsibility was "to provide Nisei with guidelines to proper behavior that would enable them to navigate safely the social conventions of the white world as well as meet the standards of their parents and the Japanese-American community." In addition, Matsumoto demonstrates how writers of this period were certainly progressive in dealing with the complexities of intergenerational issues, along with other sensitive topics such as multiethnic and multiracial relationships.[11]

Complementing Matsumoto's chapters is Leslie Ito's contribution on Japanese American women and the student relocation movement.[12] While much of the focus on the Nisei has been on the men who served in the U.S. military, many of whom were drafted directly from the internment camps, or on the "no-no" boys, who resisted the draft, young women's experiences have been examined only recently. Japanese American women were permitted to leave the camps to work in the factories, to be employed as domestic servants, and also to pursue higher education. Ito's essay examines the World War II era and the postwar years through the lenses of Japanese American college women who had much more to worry about than their majors. They sought to balance their allegiances to America while also affirming their racial identity at a time when it was extremely unpopular, even dangerous, to display one's ethnicity or to be critical of the government's policy of interning its citizens. Students were quite cognizant of being positioned as "ambassadors of goodwill" for their community. Being given this responsibility to prove that Japanese Americans could be "reintegrated" into society made them mature beyond their years. This chapter examines how they valiantly managed their lives and pursued their dreams, even beyond the war years, within the social and political confinements of the time.

Continuing this theme, the next set of chapters focuses on the historical connection between U.S. imperialism and militarism in Asia and its impact on gender relations. As a result of U.S. imperialist aggression in Asia and the Pacific during World War II, the Korean War, and the Vietnam War, the U.S. military has had a continuing presence throughout Asia with its colonization of the Philippines and establishment of military bases in Taiwan, Thailand, South Korea, and Japan.[13] This presence has resulted in sexual relations, and in some cases marriages, between Asian women and American military personnel. During World War II, Asian women married Asian American men, and many war brides from this era were Chinese women who married Chinese American soldiers. During the Korean and Vietnam Wars, more war brides entered this country, and many of them were married to non–Asian Americans. These women, who constituted the majority of immigrants during these decades, also helped to shape the immigration patterns of Asian American communities because many of them sponsored additional family members, a provision permitted with the Immigration Act of 1965. Although some of these international, transracial unions have been blissful, enduring relations, others have been marked by cultural, linguistic, social, and religious differences. The husbands have been stationed at military bases throughout the country, and as a result many of these women have been isolated from ethnic communities or even other ethnic war brides who could provide them with a support system.

In her groundbreaking project, Debbie Storrs reveals the complexities of interviewing her own mother and analyzing her life experiences as a Japanese American war bride. Her work contributes to the growing but still limited literature on the lives of Asian war brides and how their experiences were shaped by U.S. militarization, stereotypes of Asian women, and patriarchy.[14] Rather than casting her mother merely as a victim, she analyzes how her mother was a social agent in improving her life circumstances and how she found ways to resist the affronts she faced. By studying those whose lives are intimately intertwined with her own, Storrs also challenges traditional methodological practices that argue for researchers to remain distanced and neutral in order for a study to be objective and scientifically valid. As the daughter, she uses her intimate connections and knowledge to enrich the research project and to provide a nuanced, textured analysis of her mother's survival story. Storrs's mother read the material and gave her daughter suggestions for revisions; she also selected the two photographs that accompany the chapter.

The next chapter, by Suzan Ruth Travis-Robyns, reconstructs the life of Nguyen Ngoc Xuan, a Vietnamese American woman of ethnic Chinese ancestry, within the context of the Vietnam War and its aftermath.[15] Born out of rape, as a child she was beaten by her adoptive father, forced to sell food at the marketplace, and worked as a prostitute for American soldiers. In many ways, her story represents the lives of many Vietnamese women who were not ideologically invested in or supportive of the war, but were caught in its web. Merely trying to survive at a time when their war-torn country faced high inflation and agricultural displacement, these women survived by working in war-spawned industries such as prostitution. Even though she is a war bride, Xuan's experiences are typical of many Southeast Asian women refugees, the majority of whom arrived in the post-1975 period and worked diligently to support their families and to adapt culturally and linguistically in a foreign and sometimes hostile country. Unfortunately, many of their wounds, physical and mental, particularly post-traumatic stress disorder (PTSD), have not been treated because the U.S. government, which could provide funds for medical services, does not recognize them as "veterans" and because the male leadership in the ethnic communities has been unable to publically acknowledge the brutality of war on women. Xuan's story of coming to terms with her suffering and finding creative venues to heal herself and her community is comparable to Le Ly Hayslip's experience as depicted in her coauthored autobiographies and in Oliver Stone's movie based on her life.[16] Thus, this chapter is one of many beginnings to give voice to the experiences of Southeast Asian American women who continue to struggle with the consequences of war, to contend with the traumas of dislocation, and to combat silences from the larger society as well as from within their own communities.

LABOR AND GLOBAL CAPITALISM

Global capitalism, imperialism, and militarism have long shaped the contradictory subject-positions of Asian American women as both "desiring subjects" and "working subjects." Our exoticized/eroticized bodies have been sold in the transnational sex industry, our nimble fingers have been sought for various sweatshop factories located here or in export processing zones, and our ability to serve as domestic workers has made us particularly favored in the health and child care professions and in service sector occupations. Although it was our men's labor that was originally sought after, Asian American women's labor has been essential to the survival of our families and our communities, and now to the global economy. Historically, Chinese and Japanese women were forced into prostitution on the mainland and in Hawaii to serve the needs of U.S. venture capitalists who wanted to extract the most labor from Asian males at the lowest possible cost in order to shore up the developing U.S. capitalist economy.[17] United States immigration policies and laws did not allow men to bring their partners or families, although they did permit (at least initially) Asian women who emigrated to be sold into a system of enslaved prostitution in order to pacify the heterosexual Asian male workforce.[18]

As Pamela Thoma's chapter reveals, the commodification of our bodies is a worldwide phenomenon that supports global capitalism, imperialism, and militarism. The historic "Comfort Women of World War II" conference held at Georgetown University from September 30 to October 2, 1996, brought international attention to the Imperial Japanese government's complicit involvement in colonial sexual slavery, which had been systematically erased from national history and public memory. During World War II, when the Japanese military colonized Korea, Korean "comfort women" endured state-sponsored violence – torture, medical experimentation, mutilation, rape, and murder – to appease the men serving the military nation-state and its imperialist quest.[19] After filing a landmark lawsuit against Japan, three survivors who had been silenced by shame or by state denials for over fifty years were finally given the opportunity to provide testimonies about the unspeakable physical and emotional violence they suffered. The conference was a transformative moment for Asian and Asian American women. This event is part of ongoing international movements to bring attention to atrocities committed against Asian women during wartime and to make the responsible governments and nations admit to their crimes against humanity and provide compensation for hundreds of former "comfort women" from China, Indonesia, Korea, Taiwan, the Philippines, and other nations.[20]

The trafficking of Asian women as commodities in the global sex trade continues because of U.S. military presence in Asia, the sex-tour industry in Asia, and the Asian mail-order bride business.[21] The construction of Asian women as hyperfeminine erotic exotics who willingly and passively service male desires has contributed to these thriving sex industries. These lucrative businesses rely on Asian girls and women who are desperately trying to escape conditions of poverty often created by capitalist expansion in Asia. The U.S. efforts to exert political and economic control in Asia are evident in its continuing military presence. Military bases in South Korea, Okinawa, and other parts of Asia encourage prostitution to service the military personnel, and local power brokers look the other way because these bases are crucial to the survival of their economy.[22] Also profiting from these degrading images of Asian women is the U.S. tourist industry, which offers sex tours in Asia.[23] In addition, the mail-order bride business, in which men (mainly American men), can select "oriental" brides through catalogs or through the Internet, also flourishes.[24] Activist organizations like General Assembly Binding Women for Reform, Integrity, Equality, Leadership, and Action (GABRIELA) continue to work to stop the degradation and sexual exploitation of Asian women; however, it has been a struggle because local governments look the other way and victims understandably hesitate to come forward.

Asian Americans have traditionally worked in low-wage occupations, and this has affected the treatment they have received. The position of Asian women in the global economy, as well as Asian American women in the U.S. economy, has shifted significantly in the era marked by America's deindustrialization and the establishment of "export processing zones" or "free trade zones." This gendered and racialized capitalist development has increased the involvement of "Third World" women and girls in the global labor force. In fact, the reliance on low-wage female laborers has attracted foreign investments in Asia, particularly those of U.S. corporations and transnational corporations. Thus, the restructuring of global capitalism permits "mixed production" and "flexible accumulation," allowing multinational corporations to maximize profits and ultimately to exploit workers who compete on a global scale for employment. Because of this transnational flow of capital and international division of labor, these multinational corporations can obtain the most inexpensive labor force by recruiting workers in Asia, the Caribbean, and Latin America, workers who compete with immigrant women in the United States.[25] The labor of immigrant women is a highly prized commodity that is perceived to be easily exploitable because of their gendered, racialized, and citizenship status. These women are preferred in the nonunionized garment or apparel industries, in electronics assembly work, and in the service-sector economy because they are perceived to be docile, hardworking employees who are willing to labor for lower wages or in substandard working conditions.[26] Organizations such as Asian Immigrant Women Advocates, based in the San Francisco Bay area, lead the campaign to organize and unionize workers and educate the general public about the abusive conditions that persist.[27]

Charlene Tung makes powerfully visible the largely invisible emotional and physical labor of Filipina domestic workers in the live-in home health caregiving industry in southern California, a growing employer of transnational migrant women. As life expectancy for Americans increases, occupations related to elderly care and services will increase, particularly in hospitals, retirement centers, and private homes. Asian women, many of whom leave their children and families behind in their homeland, are seen as model workers and are being recruited to fill these jobs. The remittances that these transnational migrant workers send to their families in their homelands, in effect, support these economies and help pay off their national debts.[28] Both the home country and the host country benefit from the employment of these transmigrant women abroad; therefore, neither government wants to be accountable for the exploitation or abuses that do occur in this loosely monitored system.[29] United States colonial and neocolonial relations with the Philippines makes it an "ideal" source of "cheap labor," since it is assumed the workers will have some English language skills and Americanized educational training. Employers also prefer Filipinas because their immigrant status makes them less likely to complain about working conditions and easier to exploit, for example by paying them lower wages than their American counterparts.[30]

PEDAGOGY AND VOICE

Thirty years ago we were hardly a physical presence on college campuses because of racialized, gendered exclusions, and our lives were absent from the curriculum. The scholarship introduced in the early Asian American studies courses pivoted around heterosexual men, and women were seen as accessories in terms of their economic and community contributions. Crucial to the reformulation of Asian American studies has been an epistemological critique of the practice of centering our histories around men.[31] These contestations to this exclusionary knowledge continue to force scholars and the academy to reimagine the way we theorize and teach Asian American history, Asian American women's history, and Asian American gender and sexual relations.[32] The University of California, Berkeley, was the first to offer a course on Asian American women, in 1970, and now is joined by public and private institutions across the country.[33] In addition to demanding courses on Asian American women in the academy, we now encourage the hiring of faculty who can serve as mentors, create reading groups, form academic programs, establish on-campus student publications, develop admissions and retention services, and organize workshops, film series, and conferences.[34] While our representation in the academy varies across institutions, in the power hierarchy of the ivory tower, we are still rarely seen in critical decision-making positions.[35]

The formulation and reformulations of Asian American studies would certainly not be where they are today if not for the historical legacy of the Civil Rights movement; black, brown, red, and yellow power movements; and antiwar movements of the 1960s and early 1970s. Judy Chu's chapter provides an invaluable case study of team teaching one of the earliest course offerings of Asian American women's studies at the University of California, Los Angeles, in 1973.[36] She candidly discusses the conflicts and contradictions Asian American women experienced both within these movements and in the women's studies classroom, conflicts resulting from institutionalized and internalized sexism and racism. Chu also provides an important reminder about the legacy of Asian American student activists at UCLA, University of California, Berkeley, and San Francisco State University, who were among the first to establish consciousness-raising groups that created safe spaces for Asian American women to openly address questions as political and community organizers. These groups served as the impetus for the first course offerings of Asian American women's studies. These early classes, which incorporated "collectivity, consciousness-raising, and a community orientation," helped Asian American women develop as leaders, both inside and outside the academy. Chu's chapter is important to understanding the role of Asian American women within the history of the Asian American student movement and the institutionalization of Asian American studies and women's studies.

The landmark book *Asian Women,* published in 1971 by a group of Asian American women who met at University of California, Berkeley, incorporated feminist discourse into Asian American studies.[37] Collections on Asian American women have been crucial to introducing the diversity of our lives.[38] Pathbreaking monographs about ethnic women – such as Evelyn Nakano Glenn's *Issei, Nisei, War Bride,* about Japanese American women, Judy Yung's *Unbound Feet,* about Chinese American women, and Nazli Kibria's *Family Tightrope,* on Vietnamese American women – have broadened this base of knowledge.[39] Scholars such as Elaine Kim, King-Kok Cheung, Amy Ling, Wendy Ho, Sau-Ling Wong, Lisa Lowe, Traise Yamamoto, Rachel Lee, Leslie Bow, and Mari Matsuda have transformed the field of Asian American literary and cultural criticism.[40]

Our presence and theoretical perspectives transformed and challenged the academy, yet we are still met with resistance.[41] Piya Chatterjee's insightful chapter critically reflects on how our positions and locations as women of color affect our experiences in American universities. She addresses the complex pedagogical dilemma many of us encounter when we enter the classroom: it is not a question of whether or not our gender, race, ethnicity, nationality, citizenship, class, and sexuality will be read by our students, it is a matter of how they will be (mis)interpreted. As a South Asian immigrant woman, she explains in ethnographic form how she incorporates the personal as a pedagogic tool, inverts the scripts of "gendered otherness" imposed on her, and contends with the students' level of indifference and resistance. Even within the diversity of the southern California region, where it is certainly feasible to have greater cross-racial interactions than in other, seemingly homogeneous, communities, it is still possible to live racially and economically segregated lives. Students arrive in our classes indoctrinated with distortions of the racial "other," both local and global, and live in a society embedded with cultural hierarchies. For Chatterjee, engagement, dialogue, and negotiation are essential in this self-reflective, pedagogic process.[42] As academic women of Asian ancestry, we not only encounter racialized, gendered skepticism and scrutiny by the students in our classrooms, but by our colleagues as well.

Recognizing the importance of establishing intellectual links and promoting ongoing dialogues between women from varying racial back-grounds, *Frontiers* once again broke ground in the mid-nineties by pub-lishing a critically thoughtful online conversation that grew out of a panel presented at the 1995 American Studies Association meeting among five women faculty, including two Asian Americans, who teach courses on a diverse genre of American ethnic autobiographies.[43] Similar to the peda-gogical challenges raised in Piya Chatterjee's essay, Shelli B. Fowler, Tiffany Ana López, Kate Shanley, Caroline Chung Simpson, and Traise Yamamoto provide us with an engaging conversation on the self-reflective act of teach-ing and reading that critically examines the complex relationship between the text, the teacher, and her students. Constructing critical pedagogy as "performance," they share how they negotiate their own subject-positions, in which assumptions are made of their racialized bodies in the classroom. They also share their approaches in teaching students from a diversity of backgrounds in terms of geography, sexuality, economics, generation, and personal history, and present strategic interventions to contend with simple misreadings of ethnic autobiographies and inappropriate use of essentialist analogies. These five women bring their own perspective and experiences into the dialogue, and we found this exchange invaluable for its incisive criticism of the academy as well as its contribution to the larger debates on the literary canon, the production of knowledge, and epistemological frameworks.

Through these transformations in the curriculum, important intellectual links between Asian American studies and women's studies have been cre-ated; however, on a practical level these dialogues have often been tenuous. Race is often not centrally included in the dialogue within the U.S. feminist movement, and when race is included it is treated as monolithically "black," so Asian American women are often remarginalized. These exclusions and tokenizations have produced vigorous debates and protests, most evident in the establishment of alternative Asian American feminist organizations that reenvision the intersections of race, class, gender, and sexuality in the-ory and praxis.[44] Asian American women's activism and resistance in the Civil Rights and post–Civil Rights eras have challenged us to critique the traditional hierarchies that have shaped our communities. In forging bonds of cross-racial sisterhoods and developing feminist oppositional discourses, we have also been accused of abandoning our Asian American brothers in the struggle against racism.[45] Although we have made gains in grassroots organizing and mainstream politics, there is still a need for us to continue our politicization and struggles against injustices, both local and global.[46]

REPRESENTATIONS AND RESISTANCES

The colonial imagination, which is perpetuated by the mainstream media and imperialist nostalgia, has historically limited Asian American women to racialized and sexualized representations as evil dragon ladies, exotic, erotic lotus blossoms, whores with hearts of gold, submissive mail-order brides, and compliant model minorities. Given the globalization of the media and the transnational currency of U.S. popular culture, we are either culturally invisible, marginally visible, or spectacularly visible in Hollywood representations.[47] As Asian American cultural producers – artists, poets, writers, musicians, photographers, filmmakers, and cultural critics – we grapple with how to construct a new politics of representing ourselves, not only to resist ongoing hegemonic fantasies, but also to challenge and counter the damaging internalized sexist, racist, classist, and homophobic representations created by the colonized imaginations of our "own" ethnic communities. These representations affect our social, economic, political, and psychic survival. At the same time, we can now celebrate the "critical mass" of classic and contemporary literary and cultural productions by Asian American women that clearly provide both a testament to our will to survive the imperialist forces of oppression and an inspiration for the next generation of cultural producers.[48]

Rather than using a skewed and simplistic approach that solely blames Asian cultural traditions, it is more appropriate to accept that both Western and Asian patriarchy may vary yet both work to oppress Asian and Asian American women. Cultural productions cross national borders as North American culture is transmitted globally, even to remote Asian villages. Asian cultural forms can be found in the United States via broadcasts on international television channels or videotapes available at ethnic video shops. The American cooptation of Asian female images, even in recycled form, has had an impact on Asian American women. Notable recently is the popularity of the book *Memoirs of a Geisha,* by Arthur S. Golden, possibly to be made into a Hollywood movie; the reprint of *Geisha* by Liza Dalby; and pop icon Madonna's brief but symbolic cultural appropriation of the geisha image.[49] Would the public be so receptive if Madonna chose to don the blackface popularized in American minstrel shows or to adopt the gendered "black Mammy" image? As Traise Yamamoto cautions, "Into the disjuncture between visual inclusion and continued structural exclusion, the sexualization of Asian American women functions simultaneously in terms of longstanding orientalist traditions and newer proclamations of multicultural diversity, joined through the mechanism of visual fetishization."[50] In this era of transnational cultural productions and the regime of commodity capitalism, there are possibilities for intervention to disrupt the orientalist hegemony and assert our identities and pleasures on our own terms.[51]

Aki Uchida's feminist literary analysis of Lydia Minatoya's 1993 autobiographical narrative *Talking to High Monks in the Snow* addresses the complexities as well as limitations around constructing a new ethnic identity, particularly for Japanese American women.[52] The renewed popularity of Asian American women's autobiographies in the late eighties and throughout the nineties, such as Le Ly Hayslip's *When Heaven and Earth Changed Places: A Vietnamese Woman's Journey from War to Peace* (1989), Mary Paik Lee's *Quiet Odyssey: A Pioneer Korean Woman in America* (1990), Meena Alexander's *Fault Lines* (1993), Wakako Yamauchi's *Songs My Mother Taught Me: Stories, Plays, and Memoirs* (1994), Kyoko Mori's *A Dream of Water: A Memoir* (1995), Shirley Geok-lin Lim's *Among the White Moon Faces: An Asian-American Memoir of Homelands* (1996), Kyoko Mori's *Polite Lies: On Being a Woman Caught between Cultures* (1997), Grace Lee Boggs's *Living for Change: An Autobiography* (1998), Soo-Young Chin's *Doing What Had to Be Done: The Life Narrative of Dora Yum Kim* (1999), and M. Elaine Mar's *Paper Daughter: A Memoir* (1999), speaks to a decade of representations by Asian American women writers on their lived experiences and struggles. Uchida's chapter offers us a theoretically insightful feminist analysis of "how the self is constructed as a multiple, shifting, and unfinished process that rejects the traditional notion of a static and unitary identity embedded in the language of dualism and essentialism." She, moreover, argues that "[Minatoya's] text contributes to the ongoing discourse of resistance" by Asian American women writers. At the same time, Uchida's analysis does not celebrate wholesale the autobiographical construction or simplistic recovery of the female or ethnic self, identity, or heritage. Rather, she perceptively recognizes the political limitations of Minatoya's narrative in either countering dominant cultural ideologies or in "presenting a radical and liberatory vision."

Nhi Lieu's cultural critique of Vietnamese American beauty pageants deepens our critical understanding of the intricacies of community representations and identities. Ethnic beauty pageants can be read as countering our exclusion from mainstream standards of beauty and as a display of ethnic dignity; however, a close reading also reveals their reinforcement of traditional gender roles, cultural authenticity, and racial purity.[53] The bodies of the Vietnamese beauty contestants are adorned in traditional dress and are used to symbolize a nation before annexation, U.S. invasion, civil war, and dispersion of its population in other nations. This master narrative speaks to a refugee community that has shared the traumas of colonization, war, dislocation, diaspora, and resettlement. These beauty pageants allow organizers, participants, and audience members to recapture aspects of their former lives, momentarily forgetting their daily lives in America where they have to contend with economic struggles, cultural differences, linguistic difficulties, and racial discrimination. With these ethnic celebrations, they assert their ethnic pride, regain some control over their lives, and reestablish their former community status. However, in so doing, they also reestablish patriarchal ideals of enclosed nationhood and traditional gender hierarchies. Additionally, they construct a contradictory politics of representation that demands, on the one hand, that young, female contestants be "ethnically authentic," yet on the other hand privilege the Eurocentric beauty standards of "Western" facial and body features, especially through promotion of cosmetic surgery. The impact of Western political and cultural imperialism has left both a physical and emotional legacy on this diasporic community and many others as well.[54]

Future challenges include addressing the complexities of our multiple identities and considering what the consequences are when forcing us to "choose" or prioritize aspects of who we are, as if we can simply compartmentalize our identities into distinct parts. Beverly Yuen Thompson's powerful narrative asks us to reimagine spaces of self-definition by creating a new politics of representation that interrogates narrow constructions of race, gender, and sexuality. As a *hapa* and bisexual woman, she describes her personal and political journey to find "centers" where one is constantly positioned outside of even the "margins." The emergent research and literature on biracial and multiracial Asian Americans reminds us that Asian American communities have always been multiracial and that this growing population is on the forefront of reshaping the national dialogue on racialized constructions and interrogating debates on cultural authenticity.[55] This chapter complements Storrs's chapter, which is about her mother's experience as a war bride involved in an interracial marriage and how she struggled to survive and raise her multiracial children. One of the coeditors of this book was born to a Japanese American mother and an Italian American father, and the other was raised by her Vietnamese American mother and adoptive Czechoslovakian/Irish American father, so these issues resonate for us not only intellectually, but also at the very personal level. In asserting ethnic pride, monoracial Asian Americans often unintentionally neglect, silence, or offend multiracial communities. Similarly, they also intentionally and unintentionally impose heterosexist standards on the lives of lesbian, queer, and bisexual Asian Americans.[56] It is from these spaces of discovery that Thompson calls on all of us to redefine and reassert the identifier "Asian American woman."[57]

The chapters in this collection give voice to the complexities of our lived experiences and struggles both within the United States and in the transnational spaces many of us occupy. These voices remind us that long ago we broke our silences, and there is no going back. Our radical visions of moving beyond our limited subject-positions is an ongoing effort to resist and challenge the neocolonialist representations and oppressive forces imposed on us along with those we have internalized and recreated for ourselves. As coeditors, we offer voices and visions representing the rich diversity of our lives in the hopes of creating the possibilities for a new transnational public space of critically self-reflexive dialogue, strategic resistance, and alliance building. The perspectives and locations, personal and intellectual, of the authors represented here challenge the epistemological and ideological formations about Asian American women in history, in the classroom, in the global economy, in the media, and in our communities, as well as in our social and familial relationships. The cultural, economic, and political circumstances we face in making personal life decisions determine our worldview and shape the legacy and reflections we leave for the next generation.[58]

Although the fifteen chapters in this collection were all originally published before the September 11, 2001, tragedy, they bring to the foreground the complex issues this crisis has forced us to grapple with, such as individualism, nationalism, immigration, citizenship, racialized relations, militarization, and imperialism. While we are rarely or marginally included in the national political dialogue, we were among those who perished or were injured on that tragic day; we have been the victims of misdirected acts of hate-crime violence; we are part of the U.S. military forces that defend American interests; and we have called for humane, measured responses to terrorism at home and abroad.[59] The future will bring new opportunities for racialized populations given the predicted demographic growth of our communities within the context of global transformations. However, it will also bring seemingly insurmountable challenges, and we expect that *Frontiers* will continue to be engaged in presenting inclusive voices and critical perspectives. We acknowledge there is much that still needs to be addressed to present a comprehensive picture of our emergent histories, identity formations, and oppositional practices, but we hope these selections from *Frontiers* provide inspiration as well as the necessary courage for us to continue this work in the future.

Linda Trinh Võ and Marian Sciachitano

NOTES

We extend a special thank you to the general editor of *Frontiers*, Sue Armitage, for her extraordinarily skillful guidance in the editing of our original special issue volume as well as making this collection possible. We appreciate the exceptional staff that worked on the original special issue, Karen Weathermon and Tanya Gonzales, and especially Patricia Hart, who guided us through both projects with such diligence and enthusiasm. We are grateful to Mary Yu Danico, who assisted in the gathering of submissions, and Camille Roman for her helpful editorial advice. In addition, we extend our thanks to all of those with *Frontiers* who we did not work with directly but who were instrumental in publishing these chapters on Asian American women in the journal over the decades. Linda would like to give credit to her mother, Thuy Hanlon, for challenging her to find her own voice. She thanks her lifelong partner, Bill, for his loving encouragement, and their children, Aisha and Kian, for their abundant laughter and their never-ending questions, all of which begin with "why." Marian would like to thank Jo Hockenhull and Noël Sturgeon for their support and encouragement throughout the years.

1. Marian Sciachitano and Linda Trinh Võ, guest coeditors, special issue on Asian American Women, *Frontiers: A Journal of Women Studies* 21:1/2 (2000). We regret not being able to include the poetry, short fiction, artwork, and photography on and by Asian American women from this special issue or others.

2. Matsui Yayori's "Sexual Slavery in Korea," *Frontiers* 2:1 (1977): 22–30; and Diana E. H. Russell, "Report on the International Tribunal on Crimes against Women," *Frontiers* 2:1 (1977): 1–5.

3. See also Yong Soon Min, "DMZ XING" (art essay) and "Heartland" (poem), *Frontiers* 28:1 (1997): 134–39, 134–41.

4. Elaine Kim and Lisa Lowe, introduction to a special issue ("New Formations, New Questions: Asian American Studies") of *positions: east asia cultures critique* 5:2 (1997): xiii.

5. Linda Basch, Nina Glick Schiller, and Cristina Szanton Blanc, *Nations Unbound: Transnational Projects, Postcolonial Predicaments, and Deterritorialized Nation-States* (Australia: Gordon and Breach Publishers, 1994); and Aihwa Ong, *Flexible Citizen-*

ship: The Cultural Logics of Transnationality (Durham NC: Duke University Press, 1999).

6. Sucheng Chan, *Asian Americans: An Interpretative History* (Boston: Twayne Publishers, 1991); and Lisa Lowe, *Immigrant Acts: On Asian American Cultural Politics* (Durham NC: Duke University Press, 1996).

7. Lin Lean Lim and Nana Oishi, "International Labor Migration of Asian Women: Distinctive Characteristics and Policy Concerns," *Asian and Pacific Migration Journal* 5:1 (1996): 85–116.

8. Genny Lim, *Paper Angels and Bitter Cane* (Honolulu: Kalamaku Press, 1991); Him Mark Lai, Genny Lim, and Judy Yung, *Island: Poetry and History of Chinese Immigrants on Angel Island, 1910–1940* (Seattle: University of Washington Press, 1991); and M. Elaine Mar, *Paper Daughter: A Memoir* (New York: Harper Collins, 1999).

9. Judy Yung, *Unbound Feet: A Social History of Chinese Women in San Francisco* (Berkeley: University of California Press, 1995), and *Unbound Voices: A Documentary History of Chinese Women in San Francisco* (Berkeley: University of California Press, 1999). Also see Judy Yung, *Chinese Women of America: A Pictorial History* (Seattle: University of Washington Press, 1986).

10. Valerie J. Matsumoto, *Farming the Home Place: A Japanese American Community in California, 1919–1982* (Ithaca NY: Cornell University Press, 1993).

11. See also Gail Nomura, "'Peace Empowers': The Testimony of Aki Kurose, a Woman of Color in the Pacific Northwest," *Frontiers* 22:3 (2002): 75–92.

12. For more on this topic, see Gary Y. Okihiro with a contribution by Leslie Ito, *Storied Lives: Japanese American Students and World War II* (Seattle: University of Washington Press, 1999).

13. While the last U.S. military base in the Philippines was closed in 1992, as a result of the new Visiting Forces Agreement approved by the Philippine Senate in May 1999, the United States is allowed to resume military training exercises and ship visits. In 2002 there were some two thousand U.S. troops stationed in the Philippines.

14. Bok-Lim Kim, "Asian Wives of American Servicemen: Women in Shadows," *Amerasia Journal* 4:1 (1977): 91–115; Evelyn Nakano Glenn, *Issei, Nisei, War Bride: Three Generations of Japanese American Women in Domestic Service* (Philadelphia: Temple University Press, 1986); Haeyun Juliana Kim, "Voices from the Shadows: The Lives of Korean War Brides," *Amerasia Journal* 17:1 (1991): 15–30; Teresa Kay Williams, "Marriage between Japanese Women and U.S. Servicemen Since World War II," *Amerasia Journal* 17:1 (1991): 135–54; Ji-Yeon Yuh, "Out of the Shadows: Camptown Women, Military Brides, and Korean (American) Communities," *Hitting Critical Mass* 6:1 (1999): 13–33; and Caroline Chung Simpson, "'Out of an Obscure Place':

Japanese War Brides and Cultural Pluralism in the 1950s," in *An Absent Presence: Japanese Americans in Postwar American Culture, 1945–1960* (Durham NC: Duke University Press, 2001), 149–85.

15. Xuan Ngoc Nguyen (Evans) worked as a translator and is featured in the documentary video *Regret to Inform* by Barbara Sonneborn (Berkeley: Sun Fountain Productions, 1998).

16. Le Ly Hayslip with Jay Wurts, *When Heaven and Earth Changed Places: A Vietnamese Woman's Journey from War to Peace* (New York: Plume, 1989); Le Ly Hayslip with James Hayslip, *Child of War, Woman of Peace* (New York: Doubleday, 1993); and *Heaven and Earth,* directed by Oliver Stone (Warner Brothers, 1993). For other Vietnamese American women's biographies, see Monique Senderowicz, ed., *The Rubber Tree: Memoir of a Vietnamese Woman Who Was an Anti-French Guerrilla, a Publisher, and a Peace Activist* (Jefferson NC: McFarland and Company, 1994); and Duong Van Mai Elliott, *The Sacred Willow: Four Generations in the Life of a Vietnamese Family* (New York: Oxford University Press, 1999).

17. Lucie Cheng and Edna Bonacich, eds., *Labor Immigration under Capitalism: Asian Workers in the United States Before World War II* (Berkeley: University of California Press, 1984); and Evelyn Hu-DeHart, ed., *Across the Pacific: Asian Americans and Globalization* (Philadelphia: Temple University Press, 1999).

18. Benson Tong, *Unsubmissive Women: Chinese Prostitutes in Nineteenth-Century San Francisco* (Norman: University of Oklahoma Press, 1994); Yung, *Unbound Feet*; and George Anthony Peffer, *If They Don't Bring Their Women Here: Chinese Female Immigration Before Exclusion* (Urbana: University of Illinois Press, 1999).

19. Dai Sil Kim-Gibson, "They Defiled My Body, Not My Spirit: The Story of a Korean Comfort Woman, Chung SeoWoon," in *Making More Waves: New Writing by Asian American Women,* ed. Elaine H. Kim, Lilia V. Villanueva, and Asian Women United of California (Boston: Beacon Press, 1997), 177–83; Chungmoo Choi, guest editor, special issue ("The Comfort Women: Colonialism, War, and Sex") of *positions: east asia cultures critique* 5:1 (1997); and Elaine H. Kim and Chungmoo Choi, eds., *Dangerous Women: Gender and Korean Nationalism* (New York: Routledge, 1998). For an emotionally powerful documentary on this topic, see *Silence Broken: Korean Comfort Women,* by Dai Sil Kim-Gibson (Parkersburg IA: Mid-Prairie Books, 1999).

20. Maria Rosa Henson, *Comfort Woman: A Filipina's Story of Prostitution and Slavery under the Japanese Military* (Lanham MD: Rowman & Littlefield, 1999).

21. Tracy Lai, "Asian American Women: Not for Sale," in *Changing Our Power: An Introduction to Women's Studies,* ed. Jo Whitehorse Cochran, Donna Langston, and Carolyn Woodward (Dubuque IA: Kendall-Hunt, 1988), 120–27; Kamala Kempadoo and Jo Doezema, eds., *Global Sex Workers: Rights, Resistance, and Redefinition*

(New York: Routledge, 1998); Christa Wichterich, *The Globalized Woman: Reports from a Future of Inequality* (London: Zed Books, 2000); Dennis Altman, *Global Sex* (Chicago: University of Chicago Press, 2002); and Susanne Thorbek and Bandana Pattanaik, eds., *Global Prostitution: Changing Patterns in a Changing Context* (London: Zed Books, 2002).

22. Cynthia Enloe, *Bananas, Beaches, and Bases: Making Feminist Sense of International Politics* (Berkeley: University of California Press, 1990); Saundra Pollack Sturdevant and Brenda Stoltzfus, *Let the Good Times Roll: Prostitution and the U.S. Military in Asia* (New York: The New Press, 1992); Thanh-Dam Truong, *Sex, Money, and Morality: Prostitution and Tourism in Southeast Asia* (London: Zed Books, 1990); Bang-Soon Yoon, "Military Sexual Slavery: Political Agenda for Feminist Scholarship and Activism," paper prepared for the Non-Governmental Organization Forum on Women, Huairou, China, 1995; and Yuh, "Out of the Shadows." For an excellent video on the topic, see J. T. Takagi and Hye Jung Park, *The Women Outside: Korean Women and the U.S. Military* (New York: Third World Newsreel, 1995).

23. Elaine Kim, "Sex Tourism in Asia: A Reflection of Political and Economic Inequality," in *Korean Women in Transition: At Home and Abroad,* ed. Eui-Young Yu and Earl H. Phillips (Los Angeles: Center for Korean-American and Korean Studies, California State University, Los Angeles, 1987), 127–44; and Lenore Manderson and Margaret Jolly, eds., *Sites of Desire, Economies of Pleasure: Sexualities in Asia and the Pacific* (Chicago: University of Chicago Press, 1997).

24. Venny Villapando, "The Business of Selling Mail-Order Brides," in *Making Waves: An Anthology of Writings by and about Asian American Women,* ed. Asian Women United of California (Boston: Beacon Press, 1989), 318–26; and Marian Sciachitano, "'MOBS' on the Net: Critiquing the Gaze of the 'Cyber' Bride Industry," *Race, Gender and Class* 7:1 (2000): 57–69.

25. June C. Nash and Maria Patricia Fernández-Kelly, eds., *Women, Men, and the International Division of Labor* (Albany: SUNY Press, 1983); Edna Bonacich et al., eds., *Global Production: The Apparel Industry in the Pacific Rim* (Philadelphia: Temple University Press, 1994); Andrew Ross, ed., *No Sweat: Fashion, Free Trade, and the Rights of Garment Workers* (New York: Verso, 1997); and Evelyn Hu-DeHart, "Women, Work, and Globalization in Late Twentieth-Century Capitalism: Asian Women Immigrants in the United States," Working Paper Series in Cultural Studies, Ethnicity, and Race Relations (Pullman WA: Department of Comparative American Cultures, Washington State University, 1999).

26. See Chalsa Loo, *Chinatown: Most Time, Hard Time* (New York: Praeger, 1991); Miriam Ching Louie, "Immigrant Asian Women in Bay Area Garment Sweatshops: 'After Sewing, Laundry, Cleaning, and Cooking, I Have No Breath to Sing,'" *Amerasia*

Journal 18:1 (1992): 1–26; Karen Hossfeld, "Hiring Immigrant Women: Silicon Valley's 'Simple Formula,' " in *Women of Color in U.S. Society,* ed. Maxine Baca Zinn and Bonnie Thornton Dill (Philadelphia: Temple University Press, 1994), 65–93; Lisa Lowe, "Work, Immigration, Gender: Asian 'American' Women," in Kim, Villanueva, and Asian Women United of California, *Making More Waves,* 269–77; and Miriam Ching Louie, "Breaking the Cycle: Women Workers Confront Corporate Greed Globally," in *Dragon Ladies: Asian American Feminists Breathe Fire,* ed. Sonia Shah (Boston: South End Press, 1997), 121–31.

27. Miriam Ching Louie, *Sweatshop Warriors: Immigrant Women Workers Take on the Global Factory* (Cambridge MA: South End Press, 2001); and Patricia Wong Hall and Victor M. Wang, *Anti-Asian Violence in North America: Asian American and Asian Canadian Reflections on Hate, Healing and Resistance* (Walnut Creek CA: AltaMira Press, 2001).

28. Grace Chang, "The Global Trade in Filipina Workers," in Shah, *Dragon Ladies,* 132–52.

29. Nicole Constable, *Maid to Order in Hong Kong: Stories of Filipina Workers* (Ithaca NY: Cornell University Press, 1997); Grace Chang, *Disposable Domestics: Immigrant Women Workers in the Global Economy* (Cambridge MA: South End Press, 2000); Bridget Anderson, *Doing the Dirty Work?: The Global Politics of Domestic Labour* (London: Zed Books, 2000); and Rhacel Salazar Parreñas, *Servants of Globalization: Women, Migration, and Domestic Work* (Stanford: Stanford University Press, 2001).

30. Delia D. Aguilar, *Toward a Nationalist Feminism* (Quezon City, Philippines: Giraffe Books, 1998).

31. Gary Y. Okihiro, *Margins and Mainstreams: Asians in American History and Culture* (Seattle: University of Washington Press, 1994); Sylvia Yanagisako, "Transforming Orientalism: Gender, Nationality, and Class in Asian American Studies," in *Naturalizing Power: Essays in Feminist Cultural Analysis,* ed. Sylvia Yanagisako and Carol Delaney (New York: Routledge, 1995), 275–98; Yen Le Espiritu, *Asian American Women and Men: Labor, Laws, and Love* (Thousand Oaks CA: Sage Publications, 1997); and Shirley Hune, *Teaching Asian American Women's History* (Washington DC: American Historical Association, 1997).

32. May Ying Chen, "Teaching a Course on Asian American Women," in *Counterpoint: Perspectives on Asian America,* ed. Emma Gee (Los Angeles: Asian American Studies Center, University of California Los Angeles, 1976), 234–39; Judy Chu, "Asian American Women's Studies Courses: A Look Back at Our Beginnings," *Frontiers* 8:3 (1986): 96–101; King-Kok Cheung, "Reflections on Teaching Literature by American Women of Color," *Pacific Coast Philology* 25:1–2 (1990): 19–23; and Diane C. Fujino,

"Unity of Theory and Practice: Integrating Feminist Pedagogy into Asian American Studies," in *Teaching Asian America: Diversity and the Problem of Community*, ed. Lane Ryo Hirabayashi (Lanham MD: Rowman & Littlefield, 1998), 73–92.

33. Nancy InKyung Kim, "Transformative Education and Asian American Feminist Pedagogy in the General Survey Course on Asian American Women" (master's thesis, University of California, Los Angeles, 1999). Sciachitano has taught "Asian American Women's Literature" and Võ has taught "Asian American Women" at Washington State University (WSU), a campus located in a rural area. Võ also taught a similar course at Oberlin College as well as introduced a new course, "Vietnamese American Women," at her current institution, the University of California, Irvine.

34. Asian American women's organizations and conferences continue to flourish in some educational environments, but other campuses are just beginning these endeavors. For example, at WSU, we served as coadvisors for the Association of Pacific and Asian Women (APAW), established in 1995, which held its first annual Asian Pacific American Women's Conference in 1999.

35. Shirley Hune, *Asian Pacific American Women in Higher Education: Claiming Visibility and Voice* (Washington DC: Association of American Colleges and Universities, 1998).

36. Chu, "Asian American Women's Studies Courses."

37. *Asian Women* (Los Angeles: Asian American Studies Center, University of California, Los Angeles, 1971). Also see Nobuya Tsuchida, ed., *Asian and Pacific American Experiences: Women's Perspectives* (Minneapolis: Asian/Pacific American Learning Resource Center and General College, University of Minnesota, 1982).

38. Asian Women United of California, *Making Waves*; Shirley Geok-lin Lim, Mayumi Tsutakawa, and Margarita Donnelly, eds., *Forbidden Stitch: An Asian American Women's Anthology* (Corvallis OR: Calyx, 1989); Sylvia Watanabe and Carol Bruchac, eds., *Home to Stay: Asian American Women's Fiction* (Greenfield Center NY: Greenfield Review Press, 1990); Shirley Geok-lin Lim and Amy Ling, eds., *Reading the Literatures of Asian America* (Philadelphia: Temple University Press, 1992); Women of the South Asian Descent Collective, ed., *Our Feet Walk the Sky: Women of the South Asian Diaspora* (San Francisco: Aunt Lute Books, 1993); Sharon Lim-Hing, ed., *The Very Inside: An Anthology of Writings by Asian and Pacific Islander Lesbians and Bisexual Women* (Toronto: Sister Vision Press, 1994); Carol Camper, ed., *Miscegenation Blues: Voices of Mixed Race Women* (Toronto: Sister Vision Press, 1994); Sunaina Maira and Rajini Srikanth, eds., *Contours of the Heart: South Asians Map North America* (New York: The Asian American Writers' Workshop, 1996); Shah, *Dragon Ladies;* Shamita Das Dasgupta, ed., *A Patchwork Shawl: Chronicles of South Asian Women in America* (New Brunswick NJ: Rutgers University Press, 1998); Vicki Ham, ed., *Yell-Oh Girls!: Emerging Voices Explore Culture, Identity, and Growing*

INTRODUCTION xxxi

Up Asian American (New York: Quill, 2001); and Erica Harth, ed., *Last Witnesses: Reflections on the Wartime Internment of Japanese Americans* (New York: Palgrave, 2001).

39. See Mei Nakano, *Japanese American Women: Three Generations, 1890–1990* (Berkeley: Mina Press Publishing, 1990); Usha Welaratna, *Beyond the Killing Fields: Voices of Nine Cambodian Survivors in America* (Stanford: Stanford University Press, 1993); Sucheng Chan, ed., *Hmong Means Free: Life in Laos and America* (Philadelphia: Temple University Press, 1994); Lavina Dhingra Shankar and Rajini Srikanth, eds., *A Part, Yet Apart: South Asians in Asian America* (Philadelphia: Temple University Press, 1988); Sylvia Junko Yanagisako, *Transforming the Past: Tradition and Kinship among Japanese Americans* (Stanford: Stanford University Press, 1985); Glenn, *Issei, Nisei, War Bride;* Nazli Kibria, *Family Tightrope: The Changing Lives of Vietnamese Americans* (Princeton NJ: Princeton University Press, 1993); Matsumoto, *Farming the Home Place*; Nancy D. Donnelly, *Changing Lives of Refugee Hmong Women* (Seattle: University of Washington Press, 1994); MaryCarol Hopkins, *Braving a New World: Cambodian (Khmer) Refugees in an American City* (Westport CT: Bergin & Garvey, 1996); Kyeyoung Park, *The Korean American Dream: Immigrants and Small Business in New York City* (Ithaca NY: Cornell University Press, 1997); Sangeeta R. Gupta, ed., *Emerging Voices: South Asian American Women Redefine Self, Family, and Community* (Thousand Oaks CA: Sage Publications, 1999); Nancy Smith-Hefner, *Khmer American: Identity and Moral Education in a Diasporic Community* (Berkeley: University of California Press, 1999); Gloria Heyung Chun, *Of Orphans and Warriors: Inventing Chinese American Cultures and Identity* (New Brunswick NJ: Rutgers University Press, 2000); and Carolyn Chung Simpson, *An Absent Presence: Japanese Americans in Postwar American Culture, 1945–1960* (Durham NC: Duke University Press, 2001).

40. Elaine H. Kim, *Asian American Literature: An Introduction to the Writings and Their Social Context* (Philadelphia: Temple University Press, 1982); Amy Ling, *Between Worlds: Women Writers of Chinese Ancestry* (New York: Pergamon Press, 1990); King-kok Cheung, *Articulate Silences: Hisaye Yamamoto, Maxine Hong Kingston, Joy Kogawa* (Ithaca NY: Cornell University Press, 1993); Sau-ling Cynthia Wong, *Reading Asian American Literature: From Necessity to Extravagance* (Princeton NJ: Princeton University Press, 1993); Lowe, *Immigrant Acts*; Traise Yamamoto, *Masking Selves, Making Subjects: Japanese American Women, Identity, and the Body* (Berkeley: University of California Press, 1999); and Wendy Ho, *In Her Mother's House: The Politics of Asian American Mother-Daughter Writing* (Thousand Oaks CA: Sage Publications, 1999); Shirley Geok-lin Lim, Larry E. Smith, and Wimal Dissanayake, eds., *Transnational Asia Pacific: Gender, Culture, and the Public Sphere* (Urbana: University of Illinois Press, 1999); Rachel Lee, *The Americas of Asian American Literature: Gendered Fictions of Nation and Transnation* (Princeton: Princeton University Press, 1999);

Leslie Bow, *Betrayal and Other Acts of Subversion: Feminism, Sexual Politics, Asian American Women's Literature* (Princeton NJ: Princeton University Press, 2001); Patricia P. Chu, *Assimilating Asians: Gendered Strategies of Authorship in Asian America* (Durham NC: Duke University Press, 2000); and Laura Hyun Yi Kang, *Compositional Subjects: Enfiguring Asian/American Women* (Durham NC: Duke University Press, 2002). For a cultural critique and critical race theory perspective, see Mari J. Matsuda, *Where Is Your Body? And Other Essays on Race, Gender, and the Law* (Boston: Beacon Press, 1996).

41. Shirley Hune, "Higher Education as Gendered Spaces: Asian-American Women and Everyday Inequities," in *Everyday Sexism in the Third Millennium,* ed. Carol Rambo Ronai, Barbara A. Zsembik, and Joe R. Feagin (New York: Routledge, 1997), 181–96.

42. For more on how she contends with these larger issues in her own research, see Piya Chatterjee, *A Time for Tea: Women, Labor, and Post/Colonial Politics on an Indian Plantation* (Durham NC: Duke University Press, 2001).

43. Shelli B. Fowler, Tiffany Ana López, Kate Shanley, Caroline Chung Simpson, and Traise Yamamoto, "Negotiating Textual Terrain: A Conversation on Critical and Pedagogical Interventions in the Teaching of Ethnic Autobiography," *Frontiers* 17:2 (1996): 4–49.

44. Mitsuye Yamada, "Asian Pacific American Women and Feminism," in *This Bridge Called My Back: Writings by Radical Women of Color,* ed. Cherríe Moraga and Gloria Anzaldúa (New York: Kitchen Table Press, 1981), 71–78; Susie Ling, "The Mountain Movers: Asian American Women's Movement in Los Angeles," *Amerasia Journal* 15:1 (1989): 51–67; Sonia Shah, "Presenting the Blue Goddess: Toward a National Pan-Asian Feminist Agenda," in *The State of Asian America: Activism and Resistance in the 1990s,* ed. Karin Aguilar-San Juan (Boston: South End Press, 1994), 147–58; and Esther Ngan-ling Chow, "The Development of Feminist Consciousness Among Asian American Women," in *Race, Class, and Gender: Common Bonds, Different Voices,* ed. Esther Ngan-ling Chow, Doris Wilkinson, and Maxine Baca Zinn (Thousand Oaks CA: Sage Publications, 1996), 251–65.

45. King-Kok Cheung, "The Woman Warrior versus the Chinaman Pacific: Must a Chinese American Critic Choose between Feminism and Heroism?" in *Conflicts in Feminism,* ed. Marianne Hirsch and Evelyn Fox Keller (New York: Routledge, 1990), 234–51; Margaret Abraham, "Ethnicity, Gender, and Marital Violence: South Asian Women's Organizations in the United States," *Gender & Society* 9:4 (1995): 450–68; and Nilda Rimonte, "A Question of Culture: Cultural Approval of Violence against Women in the Pacific-Asian Community and the Cultural Defense," *Stanford Law Review* 43 (July 1991): 1311–26.

46. Esther Ngan-Ling Chow, "The Feminist Movement: Where Are All the Asian

American Women?" in *Making Waves,* ed. Asian Women United of California, 362–76; and Helen Zia, "Violence in Our Communities: 'Where Are the Asian Women?' " in *Making More Waves,* ed. Kim, Villanueva, and Asian Women United of California, 207–14.

47. Renee Tajima, "Lotus Blossoms Don't Bleed: Images of Asian Women," in *Making Waves*, ed. Asian Women United of California, 308–26; Trinh T. Minh-ha, *Woman, Native, Other: Writing Postcoloniality and Feminism* (Bloomington: University of Indiana Press, 1989), and *When the Moon Waxes Red: Representation, Gender, and Cultural Politics* (New York: Routledge, 1991); Himani Bannerji, "Popular Images of South Asian Women," in *Returning the Gaze: Essays on Racism, Feminism, and Politics* (Toronto: Sister Vision Press, 1993), 144–52; Sayantani DasGupta, "Glass Shawls and Long Hair," *Ms.,* March/April 1993, 76–77; Gina Marchetti, *Romance and the "Yellow Peril": Race, Sex, and Discursive Strategies in Hollywood Fiction* (Berkeley: University of California Press, 1993); Jessica Hagedorn, "Asian Women in Film: No Joy, No Luck," *Ms.,* January/February 1994, 74–79; Shirley Geok-lin Lim, "Gender Transformations in Asian/American Representations," in *Gender and Culture in Literature and Film East and West: Issues of Perception and Interpretation,* ed. Nitaya Masavisut et al. (Honolulu: University of Hawaii Press, 1994), 95–112; Darrell Y. Hamamoto, *Monitored Peril: Asian Americans and the Politics of TV Representation* (Minneapolis: University of Minnesota Press, 1994); Matthew Bernstein and Gaylyn Studlar, eds., *Visions of the East: Orientalism in Film* (New Brunswick NJ: Rutgers University Press, 1997); Jun Xing, *Asian America through the Lens: History, Representations, and Identity* (Walnut Creek CA: AltaMira Press, 1998); Robert G. Lee, *Orientals: Asian Americans in Popular Culture* (Philadelphia: Temple University Press, 1999); Darrell Y. Hamamoto and Sandra Liu, eds., *Countervisions: Asian American Film Criticism* (Philadelphia: Temple University Press, 2000); and Peter X. Feng, ed., *Screening Asian Americans* (New Brunswick NJ: Rutgers University Press, 2002).

48. Jade Snow Wong, *Fifth Chinese Daughter* (New York: Harper, 1950); Monica Sone, *Nisei Daughter* (Seattle: University of Washington Press, 1953); Maxine Hong Kingston, *The Woman Warrior: Memoirs of Girlhood Among Ghosts* (New York: Random House, 1975); Akemi Kikumura, *Through Harsh Winters: The Life of a Japanese Immigrant Woman* (Novato CA: Chandler and Sharp, 1981); Ruthanne Lum McCunn, *Thousand Pieces of Gold: A Biographical Novel* (Boston: Beacon Press, 1981); Yoshiko Uchida, *Desert Exile: The Uprooting of a Japanese American Family* (Seattle: University of Washington Press, 1982); Miné Okubo, *Citizen 13660* (Seattle: University of Washington Press, 1983); Kitty Tsui, *Words of a Woman Who Breathes Fire* (San Francisco: Spinsters, 1983); Willyce Kim, *Dancer Dawkins and the California Kid* (Boston: Alyson, 1985); Nellie Wong, *Death of Long Steam Lady* (Albuquerque:

University of New Mexico Press, 1986); Kim Ronyoung, *Clay Walls* (New York: Permanent Press, 1986); Merle Woo, *Yellow Woman Speaks* (Seattle: Radical Women, 1986); Yoshiko Uchida, *Picture Bride* (New York: Simon & Schuster, 1987); Cynthia Kadohata, *The Floating World* (New York: Viking, 1989); Mary Paik Lee, ed., *Quiet Odyssey: A Pioneer Korean Woman in America* (Seattle: University of Washington Press, 1990); Jessica Hagedorn, *Dogeaters* (New York: Penguin, 1991); Lydia Yuri Minatoya, *Talking to High Monks in the Snow* (New York: HarperPerennial, 1993); Meena Alexander, *Fault Lines: A Memoir* (New York: Feminist Press of CUNY, 1993); Wakako Yamauchi, *Songs My Mother Taught Me: Stories, Plays, and Memoirs* (New York: Feminist Press of CUNY, 1994); Velina Hasu Houston, ed., *The Politics of Life: Four Plays by Asian American Women* (Philadelphia: Temple University Press, 1993); Fae Myenne Ng, *Bone* (New York: Hyperion, 1993); Roberta Uno, ed., *Unbroken Thread: An Anthology of Plays by Asian American Women* (Amherst: University of Massachusetts Press, 1993); K. Connie Kang, *Home Was the Land of Morning Calm: A Saga of a Korean-American Family* (Reading MA: Addison-Wesley, 1995); Lisa See, *On Gold Mountain: The One-Hundred-Year Odyssey of My Chinese-American Family* (New York: Vintage Books, 1996); Chitra Bannerjee Divakaruni, *Arranged Marriage: Stories* (New York: Anchor Books, Doubleday, 1995); Sui Sin Far, *Mrs. Spring Fragance and Other Writings,* ed. Amy Ling and Annette White-Parks (Urbana: University of Illinois Press, 1995); Theresa Hak Kyung Cha, *Dictée* (Berkeley: Third Woman Press, 1995); Kyoko Mori, *The Dream of Water: A Memoir* (New York: Henry Holt, 1995); Juliana Chang, ed., *Quiet Fire: A Historical Anthology of Asian American Poetry, 1892– 1970* (Philadelphia: Temple University Press, 1996); Shirley Geok-lin Lim, *Among the White Moon Faces: An Asian-American Memoir of Homelands* (New York: Feminist Press of CUNY, 1996); M. Evelina Galang, *Her Wild American Self* (Minneapolis: Coffeehouse Press, 1996); Helie Lee, *Still Life with Rice: A Young American Woman Discovers the Life and Legacy of Her Korean Grandmother* (New York: Scribner, 1996); Kyoko Mori, *Polite Lies: On Being a Woman Caught between Cultures* (New York: Henry Holt, 1997); Chitra Bannerjee Divakaruni, *The Mistress of Spices* (New York: Anchor Books, 1997); Catherine Lu, *Oriental Girls Desire Romance* (New York: Kaya, 1997); Nora Okja Keller, *Comfort Woman* (New York: The Viking Press, 1997); Patti Kim, *A Cab Called Reliable* (New York: St. Martin's Griffin, 1997); Hilary Tham, *Lane with No Name: Memoirs & Poems of a Malaysian-Chinese Girlhood* (Boulder CO: Lynne Rienner, 1997); Mitsuye Yamada, *Camp Notes and Other Writings* (New Brunswick NJ: Rutgers University Press, 1998); Barbara Tran, Monique T. D. Truong, and Luu Truong Khoi, eds., *Watermark: Vietnamese American Poetry and Prose* (New York: The Asian American Writers' Workshop, 1998); Mei Ng's *Eating Chinese Food Naked* (New York: Scribner, 1998); Ruth L. Ozeki, *My Year of Meats* (New York: The Viking Press, 1998); Grace Lee Boggs, *Living for Change: An Autobiography*

(Minneapolis: University of Minnesota Press, 1998); Soo-Young Chin, *Doing What Had to Be Done: The Life Narrative of Dora Yum Kim* (Philadelphia: Temple University Press, 1999); V. K. Mina, *The Splintered Day* (London: The Serpent's Tail, 1999); Frances Park, *When My Sister Was Cleopatra Moon* (New York: Hyperion, 2000); Kitchen Table Collective, ed., *Bolo! Bolo!: A Collection of Writings by Second Generation South Asians Living in North America* (Mississauga, Ontario: South Asian Professionals Networking Association, 2000); Loung Ung, *First They Killed My Father: A Daughter of Cambodia Remembers* (New York: HarperCollins, 2000); Christina Chiu, *Troublemaker and Other Saints* (New York: Berkeley Books, 2001); Diana Birchall, *Onoto Watanna: The Story of Winnifred Eaton* (Urbana: University of Illinois Press, 2001); Margaret Cho, *I'm the One That I Want* (New York: Ballantine Books, 2001); and Nora Okja Keller, *Fox Girl* (New York: Viking, 2002).

49. Arthur S. Golden, *Memoirs of a Geisha: A Novel* (New York: Alfred A. Knopf, 1997); and Liza Crihfield Dalby, *Geisha* (Berkeley: University of California Press, 1983).

50. Traise Yamamoto, "In/Visible Difference: Asian American Women and the Politics of Spectacle," *Race, Class, and Gender* 7:1 (2000): 53.

51. Dorrine Kondo, *About Face: Crafting Race in Fashion and Theater* (New York: Routledge, 1997).

52. Aki Uchida, "Reconstructing Identity: The Autobiographical Self of a Japanese American Woman in Lydia Minatoya's *Talking to High Monks in the Snow*," *Frontiers* 19:1 (1998): 124–45. See also Yamamoto, *Masking Selves, Making Subjects.*

53. For more on Asian ethnic beauty pageants, see also Rick Bonus, *Locating Filipino Americans: Ethnicity and the Cultural Politics of Space* (Philadelphia: Temple University Press, 2000); Shilpa Davé, "'Community Beauty': Transnational Performances and Cultural Citizenship in 'Miss India Georgia,'" *Lit: Literature Interpretation Theory* 12:3 (2001): 335–58; and Rebecca Chiyoko King, "'Eligible' to Be Japanese American: Multiraciality in Basketball Leagues and Beauty Pageants," in *Contemporary Asian American Communities: Intersections and Divergences,* ed. Linda Trinh Võ and Rick Bonus (Philadelphia: Temple University Press, 2002): 120–33.

54. Hayslip, *When Heaven and Earth Changed Places;* and Colleen Ballerino Cohen, Richard Wilk, and Beverly Stoeltje, eds., *Beauty Queens on the Global Stage: Gender, Contests, and Power* (New York: Routledge, 1996).

55. Maria P. P. Root, ed., *Racially Mixed People in America* (Newbury Park CA: Sage Publications, 1992), and *The Multiracial Experience: Racial Borders as the New Frontier* (Thousand Oaks CA: Sage Publications, 1996); Velina Hasu Houston and Teresa K. Williams, guest coeditors, "No Passing Zone: The Artistic and Discursive Voices of Asian-Descent Multiracials," *Amerasia Journal* 23:1 (1997); Paisley Rekdal, *The Night My Mother Met Bruce Lee: Observations on Not Fitting In* (New York: Pan-

theon Books, 2000); and Teresa Williams-León and Cynthia Nakashima, eds., *The Sum of Our Parts: Mixed Heritage Asian Americans* (Philadelphia: Temple University Press, 2002).

56. Dana Takagi, "Maiden Voyage: Excursion into Sexuality and Identity Politics in Asian America," *Amerasia Journal* 20:1 (1994): 1–17; Russell Leong, ed., *Asian American Sexualities: Dimensions of the Gay and Lesbian Experience* (New York: Routledge, 1996); JeeYeun Lee, "Why Suzie Wong Is Not a Lesbian: Asian and Asian American Lesbian and Bisexual Women and Femme/Butch/Gender Identities," in *Queer Studies: A Lesbian, Gay, Bisexual, and Transgender Anthology,* ed. Brett Beemyn and Mickey Eliason (New York: New York University Press, 1996), 115–32; and David L. Eng and Alice Y. Hom, eds., *Q&A: Queer in Asian America* (Philadelphia: Temple University Press, 1998).

57. See Loraine Hutchins and Lani Kaahumanu, eds., *Bi Any Other Name: Bisexual People Speak Out* (Los Angeles: Alyson Publications, 1991); Margaret Mihee Choe, "Our Selves, Growing Whole," in *Closer to Home: Bisexuality and Feminism,* ed. Elizabeth Reba Weise (Seattle: Seal Press, 1992), 20–23; Christine T. Lipat et al., "Tomboy, Dyke, Lezzie, and Bi: Filipina Lesbian and Bisexual Women Speak Out," in *Filipino Americans: Transformation and Identity,* ed. Maria P. P. Root (Thousand Oaks CA: Sage Publications, 1997), 230–46.

58. Claire S. Chow, *Leaving Deep Water: The Lives of Asian American Women at the Crossroads of Two Cultures* (New York: Dutton, 1998); and Phoebe Eng, *Warrior Lessons: An Asian American Woman's Journey into Power* (New York: Pocket Books, 1999).

59. Special issue ("After Words: Who Speaks on War, Justice, and Peace?") of *Amerasia Journal* 27:3 and 28:1 (2002).

Asian American Women

"A Bowlful of Tears"

Chinese Women Immigrants on Angel Island

Detained in this wooden house for several tens of days
Because of the Mexican exclusion laws.
It's a pity heroes have no place to exercise their prowess.
I can only await the word so I can snap my whip and gallop.[1]
From this moment on I bid farewell to this building.
All of my fellow villagers are rejoicing like me.
But don't fall for all this Western façade.
Even if it is jade-carved, it is still a cage.

    Anonymous Angel Island immigrant, translated by Genny Lim

In the quiet of night I heard the faint shrieking of wind,
And out of this landscape of visions and shadows a poem grew.
The floating clouds, the fog, darken the sky.
The moon shines softly as the insects chirp.
Grief and bitterness are sent by heaven.
A lonely shadow sits, leaning by the window.

    Yee of Toishan, translated by Genny Lim

Although there was thought to be little recorded about life on Angel Island for thousands of Chinese immigrants who were detained there between 1910 and 1941, the recently discovered calligraphy scratched on the walls of the Immigration Station movingly describes the feelings and experiences of the detainees.[2]

In 1975 I visited the Immigration Station for the first time. I shall never forget the sad emotions that overwhelmed me as I walked through the dark, empty rooms trying to imagine what this place meant to the countless number of Chinese immigrants who had passed through. I was most touched by the many poems, like those above, still visible on the walls, a testament to the sufferings of our parents and grandparents, some of whom are still alive.

Awareness that most of the living detainees were in their seventies and eighties lent urgency to the task of recording their experiences.[3] We began by approaching our own relatives. Even they were reluctant to talk about Angel Island, so painful was the experience for them. We pursued leads from friends, community agencies, and the Immigration Department. From our interviews we can begin to piece together a picture of life on Angel Island.

After twenty days at sea, often accompanied by seasickness, new Chinese immigrants arriving at San Francisco were transferred to a small boat and taken to Angel Island – a small island in San Francisco Bay. They were told to leave most of their luggage at a storage shed and were herded to the detention barracks. "About ten of us were taken to a big room and ordered to strip naked for an examination. We were told to give samples of urine and feces. Since we had not been warned ahead of time, some of us couldn't. The examination took about one hour and was cursory. We felt extremely embarrassed, not being accustomed to appearing naked in public."[4]

The immigrants were then detained on Angel Island for processing and interrogation. Under the Chinese Exclusion Act of 1882 laborers and their families were not allowed to enter the United States; only merchants and their relatives, including their wives and daughters, were permitted entry. It was not until 1943, when the Chinese Exclusion Act was finally repealed, that Chinese immigrants were allowed to enter the United States and apply for naturalization. Because of these immigration restrictions, all immigrants were interrogated at length to prove that their papers were not fraudulent.

The fortunate ones usually stayed but a few weeks. Some, through bribery, were detained only briefly.[5] One woman said she was released in three days because six-hundred dollars was given to the people in charge. "If they knew you had used 'black money,' they were nicer to you. . . . We were permitted to take our luggage with us, while everyone else had to leave theirs in storage. When I was to leave, they notified me early and helped me get my things together."

The unfortunate ones were detained for long periods; those who failed the interrogation often would stay for six months or a year while their lawyers appealed their cases in Washington DC. One woman stayed for twenty months, only to be deported at the end of her wait. According to one Immigration Inspector, 5 percent to 15 percent of those detained were deported.

Although they had not committed any crimes, all the immigrant detainees were locked in their quarters and only allowed to walk to the storage shed once a week to retrieve luggage. Men and women lived in separate quarters. They slept on two- or three-tier bunk beds, depending on how crowded it was. In the men's quarters, the number ranged from forty to over one hundred at certain times. In the women's quarters, the number rarely exceeded thirty. The women, being fewer in number, were not as organized as the men, who had formed a Self-Governing Organization. Nor were they as active. For pastimes, one woman told us, "After meals, some knit, read newspapers, wrote letters, then slept. When you got up, it was time to eat again. Eat and sleep. In between, people cried."

Another woman told us, "Some of the ladies who were there for a long time finished a lot of knitting projects. If you didn't do anything, you didn't do anything. That's why, in just two weeks, I was so disgusted and bored of just sitting around! There wasn't anything special about it. Day in, day out, the same kind of thing."

Some women had their young sons with them in the barracks. If the boys were over ten, they usually were assigned to the men's quarters. One woman interviewed remembered fearing that her son would be adversely influenced by prostitutes in the women's quarters.

"There were all types of women living there. There were prostitutes, too. Some had been confined there for two or three years. They could see that my son who was fourteen was a pretty big boy. 'Come over here and I'll give you a present!' one of them said. After that I followed my son everywhere! I went with him to the bathroom; wherever he went, I followed. I didn't dare let him go anywhere alone."

The women, like the men, were not allowed any visitors prior to the interrogation, for fear that coaching information for the interrogation would be smuggled in for them to study. But missionaries were allowed to visit. Most of the women interviewed remember Katharine Maurer, alias the "Angel of Angel Island." She spent many years on Angel Island comforting, translating, and providing information and needlework materials to the women.

At one time, women were allowed to go for walks around the island once a week. During other periods, we were told, they were given dominoes to play with. But most of the time, they sat on their beds in the locked room and idled away the time. There was generally an atmosphere of gloom as the women anguished over their fate. One factor that prevented their comforting one another was differences in the dialects they spoke. For example, those who spoke Sam Yup could not communicate with those who spoke Sze Yup.

Said one woman, "At that time, there wasn't much to say because we were the newcomers. Sometimes, Chinese tend to discriminate. We were Sam Yup and didn't know them. When we arrived, we were kind of shy and distant, so there really wasn't much to say."

In order to keep the men and women separated, they were scheduled to eat at different times in the dining room downstairs. Almost everyone we interviewed said there was enough to eat, but that the food was tasteless.

"The squash were all chopped and thrown together like pig slop," one woman told us. "The pork was in big, big chunks. Everything thrown into a big bowl that resembled a wash tub, left there for you to eat or not. They just steamed the food till it was like a soupy stew. After looking at it, you'd lose your appetite."

We learned from a Chinese cook who worked there from 1923 to 1925 that meals usually included soup, salted fish, and one of the following with rice: vermicelli and pork, dried bean curd and pork, potatoes and beef, dried greens, or sand dab. The steamship company paid for the meals. "The food was cheap and of the worst quality," he said. He, along with the other Chinese kitchen help, did not eat the same food they cooked for the detainees.

In 1923, he recalled, there was a riot protesting the poor food. "Dishes were thrown all over, and the Chinese Consul General came to explain that the menu was fixed by government agreement. The rioters were forced into their quarters by soldiers. They refused food for three days." But no change in the quality of food resulted.

The women told us that they had relatives send food from San Francisco to supplement the poor food on Angel Island. Roast duck and chicken, barbequed pork, and sausages were sent to both men and women. There was also a store during certain periods that sold canned food and snacks.

Since the interrogation process was what determined whether the immigrants would be allowed entry or not and also determined how long they would be detained, everyone dreaded the interrogation session and remembered that experience most vividly of all. Usually, there were two inspectors, an interpreter, and a recorder present. One inspector we interviewed told us that he suspected that over 90 percent of the detainees were entering on fraudulent papers. It was his duty to prove these suspicions by asking detailed questions about the detainee's background.

Because of the Exclusion Laws, many Chinese immigrants were forced to lie and come to the United States as "paper sons." The routine functioned in this way: Each time an immigrant returned to China for a visit, he reported the birth of a son. Thus, immigration slots were created and later sold to and used by fellow countrymen to come to America as either the sons of merchants or American citizens. There are known cases of fathers reporting daughters born in China as sons to American officials so that another male could later come to America as a paper son.

In order to catch these illegal entrants, detainees were asked questions regarding the layout of their village and their house, and their family background, going back two or three generations. They were expected to know and relate the number of steps in the house, the burial sites of their grandparents and the directions in which they faced, the number of houses in the village and their arrangement, the names of the neighbors, a description of the village market, incidents that occurred during the father's last visit home, and other such details.

In preparation for the interrogation, most detainees studied "coaching books," which were sent to them prior to their coming to America. Many took the coaching information on board the ship, but as soon as they approached Hawaii, they tore it into pieces and threw it overboard. Said one detainee, "There were more than ten pages of coaching information sent to me by my father, which included information on the family relationships, the village, and living quarters. There were coaching specialists in San Francisco who pointed out the important questions and details. Sample standard questions were on sale. But it could be very tricky, especially when they [didn't] ask the essentials, but instead, "Was there a clock?" or "Who was in the family photos?"

The inspectors checked the answers of the detainees against those of the witnesses. When unexpected questions came up, word was transmitted to the detainees from witnesses through the Chinese kitchen help, who took turns going to San Francisco on their days off. They would come back with messages, which they hid in the food. If they should be caught, all detainees present were to fight to prevent confiscation of the message. The *San Francisco Chronicle* of March 20, 1928, reported an incident of a matron being physically attacked when she attempted to intercept such a message.

The two immigration inspectors we interviewed both felt that the interrogation, as conducted, was the only fair way Immigration could have determined the immigrant's legal right to enter the United States. "We asked them what legitimate children ought to know," said one inspector. According to one of the inspectors, "When in doubt about the answers, we always reinterrogated the detainee."

Yet even real children sometimes failed the interrogation. One real son told us he failed because he said the floor under his bed was brick, and his father testified it was dirt. "It was a dirt floor and then changed to brick when my father left for America." That erroneous answer, coupled with a few other discrepancies, caused him to fail the interrogation.

Because of the cross-checking, each case usually took two to three days. The detainees were then notified. One woman remembered that the guard came and called out a name followed by the Chinese words "ho sai guy," which meant "good fortune." The fortunate one would then gather his or her belongings and go to San Francisco. Inevitably, those left behind experienced a bittersweet mixture of joy and self-pity. "Whenever we saw anyone leaving, we would cry, especially those of us who had been there a long time," she said. "I must have cried a bowlful during my stay at Angel Island. I was forced to come to America and marry a man I had never seen before. The Japanese were bombing us, and there was nowhere else to go. My mother wanted me to come to America so that I could bring the family over later."

NOTES

1. Many foreigners were expelled from the country during the Mexican Revolution of 1910, including the Chinese. Those expelled then came to the United States, were barred entry, and detained on Angel Island to await their return to China. Author is awaiting news of release.

2. Angel Island State Park ranger Alexander Weiss first noticed writings carved all over the walls of the old immigration building in May 1970 and immediately recognized their cultural and historical significance. None of his superiors shared his enthusiasm; the building was earmarked for destruction. So, in 1972 Weiss contacted Dr. George Araki of San Francisco State University, who with Mak Takahashi photographed every inch of wall with poetry on it. They alerted various Asian American studies departments, and soon the Angel Island Immigration Station Historical Advisory Committee was formed by volunteers from the Chinese community. Their efforts to save the remains of the Immigration Station resulted in a state appropriation of $250,000 toward the restoration of the detention barracks.

3. In an attempt to record this relatively unknown beginning of Chinese American history, Genny Lim, a poet, Him Mark Lai, a historian, and I, a librarian, started

collaboration on a book that would include translations of the poems, oral history interviews, and historical background. We interviewed over twenty-five detainees, two interpreters, one cook, and two inspectors. Two detainees provided us with collections of poems copied off the walls during their stay.

4. During one period, detainees were examined for hookworm and liver fluke.

5. In 1917 a graft ring was exposed, and several immigration officers were indicted and convicted; twenty-five were dismissed or transferred.

Frontiers 2:2 (1977): 52–55.

"It is hard to be born a woman but hopeless to be born a Chinese"

The Life and Times of Flora Belle Jan

JUDY YUNG

In 1924 the U.S. Congress passed the National Origins Quota Act, aimed at excluding undesirable immigrants, namely those from southern and eastern Europe, and all aliens ineligible for citizenship, specifically the Chinese, Japanese, and Koreans. That same year, a group of sociologists was investigating the "oriental problem," or the causes of racial conflict on the Pacific Coast. Under the direction of Robert E. Park of the University of Chicago, the Survey of Race Relations staff employed the life histories method, interviewing over three hundred predominantly Chinese and Japanese Americans about their early lives, immigration experiences, aspirations, world views, cultural conflicts, and relationships with other groups.[1] Among them was Flora Belle Jan, the seventeen-year-old daughter of the proprietor of the Yet Far Low chop suey restaurant in Fresno's China Alley. In a one-hour interview with investigator Merle Davis held at her father's restaurant, Flora Belle said, "When I was a little girl, I grew to dislike the conventionality and rules of Chinese life. The superstitions and customs seemed ridiculous to me. My parents have wanted me to grow up a good Chinese girl, but I am an American and I can't accept all the old Chinese ways and ideas. A few years ago when my Mother took me to worship at the shrine of my ancestor and offer a plate of food, I decided it was time to stop this foolish custom. So I got up and slammed down the rice in front of the idol and said, 'So long Old Top, I don't believe in you anyway.' My mother didn't like it a little bit."[2] As she explained further, it was not just Chinese conventions that she disliked and attacked, but American hypocrisy as well. Flora Belle told Davis that she had already written an article in the local newspaper poking fun at her Chinese male friends ("The Sheiks of Chinatown") and a skit that

Flora Belle Jan in 1925. Courtesy of Flora Belle Jan's family.

ridiculed the modern woman in American society ("Old Mother Grundy and Her Brood of Unbaptized Nuns"). She also criticized the "snobbishness" of sorority girls at her college for allowing only rich girls into their organizations, adding matter-of-factly, "Of course being a Chinese girl, I'm not eligible to membership in a sorority, but some of the girls are awfully good to me."[3]

Davis was evidently fascinated by Flora Belle's keen intellect, outgoing personality, and unconventional outlook, for he quickly wrote Park that "Flora Belle is the only Oriental in town apparently who has the charm, wit and nerve to enter good White society. . . . She is both a horror and source of pride to her staid Chinese friends, and is quite the talk of American town."[4] In other words, she was living proof that contrary to popular nativist and racist opinions, Asians were assimilable and could become good Americans. She therefore confirmed Park's theory that all groups, regardless of race or ethnicity, would eventually become integrated into mainstream American life, according to his postulated race relations cycle of contact, conflict, accommodation, and assimilation. To become assimilated, in Park's view, meant Anglo conformity and the erasure of one's ethnicity.[5]

Clearly, here was a Chinese American woman who stood out among her second-generation peers. On the whole, American-born Chinese who came of age in the 1920s aspired to become acculturated or adapted to American middle-class life.[6] They were, after all, U.S. citizens by birth, educated in American public schools, and influenced by their teachers, peers, and the popular media to be Westernized in appearance, outlook, and lifestyle. However, their ability to acculturate was constrained by intergenerational and cultural conflicts at home, and racism, sexism, and economic segmentation in the larger society. Having to negotiate between cultures, between American ideals of democracy and the realities of socioeconomic and political exclusion, Chinese Americans, like their Mexican American and Japanese American contemporaries, responded in a variety of ways based on the interplay of historical forces, cultural values, family circumstances, and individual personalities.[7] Many who were busy with survival just toed the line, acquiescing to the expectations of conservative parents and the limitations placed on them by the larger society. The majority of second-generation Chinese Americans chose to adopt a bicultural lifestyle or a blend of what they took to be "the best of the East and the West" while maintaining a segregated existence from mainstream society. Some, imbued with a strong sense of Chinese nationalism, looked to China for gainful employment, social acceptance, and political participation.[8] Few rebelled as Flora Belle

Jan did in rejecting Chinese customs, claiming an American identity, and critiquing social hypocrisy among her peers. She was what was called a "flapper" in the Jazz Age of the 1920s – a woman who defied social control and conventions, who was modern, independent, sophisticated, and frank in speech, dress, morals, and lifestyle.[9]

At this time the only well-known Chinese American flapper was Anna May Wong, who broke convention by becoming a Hollywood actress. She appeared in *The Thief of Baghdad* (1924) and made more than one hundred films in her thirty-seven-year career, most of which typecasted her in the limited role of "oriental villainess." The image she projected in the movie magazines, however, was that of a beautiful and modern woman who lived in her own apartment, dressed in the most up-to-date fashion, and spoke the latest slang.[10] Although they never met, Flora Belle, when shown some of these articles, remarked, "More power to any Chinese girl who dares to buck the conventions."[11] In her own way, Flora Belle was just as unconventional, independent, and frank. She made her "flapperism" known through her pen, which she wielded with vengeance, leaving behind a trail of letters, romantic poems, short stories, and caustic articles that were published in the *Fresno Bee, San Francisco Examiner,* and *Chinese Students' Monthly.* Her plan to become a famous writer, however, was cut short in 1932, when she went to live in China with her husband. There she experienced transnational dislocation, the hardships and turmoil of war, job discrimination, and a deteriorating health condition caused by stress, a number of abortions, and a difficult childbirth. She passed away in 1950, a year after she returned to the United States.

What made Flora Belle Jan such a daring rebel for her time and how did she negotiate an identity amid generational and gender conflict at home, racism and sexism in American society, and socioeconomic dislocation in war-torn China? Based on interviews that I conducted with three family members (Flora Belle's sister and daughters), letters that Flora Belle wrote to her childhood friend Ludmelia Holstein from 1918 to 1949,[12] and her published writings, I hope to reconstruct Flora Belle Jan's life story and show how history, culture, power, and personality shaped her identity at different points of her life.[13] By so doing, we can come to appreciate the complexities, contradictions, conflicts, and constraints of Flora Belle Jan's life and times as well as the diverse ways that her generation chose to deal with them. At the same time, her story provides us with a multiracial dimension to our understanding of the flapper generation, which led the cultural revolution in the 1920s and ushered America into the modern age.[14] Ultimately, while

Robert E. Park saw Flora Belle Jan as a confirmation of his assimilation theory, her outcome proved him wrong. As acculturated as she was to the American way of life, she could not assimilate as long as the dominant group excluded her on the basis of race.[15] Caught in the webs of two cultures and marginalized by American and Chinese society as well as the Chinese American community, Flora Belle sought to define her own identity, to find her own cultural niche. Her life story and writings reveal a complicated individual, a noteworthy social critic, a talented writer, and a feminist ahead of her time.

Flora Belle Jan was born on September 22, 1906, in Fresno, California. Her parents were immigrants from Guangdong Province in southeast China and operated the Yet Far Low restaurant in China Alley. They had a total of eight children – five girls and three boys. Flora Belle was their third child and oldest daughter.

As Flora Belle's sister Bessie recalls, the family grew up in a poor but integrated neighborhood of Mexicans, Japanese, blacks, and European immigrants. All the children were expected to help at the restaurant and with the housework, but there was time for visits to the public library, music lessons, and church activities. "We didn't have any discipline, advice, or anything [from the parents]," said Bessie. "We just grew up."[16] The father worked long hours at the restaurant, and the mother was described as being old-fashioned, superstitious, and in failing health. Yet, they evidently did try to maintain some parental control over their children. According to letters that she wrote her best girlfriend Ludy (Ludmelia Holstein), Flora Belle often had disagreements with her parents over her aspirations and behavior. They did not approve of her writing, her plans to go away to college, or her active social life. At fourteen, when she was scolded for leaving home to visit relatives in San Francisco without their permission, she wrote Ludy:

Since I'm just back from a 2-weeks' trip, I have loads of work to do and besides, even if I haven't, I'll have to stick around the house because that mother in this house is continually nagging, and Dad says that he'll be glad if I never come back. Yes, Lud, he means that, and I'm, oh, I'm just *ill* about it. He even told me to buy my own stamps in the future. He isn't home now and didn't tell me – but mother – and she, naturally, told everything. I got six dollars to go to "H," and he scolded. Oh Lud, really I wish I were dead, even in spite of my advice to you. When I went to "B" [Berkeley] I got loaded with patriotism, and now my ambition is to graduate from U. of C. [University of California] and go back [to China] and teach. Lucy told me that (She's been back there) teachers were in terrible demand in China now. Oh, Lud, help me! I want to get thru, and out of this house forever! I *hate* my parents, *both,* now, and I want to show them that I can do something in spite of their dog-gone skepticism, old-fashionism, and unpardonable unparentliness. Ludy, will you help me? Mother, or that woman, rather, has just finished saying for the ninth time, "Why did I come back for? What am I doing in this house?" Ludy, if you only knew! Goodnight, dear chum. Hope to see you soon. Love from Flo.[17]

Like most Chinese immigrant parents, her parents wanted unquestioning obedience from their daughter and control over her comings and goings. But, as the above letter shows, they had difficulty communicating this to Flora Belle, who, resentful of their authoritarian ways, was already considering her options, including "going back" to China to teach, as some of her peers were doing. Although they had never been in China before, the tendency was for the second generation to talk about "going back" because their parents and America's discriminatory practices had led them to believe that they belonged in China, not America. Yet, throughout her life and in her writings, Flora Belle always identified with being an American.

Admittedly, Flora Belle was a difficult daughter to manage and quite different from any of her siblings and peers. Young Chinese American women then were busy helping their families make ends meet and, aware of racism and sexism, looking toward developing some practical job skill or marriage for economic security, but not Flora Belle. She was planning on college and a writing career. One reason for the difference may have been her geographic location. In contrast to the segregated life of Chinese Americans in San Francisco, for example, living in Fresno provided more opportunities for someone like Flora Belle to interact with the larger society. As her letters to Ludy reveal, she was more influenced by books, popular culture, her teachers, and peers than by her family upbringing. According to her sister Bessie, Flora Belle was the ambitious and outgoing one in the family, the only one to graduate from college. She was studious, resourceful, had a vivid imagination and flair for writing, was popular with boys, and was regarded as special by many of her teachers. "She kept up friendships with her teachers," her sister said. "They liked her. All through her whole life, they would write her when she was in China, wherever she was."[18] An avid reader, Flora Belle was always going to the library or buying books with money earned from her part-time jobs as a house cleaner, factory worker, or salesgirl. At twelve, she was reading *Huckleberry Finn* and *Tom Sawyer,* corresponding with a number of girlfriends of different ethnic backgrounds about books, China Alley, and boys, and writing stories, poetry, and songs.

Encouraged by her teachers and friends, she wanted to become a famous writer. When admonished by Ludy for taking too much interest in boys, she wrote back, "Oh, dear me! Please, dear chum, *don't* say such an awful, awful thing. You are going to discourage me, utterly dishearten me, and take away all my ambition. *Don't* say that I will be married before you finish college. It will be impossible to adapt myself to a settled-down condition. Oh, how can I bear it, to be a mother and take care of children and live an uneventful life, and die, 'unwept, unhonored, and unsung,' by the world of Fame; only by friends and relatives! No, Ludy dear, I can not, simply will not do it. You must encourage me, and tell me constantly that I must achieve fame and fortune before I consider my task is done."[19]

Flora Belle was serious about pursuing a career in writing. She joined literary clubs, worked on student publications and as a newspaper correspondent, and submitted poems and stories for publication. But her attention was easily diverted by her love for fashion, romance, and a good time out – values promoted by the mass media during a period of postwar prosperity and consumerism. Indeed, as Vicki Ruiz points out in her essay on Mexican American flappers, U.S. consumer culture served as a catalyst for change, affirming women's desires for greater autonomy and a freer heterosexual environment.[20] Because of strict parents or the reality of poverty and prejudice, few could become the flappers they saw on the silver screen or read about in magazines, but Flora Belle could, to a certain extent. Her parents may have been strict, but they were either too busy with work or did not know how to keep her under control. Although the family was poor when she was born, living conditions improved after her father's restaurant business began to prosper. What spending money she got from her parents, when combined with the money she earned from part-time jobs, allowed her to indulge her interests in reading, writing, playing tennis, and dressing fashionably. To outfit herself as a bridesmaid for a wedding when she was fourteen, she wrote Ludy, "I bought my own white kid shoes. They're *high heel* and have a ribbon bow; very much in style now. I know you will be shocked, but why not? – It's my own money, not mother's nor daddy's. It's a fourteen-dollar shoe, but being on sale, it only cost me ten dollars."[21]

For the (Chinese American) Native Sons' Dance in San Francisco, she went out and bought "a stunning $27.50 blue tricotine suit, blue and gray chin-hat and veil, and two-toned gray suede shoes."[22] At one point, she admitted to taking money from her father's cash register to pay for her extravagant purchases. This is how she rationalized it to Ludy: "You must think I'm awful, and your opinion is justified, but dear girl, let me explain our Chinese Girls' Situation to you. Our mothers don't believe in pampering their daughters with too many American clothes, so we, in order to keep pace with Dame Fashion, must resort to schemes and stealing to be thoroughly up-to-date. Literally, 'we lie to live.' "[23]

Her brazen behavior with boys and outspoken criticism of social conventions were other markings of her flapper identity. This was noted by her Sunday school teacher, Amy Purcell, in an interview with Merle Davis:

She is an unique girl. Very keen, unconventional, bright student, good writer. . . . She writes satires and take-offs on Chinese life and customs, and has roused much opposition in her family and in the Chinese community. She wrote for the *Fresno Republican* such caustic articles on Chinatown that the Tongs compelled her to stop. . . . She would like to go on with her education at the University of California, but her parents objected. She needs the advice and help of a good friend. She runs around with the native young Chinese boys, who are as American as she. Last night I saw her go tearing along in a big car with a boy's arm around her neck. At the same time I think Flora Belle is amply able to take care of herself and will not get into serious trouble.[24]

Purcell also observed in the interview that Flora Belle was as critical of Christianity as she was of Chinese religion and customs. She no longer attended Sunday school and "openly scoffs at Christianity and our mission." Flora Belle said as much in one of her letters to Ludy:

Miss Purcell told me she was going to Asilomar in August with her chum for a vacation; and she asked me if I would like to go. "Of course," I said. Then she told me it'd cost about twenty dollars. . . . And Lud-melia! – she darkened the horizon by saying there would be *Bible Study* in the afternoons. I didn't say a word; but I just know in my secret heart that I *won't* spend twenty dollars to go to a religious convention. I'd rather be a vamp and have a Theda Bar-ist time in S.F., and besides, is there a mortal in this world who could live through the tortuous month of July, without a single bit of excitement and suddenly find herself in the tame regions of a religious camp?!!! No-sirree!![25]

As her letters written during her adolescent years indicate, she was no different from other flappers who defined "excitement" as dating and partying. At the age of eleven, she wrote about going out on an automobile ride with a girl and some boys.[26] At thirteen, she wrote that G. had bitten her in several places and called her his "F" (Future).[27] A stream of Chinese American boys pursued her, and she wrote about going out with them for automobile rides, dances, and picnics. In high school she was the only female officer in the

Chinese Students' Club, and when her play, "Miss Flapper Vampire," was performed at the YWCA she created an uproar by dancing with white boys and inviting her white girlfriends to dance with the Chinese boys.[28] Aside from mentioning that she saw no harm in "necking" with boys, there is no indication that she was as sexually permissive as flappers were reputed to be. Nor was she into smoking or drinking. A number of times she wrote Ludy about how she cleverly avoided meeting a suitor alone in the park or how she worked around the efforts of some boys to get her drunk at a party. Flora Belle evidently set her own moral standards somewhere between those of her parents and those of her notorious peers.

Her published writings at this time show Flora Belle to be a romantic dreamer with a vivid imagination. The heroines in her stories have much to say about Flora Belle's own self-image and pursuits in life. In the story "Romance on the Roof," Maizie Edmunds ("the bewitching, dark-haired, dark-eyed, rosy-cheeked, 'slangy' girl of the tenements") is discovered by Ted Hilton ("a captivating young man with wavy auburn hair, dark violet eyes, and a complexion that indicated the athlete") while singing on a rooftop in the slums. Conveniently, Ted happens to be the son of a philanthropist and offers to finance her studies at a music conservatory. But rather than accept his help, Maizie succeeds on her own. The story ends with their chance meeting five years later at her debut performance as a budding opera singer.

It was after the reception and on the roof garden of a famous hotel. The night was coal black, but the flowers in the baskets were snow white. Dark-haired, glowing-eyed Maizie stood like a queen in a gown of shimmering white, looking at Ted, and smiling.

"It is like a dream to see you again," she said. "I tried hard to succeed so that somewhere in the distance you would hear of me, and be glad."

"It is not a dream. It is real," said Ted, taking her hand. "You will never go away again, will you?"

And Maizie answered, "No, unless you go with me."[29]

In another short story, titled "Afraid of the Dark," the heroine Ming Toy closely resembles Flora Belle in a number of revealing ways. Ming Toy is the daughter of a "chop suey palace proprietor" in Chinatown Alley. She is beautiful and brazen, refusing to honor her ancestors, traveling alone in a sleeper car on a train, writing outrageous stories about Chinatown society, behaving like an American flapper, and leaving home for a college education. Moreover, "Ming Toy has never seen China and has no desire to see China. Ming Toy was born in Chinatown, but she has no desire to live in Chinatown. Ming Toy is an American." One night she is found cowering on the steps of a university building because she is afraid to go home in the dark. Here the story becomes even more imaginative: Ming Toy is afraid of the dark because that is when she sees the Chinese ghosts that once haunted her grandfather. But what she doesn't know is that her grandfather was the village executioner and these ghosts were ghosts of the men he executed. And because of that, he was driven to insanity before he died – a story that no one dares tell Ming Toy for fear of disgracing her.[30]

Aside from writing such fanciful short stories for student publications, Flora Belle also submitted articles to local newspapers. On March 27, 1924, she began a short stint with the *San Francisco Examiner,* which billed her as a "Chinese flapper [who] has roped and tied the English language in a manner that would have made Noah Webster marvel."[31] In these articles, Flora Belle went out of her way to write in English slang and showcase her views on Chinese American life "for the edification and entertainment" of the *Examiner* readers. Although her article "Chinatown Sheiks Are Modest Lot" was criticized by some of her peers for being harmful to their image, it might have actually helped to break stereotypes of American-born Chinese men.[32] Contrary to the prevailing images of the emasculated Chinese coolie or the diabolical Fu Manchu, they knew how to "shimmy 'Chicago,' and tango . . . buy candy for the Shebas, take them to the theater, sing them all kinds of 'I've got the blues' songs, and do everything else that American sheiks indulge in; but they'll be dawgoned if they want the world to know about them!" Furthermore, "Oriental sheiks do not pollute their vocabulary with expressions like 'bees' knees,' 'fleas' whiskers,' and 'come on, babe, let's cheese it to the Saturday night hop.' " Rather, they knew the graces of etiquette, enjoyed writers like Gertrude Atherton and Ruby Ayres, and were not pretentious about being highbrow. "But say," she concluded defensively, "if anyone insinuates that they are a million miles from the highbrow, I'll take off my French heels and knock him for a set of mah jongg!"[33] But the *Examiner* was not impressed. She was soon let go for being "too inexperienced for a metropolitan daily."[34]

Upon graduating from Fresno Junior College, Flora Belle moved to San Francisco to pursue her dreams of attending the University of California at Berkeley and becoming a journalist. Although increasing numbers of American women were attending college in the 1920s, there were few Chinese Americans among them because of the prohibitive costs involved and the dim possibilities of any of them finding a job in any professional field upon graduation. Among the Chinese Americans who attended college, most of the men chose to major in engineering, chemistry, and the biological sciences, and the women chose to concentrate in the social sciences and medical fields. Very few pursued the literary arts, as Flora Belle did.[35] To support herself through college, Flora Belle worked first in a Japanese ice cream parlor and later as a check girl at the Mandarin Cafe, jobs that were not considered respectable by Chinatown standards. "My brother says all Chinatown is horrified," she wrote Ludy, "but I merely retorted: Horrified, why? Because their own lives are so saintly that the sight of a girl behind a soft drink counter would give them paralysis of their nerves?"[36]

Living on her own in the city gave Flora Belle free rein to indulge her youthful whims, although she faithfully wrote Chinese letters home to her father. She joined the Chinese Students' Club, signed up to write for the college newspaper, went to fraternity parties, and competed for the title of Chinatown queen.[37] Although she was known as "the belle of Berkeley" among her Chinese American peers, she found it difficult to take part in the flapper movement on the college campus. As in Fresno, she could not join any of the white sororities or date any of the white fraternity boys, an issue that she later takes up in her short story "Transplanted Flower Blossoms."[38] Within a year, too much partying, automobile rides, romantic relationships (once with an engaged man, another time with a Japanese American), and "scandalous" articles had earned her a bad reputation in the close-knit, conservative Chinatown community. She had just met Robert E. Park through her employer at the Mandarin Cafe and, at his suggestion, decided to transfer to the University of Chicago.[39] As she reported to Ludy:

And, Ludy, listen to this – I have been out with so many people for the past few years that I can't help but be known and notorious, and those that I meet now, whom I really care to associate with, feel that I am a friend to too many people, and I cannot be limited to them, so better friendships are impossible. I put this mildly. My reputation, while not at stake, is winked at by many people. I didn't use to care – but I can't help it now. Of course I am *never* so wicked as they regard me – but what is the use of virtue when it isn't recognized? Anyway, I am tired of everybody here – and I want to go away to Chicago, where the distractions of the multitude will not hurt me. There I can perhaps write, and become a worthwhile personage. Here – mediocrity and the lowering influence of the masses are harmful. There is no incentive to rise, one has to be like the others or be criticized.[40]

In Chicago, Flora Belle lived with the Parks and worked part-time as a waitress at the Guardwell Tearoom while attending the university. As she complained to Ludy, it was not easy work: "I have been waiting on tables (the hardest, most nerve-wrecking job in the world). But Mrs. Hernick, the proprietor, thinks I am too slow and so last night she made me carry biscuits and water. I dropped the tray full of glasses and cut my hand and she sent me home."[41] Fortunately, she ran into a relative who owned a restaurant and who insisted on giving her some financial assistance "in return for the help my aunt and uncle gave him when he was younger and needed money," she wrote Ludy.[42] So, according to plan, Flora Belle pursued writing. She became literary editor of the *Chinese Students' Monthly,* joined the Poetry Circle, American Literary Association, and Order of Book Fellows, and was a feature writer for the *Chicago Daily News.* Her story "Murdered by a Chinese Slave Dealer" was published in *Real Detective Stories.*[43] And she evidently fell in and out of love, for many of the poems and short stories that she wrote during this period made references to herself as a "pure lily" in search of the perfect love, only to be repeatedly disappointed by empty promises.[44] At twenty, she was already writing in the voice of someone who had experienced the vicissitudes of life and unrequited love:

PLEASE, GOD

Please, God, will you create a soul
Again for me?
I want my present soul to mold –
To cease to be.

My soul has veins that hold just tears,
And when released
They flood my eyes, my face, my hair,
And will not cease.

I want a soul that cannot feel
Nor hate, nor love.
Nor sympathize nor want to steal
The things of love.

My ideal soul will not regret
Nor dream nor sigh.
Then disillusion cannot let
The tear gates fly.

Please God, if you can't make that soul,
Don't let me weep
For a better one; just take this soul,
And give me sleep.[45]

Yet, she still continued to identify herself as an American flapper. In an article that she wrote in *The Chinese Christian Student* called "Chinese Girls of the East and West," she remarked on the "peculiar" appearances and behavior of female students from China at the University of Chicago: "They are shy and retiring, their hair is seldom artistically arranged, they have little sense of color harmony, they lack campus spirit, they have no style whatsoever." In comparison, native-born coeds like herself "powder and rouge, marcel their hair, trip gaily on impossible French heels, talk slang, flirt openly with boys, dance, drive cars, and go out late, unchaperoned." As she explained the difference, the ideals and standards of each group were molded by the world around them. For those native-born like herself who found "standards of the East lacking, they naturally would adopt the best that they can find in the country of their birth."[46]

Most importantly, Flora Belle fulfilled her goal of graduating from college with a degree in journalism, quite an accomplishment for a Chinese American woman. There was only one other Chinese American journalist at the time – Louise Leung, who had just been hired by the *Los Angeles Record* as a reporter.[47] Flora Belle was finally in a good position to launch her literary career, but then she fell in love with a handsome graduate student from Henan Province, China, who was studying psychology at the University of Chicago, and decided to marry him.

Interestingly enough, her husband strongly resembles Lang-Toa in her short story "Transplanted Flower Blossoms" as much as Flora Belle resembles the heroine Ah Moy. The story opens with Ah Moy's parents leaving China for America. Ah Moy is born soon after their arrival, and they attempt to raise her to be a gentle Chinese lady skilled in the domestic arts. But influenced by what she learns in school, Ah Moy rebels, saying, "I can't be a thorough Chinese, not here in America." She insists on her flapper ways, refuses to be arranged in marriage, and leaves home to attend college. After being jilted by Jimmy Hilton, a "tall American youth with deep brown eyes and chestnut hair," and pursued by a summer job employer who turns out to be a married man, Ah Moy meets and falls in love with Lang-Toa, a student from China who is described as "unusually tall, unusually fair, with eyes more Occidental than Chinese, and a mouth that suggested the chiseled perfection of the imaginary lover of the willow plate." When he proposes marriage, Ah Moy wavers over the prospect of living with him in China – "the land of ancient and established traditions, of sordid realities." But when he agrees to bring her back should China not suit her, she finally accepts his offer of marriage:

Ah Moy was thrilled: she felt submerged in the light of his eyes. She had not expected this: to her the thought of going back to China had meant the end of happiness. He had said she could come back. It was a safe venture.

"What is your answer, Ah Moy?" asked Lang-Toa again.

Ah Moy went to a table and plucked a Chinese lily from a bowl. Smiling, she offered it to Lang-Toa. "This is my way of answering," she said. "Mother, don't you believe that love is like this flower – not that it dies, but that it is pure?"[48]

Like Ah Moy, Flora Belle also had reservations about living in China. Although she had mentioned earlier in a letter to Ludy that she had plans to go teach English in China, it was only in order to escape her restrictive home life, not for nationalist reasons or employment opportunites as in the case of her Chinese American peers.[49] In fact, Flora Belle was rather dubious about whether Chinese Americans could really find success and happiness in the fatherland, as she indicated in her article on the differences between the China-born and the American-born.[50] She apparently also knew that she, for one, was too much of an American flapper to ever adapt to life in China. When Ah Moy's father threatens to send her to China, she replies, "If I should go back to China, I'd feel lost because I have been with Americans for eight[een] years. You see, father, I can't go back."[51] According to her daughters, Flora Belle really had little choice in the matter because their father had every intention of returning to China for work once he completed his education.[52]

Continuing where Ah Moy's story ends, Flora Belle's marriage was far from perfect; her husband did not always prove to be as considerate and understanding as Lang-Toa. While he finished up his graduate studies at the University of Chicago, Flora Belle worked at odd jobs to support him. They had a son a year after their marriage. Then because he irresponsibly refused to practice birth control, Flora was forced to undergo five abortions within four years, resulting in the deterioration of her health. As she later confided in a letter to Ludy:

I have been thinking that I have given the six best years of my life to a man who is not worth it. I have just found out through reflection the reason for our having made no progress in life since [my husband] and I met. Everything I began, everything I attempted was doomed to failure. When I first met him, I was idealistic and enthusiastic and ambitious. I had a body that was sound and healthy. Now I am completely disillusioned, entirely lacking any enthusiasm and utterly devoid of ambition. And my poor body is a mass of nerves and pain. . . . I had my first abortion in September, 1928, at a time when I was pathetically struggling with some editorial work for which I was never paid. The next abortion came the following spring. Then in September, 1929, I was fortunate enough to get a job at the Methodist Book Concern, the salary from which helped [my husband] to go back to school. In January, 1930, I had my third abortion. My memory is a bit hazy but I think the fourth came in December of 1931. I struggled with contraceptives, begged [my husband] to use condoms for added precaution but he stubbornly refused. Then I had a fifth abortion in January, 1932. For these abortions, I have pawned my mother's jewelry, modelled in art schools, slaved at office routine, stood the boresome company of a Chinese newspaper editor whom I taught English, neglected [my son] to go out to work, gone without the decencies of life and the clothes I long for with all the fever of youth. Why have I had to undergo this torture? Because of a man who prides himself on his intelligence that is hopelessly lacking in understanding.[53]

Why did she tolerate this, especially in light of the sexually liberating times when divorce rates were on the rise and women were taking the initiative in controlling their sex lives? It is likely that, similar to the Nisei women in Seattle that Sylvia Yanagisako studied, Flora Belle regarded her marriage as a synthesis between the opposing categories of American and Chinese marriage; that is, romantic love entered into the relationship but so did a degree of duty and commitment.[54] According to their older daughter, "There were times when they seemed very happy to me, and there were times when they fought and she was rather mercurial."[55] Although their marriage was stormy, the subject of divorce never came up in her letters to Ludmelia, probably because of her strong sense of duty and obligation. At a high point in their marriage, she wrote Ludy, "I admire [my husband] more than ever. I appreciate what he has had to endure and he cares more and more for me. He won't even look at anyone else. We get along very well on the whole except for my occasional fits of temper."[56] It was apparently not easy living with a temperamental flapper like Flora Belle.

Remarkably, between her numerous abortions Flora Belle managed to juggle her work and household responsibilities and support her husband through graduate school. "Dishwashing and parading around with the vacuum cleaner *will not* last forever!" she wrote Robert E. Park. "I would not advise any one to plunge into domesticity if one has ambitions for a career."[57] Nevertheless, this period of her life proved to be the most productive in terms of her literary career. She made time in her busy schedule to write poetry, short stories, and articles for the *Chinese Students' Monthly, Chinese Christian Student,* and *Chicago Daily News.* Indeed, she considered reading and writing poetry therapeutic. "There is nothing like poetry," she added in a postscript to Park. "When it is graceful and cheerful, it makes us glad. When it is melancholy and pessimistic, it chimes in with our moods. It is the best escape from *Life!*"[58] One poem, in particular, showed her newfound appreciation for Chinese motherhood, perhaps because her own mother, whom she had never spoken well of in her letters, had recently been committed to a state mental institution; or it could have been because she herself had become a mother. Regardless, the following poem is one of the few times that Flora Belle had anything positive to say about Chinese culture.

TO A CHINESE MOTHER

Small in stature, glossy-haired,
Young in face, though wan.
Forgotten have you how you fared
In your bridal caravan?

Skin of velvet, luscious eyes,
Wide in childlike gaze –
How are you able to disguise
The sorrow of those tortured days?

Was love a duty, or duty, love,
When brides were tagged a price
And sent to market in a drove
Fat purses to entice?

Ten years have gone, and you are free,
Your sons your only care.
How could those years of slavery
Still leave you young and fair?

You smile at questions, shake your head,
And work the silken floss
Of the multi-colored petal threads.
ute, on the years you've lost.

Can it be you think it folly
o mourn over what must be.
That our lives are mapped out wholly
By the Gods of Destiny?

If from your face, serene and calm,
I can gain your philosophy,
I would fear no torrents of grief or pain.
From all desires would I be free![59]

In 1932, a year after her husband received his Ph.D. in psychology, the couple and their four-year-old son sailed for China, but only after Flora Belle had insured that she would be able to return to the United States. By marrying "an alien ineligible to citizenship" she had lost her U.S. citizenship according to the Cable Act of 1922, a racist piece of legislation aimed at discouraging Chinese immigration and family life in America. A 1931 amendment to the Cable Act, thanks to the political efforts of the Chinese American Citizens Alliance, made it possible for her to regain her citizenship through naturalization.[60] The only problem was that she did not hold a birth certificate because there was no doctor present at her birth. As she explained in a letter to Ludmelia: "I must have my birth certificate. After that, I must apply for citizenship since I lost it by marrying an alien according to a recent law. I am permitted to apply for it by paying a $10 fee and passing an examination, providing that I have my birth certificate. I must go through this before I ever dare leave America because once I am out of the country, as an alien, I'll have a devil of a time trying to get back. And I know that I will always want to come back because it is my home."[61] Fortunately, the judge believed her and allowed her to "repatriate" even without the birth certificate.[62] As indicated by this letter, despite efforts on the part of the U.S. government to exclude her, Flora Belle still held on to her identity as an American and to the United States as her home.

Although the family left the United States in debt, their first years in China were relatively good ones. Her husband was able to find a position at the

Catholic University in Beijing, where he taught psychology and statistics, and on his salary alone they were able to rent a nice house with a courtyard, hire a cook and four house servants, and live a comfortable life. But Flora Belle refused to adapt to life in China. According to her older daughter, born in Beijing in 1934, "The years in Peking were good ones for my father but not particularly for my mother, mainly because she was an American and she did not like China. She could neither read nor write the language. She also had many pregnancies which were very detrimental to her health. So on the whole, she was not happy in China. She didn't like the country. She thought it was filthy. She boiled everything. She was always interfering in the kitchen because she thought the servants were too dirty for her standards."[63] Flora Belle refused to learn Mandarin Chinese or associate with the Chinese elite, whom she found "snobbish." Instead, she insisted on speaking English at home, dressing the children in American clothes, cooking and eating American food, and inviting English-speaking diplomats, business people, and students to parties that she hosted. Her younger daughter, born in Beijing in 1938, remembers her mother making American candy and doughnuts and taking her to see American movies like *Bambi*, westerns, and Jane Powell musicals.[64] In contrast to other Chinese Americans who were better prepared for life in China and thus able to effect rapid social and occupational mobility there, Flora Belle was a social misfit.[65] She was also driven to work and to write, making her life more hectic than it needed to be. "She was not a contented housewife," her older daughter remarked.[66]

It didn't help matters that war broke out in China while she was there. In her letters to Ludy, Flora Belle spoke of these trying times, of how the outbreak of Japanese hostilities in the country severed communication with the outside world, caused a food scarcity, and inflated the cost of living. In addition, a complicated pregnancy and difficult childbirth took its toll on her health and nerves. At one point, she was hospitalized and diagnosed as having a kidney infection, anemia, and high blood pressure. "This past year has been a year of judgement upon me," she wrote Ludy. "I survived for what reason I do not know. But at least pain and illness will bring me one kind of freedom – sterility." (In poor health at the time of her third child's birth, she had her tubes tied.) "And with that freedom, I hope to come back to America to remake my shattered life."[67]

But her plans to return home were thwarted by the escalation of war. The worst was yet to come. One year later, she wrote, "I am dumb before the chaos and confusion that confronts me." Their family life had been totally disrupted by the war. Driven out of their home in Beijing, they moved to

Xian, Chongqing, and then Shanghai. At one point, their son boarded in a high school in Xian, the older daughter in a middle high school in Nankai (ten miles away from Chongqing), the younger daughter in a missionary primary school on the south shore, her husband held a government job in Chongqing, and Flora Belle lived on the outskirts of town in a rat-infested room with a leaky roof close to the U.S. Office of War Information, where she worked as a secretary. Their combined salaries could not keep up with the inflated cost of living. They owed the university for medical bills, and food prices were rising so fast that "we don't have a cent even to buy a pair of stockings with," she wrote Ludy, who managed to send her care packages.[68]

Compounding her problems was the job discrimination she faced as a Chinese American and woman journalist in China. Because of her Chinese language limitations, she could only find work with English-language publications and firms – the *Shanghai Herald, Daily Tribune, China Weekly Review,* China National Aviation Corporation, and the Office of War Information. Her letters to Ludmelia were filled with complaints about white male supervisors who treated her unfairly in terms of work assignments, wages, and promotional opportunities. While employed at the Office of War Information (later changed to U.S. Information Service), she wrote Ludy:

My education and previous experience were not considered when I came here. I was given a stenographic test like any China born and I was paid like them. Although after one month of work as a permanent staff member, I was given a $24 raise U.S. because I had shown efficiency. I am still getting a smaller salary than four other girls, two of whom have never been out of China. All around me are staff members who are no older than I and who are no better educated, who hold executive positions with four times my salary, good living quarters, and a living allowance. You wonder I am dissatisfied? It is hard to be born a woman but hopeless to be born a Chinese. There is nothing to hold me here. I shall go at an instance's notice.[69]

Holding a superior attitude toward the local Chinese and toward American employees whom she considered less qualified, she came smack against the harsh reality of racism and sexism in the work world. From her own marital relationship, she also came to a new realization about her racial identity: "I have much respect and affection for him [her husband] but can never be completely happy married to a Chinese as I have a white complex," she wrote Ludy.[70]

As desperate times continued with the ongoing war and as she watched others less worthy reap benefits and rewards because they were white men or because they were women who knew how to flatter the boss, she became more cynical and determined to return home:

I have become philosophic about life and somewhat of a social recluse. I don't have the acute enthusiasm of my youth, nor the abysmal disappointments. I have learned to control my temper and am generally calm and collected. Often I wonder about what pays off in this mortal world and what price, talent and ability and conscientious effort? Our values are all wrong. What usually counts most is hidden and unrecognized. What pays off is vulgar, shallow, and cheap. . . . Somewhere, Ludy, there are green hills, calm blue skies, a musical running brook, a cow grazing contentedly on the pasture, and a clean white cottage where peace and goodness dwell. I shall not give up until I find this place on this awesome, other earth. I cannot say when I am coming back to America, but I shall come if it is just to die.[71]

Realizing that her earlier reservations about China had proven correct – she would never belong there[72] – Flora Belle had tried a number of times to return home to the United States, only to be met with emigration barriers of one kind or another. During the war years the Japanese authorities, who did not recognize dual citizenship, refused to let her leave. Then after the war was over, Flora Belle had a change of heart, placing her family's interest above her own. After all, her husband and three children had all grown up in China and belonged there even if she did not. On the other hand, if they did not return to the United States soon, the girls would lose their right to U.S. citizenship and a chance "to live in a well-ordered world where they can study and learn a profession."[73] As conditions in China remained unstable and civil war between the communists and nationalists broke out, she made preparations to leave. Her husband and son were unsuccessful in gaining permission to accompany her, but they all agreed it was best for her and the two daughters to leave first.[74]

The prospect of returning home refueled Flora Belle's ambitions to pursue a writing career. Newswriting would be the means by which she would support herself and her daughters in the United States. She made plans in her mind to "some day [find happiness] in an independent literary effort, and still further in the future, in some kind of sociological work that will help repay the world for the blessings it has given me."[75] Prior to departing, she began making contacts through her employers in China with news and travel agencies in the United States. She wrote Ludmelia about the exciting prospects of working for United Press International or Pan American Airways, both of which had expressed interest in her. According to her younger daughter, her typewriter – the one thing she insisted her husband buy for her in China – remained her constant companion during their voyage home from Shanghai to San Francisco in December 1948.[76]

After a brief visit with her family in San Francisco, they went to live with Ludy in Yuma, Arizona, where Flora Belle found work as a secretary and spent all her spare moments composing at her typewriter. But her health never recovered from the hardships she had suffered in China. On January 22, 1950, at the age of forty-three, Flora Belle Jan died of high blood pressure and kidney failure. Her children had inscribed on her gravestone "A journalist and feminist before her time. A talent and beauty extinguished in her prime. Our beloved mother."

Flora Belle Jan's worst fear – that she would "live an uneventful life, and die, 'unwept, unhonored, and unsung,' by the world of Fame" – was not unfounded given the socioeconomic and political barriers she had to confront both in the United States and China. Although she did not achieve literary fame, she did live an eventful life as an American flapper who rebelled against both Chinese and American conventionality and social restraints. As her correspondence and publications indicate, she was a talented writer, a noteworthy social critic, and a strong woman who stood up for what she believed in. Despite the constraints of her time, she lived life to its fullest, held on to her American identity and dreams, and left a legacy of writings about her time and generation for posterity. Her life story reminds us of the different responses that Chinese Americans have brought to bear on cultural conflicts and of the high costs that women of color have had to pay for the racial and gender inequities of our society. As well, Flora Belle Jan's biography illuminates the transformation of identity at different points in one's life due to the interplay of history, culture, power, and personality. And finally, it points to the diversity of experiences that make up Chinese America and the flapper generation of the 1920s.

NOTES

My special thanks to the following colleagues for their helpful suggestions on this article: Colleen Fong, Ruthanne Lum McCunn, Valerie Matsumoto, Peggy Pascoe, Mitziko Sawada, K. Scott Wong, Shelley Wong, and Henry Yu.

1. Funded by the Institute of Social and Religious Studies in New York and other private donations, the Survey of Race Relations was to gather useful information that would hopefully lead to improved race relations in the United States. However, the

research project terminated in 1925, two years after it started, for lack of funds. One set of the Survey's reports, correspondence, and interview transcripts was deposited at the Hoover Institution on War, Revolution, and Peace at Stanford University (hereafter cited as SRR). Two key players in the project eventually published books based on the work of the Survey: Eliot Grinnell Mears, *Resident Orientals on the American Pacific Coast: Their Legal and Economic Status* (Chicago: University of Chicago Press, 1928) and William Carlson Smith, *Americans in Process: A Study of Our Citizens of Oriental Ancestry* (Ann Arbor: Edwards Brothers, 1937). For an intellectual history of Park and the institutional construction of the "oriental problem," see Henry Yu, "Thinking about Orientals: A History of Race, Migration, and Modernity in Twentieth-Century America" (Ph.D. diss., Princeton University, 1995).

2. "Interview with Flora Belle Jan, Daughter of Proprietor of the 'Yet Far Low' Chop Suey Restaurant, Tulare St. and China Alley, Fresno," box 28, folder 225, 1924, SRR.

3. "Interview with Flora Belle Jan, Daughter of Proprietor."

4. Merle Davis correspondence to Dr. Robert E. Park, June 1, 1924, box 12, SRR.

5. Robert E. Park, *Race and Culture* (Glencoe IL: Free Press, 1950). For a discussion of Flora Belle Jan as a confirmation of Park's assimilation theory, see Yu, "Thinking about Orientals," 41–54. Flora Belle Jan's life story and writings are also discussed in Judy Yung, *Unbound Feet: A Social History of Chinese Women in San Francisco* (Berkeley: University of California Press, 1995), chapter 3, and *Unbound Voices: A Documentary History of Chinese Women in San Francisco* (Berkeley: University of California Press, 1999).

6. I take this meaning of acculturation from Eileen H. Tamura's study of second-generation Japanese Americans in Hawaii, in which she makes a clear distinction between acculturation and Americanization: "Acculturation refers to the adaptation of a group to American middle-class norms and assumes that the process entails the persistence of ethnic identity. Americanization, on the other hand, refers to the organized effort during and following World War I to compel immigrants and their children to adopt certain Anglo-American ways while remaining at the bottom of socioeconomic strata of American society" (*Americanization, Acculturation, and Ethnic Identity: The Nisei Generation in Hawaii* [Urbana and Chicago: University of Illinois Press, 1994], 52). Her study clearly shows that the Nisei in Hawaii gradually acculturated into American life while retaining elements of their Japanese heritage.

7. See George J. Sanchez, *Becoming Mexican American: Ethnicity, Culture, and Identity in Chicano Los Angeles, 1900–1945* (New York: Oxford University Press, 1993); Vicki Ruiz, "'La Malinche Tortilla Factory': Negotiating the Iconography of Americanization, 1920–1950," in *Privileging Positions: The Sites of Asian American Studies,* ed. Gary Okihiro, et al. (Pullman: Washington State University Press, 1995), 201–

16; and "'Star Struck': Acculturation, Adolescence, and Mexican American Women, 1920–1950," in *Small Worlds: Children and Adolescents in America, 1850–1950,* ed. Elliott West and Paula Petrik (Lawrence: University Press of Kansas, 1992), 61–80; Tamura, *Americanization, Acculturation, and Ethnic Identity;* and Valerie Matsumoto, "Desperately Seeking 'Deirdre': Gender Roles, Multicultural Relations, and Nisei Women Writers of the 1930s," *Frontiers*12:1 (1991): 19–32.

8. For studies on the acculturation of second-generation Chinese Americans, see Kit King Louis, "A Study of American-born and American-reared Chinese in Los Angeles" (master's thesis, University of Southern California, 1931); Marjorie Lee, "Hu-Jee: The Forgotten Second Generation of Chinese Americans, 1930–1950" (master's thesis, University of California, Los Angeles, 1984); and Yung, *Unbound Feet,* chapter 3.

9. For an examination of youth culture in the 1920s, see Paula Fass, *The Damned and the Beautiful: American Youth in the 1920s* (New York: Oxford University Press, 1977); John D'Emilio and Estelle Freedman, *Intimate Matters: A History of Sexuality in America* (New York: Harper and Row, 1988); Vicki Ruiz, "The Flapper and the Chaperone: Historical Memory among Mexican-American Women," in *Seeking Common Ground: Multidisciplinary Studies of Immigrant Women in the United States,* ed. Donna Gabaccia (Westport CT: Greenwood Press, 1992), 141–57; and Valerie Matsumoto, "Japanese American Women and the Creation of Urban Nisei Culture in the 1930s," in *Over the Edge: Remapping Western Experiences,* ed. Valerie J. Matsumoto and Blake Allmendinger (Berkeley: University of California Press, 1999).

10. See Judy Chu, "Anna May Wong," *Counterpoint: Perspectives on Asian America,* ed. Emma Gee (Los Angeles: Asian American Studies Center, University of California, 1976), 284–88; and Alice L. Tilderley, " 'I Am Lucky That I Am Chinese,' " *San Francisco Chronicle,* June 3, 1928, 13.

11. Letter from Flora Belle Jan to Ludmelia Holstein, September 21, 1931.

12. Ludmelia Holstein was born in Fresno, California, in 1905 and died of a stroke in Yuma, Arizona, in 1976 at the age of seventy-one. She had been Flora Belle's confidante since grammar school. The two shared life experiences and aspirations to become famous writers throughout Flora Belle's lifetime. After Flora Belle's death in 1950, Holstein returned all of Flora Belle's letters to her older daughter, who later generously shared some of them with me.

13. Here I am borrowing from cultural critic Stuart Hall, who wrote that cultural identity is as much a matter of becoming as being: "Cultural identities come from somewhere, have histories. But, like everything which is historical, they undergo constant transformation. Far from being eternally fixed in some essentialised past, they are subject to the continous 'play' of history, culture and power." By "power" he means the dominant group's power "to make us see and experience *ourselves* as

'Other.' " See Stuart Hall, "Cultural Identity and Diaspora," in *Identity: Community, Culture, Difference*, ed. Jonathan Rutherford (London: Lawrence and Wishart, 1990), 225.

14. Most literature on youth culture of the 1920s, such as Fass's *The Damned and the Beautiful*, have failed to address other groups outside of white, middle-class youths. For studies on Mexican American and Japanese American flappers, see Ruiz, "The Flapper and the Chaperone," and Matsumoto, "Japanese American Women and the Creation of Urban Nisei Culture in the 1930s."

15. Here I am making a distinction between acculturation and assimilation according to Milton M. Gordon's *Assimilation in American Life: The Role of Race, Religion, and National Origin* (New York: Oxford University Press, 1964), in which he argues that a group can acculturate (change values, customs, and cultural forms) but not assimilate (change primary and institutional relationships) unless it is accepted and allowed to do so by the dominant group.

16. Bessie Hung, interview with author, June 30, 1989.

17. Letter from Flora Belle to Holstein, July 17, 1921.

18. Bessie Hung interview, June 30, 1989.

19. Letter from Flora Belle to Holstein, August 20, 1920.

20. See Ruiz, "The Flapper and the Chaperone," 149–51.

21. Letter from Flora Belle to Holstein, August 20, 1920.

22. Letter from Flora Belle to Holstein, August 17, 1921.

23. Letter from Flora Belle to Holstein, August 17, 1921.

24. "Flora Belle Jan," box 9, folder 9, 1925, SRR.

25. Letter from Flora Belle to Holstein, June 28, 1920.

26. Letter from Flora Belle to Holstein, September 3, 1918.

27. Letter from Flora Belle to Holstein, August 20, 1920.

28. According to Merle Davis's letter to Robert E. Park, "There is now quite a furore in the town at this breaking of cast and the Y. W. C. A. is catching it." See Merle Davis correspondence to Dr. Robert E. Park, SRR.

29. Flora Belle Jan, "Romance on the Roof," *The Trailmaker*, March 1924, 55–58.

30. Flora Belle Jan, "Afraid of the Dark," *The Interpreter*, September 1927, 17–19. There is a Chinese belief that people who die before their time, such as murder victims or suicides, often return as malicious ghosts to haunt those from whom they seek revenge.

31. *San Francisco Examiner*, March 27, 1924, 9.

32. According to Amy Purcell, the story created such a commotion among some of the Chinese male students that they fought over it. Some felt Flora Belle had attacked the honor of China; others felt that it was a ridiculous caricature of Chinese American life. See "Flora Belle Jan," box 9, SRR. Later, in a letter to Ludy from

San Francisco dated July 6, 1924, Flora Belle wrote, "A worker at the Y. W. C. A. disapproves of my articles – said they did more harm than good. So do other people – but, who's paying me – the 'Y' or the Ex.!! Can't be worried!"

33. Flora Belle Jan, "Chinatown Sheiks Are Modest Lot: Eschew Slang, Love-Moaning Blues," *San Francisco Examiner,* March 27, 1924, 9.

34. Letter from Flora Belle to Holstein, July 16, 1924.

35. See Beulah Ong Kwoh, "Occupational Status of the American-born Chinese College Graduates" (master's thesis, University of Chicago, 1947).

36. Letter from Flora Belle to Holstein, July 18, 1924.

37. "Chinese Girls Vie for Fete Queen Honors," *San Francisco Examiner,* April 5, 1925, 13.

38. Flora Belle Jan, "Transplanted Flower Blossoms," *The Chinese Students' Monthly* 24:7 (1929): 324–28, and 24:8 (1929): 351–66.

39. Park took an interest in mentoring Chinese and Japanese American students to pursue higher education. A significant number of them were recruited to the University of Chicago to study sociology with him. See Yu, "Thinking about Orientals."

40. Letter from Flora Belle to Holstein, November 27, 1925.

41. Letter from Flora Belle to Holstein, January 9, 1926.

42. Letter from Flora Belle to Holstein, January 24, 1926.

43. "Fresno Girl Wins Success as Feature, Story Writer," *Fresno Bee,* June 23, 1932.

44. See "To the One Who Supplanted Me," *Chinese Students' Monthly* 23:8 (1928): 58; "Self Delight," *Chinese Students' Monthly* 24:4 (1929): 170; "Transplanted Flower Blossoms," *Chinese Students' Monthly* 24:7 (1929): 324–28; "Vows," *Chinese Students' Monthly* 24:8 (1929): 349; "The Absolute," *Chinese Students' Monthly* 24:8 (1929): 366; and "Tragedy Found in Painting – Artist Goes; Maid Dies of Love – Famous Masterpiece Here," *Chinese Students' Monthly* 25:1 (1929): 60–61.

45. Flora Belle Jan, "Two Poems," *The Survey* 56:3 (1926): 164.

46. Flora Belle Jan, "Strangers Who Have Met – Chinese Girls of the East and West," *The Chinese Christian Student* 2 (1927): 10–11.

47. See Louise Leung Larson, *Sweet Bamboo: Saga of a Chinese American Family* (Los Angeles: Chinese Historical Society of Southern California, 1989), 213–15, and *Linking Our Lives: Chinese American Women of Los Angeles: A Joint Project of Asian American Studies Center, UCLA, and the Chinese Historical Society of Southern California* (Los Angeles: Chinese Historical Society of Southern California, 1984), 73–74.

48. Flora Belle Jan, "Transplanted Flower Blossoms," 366.

49. Most second-generation Chinese Americans who went to China in the 1920s and 1930s did so not only out of frustration over racial discrimination in America but also in answer to China's call for help in building a stronger nation. For a

discussion of the Chinese American debate over "Does my future lie in China or America?" see Yung, *Unbound Feet,* 157–60.

50. Flora Belle Jan, "Strangers Who Have Met," 10.

51. Flora Belle Jan, "Transplanted Flower Blossoms," 325.

52. Flora Belle Jan's daughters' and husband's names are withheld by request of the daughters, interview with author, August 6, 1989.

53. Letter from Flora Belle to Holstein, January 20, 1934.

54. See Sylvia Junko Yanagisako, *Transforming the Past: Tradition and Kinship among Japanese Americans* (Palo Alto: Stanford University Press, 1985), 107–9.

55. Interview with daughters, August 6, 1989.

56. Letter from Flora Belle to Holstein, February 11, 1929.

57. Letter from Flora Belle Jan to Robert E. Park, January 13, 1927, Robert Ezra Park Papers, Joseph Regenstein Special Collections, University of Chicago. I am indebted to Henry Yu for sharing this letter with me.

58. Letter from Flora Belle to Park, January 13, 1927.

59. Flora Belle Jan, "To a Chinese Mother," *The Chinese Students' Monthly* 25:4 (1930): 160.

60. For a discussion of the Cable Act and its effect on Chinese American women, see Sucheng Chan, "The Exclusion of Chinese Women, 1870–1943," in *Entry Denied: Exclusion and the Chinese Community in America, 1882–1943,* ed. Sucheng Chan (Philadelphia: Temple University Press, 1991), 128–29; and Yung, *Unbound Feet,* 168–69.

61. Letter from Flora Belle to Holstein, September 23, 1931.

62. Flora Belle Jan, folder 2070/174, Chinese Departure Case Files, Chicago District Office, Immigration and Naturalization Service, National Archives, Chicago, Illinois. I am indebted to Henry Yu for sharing this file with me.

63. Interview with daughters, August 6, 1989.

64. Interview with daughters, August 6, 1989.

65. For a discussion of how other Chinese Americans adapted to life in China, see Yung, *Unbound Feet,* 144–46.

66. Interview with daughters, August 6, 1989.

67. Letter from Flora Belle to Holstein, November 30, 1938.

68. Letter from Flora Belle to Holstein, September 5, 1939.

69. Letter from Flora Belle to Holstein, December 22, 1944.

70. Letter from Flora Belle to Holstein, April, 1945.

71. Letter from Flora Belle to Holstein, July 16, 1947.

72. In a letter to Ludy dated October, 1937, she had written, "So fiery and mercurial and temperamental as she [her older daughter] is, she will never get along in China just as I didn't."

73. Letter from Flora Belle to Holstein, December 3, 1948. The Nationality Act of 1940 stipulated that a person born outside the United States of a parent who is a U.S. citizen can claim derivative citizenship providing that child resides in the United States for five years between the ages of thirteen and twenty-one years.

74. The son, being a U.S. citizen, was soon able to join his mother and sisters. Flora Belle's husband, however, was only able to emigrate after her death in 1950 as the surviving parent of two minor children.

75. Letter from Flora Belle to Holstein, June 21, 1945. Flora Belle had always wanted to fulfill Park's expectations of her. When she heard of his death in 1944, she wrote to Ludmelia, "I was very depressed by a letter from Mrs. Robert E. Park, who told me of Dr. Park's death. . . . The underlining reason for my depression was that I had not accomplished anything during his lifetime. He had expected so much of me and had hope that I would write something worthwhile, but here I am beginning all over again, somebody's stand-on with security as far away as Mars" (December 1944).

76. Interview with daughters, August 6, 1989. In a letter to Ludy in October, 1937, Flora Belle wrote, "This very typewriter I am using – a good portable Corona – was loaned by a friend who sympathized with my ambitions and was willing to let me take it to America to use. But I will not merely borrow it. I want [my husband] to buy it for me. He has agreed and will pay for it later."

Frontiers 18:3 (1997): 66–91.

Japanese American Women during World War II

VALERIE MATSUMOTO

> The life here cannot be expressed. Sometimes, we are resigned to it, but when we see the barbed wire fences and the sentry tower with floodlights, it gives us a feeling of being prisoners in a "concentration camp." We try to be happy and yet oftentimes a gloominess does creep in. When I see the "I'm an American" editorial and write-ups, the "equality of race etc." – it seems to be mocking us in our faces. I just wonder if all the sacrifices and hard labor on [the] part of our parents has gone up to leave nothing to show for it?
>
> – *Letter from Shizuko Horiuchi, Pomona Assembly Center, May 24, 1942*

Thirty years after her relocation camp internment, another Nisei woman, the artist Miné Okubo, observed, "The impact of the evacuation is not on the material and the physical. It is something far deeper. It is the effect on the spirit."[1] Describing the lives of Japanese American women during World War II and assessing the effects of the camp experience on the spirit are complex tasks: Factors such as age, generation, personality, and family background interweave and preclude simple generalizations. In these relocation camps Japanese American women faced severe racism and traumatic family strain, but the experience also fostered changes in their lives: more leisure for older women, equal pay with men for working women, disintegration of traditional patterns of arranged marriages, and, ultimately, new opportunities for travel, work, and education for the younger woman.

I will examine the lives of Japanese American women during the trying war years, focusing on the second generation – the Nisei – whose work and education were most affected. The Nisei women entered college and ventured into new areas of work in unfamiliar regions of the country, sustained by fortitude, family ties, discipline, and humor. My understanding of their history derives from several collections of internees' letters, assembly center and relocation camp newspapers, census records, and taped oral history interviews that I conducted with eighty-four Nisei (second generation) and eleven Issei (first generation). Two-thirds of these interviews were with women.

The personal letters, which comprise a major portion of my research, were written in English by Nisei women in their late teens and twenties. Their writing reflects the experience and concerns of their age group. It is important, however, to remember that they wrote these letters to Caucasian friends and sponsors during a time of great insecurity and psychological and economic hardship. In their struggle to be accepted as American citizens, the interned Japanese Americans were likely to minimize their suffering in the camps and to try to project a positive image of their adjustment to the traumatic conditions.

PREWAR BACKGROUND

A century ago, male Japanese workers began to arrive on American shores, dreaming of making fortunes that would enable them to return to their homeland in triumph. For many, the fortune did not materialize, and the shape of the dream changed: They developed stakes in small farms and businesses and, together with wives brought from Japan, established families and communities.

The majority of Japanese women – over thirty-three thousand immigrants – entered the United States between 1908 and 1924.[2] The "Gentlemen's Agreement" of 1908 restricted the entry of male Japanese laborers into the country but sanctioned the immigration of parents, wives, and children of laborers already residing in the United States. The Immigration Act of 1924 excluded Japanese immigration altogether.

Some Japanese women traveled to reunite with husbands; others journeyed to America as newlyweds with men who had returned to Japan to find wives. Still others came alone as picture brides to join Issei men who sought to avoid army conscription or excessive travel expenses; their family-arranged marriages deviated from social convention only by the absence of the groom from the *miai* (preliminary meeting of prospective spouses) and wedding ceremony.[3] Once settled, these women confronted unfamiliar clothing, food, language, and customs as well as life with husbands who were, in many cases, strangers and often ten to fifteen years their seniors.

Most Issei women migrated to rural areas of the West. Some lived with their husbands in labor camps, which provided workers for the railroad industry, the lumber mills of the Pacific Northwest, and the Alaskan salmon canneries.[4] They also farmed with their husbands as cash or share tenants, particularly in California where Japanese immigrant agriculture began to flourish. In urban areas, women worked as domestics[5] or helped their husbands run small businesses such as laundries, bath houses, restaurants, pool halls, boarding houses, grocery stores, curio shops, bakeries, and plant nurseries. Except for the few who married well-to-do professionals or merchants, the majority of Issei women unceasingly toiled both inside and outside the home. They were always the first to rise in the morning and the last to go to bed at night.

The majority of the Issei's children, the Nisei, were born between 1910 and 1940. Both girls and boys were incorporated into the family economy early, especially those living on farms. They took care of their younger siblings, fed the farm animals, heated water for the *furo* (Japanese bath), and worked in the fields before and after school – hoeing weeds, irrigating, and driving tractors. Daughters helped with cooking and cleaning. In addition, all were expected to devote time to their studies: the Issei instilled in their children a deep respect for education and authority. They repeatedly admonished the Nisei not to bring disgrace upon the family or community and exhorted them to do their best in everything.

The Nisei grew up integrating both the Japanese ways of their parents and the mainstream customs of their non-Japanese friends and classmates – not always an easy process given the deeply rooted prejudice and discrimination they faced as a tiny, easily identified minority. Because of the wide age range among them and the diversity of their early experiences in various urban and rural areas, it is difficult to generalize about the Nisei. Most grew up speaking Japanese with their parents and English with their siblings, friends, and teachers. Regardless of whether they were Buddhist or Christian, they celebrated the New Year with traditional foods and visiting, as well as Christmas and Thanksgiving. Girls learned to knit, sew, and embroider, and some took lessons in *odori* (folk dancing). The Nisei, many of whom were adolescents during the 1940s, also listened to the *Hit Parade*, Jack Benny, and *Gangbusters* on the radio, learned to jitterbug, played kick-the-can and baseball, and read the same popular books and magazines as their non-Japanese peers.

The Issei were strict and not inclined to open displays of affection toward their children, but the Nisei were conscious of their parents' concern for them and for the family. This sense of family strength and responsibility helped to sustain the Issei and Nisei through years of economic hardship and discrimination: the West Coast anti-Japanese movement of the early 1920s, the Depression of the 1930s, and the most drastic ordeal – the chaotic uprooting of the World War II evacuation, internment, and resettlement.

EVACUATION AND CAMP EXPERIENCE

The bombing of Pearl Harbor on December 7, 1941, unleashed war between the United States and Japan and triggered a wave of hostility against Japanese Americans. On December 8, the financial resources of the Issei were frozen, and the Federal Bureau of Investigation began to seize Issei community leaders thought to be strongly pro-Japanese. Rumors spread that the Japanese in Hawaii had aided the attack on Pearl Harbor, fueling fears of "fifth column" activity on the West Coast. Politicians and the press clamored for restrictions against Japanese Americans, and their economic competitors saw the chance to gain control of Japanese American farms and businesses.

Despite some official doubts and some differences of opinion among military heads regarding the necessity of removing Japanese Americans from the West Coast, in the end the opinions of civilian leaders and Lieutenant General John L. DeWitt – head of the Western Defense Command – Assistant Secretary of War John McCloy, and Secretary of War Henry Stimson prevailed. On February 19, 1942, President Franklin Delano Roosevelt signed Executive Order 9066, arbitrarily suspending the civil rights of American citizens by authorizing the removal of 110,000 Japanese and their American-born children from the western half of the Pacific Coastal States and the southern third of Arizona.[6]

During the bewildering months before evacuation, the Japanese Americans were subject to curfews and to unannounced searches at all hours for "contraband" weapons, radios, and cameras; in desperation and fear, many people destroyed their belongings from Japan, including treasured heirlooms, books, and photographs. Some families moved voluntarily from the Western Defense zone, but many stayed, believing that all areas would eventually be restricted or fearing hostility in neighboring states.

Involuntary evacuation began in the spring of 1942. Families received a scant week's notice in which to "wind up their affairs, store or sell their possessions, close up their businesses and homes, and show up at an assembly point for transportation to an assembly center."[7] Each person was allowed to bring only as many clothes and personal items as he or she could carry to the temporary assembly centers that had been hastily constructed at fairgrounds, race tracks, and Civilian Conservation Corps camps: twelve in California, one in Oregon, and one in Washington.

The rapidity of evacuation left many Japanese Americans numb; one Nisei noted that "a queer lump came to my throat. Nothing else came to my mind, it was just blank. Everything happened too soon, I guess."[8] As the realization of leaving home, friends, and neighborhood sank in, the numbness gave way to bewilderment. A teenager at the Santa Anita Assembly Center wrote, "I felt lost after I left Mountain View [California]. I thought that we could go back but instead look where we are."[9] Upon arrival at the assembly centers, even the Nisei from large urban communities found themselves surrounded by more Japanese than they had ever before seen. For Mary Okumura, the whole experience seemed overwhelming at first: "Just about every night, there is something going on but I rather stay home because I am just new here & don't know very much around. As for the people I met so many all ready, I don't remember any. I am not even going to try to remember names because its just impossible here."[10]

A Nisei from a community where there were few Japanese felt differently about her arrival at the Merced Assembly Center: "I guess at that age it was sort of fun for me really [rather] than tragic, because for the first time I got to see young [Japanese] people. . . . We signed up to work in the mess hall – we got to meet everybody that way."[11]

Overlying the mixed feelings of anxiety, anger, shame, and confusion was resignation. As a relatively small minority caught in a storm of turbulent events that destroyed their individual and community security, there was little the Japanese Americans could do but shrug and say, "*Shikata ga nai*," or "It can't be helped," the implication being that the situation must be endured. The phrase lingered on many lips when the Issei, Nisei, and the young Sansei (third generation) children prepared for the move – which was completed by November 1942 – to the ten permanent relocation camps organized by the War Relocation Authority: Topaz, Utah; Poston and Gila River, Arizona; Amache, Colorado; Manzanar and Tule Lake, California; Heart Mountain, Wyoming; Minidoka, Idaho; Denson and Rohwer, Arkansas.[12] Denson and Rohwer were located in the swampy lowlands of Arkansas; the other camps were in desolate desert or semi-desert areas subject to dust storms and extreme temperatures reflected in the nicknames given to the three sections of the Poston Camp: Toaston, Roaston, and Duston.

The conditions of camp life profoundly altered family relations and affected women of all ages and backgrounds. Family unity deteriorated in the crude communal facilities and cramped barracks. The unceasing battle with the elements, the poor food, the shortages of toilet tissue and milk, coupled with wartime profiteering and mismanagement, and the sense of injustice and frustration took their toll on a people uprooted, far from home.

The standard housing in the camps was a spartan barracks, about twenty feet by one hundred feet, divided into four to six rooms furnished with steel army cots. Initially each single room, or "apartment," housed an average of eight persons; individuals without kin nearby were often moved in with smaller families. Because the partitions between apartments did not reach the ceiling, even the smallest noises traveled freely from one end of the building to the other. There were usually fourteen barracks in each block, and each block had its own mess hall, laundry, latrine, shower facilities, and recreation room.

Because of the discomfort, noise, and lack of privacy, which "made a single symphony of yours and your neighbors' loves, hates, and joys,"[13] the barracks often became merely a place to "hang your hat" and sleep. As Jeanne Wakatsuki Houston records in her autobiography, *Farewell to Manzanar*, many family members began to spend less time together in the crowded barracks. The even greater lack of privacy in the latrine and shower facilities necessitated adjustments in former notions of modesty. There were no partitions in the shower room, and the latrine consisted of two rows of partitioned toilets "with nothing in front of you, just on the sides. Lots of people were not used to those kind of facilities, so [they'd] either go early in the morning when people were not around, or go real late at night. . . . It was really something until you got used to it."[14]

The large communal mess halls also encouraged family disunity as family members gradually began to eat separately: mothers with small children, fathers with other men, and older children with their peers. "Table manners were forgotten," observed Miné Okubo. "Guzzle, guzzle, guzzle; hurry, hurry, hurry. Family life was lacking. Everyone ate wherever he or she pleased."[15] Some strategies were developed for preserving family unity. The Amache Camp responded in part by assigning each family a particular table in the mess hall. Some families took the food back to their barracks so that they might eat together. But these measures were not always feasible in the face of varying work schedules; the odd hours of those assigned to shifts in the mess halls and infirmaries often made it impossible for the family to sit down together for meals.

Newspaper reports about how Japanese Americans were living in luxurious conditions angered evacuees struggling to adjust to cramped quarters and crude communal facilities. A married woman with a family wrote from Heart Mountain: "Last weekend, we had an awful cold wave and it was about 20° to 30° below zero. In such a weather, it's terrible to try going even to the bath and latrine house. . . . It really aggravates me to hear some politicians say we Japanese are being coddled, for *it isn't so*!! We're on ration as much as outsiders are. I'd say welcome to anyone to try living behind barbed wire and be cooped in 20 ft. by 20 ft. room. . . . We do our sleeping, dressing, ironing, hanging up our clothes in this one room."[16]

After the first numbness of disorientation, the evacuees set about making their situation bearable, creating as much order in their lives as possible. With blankets they partitioned their apartments into tiny rooms and created benches, tables, and shelves from scrap lumber left over from barracks construction; victory gardens and flower patches appeared. Evacuees also took advantage of the opportunity to taste freedom when they received temporary permits to go shopping in nearby towns. These were memorable occasions. A Heart Mountain Nisei described in 1944 what such a trip meant to her:

For the first time since being behind the fences, I managed to go out shopping to Billings, Montana – a trip about 4 hours ride on train and bus. . . . It was quite a mental relief to breathe the air on the outside. . . . And was it an undescribable sensation to be able to be dressed up and walk the pavements with my high heel shoes!! You just can't imagine how full we are of pent-up emotions until we leave the camp behind us and see the highway ahead of us. A trip like that will keep us from becoming mentally narrow. And without much privacy, you can imagine how much people will become dull.[17]

Despite the best efforts of the evacuees to restore order to their disrupted world, camp conditions prevented replication of their prewar lives. Women's work experiences, for example, changed in complex ways during the years of internment. Each camp offered a wide range of jobs, resulting from the organization of the camps as model cities administered through a series of departments headed by Caucasian administrators. The departments handled everything from accounting, agriculture, education, and medical care to mess hall service and the weekly newspaper. The scramble for jobs began early in the assembly centers and camps, and all able-bodied persons were expected to work.

Even before the war many family members had worked, but now children and parents, men and women, all received the same low wages. In the relocation camps, doctors, teachers, and other professionals were at the top of the pay scale, earning nineteen dollars per month. The majority of workers received sixteen dollars, and apprentices earned twelve dollars. The new equity in pay and the variety of available jobs gave many women unprecedented opportunities for experimentation, as illustrated by one woman's account of her family's work in Poston: "First I wanted to find art work, but I didn't last too long because it wasn't very interesting . . . so I worked in the mess hall, but that wasn't for me, so I went to the accounting department – time-keeping – and I enjoyed that, so I stayed there. . . . My dad . . . went to a shoe shop . . . and then he was block gardener. . . . He got $16. . . . [My sister] was secretary for the block manager; then she went to the optometry department. She was assistant optometrist; she fixed all the glasses and fitted them. . . . That was $16."[18]

As early as 1942, the War Relocation Authority began to release evacuees temporarily from the centers and camps to do voluntary seasonal farm work in neighboring areas hard hit by the wartime labor shortage. The work was arduous, as one young woman discovered when she left Topaz to take a job plucking turkeys:

The smell is terrific until you get used to it. . . . We all wore gunny sacks around our waist, had a small knife and plucked off the fine feathers.

This is about the hardest work that many of us have done – but without a murmur of complaint we worked 8 hours through the first day without a pause.

We were all so tired that we didn't even feel like eating. . . . Our fingers and wrists were just aching, and I just dreamt of turkeys and more turkeys.[19]

Work conditions varied from situation to situation, and some exploitative farmers refused to pay the Japanese Americans after they had finished beet topping or fruit picking. One worker noted that the degree of friendliness on the employer's part decreased as the harvest neared completion. Nonetheless, many workers, like the turkey plucker, concluded that "even if the work is hard, it is worth the freedom we are allowed."

Camp life increased the leisure of many evacuees. A good number of Issei women, accustomed to long days of work inside and outside the home, found that the communally prepared meals and limited living quarters provided them with spare time. Many availed themselves of the opportunity to attend adult classes taught by both evacuees and non-Japanese. Courses involving handcrafts and traditional Japanese arts such as flower arrangement, sewing, painting, calligraphy, and wood carving became immensely popular as an overwhelming number of people turned to art for recreation and self-expression. Some of these subjects were viewed as hobbies and leisure activities by those who taught them, but to the Issei women they represented access to new skills and a means to contribute to the material comfort of the family.

The evacuees also filled their time with Buddhist and Christian church meetings, theatrical productions, cultural programs, athletic events, and visits with friends. All family members spent more time than ever before in the company of their peers. Nisei from isolated rural areas were exposed to the ideas, styles, and pastimes of the more sophisticated urban youth; in camp they had the time and opportunity to socialize – at work, school, dances, sports events, and parties – in an almost entirely Japanese American environment. Gone were the restrictions of distance, lack of transportation, interracial uneasiness, and the dawn-to-dusk exigencies of field work.

Like their noninterned contemporaries, most young Nisei women en-visioned a future of marriage and children. They – and their parents – anticipated that they would marry other Japanese Americans, but these young women, also expected to choose their own husbands and to marry "for love." This mainstream American ideal of marriage differed greatly from the Issei's view of love as a bond that might evolve over the course of an arranged marriage that was firmly rooted in less romantic notions of compatibility and responsibility. The discrepancy between Issei and Ni-sei conceptions of love and marriage had sturdy prewar roots; internment fostered further divergence from the old customs of arranged marriage.

In the artificial hothouse of camp, Nisei romances often bloomed quickly. As Nisei men left to prove their loyalty to the United States in the 442nd Combat Team and the 100th Battalion, young Japanese Americans strove to grasp what happiness and security they could, given the uncertainties of the future. Lily Shoji, in her "Fem-a-lites" newspaper column, commented upon the "changing world" and advised Nisei women: "This is the day of sudden dates, of blind dates on the up-and-up, so let the flash of a uniform be a signal to you to be ready for any emergency. . . . Romance is blossoming with the emotion and urgency of war."[20]

In keeping with this atmosphere, camp newspaper columns like Shoji's in *The Mercedian*, *The Daily Tulean Dispatch*'s "Strictly Feminine," and the *Poston Chronicle*'s "Fashionotes" gave their Nisei readers countless suggestions on how to impress boys, care for their complexions, and choose the latest fashions. These evacuee-authored columns thus mirrored the mainstream girls' periodicals of the time. Such fashion news may seem incongruous in the context of an internment camp whose inmates had little choice in clothing beyond what they could find in the Montgomery Ward or Sears and Roebuck mail-order catalogues. These columns, however, reflect women's efforts to remain in touch with the world outside the barbed wire fence; they reflect as well women's attempt to maintain morale in a drab, depressing environment. "There's something about color in clothes," speculated Tule Lake columnist "Yuri"; "Singing colors have a heart-building effect. . . . Color is a stimulant we need – both for its effect on ourselves and on others."[21]

The evacuees' fashion columns addressed practical as well as aesthetic concerns, reflecting the dusty realities of camp life. In this vein, Mitzi Sugita of the Poston Sewing Department praised the "Latest Fashion for Women Today – Slacks," drawing special attention to overalls; she assured her readers that these "digging duds"[22] were not only winsome and workable but also possessed the virtues of being inexpensive and requiring little ironing.

The columnists' concern with the practical aspects of fashion extended beyond the confines of the camps, as women began to leave for life on the outside – an opportunity increasingly available after 1943. Sugita told prospective operatives, "If you are one of the many thousands of women now entering in commercial and industrial work, your required uniform is based on slacks, safe and streamlined. It is very important that they be durable, trim and attractive."[23] Women heading for clerical positions or college were more likely to heed Marii Kyogoku's admonitions to invest in "really nice things," with an eye to "simple lines which are good practically forever."[24]

RESETTLEMENT: COLLEGE AND WORK

Relocation began slowly in 1942. Among the first to venture out of the camps were college students, assisted by the National Japanese American Student Relocation Council, a nongovernmental agency that provided invaluable placement aid to 4,084 Nisei in the years 1942–1946.[25] Founded in 1942 by concerned educators, this organization persuaded institutions outside the restricted Western Defense zone to accept Nisei students and facilitated their admissions and leave clearances. A study of the first four hundred students to leave camp showed that a third of them were women.[26] Because of the cumbersome screening process, few other evacuees departed on indefinite leave before 1943. In that year, the War Relocation Authority tried to expedite the clearance procedure by broadening an army registration program aimed at Nisei males to include all adults. With this policy change, the migration from the camps steadily increased.[27]

Many Nisei, among them a large number of women, were anxious to leave the limbo of camp and return "to normal life again."[28] With all its work, social events, and cultural activities, camp was still an artificial, limited environment. It was stifling "to see nothing but the same barracks, mess halls, and other houses, row after row, day in and day out, it gives us the feeling that we're missing all the freedom and liberty."[29] An aspiring teacher wrote, "Mother and father do not want me to go out. However, I want to go so very much that sometimes I feel that I'd go even if they disowned me. What shall I do? I realize the hard living conditions outside but I think I can take it."[30] Women's developing sense of independence in the camp environment and their growing awareness of their abilities as workers contributed to their self-confidence and hence their desire to leave. Significantly, Issei parents, despite initial reluctance, were gradually beginning to sanction their daughters' departures for education and employment in the Midwest and East. One Nisei noted: "[Father] became more broad-minded in the relocation center. He was more mellow in his ways. . . . At first he didn't want me to relocate, but he gave in. . . . I said I wanted to go [to Chicago] with my friend, so he helped me pack. He didn't say I could go . . . but he helped me pack, so I thought, 'Well, he didn't say no.' "[31]

The decision to relocate was a difficult one. It was compounded for some women because they felt obligated to stay and care for elderly or infirm parents, like the Heart Mountain Nisei who observed wistfully, "It's getting so more and more of the girls and boys are leaving camp, and I sure wish I could but mother's getting on and I just can't leave her."[32] Many internees worried about their acceptance in the outside world. The Nisei considered themselves American citizens, and they had an allegiance to the land of their birth: "The teaching and love of one's own birth place, one's own country was . . . strongly impressed upon my mind as a child. So even though California may deny our rights of birth, I shall ever love her soil."[33] But evacuation had taught the Japanese Americans that in the eyes of many of their fellow Americans, theirs was the face of the enemy. Many Nisei were torn by mixed feelings of shame, frustration, and bitterness at the denial of their civil rights. These factors created an atmosphere of anxiety that surrounded those who contemplated resettlement: "A feeling of uncertainty hung over the camp; we were worried about the future. Plans were made and remade, as we tried to decide what to do. Some were ready to risk anything to get away. Others feared to leave the protection of the camp."[34]

Thus, those first college students were the scouts whose letters back to camp marked pathways for others to follow. May Yoshino sent a favorable report to her family in Topaz from the nearby University of Utah, indicating that there were "plenty of schoolgirl jobs for those who want to study at the University."[35] Correspondence from other Nisei students shows that although they succeeded at making the dual transition from high school to college and from camp to the outside world, they were not without anxieties as to whether they could handle the study load and the reactions of the Caucasians around them. One student at Drake University in Iowa wrote to her interned sister about a professor's reaction to her autobiographical essay, "Evacuation": "Today Mr. – , the English teacher that scares me, told me that the theme that I wrote the other day was very interesting. . . . You could just imagine how wonderful and happy *I* was to know that he liked it a little bit. . . . I've been awfully busy trying to catch up on work and the work is *so* different from high school. I think that little by little I'm beginning to adjust myself to college life."[36]

Several incidents of hostility did occur, but the reception of the Nisei students at colleges and universities was generally warm. Topaz readers of *Trek* magazine could draw encouragement from Lillian Ota's "Campus Report." Ota, a Wellesley student, reassured them: "During the first few days you'll be invited by the college to teas and receptions. Before long you'll lose the awkwardness you might feel at such doings after the months of abnormal life at evacuation centers."[37] Although Ota had not noticed "that my being a 'Jap' has made much difference on the campus itself," she offered cautionary and pragmatic advice to the Nisei, suggesting the burden of responsibility these relocated students felt, as well as the problem of communicating their experiences and emotions to Caucasians. "It is scarcely necessary to point out that those who have probably never seen a nisei before will get their impression of the nisei as a whole from the relocated students. It won't do you or your family and friends much good to dwell on what you consider injustices when you are questioned about evacuation. Rather, stress the contributions of [our] people to the nation's war effort."[38] Given the tenor of the times and the situation of their families, the pioneers in resettlement had little choice but to repress their anger and minimize the amount of racist hostility they encountered.

In her article "a la mode," Marii Kyogoku also offered survival tips to the departing Nisei, ever conscious that they were on trial not only as individuals but as representatives of their families and their generation. She suggested criteria for choosing clothes and provided hints on adjustment to food rationing. Kyogoku especially urged the evacuees to improve their table manners, which had been adversely affected by the "unnatural food and atmosphere" of mess hall dining:

You should start rehearsing for the great outside by bringing your own utensils to the dining hall. Its an aid to normality to be able to eat your jello with a spoon and well worth the dishwashing which it involves. All of us eat much too fast. Eat more slowly. All this practicing should be done so that proper manners will seem natural to you. If you do this, you won't get stagefright and spill your water glass, or make bread pills and hardly dare to eat when you have your first meal away from the centers and in the midst of scrutinizing Caucasian eyes. [39]

Armed with advice and drawn by encouraging reports, increasing numbers of women students left camp. A postwar study of a group of a thousand relocated students showed that 40 percent were women. [40] The field of nursing was particularly attractive to Nisei women; after the first few students disproved the hospital administration's fears of their patients' hostility, acceptance of Nisei into nursing schools grew. By July 1944, there were more than three hundred Nisei women in over a hundred nursing programs in twenty-four states. [41] One such student wrote from the Asbury Hospital in Minneapolis: "Work here isn't too hard and I enjoy it very much. The patients are very nice people and I haven't had any trouble as yet. They do give us a funny stare at the beginning but after a day or so we receive the best compliments." [42]

The trickle of migration from the camps grew into a steady stream by 1943, as the War Relocation Authority developed its resettlement program to aid evacuees in finding housing and employment in the East and Midwest. A resettlement bulletin published by the Advisory Committee for Evacuees described "who is relocating": "Mostly younger men and women, in their 20s or 30s; mostly single persons or couples with one or two children, or men with larger families who come out alone first to scout opportunities and to secure a foothold, planning to call wife and children later. Most relocated evacuees have parents or relatives whom they hope and plan to bring out 'when we get re-established.' " [43]

In early 1945, the War Department ended the exclusion of the Japanese Americans from the West Coast, and the War Relocation Authority announced that the camps would be closed within the year. By this time, 37 percent of the evacuees of sixteen years or older had already relocated, including 63 percent of the Nisei women in that age group. [44]

For Nisei women, like their non-Japanese sisters, the wartime labor shortage opened the door into industrial, clerical, and managerial occupations. Prior to the war, racism had excluded the Japanese Americans from most white-collar clerical and sales positions, and, according to sociologist Evelyn Nakano Glenn, "The most common form of nonagricultural employment for the immigrant women (issei) and their American-born daughters (nisei) was domestic service."[45] The highest percentage of job offers for both men and women continued to be requests for domestic workers. In July 1943, the Kansas City branch of the War Relocation Authority noted that 45 percent of requests for workers were for domestics, and the Milwaukee office cited 61 percent.[46] However, Nisei women also found jobs as secretaries, typists, file clerks, beauticians, and factory workers. By 1950, 47 percent of employed Japanese American women were clerical and sales workers and operatives; only 10 percent were in domestic service.[47] The World War II decade, then, marked a turning point for Japanese American women in the labor force.

Whether they were students or workers, and regardless of where they went or how prepared they were to meet the outside world, Nisei women found that leaving camp meant enormous change in their lives. Even someone as confident as Marii Kyogoku, the author of much relocation advice, found that reentry into the Caucasian-dominated world beyond the barbed wire fence was not a simple matter of stepping back into old shoes. Leaving the camps – like entering them – meant major changes in psychological perspective and self-image. "I had thought that because before evacuation I had adjusted myself rather well in a Caucasian society, I would go right back into my former frame of mind. I have found, however, that though the center became unreal and was as if it had never existed as soon as I got on the train at Delta, I was never so self-conscious in all my life." Kyogoku was amazed to see so many men and women in uniform and, despite her "proper" dining preparation, felt strange sitting at a table set with clean linen and a full set of silverware. "I felt a diffidence at facing all these people and things, which was most unusual. Slowly things have come to seem natural, though I am still excited by the sounds of the busy city and thrilled every time I see a street lined with trees, I no longer feel that I am the cynosure of all eyes."[48] Like Kyogoku, many Nisei women discovered that relocation meant adjustment to "a life different from our former as well as present way of living"[49] and, as such, posed a challenge. Their experiences in meeting this challenge were as diverse as their jobs and living situations.

"I live at the Eleanor Club No. 5 which is located on the west side," wrote Mary Sonoda, working with the American Friends Service Committee in Chicago:

I pay $1 per day for room and two meals a day. I also have maid service. I do not think that one can manage all this for $1 unless one lives in a place like this which houses thousands of working girls in the city. . . . I am the only Japanese here at present. . . . The residents and the staff are wonderful to me. . . . I am constantly being entertained by one person or another.

The people in Chicago are extremely friendly. Even with the *Tribune* screaming awful headlines concerning the recent execution of American soldiers in Japan, people kept their heads. On street cars, at stores, everywhere, one finds innumerable evidence of good will.[50]

Chicago the location of the first War Relocation Authority field office for supervision of resettlement in the Midwest, attracted the largest number of evacuees. Not all found their working environment as congenial as Mary Sonoda did. Smoot Katow, a Nisei man in Chicago, painted "another side of the picture": "I met one of the Edgewater Beach girls. . . . From what she said it was my impression that the girls are not very happy. The hotel work is too hard, according to this girl. In fact, they are losing weight and one girl became sick with overwork. They have to clean about fifteen suites a day, scrubbing the floors on their hands and knees. . . . It seems the management is out to use labor as labor only. . . . The outside world is just as tough as it ever was."[51] These variations in living and work conditions and wages encouraged – and sometimes necessitated – a certain amount of job experimentation among the Nisei.

Many relocating Japanese Americans received moral and material assistance from a number of service organizations and religious groups, particularly the Presbyterians, the Methodists, the Society of Friends, and the Young Women's Christian Association. One such Nisei, Dorcas Asano, enthusiastically described to a Quaker sponsor her activities in the big city:

Since receiving your application for hostel accommodation, I have decided to come to New York and I am really glad for the opportunity to be able to resume the normal civilized life after a year's confinement in camp. New York is really a city of dreams and we are enjoying every minute working in offices, rushing back and forth to work in the ever-speeding sub-way trains, counting our ration points, buying war bonds, going to church, seeing the latest shows, plays, operas, making many new friends and living like our neighbors in the war time. I only wish more of my friends who are behind the fence will take advantage of the many helpful hands offered to them.[52]

The Nisei also derived support and strength from networks – formed before and during internment – of friends and relatives. The homes of those who relocated first became way stations for others as they made the transition into new communities and jobs. In 1944, soon after she obtained a place to stay in New York City, Miné Okubo found that "many of the other evacuees relocating in New York came ringing my doorbell. They were sleeping all over the floor!"[53] Single women often accompanied or joined sisters, brothers, and friends as many interconnecting grapevines carried news of likely jobs, housing, and friendly communities. Ayako Kanemura, for instance, found a job painting Hummel figurines in Chicago; a letter of recommendation from a friend enabled her "to get my foot into the door and then all my friends followed and joined me."[54] Although they were farther from their families than ever before, Nisei women maintained warm ties of affection and concern, and those who had the means to do so continued to play a role in the family economy, remitting a portion of their earnings to their families in or out of camp, and to siblings in school.

Elizabeth Ogata's family exemplifies several patterns of resettlement and the maintenance of family ties within them. In October 1944, her parents were living with her brother Harry who had begun to farm in Springville, Utah; another brother and sister were attending Union College in Lincoln, Nebraska. Elisabeth herself had moved to Minneapolis to join a brother in the army, and she was working as an operative making pajamas. "Minn. is a beautiful place," she wrote, "and the people are so nice. . . . I thought I'd never find anywhere I would feel at home as I did in Mt. View [California], but I have changed my mind."[55] Like Elizabeth, a good number of the thirty-five thousand relocated Japanese Americans were favorably impressed by their new homes and decided to stay.

The war years had complex and profound effects upon Japanese Americans, uprooting their communities and causing severe psychological and emotional damage. The vast majority returned to the West Coast at the end of the war in 1945 – a move that, like the initial evacuation, was a grueling test of flexibility and fortitude. Even with the assistance of old friends and service organizations, the transition was taxing and painful; the end of the war meant not only long-awaited freedom but more battles to be fought in social, academic, and economic arenas. The Japanese Americans faced hostility, crude living conditions, and a struggle for jobs. Few evacuees received any compensation for their financial losses, estimated conservatively at $400 million, because Congress decided to appropriate only $38 million for the settlement of claims.[56] It is even harder to place a figure on the toll taken in emotional shock, self-blame, broken dreams, and insecurity. One Japanese

American woman still sees in her nightmares the watchtower searchlights that troubled her sleep forty years ago.

The war altered Japanese American women's lives in complicated ways. In general, evacuation and relocation accelerated earlier trends that differentiated the Nisei from their parents. Although most young women, like their mothers and non-Japanese peers, anticipated a future centered around a husband and children, they had already felt the influence of mainstream middle-class values of love and marriage and quickly moved away from the pattern of arranged marriage in the camps. There, increased peer group activities and the relaxation of parental authority gave them more independence. The Nisei women's expectations of marriage became more akin to the companionate ideals of their peers than to those of the Issei.

As before the war, many Nisei women worked in camp, but the new parity in wages they received altered family dynamics. And though they expected to contribute to the family economy, a large number did so in settings far from the family, availing themselves of opportunities provided by the student and worker relocation programs. In meeting the challenges facing them, Nisei women drew not only upon the disciplined strength inculcated by their Issei parents but also upon firmly rooted support networks and the greater measure of self-reliance and independence that they developed during the crucible of the war years.

NOTES

For their invaluable assistance with this paper, I would like to thank Estelle Freedman, Mary Rothschild, and members of the women's history dissertation reading group at Stanford University – Sue Cobble, Gary Sue Goodman, Yukiko Hanawa, Gail Hershatter, Emily Honig, Susan Johnson, Sue Lynn, Joanne Meyerowitz, Peggy Pascoe, Linda Schott, Frances Taylor, and Karen Anderson.

1. Miné Okubo, *Miné Okubo: An American Experience*, exhibition catalogue (Oakland: Oakland Museum, 1972), 36.

2. The very first Japanese women to arrive in the United States before the turn of the century were the *ameyuki-san* – prostitutes – of whose lives little is known. For information, see Yuji Ichioka, "Ameyuki-san: Japanese Prostitutes in Nineteenth Century America," *Amerasia Journal* 4:1 (1977). A few references to the *ameyuki-san* appear in Mildred Crowl Martin's biography, *Chinatown's Angry Angel: The Story of Donaldina Cameron* (Palo Alto: Pacific Books, 1977).

3. In Japan, marriage was legally the transfer of a woman's name from her father's registry to that of the groom's family. Even through the Meiji Era there was

enormous diversity in the time period of this formalization; it might occur as early as several days before the wedding ceremony or as late as seven or more years later, by which time the bride should have produced several sons and proved herself to be a good wife and daughter-in-law. For a detailed cross-cultural history of the Issei women, see Yukiko Hanawa, "The Several Worlds of Issei Women," California State University at Long Beach (master thesis, 1982).

4. Yuji Ichioka, "*Amerika Nadeshiko*: Japanese Immigrant Women in the United States, 1900–1924," *Pacific Historical Review* 69:2 (1980): 343.

5. Evelyn Nakano Glenn has examined the lives of Issei and Nisei domestic workers in the prewar period in her study "The Dialectics of Wage Work: Japanese-American Women and Domestic Servants, 1905–1940," *Feminist Studies* 6:3 (1980): 432–71.

6. Sources on evacuation: Robert A. Wilson and Bill Hosokawa, *East to America: A History of the Japanese in the United States* (New York: William Morrow, 1980); Audrie Girdner and Anne Loftis, *The Great Betrayal: The Evacuation of the Japanese-Americans during World War II* (Toronto: Macmillan, 1969); Daisuke Kitagawa, *Issei and Nisei: The Internment Years* (New York: Seabury Press, 1967) and Roger Daniels, *The Decision to Relocate the Japanese Americans* (Philadelphia: J. B. Lippincott, 1975).

7. Wilson and Hosokawa, *East to America*, 208.

8. Bettie to Mrs. Jack Shoup, June 3, 1942, Mrs. Jack Shoup Collection, Hoover Institution Archives (hereafter referred to as HIA), Stanford, California.

9. May Nakamoto to Mrs. Jack Shoup, November 30, 1942, Mrs. Jack Shoup Collection, HIA.

10. Mary Okumura to Mrs. Jack Shoup, May 30, 1942, Mrs. Jack Shoup Collection, HIA.

11. Miye Baba, personal interview, February 10, 1982, Turlock, California.

12. Many of the Japanese community leaders arrested by the FBI before the evacuation were interned in special all-male camps in North Dakota, Louisiana, and New Mexico. Some Japanese Americans living outside the perimeter of the Western Defense zone in Arizona, Utah, etc. were not interned.

13. Miné Okubo, *Citizen 13660* (New York: Columbia University Press, 1946) 66.

14. Chieko Kimura, personal interview, April 9, 1978, Glendale, Arizona.

15. Okubo, *Citizen 13660*, 89.

16. Shizuko Horiuchi to Henriette Von Blon, January 24, 1943, Henriette Von Blon Collection, HIA.

17. Shizuko Horiuchi to Henriette Von Blon, January 5, 1944, Henriette Von Blon Collection, HIA.

18. Ayako Kanemura, personal interview, March 10, 1978, Glendale, Arizona.

19. Anonymous, *Topaz Times*, October 24, 1942, 3.

20. Lily Shoji, "Fem-a-lites," *The Mercedian*, August 7, 1942, 4.

21. "Yuri," "Strictly Feminine," September 29, 1942, 2.

22. Mitzi Sugita, "Latest Fashion for Women Today – Slacks," *Poston Chronicle*, June 13, 1943, 1.

23. Sugita, "Latest Fashion for Women Today."

24. Marii Kyogoku, "a la mode," *Trek*, February 1943, 38.

25. From 1942 to the end of 1945 the Council allocated about $240,000 in scholarships, most of which were provided through the donations of churches and the World Student Service Fund. The average grant per student was $156.73, which in that era was a major contribution toward the cost of higher education (National Japanese American Student Relocation Council, Minutes of the Executive Committee Meeting, Philadelphia, Pennsylvania, December 19, 1945).

26. Robert O'Brien, *The College Nisei* (Palo Alto: Pacific Books 1949), 73–74.

27. The disastrous consequences of the poorly conceived clearance procedure have been examined by Wilson and Hosokawa. *East to America*, 226–27; and Girdner and Loftis, *The Great Betrayal*, 342–43.

28. May Nakamoto to Mrs. Jack Shoup, November 20, 1943, Mrs. Jack Shoup Collection, HIA.

29. Shizuko Horiuchi to Henriette Von Blon, December 27, 1942, Henriette Von Blon Collection, HIA.

30. Toshiko Imada to Margaret Cosgrave Sowers, January 16, 1943, Margaret Cosgrave Sowers Collection, HIA.

31. Ayako Kanemura, personal interview, March 24, 1978, Glendale, Arizona.

32. Kathy Ishikawa to Mrs. Jack Shoup, June 14, 1942, Mrs. Jack Shoup Collection, HIA.

33. Anonymous Nisei nurse in Poston Camp to Margaret Finley, May 5, 1943, Margaret Finley Collection, HIA.

34. Okubo, *Citizen 13660*, 139.

35. *Topaz Times*, October 24, 1942, 3.

36. Masako Ono to Atsuko Ono, September 28, 1942, Margaret Cosgrave Sowers Collection, HIA. Prior to the war, few Nisei had college experience: The 1940 census lists 674 second-generation women and 1,507 men who had attended or were attending college.

37. Lillian Ota, "Campus Report," *Trek* February 1943, 33.

38. Ota, "Campus Report," 33–34.

39. Kyogoku, "a la mode," 39.

40. O'Brien, *The College Nisei*, 84.

41. O'Brien, *The College Nisei*, 85–86.

42. Grace Tanabe to Josephine Duveneck, February 16, 1944, Conard-Duveneck Collection, HIA.

43. Advisory Committee for Evacuees, *Resettlement Bulletin*, April 1943, 2.

44. Leonard Broom and Ruth Riemer, *Removal and Return: The Socio-Economic Effects of the War on Japanese Americans* (Berkeley: University of California Press, 1949), 36.

45. Glenn, "The Dialectics of Wage Work," 432.

46. Advisory Committee for evacuees, *Resettlement Bulletin*, July 1943, 3.

47. 1950 United States Census, Special Report.

48. Marii Kyogoku, *Resettlement Bulletin*, July 1943, 5.

49. Kyogoku, "a la mode," 39.

50. *Poston Chronicle*, May 23, 1943, 1.

51. *Poston Chronicle*, May 23, 1943.

52. Dorcas Asano to Josephine Duveneck, January 22, 1944, Conard-Duveneck Collection, HIA.

53. Okubo, *An American Experience*, 41.

54. Ayako Kanemura, personal interview, March 24, 1978, Glendale, Arizona.

55. Elizabeth Ogata to Mrs. Jack Shoup, October 1, 1944, Mrs. Jack Shoup Collection, HIA.

56. Susan M. Hartmann, *The Home Front and Beyond: American Women in the 1940s* (Boston: Twayne Publishers, 1982), 126. There is some debate regarding the origins of the assessment of evacuee losses at $400 million. However, a study by the Commission on Wartime Relocation and Internment of Civilians has estimated that the Japanese Americans lost between $149 million and $370 million in 1945 dollars, and between $810 million and $2 billion in 1983 dollars. See the *San Francisco Chronicle*, June 16, 1983, 12.

Frontiers 8:1 (1984): 6–14.

Desperately Seeking "Deirdre"

Gender Roles, Multicultural Relations, and Nisei Women Writers of the 1930s

VALERIE MATSUMOTO

In July 1941, as wartime tensions rose in the United States, a second-generation Japanese American woman poet, Toyo Suyemoto, wrote:

> Out of the anguish of my heart
> There must come gentle peace
> That will bid wayward grief
> And troubled thoughts to cease.
>
> When one by one, old sorrows pass
> And I know my own will,
> Let not the spirit fear again
> Or let my songs grow still.[1]

The World War II internment of the Japanese Americans in concentration camps would swallow up many of the "songs" pouring forth from the second-generation, or Nisei, women writers of the 1930s, like Suyemoto. Indeed, the postwar silence of the hardscrabble resettlement years of the 1940s and the cold war era's discouragement of celebrating ethnicity have obscured the vitality and creative ferment of the prewar Japanese American literati. Their writings provide many windows onto the cultural diversity of life in the West Coast. Viewed through the lens of Nisei efforts to shape ethnic culture, the dynamics of interracial/interethnic relations and gender roles come into provocative focus.

Until recently, very little attention – scholarly or otherwise – has been paid to this prewar literature.[2] I first became aware of the flood of poetry, fiction, articles, and essays by the Nisei in the vernacular press (as they called it) when, a few years ago, Nisei activist Chizu Iiyama drew my attention to the etiquette advice column written by "Deirdre," a Japanese American "Dear Abby" of the 1930s, for a San Francisco Japanese American newspaper, the *New World–Sun*. The more I delved into the background of the witty and opinionated "Deirdre," the more aware I became of the active network of Japanese American women and men writers and the breadth of the cultural and social issues they tackled. Like a gumshoe of the 1930s detective thrillers, I became enmeshed in a seemingly endless search for clues and leads, running into the classic dead ends of memory loss, the destruction of personal papers, and potential informants who disappeared due to death or change of name. And, like a detective, I found that the primary research brings to light a host of intriguing theoretical questions.[3]

In this chapter I will draw upon the work of a number of these writers – and Deirdre's in particular – as a way to discuss some of the interpretive issues that emerge as one does documentary research. What I have found is suggestive rather than conclusive, but even at this early stage, the project raises speculations regarding the attempt to create and promote ethnic culture, the search for role models, and the tension of women's dreams caught between gender-role expectations and the economic realities of a racially discriminatory society.

Throughout the nineteenth and twentieth centuries U.S. women have looked to advice literature for moral guidance and etiquette, from Victorian arbiters like *Godey's Lady's Book* to the modern-day columns and manuals of Abigail Van Buren, Ann Landers, Miss Manners, the Mayflower Madam, and others. It was within this long tradition that Deirdre promised to address the social problems facing the second generation and stated that she would be "happy to answer any question put her concerning family affairs, love and other sex problems, social etiquette, and other personal questions."[4]

However, Deirdre's situation, as advice columnist of the *New World–Sun* from 1935 to 1941, was far more complex than that of mainstream etiquette mavens. Her task was to provide the Nisei with guidelines for proper behavior that would enable them to navigate safely the social conventions of the white world as well as to meet the standards of their parents and the Japanese American community. She also had to tailor her advice to racial ethnic readers grappling with complex issues such as interracial relations and dating, whether to resist arranged marriage in favor of love matches, and how to reconcile conflicts between marriage and career. With considerable panache, Deirdre briefed her readers on dinner place settings and the mechanics of a proper bow, mediated lengthy pen battles between readers with opposing views, and dispensed brisk advice to the shy, lovelorn, and confused.

Who was Deirdre? Some sleuthing by Nisei activist and writer Nikki Sawada Bridges revealed that her real name was Mary "Mollie" Oyama Mittwer and that she was retired and living with her daughter in southern California. From talking with Vicki Mittwer Littman, her daughter, and other Nisei journalists, I learned that Mary Oyama Mittwer did more than pen advice columns: As one of the most prolific and energetic Nisei writers, she contributed articles, interviews, poetry and regular columns to nearly all of the major Japanese American newspapers, as well as to the Nisei magazine *Current Life* and to *Common Ground*, a liberal journal that provided a rare forum open to ethnic voices.

Mary Oyama was born in 1907, in Fairfield, California, the oldest daughter in a family of six children. According to her brother Joe and daughter Vicki, the warm encouragement she received from Caucasian teachers nurtured her confidence and writing skills. She graduated from Sacramento High School in 1925 and from the San Francisco National Training School (a Methodist school for training missionaries) in 1928. After a short stint of studying journalism at University of Southern California around 1931, Oyama moved briefly to Seattle and then moved to Los Angeles. There, she developed as a prolific writer for a host of papers, including the *Kashu Mainichi* and the *Rafu Shimpo* in Los Angeles and the *Nichibei* and the *Shin-Sekai* in San Francisco.

Pursuing the thread of Mary Oyama's career revealed not only the energy of the Nisei writers but also how many of them were women. A 1940 article in *Current Life* on "Who's Who in the Nisei Literary World" profiled fifteen men and nine women, including Mary Oyama, who was described as "earnestly interested in promoting better race understanding" and as "an affectionate young matron – poised, neat, with a tranquil charm all her own."[5] These columnists, poets, fiction authors, and fashion editors published energetically in the vernacular press, experimenting with form and style in the process of developing their own voices. Many adopted a flippant and brash jazz style; Hisaye Yamamoto poked fun at lyric convention in humorous poems with latin titles, and Toyo Suyemoto limned her subjects in powerful austere rhymes, stating:

. . . all that I can give to you
Is simple speech of everyday . . .
Words stripped and stark like life and death
Wherein you stand midway.[6]

These writers explored a range of sensitive and timely subjects, as well as styles. Interracial relations, interethnic prejudice, and women's roles in the Japanese American family provided grist for their mills. Mary Oyama, in the guise of Deirdre, pushed especially hard for more political involvement by "Alice Nisei," as well as for harmonious interracial relations and women's pursuit of independence and personal goals. In many ways, such "New Woman" sentiments were embodied in Oyama's own life: she pieced together a full-time journalism job by writing for many papers in a range of different formats. Leaving in her wake a string of beaus, she married at the age of thirty, late for a Nisei. Her husband, Frederick Mittwer, a handsome linotypist for the *Rafu Shimpo* newspaper, was a Japan-born man of Caucasian and Japanese parentage.

Oyama's writings and her life illustrate the tensions confronting Nisei women who dreamed of careers as well as marriage. Though Deirdre encouraged ambitious readers, in 1990s terms, "to do it all," she also permitted herself to grumble that "Housewives Have No Spare Time" in a 1939 column. Her complaint presaged the discontent Betty Friedan would later examine in *The Feminine Mystique*. "Domesticity," Oyama found, "seems to allow less time for self-improvement . . . than regular routine work outside. . . . As hard as I'm toiling around the house, my folks complain and think that I'm not doing enough. It's aggravating, really."[7]

Gender-role expectations were not the only hurdle Nisei women faced. Of the many Japanese American young women energetically penning articles, stories, and poems for the vernacular press, few ever made inroads into the mainstream media. Mary Oyama, writing for *Common Ground*, and Hisaye Yamamoto, whose fiction later appeared in *Harper's Bazaar* and *Martha Foley's Best American Short Stories*, were among the exceptions. In this sense, the writers' situation mirrored that of Nisei and other ethnic women who found it difficult to obtain work outside the ethnic community. In addition, their careers met the devastating roadblock of World War II internment, the painful net of many dreams.

The concerns aired in Deirdre's column, as well as the themes elaborated by the literati, suggest that for the Nisei, cultural crossroads were the inescapable locations of daily life. Although the Japanese American community monitored their behavior as modest, industrious *musuko* (sons) and *musume* (daughters), public schooling provided another arena of interaction with non–Asian American teachers and classmates. The daily routine of most Nisei children – the majority of whom were born between 1910 and 1940 – revolved around work and education. Many worked in the fields or the family business before school, attended Japanese language class after public school finished, and then returned home, where further chores awaited. Whether urban or rural, they often acted as intermediaries between their immigrant parents and the dominant society, being called upon to develop translation skills early on. And the younger members of the second generation looked to older Nisei like Deirdre for guidance in negotiating the demands of immigrant parents and the surrounding society.

The offerings of the Japanese American press during the 1930s and on into the early 1940s evidence the rich diversity of cultural influences permeating the lives of the Nisei. The second generation, most of them able to speak but not read Japanese, pored over growing English sections in the vernacular newspapers. A young reader might follow the comic strip adventures of "Tarzan and the Golden Lion," as well as the exploits of local Nisei baseball and basketball teams, or join a Nisei pen pal club. For older readers, the sections included Buddhist and Christian church news, articles on U.S.-Japan relations, and articles on women's status and concerns in the United States. Women as well as men enthusiastically submitted poetry and fiction, and they sought advice from the outspoken Deirdre.

The photographs of movie stars and the fashion columns particularly reflected the impact of mainstream society. Like other U.S. women, the Nisei might try to determine what "Hollywood type" they were and then attempt to enhance their best features accordingly. As one fashion columnist advised, "If you have broad Garboesque shoulders – softly tailored lines will streamline your size. . . . If you are small with a Constance Bennett chin – tall hats give you a lift with a lean look."[8] Incidentally, the fashion page in the Nisei magazine *Current Life* always featured Japanese American models wearing the latest styles, usually available at "Kiyo's Dress Shop."

The English section of the newspapers also reflected the culinary diversity for which California is famous. Women readers shared a variety of recipes, ranging from sukiyaki and *kuromame* ("black beans") to *bok choy chow yuk*, fruit cake, and cream puffs. Mothers might glean helpful hints to add pizzazz to *kanten*, a Japanese gelatin, by putting in bits of canned pineapple, or to give their children a healthy snack of Wheaties.

In addition, Nisei fiction writers charted the multicultural landscape of their generation. For example, issues of gender and race permeate the short stories of Hisaye Yamamoto, one of the most widely acclaimed Japanese American writers. Born in southern California in 1921, Yamamoto began writing as a teenager, submitting poems and essays – under the pseudonym "Napoleon" – to the ethnic press in the 1930s and 1940s. During her World War II internment in Arizona, she wrote for the *Poston Chronicle*, the concentration camp newspaper. Her fiction found receptive mainstream and Japanese American audiences in the postwar years.[9] These short stories have delineated the multicultural flavor of prewar life in both city and country: the repertoire of treats to be enjoyed in Little Tokyo in Los Angeles included Eskimo Pies purchased on the street and popular *China-meshi* ("Chinese food") as well as sushi and Japanese confections. Interethnic relations weave through the stories, whether in the form of remedies sold by a Korean herbalist, an affair between a Pilipino hired hand and an Issei woman, or a Nisei teenager's first kiss from a Chicano schoolmate and harvest worker. For Yamamoto's characters, as for Deirdre's readers, the dynamics of romantic relations exposed the interethnic/interracial and gender-role tensions faced by the Nisei.

Marriage was a recurrent theme in Deirdre's column.[10] Nisei readers engaged in spirited discourse over the merits of mainstream "love marriage" versus the arranged matches expected by many Issei parents, and they debated the ramifications of marrying a farmer, especially for urban women. Both men and women – protected by the anonymity of pseudonyms like "Voice of the Rockies," "Modern Miss," and "Farmer Bob" – set forth the attributes they hoped to find in a mate. Their letters evidence the influence of mainstream ideals of romantic affection and companionate marriage, which deviated considerably from the Issei's marital expectations. As Deirdre and one female correspondent agreed, "This marriage business comes to 'a question of loving someone.' "[11] The later findings of anthropologist Sylvia Yanagisako have documented the development of Nisei marriage as a compromise between Japanese and American ideals, valorizing love and affection but not at the expense of duty and commitment.[12]

Tensions surrounding the issues of courtship and marriage were compounded when the factor of race entered the picture. The dominant society's opposition to interracial marriage made the unions of Asians or African Americans with whites illegal under California's miscegenation laws until 1948.[13] Given this prohibition and the Japanese American community's own disapproval of intermarriage, it is not surprising that the topic was a sensitive one for the Nisei. In such a context, the Nisei's discussion of interracial/interethnic dating and relationships reveals complicated junctures of race, gender, and class. Short stories, articles, and Deirdre's column shed light on Japanese American perceptions of ethnicity and identity, as well as ambivalence about mainstream and ethnic cultural norms regarding male and female standards.

Though the white population might have lumped all Asian Americans into one category, regardless of cultural differences and historic enmities, Asian Americans themselves drew distinctions. Nisei critiques of Japanese American prejudices indicate the prevalence of such attitudes. In this vein, one Nisei wrote to ask Deirdre's opinion of Japanese Americans who dated Chinese or "young people of other nationalities." The irate author was prompted to write after overhearing his sister stigmatized for dating a Chinese American, "as if that were a great social crime."[14] He criticized the Japanese American community for narrow-mindedness and intolerance, and defended his sister's friend as a well-educated, widely traveled, third-generation U.S. citizen. At the same time, he was quick to mention that his sister's date was "perfectly platonic," thereby skirting the issue of interethnic sexual relations while claiming the right of association. Less ambiguously, Jeanne Nishimori's short story titled "I Cannot Marry Thee," bitingly indicated the prejudice of a male protagonist – presumably Nisei – who felt attracted to a woman he met on the bus until he learned that she was a Chinese American.[15]

Although Deirdre, who supported interracial dating, may not have been representative of Japanese Americans, her writing on this subject revealed the social matrix of the issue. In 1935, she wrote in a positive tone about a Nisei woman's dating a white male whom the columnist described as "well-educated, charming and extremely nice-looking."[16] His "utter lack of prejudice" she attributed to the fact that he came from a less prejudiced state than California. Like the Nisei man who defended his sister's right to date a Chinese American, Deirdre sought to remove the issue from the troubling realm of erotic attraction to the less threatening ground of casual camaraderie. The columnist was quick to establish that, although he was a "nice chap," the Nisei woman was not in love with him but regarded him as a "pal." Indeed the woman said that she considered herself "too young to be thinking about such things" – although clearly this did not stop her, Deirdre, or Deirdre's readers from doing so. The woman also said she supposed that her Japanese American friends considered her "eccentric" for dating a Caucasian but declared, "It's about time we Nisei and we Japanese got over our prejudices. You must admit that a lot of us have them, too." Again, careful ambiguity and mixed messages like the endorsement of nonromantic friendship in conjunction with the mention of the "charm" of the attractive interracial couple suggest the tensions within and outside the ethnic community in regard to such relations. We are reminded simultaneously of the strength of prevailing norms and the presence of a small minority who pushed against sociocultural boundaries, both ethnic and mainstream.

Although the dominant society might regard racial ethnic people as inferior – the cornerstone of the argument against interracial unions – this did not always translate into minority acceptance of such views. Neither did their being subject to racial discrimination necessarily prevent them from holding their own prejudices, as Deirdre's subject asserted. Contrary to mainstream eugenic objections to intermarriage, Japanese Americans did not accept notions of their presumed physiological deficiency. As Charles Kikuchi said, "In regard to intermarriage, most of the Nisei oppose it on sociological and economic lines, but not on biological lines." Rather, he stated, "They are proud of their ancestry and do not consider themselves as products of an inferior race."[17] However, the terminology of ethnicity evidenced the unequal sense of entitlement in U.S. society: while the Japanese Americans referred to themselves as "Nisei" or "Japanese," the term "American" was usually synonymous with "white." Caucasians were also occasionally called *hakujin* (literally, "white person").

The Nisei's integration of popular cultural beliefs and the values of the Issei did not always proceed smoothly. At least one epistolary debate in Deirdre's column suggested the cultural conflict faced by Nisei seeking to reconcile two sets of sometimes incompatible norms. In this case, friction over standards of appropriate female behavior became cast in ethnic terms. Through the forum of Deirdre's column, a reader calling himself "Bachelor Bob" castigated Nisei women as "dead and uninteresting in comparison to American girls."[18] "Matsu-chan," a rural teenager, responded by asking, "Don't you think the 'hakujin' girls are a little too talkative and lively? . . . What would our parents think of us if we suddenly became like the 'hakujins' – running wild, etc?" She added, perhaps to get his goat, "The Nisei boys, too, seem dead to me." This exchange, though brief, exemplifies the linkage of issues of gender and ethnicity.

The lively English section of the vernacular newspapers and Nisei fiction allow us to glimpse the diversity surrounding the Nisei, and the complex themes of race and gender with which they grappled. A small but active network of writers energetically sought to create and promote a distinctive Japanese American culture. Growing up in the U.S. West exposed them to many cultural influences and, I think, spurred the literati to experiment with form and content as they tried to define themselves and their role in U.S. society.

The Nisei literati had a strong consciousness of themselves as a generation, and the subject of "the Nisei problem" figured largely in many of their articles and editorials. The "Nisei problem" was a catchall term encompassing the social and economic limitations the Japanese Americans faced. A 1935 editorial in the *Hokubei Asahi* newspaper noted that, despite the fact that the Nisei were in essence no different from other second-generation ethnic people in the United States, "The welter of dilemmas such as whether or not they should be Americans or Japanese, and whether they should seek a career in Japan or America, have proved somewhat of a handicap, not typical to other immigrants."[19] Such editorials and letters to the newspapers gave the Nisei an outlet to vent their frustrations at being perceived as foreigners and treated like second-class citizens.

Many of the literati strongly critiqued racism as the main obstacle to their full participation and acceptance in the larger society. When an Englishman wrote to "Dear Deirdre" to discuss whether the Nisei could be assimilated into U.S. life, she responded, "One of our Nisei boys said frankly, 'you see, it isn't a question of: "Can the Nisei become assimilated" for we already are quite thoroughly Americanized and we have learned quickly and readily how to adapt ourselves to American life; rather it is a question of: "How far are the Americans willing to LET US BECOME ASSIMILATED." ' "[20] Another Nisei added, "The Americans sometimes accuse us of not becoming thoroughly assimilated, little realizing that they themselves have set up certain restrictions which limit our capacity for assimilating. Take, for instance, the law which prohibits marriages between the Occidentals and Orientals."[21] Deirdre also cited the barring of Japanese Americans from certain restaurants, public swimming pools, and other facilities.

Although the Nisei writers maintained a critique of U.S. racism, they also believed that part of the answer to the "Nisei problem" lay in their own hands. As the *Hokubei Asahi* editor concluded, "Something new must be created by the Nisei – and by only them."[22] Somewhat like the writers of the Harlem Renaissance of the 1920s, the Japanese American literati sought to shape and promote their own culture, exhorting each other to "find a way of their own." Mary Oyama was one of the cofounders of the League of Nisei Artists and Writers, a group that met weekly at her house to foster this creative effort, organizing themselves like the League of American Writers.

What heroes and models inspired the Nisei? In pursuing the answer to this question, additional evidence of the cultural diversity of the West Coast is revealed, as well as clues about how the Japanese Americans thought about themselves as racial ethnic Americans. Examining this issue also raises even more questions about how racial-ethnic and/or ethnic groups perceive each other. The Nisei, in their attempt to create something new, cast about for role models. Mary Oyama, in a series of interviews for *Current Life* magazine, presented other ethnic Americans and the children of immigrants to stimulate her readers. One such potential role model was Leon Surmelian, a writer Oyama described as "An Armenian Nisei," whose articles about the "second-generation problem" of the Armenian Americans reminded her of the "Nisei problem." Upon learning that Surmelian lived in Hollywood, Oyama promptly invited him and several Japanese Americans to her house for a bull session. "Over the tea-cups and rice-cookies," as she puts it, "everything under the sun was discussed: Buddhism, Christianity, . . . the Nisei, interracial marriage, racial background of the Japanese people, Protestantism, Catholicism."[23] Oyama relayed Surmelian's sympathy with the Japanese Americans and the "Nisei problems," which she viewed as "really the common problems of all racial minority groups here in the United States."[24]

Oyama's writing reflected her strong concerns regarding multicultural relations. She never tired of trying to push her readers to "mix" socially with non-Japanese and to politicize her readers – as racial minority people and as citizens. For example, in July 1941, she interviewed the Italian American writer John Fante, whom she called "a Nisei like the rest of us, as he was born in the United States."[25] Oyama, in her breezy prose, deftly drew attention to another interethnic issue by focusing the article on a story by Fante that had appeared in the *Saturday Evening Post*. The story, centering around a Filipino man, had met with strong criticism from the Filipino American intelligentsia. Fante sheepishly admitted to Oyama that he had, indeed, learned more about Filipinos *after* he wrote the story.

William Saroyan held particular appeal for the Nisei writers, who mentioned him frequently. They drew encouragement from his assurance that "each of us is a Nisei," as well as from his exhortation to write. "The life of the Japanese in California is rich and full of American fables that need to be told to other Americans," he urged. "They must be written by those who lived them in order to become a part of the whole American life."[26] Words of support from such an acclaimed ethnic author must have meant a great deal to the Nisei, struggling to develop a voice and to reach a wider audience.

The Nisei literati's choice of role models raises further speculations. They were clearly drawn to ethnic individuals like the Italian American Fante and the Armenian American William Saroyan. But what about African American authors and artists? Why the Armenian Americans and Italian Americans? Perhaps regional visibility was a factor since many Armenian and Italian immigrants had settled in California at the turn of the century, when the majority of the Japanese arrived. For a brief period, the Armenians had shared the legal kinship of being categorized as "Orientals" in California. Fante, Saroyan, and Surmelian were also the children of immigrants, like the Nisei. There were far fewer blacks in the West, and the Harlem Renaissance (in the pretelevision era) had been a dazzling eastern regional development. Also, prejudice against African Americans may have prevented some Japanese Americans from viewing them as models to emulate. The choice of role models certainly poses further questions regarding interethnic relations and perceptions. Nonetheless, it is clear that Nisei writers looked both into their own community and out into the large society for inspiration in grappling with the articulation of a distinctive American ethnic identity.

By 1940, however, the lively discussion of literary aspirations, gender roles, and intergenerational dynamics that filled the columns of the 1930s dwindled as impending war between the United States and Japan intensified the "Nisei problem." Political concerns overshadowed other issues. Tones of insecurity and vulnerability infused the writings of the Nisei, reflecting their position. Toyo Suyemoto's metaphors took on larger meaning in this uncertain time:

> I know I must learn to accept,
> Not question overmuch
> Lest I forget myself
> And try to clutch
> At beauty never meant for me,
> Till slipping fingers seize
> A blade of grass or two
> And find some ease
> In nearness of familiar things –
> But even these betray
> The heart at length, for they
> Will pass away.[27]

The Japanese Americans left familiar things far behind them when they were sent to the concentration camps. World War II has been the focus of Japanese American history, encompassing a lion's share of the scholarship – a focus that, while important, has obscured the richness of prewar creativity. Examining the work of Mary Oyama and her literary sisters not only brings to light the talents and concerns of the Nisei, but also opens up critical questions regarding relations among racial ethnic groups, the impact of regional influences on ethnic culture, and the challenges faced by women seeking their niche in both mainstream U.S. society and the ethnic community.

NOTES

1. Toyo Suyemoto, "Afterwards," *Current Life: The Magazine for the American Born Japanese*, July 1941, 6. For a thoughtful examination of Suyemoto's wartime poetry, see Susan Schweik, "The 'Pre-Poetics' of Internment: The Example of Toyo Suyemoto," *American Literary History* (spring 1989): 89–109.

2. Since the original publication of this article in 1991, several books have been published that include the work of Japanese American authors or reference it, including Jeffery Paul, ed., *The Big Aiiieeeee! An Anthology of Chinese American and Japanese American* (New York: Meridan, 1991); King-Kok Cheung and Stan Yogi, *Asian American Literature: An Annotated Bibliography* (New York: Modern Language Association of America, 1988); and Yuji Ichioka et al., comp., *A Buried Past: An Annotated Bibliography of the Japanese American Research Project Collection* (Berkeley: University of California Press, 1974). Hisaye Yamamoto, *Seventeen Syllables and Other Stories*, originally published by Kitchen Table in 1988, now appears in a revised and expanded edition (New Brunswick NJ: Rutgers University Press, 2001).

3. I am grateful to Vicki Littman, Mary Oyama Mittwer, Lily and Yasuo Sasaki, Joe and Clem Oyama, Nikki Sawada Bridges, Chizu Iiyama, Hisaye Yamamoto, and Seizo Oka for generously sharing their history. For their valuable insights, I wish to thank Peggy Pascoe, Vicki Ruíz, Glenn Omatsu, Elaine Kim, Evelyn Nakano Glenn, Moira Roth, and Stan Yogi. I am also indebted to the Humanities Institute and the Women's Studies Program at the University of California, Davis, for their support of my research.

4. *Hokubei Asahi*, January 5, 1935.

5. Kenny Murase, "Who's Who in the Nisei Literary World," *Current Life: The Magazine for the American Born Japanese*, October 1940, 8.

6. Toyo Suyemoto, "Praise," *New World–Sun*, June 23, 1941.

7. *New World–Sun*, January 12, 1939.

8. *Current Life: The Magazine for the American Born Japanese*, January 1941, 11.

(In November 1941, the magazine changed its subtitle to *The Only National Nisei Magazine*.)

9. For more information about Hisaye Yamamoto, see King-Kok Cheung's insightful biography and critical introduction to Yamamoto's fiction collection, *Seventeen Syllables and Other Stories*, xi–xxv.

10. I have discussed Nisei ideas regarding marriage at greater length in a paper entitled "From Aunt Tsugi to Dear Deirdre: Japanese American Women, Acculturation, and Ethnic Identity, 1930–1941," presented at the Berkshire Conference of Women's History, Wellesley College, Wellesley, Massachusetts, 1987.

11. *New World–Sun*, February 11, 1937.

12. Sylvia Yanagisako, *Transforming the Past: Tradition and Kinship Among Japanese Americans* (Stanford: Stanford University Press, 1985), 107–8.

13. For a detailed examination of antimiscegenation laws and their application to Asian Americans, see Megumi Dick Osumi, "Asians and California's Anti-Miscegenation Laws," *Asian and Pacific American Experiences: Women's Perspectives*, ed. Nobuya Tsuchida (Minneapolis: Asian/Pacific American Learning Resource Center and General College, University of Minnesota, 1982) 1–37.

14. *New World–Sun*, October 10, 1935.

15. *Current Life: The Magazine for the American Born Japanese*, March 1941, 12.

16. *New World–Sun*, October 3, 1935.

17. Charles Kikuchi, "The Nisei and Marriage," *Current Life: The Magazine for the American Born Japanese*, August 1941, 8.

18. *New World–Sun*, October 25, 1935.

19. *Hokubei Asahi*, January 1, 1935.

20. *Hokubei Asahi*, October 23, 1936.

21. *Hokubei Asahi*, October 23, 1936.

22. *Hokubei Asahi*, January 1, 1935.

23. *Current Life: The Magazine for the American Born Japanese*, April 1941, 10.

24. *Current Life: The Magazine for the American Born Japanese*, April 1941, 10.

25. *Current Life: The Magazine for the American Born Japanese*, July 1941, 13.

26. *Current Life: The Magazine for the American Born Japanese*, May 1941, 8.

27. Toyo Suyemoto, "Hae Quoque," *Current Life: The Magazine for the American Born Japanese*, August 1941, 10.

Frontiers 12:1 (1991): 19–32. Permission to reprint Toyo Suyemoto's poetry is granted by the author.

Japanese American Women and the Student Relocation Movement, 1942–1945

LESLIE A. ITO

Michi Nishiura Weglyn was fifteen when President Franklin Delano Roosevelt issued Executive Order 9066 in February of 1942.[1] Nishiura's high school education was interrupted and her family's life of farming in rural Brentwood, California, was terminated when the United States government sent the Nishiura family and 120,000 other innocent Japanese Americans to concentration camps and stripped them of their civil liberties. The Nishiuras were incarcerated at Gila River Relocation Center, one of the ten concentration camps in the U.S. interior.[2] While in camp for nearly four years, Nishiura's father did stoop labor on a local farm, earning sixteen dollars a month, and her mother worked in the camp mess hall.[3] For Nishiura and other Nisei (second-generation Japanese American) students, makeshift high schools were established in the camps that provided minimal public schooling. However, once Nishiura graduated from high school, her future and the option of continuing her education became uncertain. Fortunately, a group of concerned educators, along with religious organizations such as the Quaker-based American Friends Service Committee, had formed the National Japanese American Student Relocation Council (NJASRC). In 1944, she was able to acquire government security clearance to leave the center and was admitted to Mount Holyoke College on a full scholarship.

Nishiura's story caught my attention while I was attending Mount Holyoke College. At first, I was merely intrigued by the idea of Michi Nishiura Weglyn, author of *Years of Infamy* and one of the most important contributors to Japanese American history, having attended my college. I learned later that three Japanese Americans attended the small women's college in western Massachusetts in the 1940s. As I began research on the history of Japanese American students like Nishiura, I discovered that an entire group of Nisei students left the camps to attend college in the Midwest and East Coast and that their stories were much deeper and more complex than the merely geographic and cultural contrasts and conflicts that they encountered. Further research also revealed that of the Nisei students attending college, roughly 39 percent were women.[4] These statistics astounded me and helped me realize that the Nisei students' history could not be examined solely within the confines of race or gender, but must be analyzed within the contexts of both. In this chapter I will discuss how societal and parental pressures urged the Nisei women students not only to earn a higher degree but also to become representatives of the Japanese American community behind the barbed wire fences. I will also show how gender and race further defined the Nisei women's multiple roles.

I begin by exploring the complex lives of these Nisei women students on the basis of gender and sexism, race and racism, and citizenship and loyalty. During the war Japanese Americans faced scrutiny that went beyond racism, as the United States government challenged their national loyalty despite their U.S. citizenship. I will also examine how the women students struggled to address the dichotomy between social agency and constraints within an institutional structure.

OUTSIDE ASSISTANCE

In response to the educational crisis that the Nisei college students faced within the concentration camps, influential educators, religious leaders, and a small number of Japanese American community members formed the NJASRC, the nongovernmental committee that was the driving force behind the movement from camps to colleges. Between the spring of 1942 and 1945, a total of 5,522 Nisei were enrolled in over 529 colleges and universities in the Midwest and East Coast, most receiving some type of assistance from the NJASRC.[5] As the War Relocation Authority (WRA) prepared to release Japanese Americans from the concentration camps, and particularly after the federal government revoked the mass exclusion orders in December of 1944, the WRA also set the agenda and defined the role that these students would play as representatives of the Japanese American community in anticipation of Japanese American resettlement.

The NJASRC strove to create a controlled environment that fostered students' success and insured that they would portray a positive image to the rest of America. The NJASRC identified colleges and universities that would allow Japanese American students to attend, practiced "building morale" and "sustaining faith" in Nisei high school students in order to encourage them to continue their education, and helped them fill out applications. The NJASRC and the government's ultimate agenda was to build the faith and morale of students so that their families would also regain optimism and eventually follow their children to the Midwest and East Coast – away from the West Coast, where they had originally lived.[6]

Although the NJASRC had an agenda for these students that reached beyond their academic success and focused more on rebuilding trust and optimism, most students were thankful to the organization for assisting them. Kay Oshiyama, who attended college in Ohio, regarded the NJASRC as a "blessing" and wrote, "It was the Council's diligence and patience in its effort to help us that brought back the fire and enthusiasm to continue where I left off."[7] Letters like Oshiyama's inundate the official files of the NJASRC, and such appreciation is echoed in many of the Nisei students' oral histories. It is true that without the NJASRC's help and the bravery of the pioneer students who ventured off to colleges in the first group of two hundred, many Nisei minds would have withered behind the barbed-wire fences. Yet further analysis of the methods employed by the NJASRC to choose the students who went to college and its political agenda for dispersing them across the country reveals that the NJASRC's objective was not only to aid in the Nisei's education, but to produce model representatives, or ambassadors, of the incarcerated Japanese American community.

In order to form this model group, the NJASRC evaluated the students' eligibility based not only on scholarship, personal records, recommendations, and financial aid status, but also on the questionnaire form completed by every applicant.[8] The NJASRC used the questionnaire to assess the students based on two criteria: dependability and adaptability. However, these two qualities were not evaluated solely within an academic environment, but more specifically with the intention of forming a network of Japanese American representatives who would both assimilate into American college life and reverse the negative wartime image of Japanese Americans.

The NJASRC's selection process intentionally constructed a controlled model to be sent out to participating college campuses, and it is thus no surprise that these students had few problems adjusting to college life. As Robert O'Brien notes, according to a survey taken of the first four hundred Nisei students to relocate, they averaged a "B" grade-point average after their first year of college and were also involved in a wide range of extracurricular activities.[9] The idea of assimilation was key to forming this elite group because the NJASRC expected these group members to dispel the Japanese American's negative wartime image.

Many of the colleges favored Japanese American female students over male students because they believed that women attracted less suspicion of espionage and wartime paranoia.[10] This rationale essentially opened up greater opportunities to those who might have been previously discriminated against because of gender; however, it is also evident that colleges could not make the distinction between Japan, the enemy, and the American-born Japanese. As unjustified fear of espionage and distrust associated with people of Japanese ancestry continued to plague the nation, gender bias reinforced the patriarchal notion of women's passivity.

The NJASRC and the WRA strongly influenced the Nisei students by encouraging them to believe that the program was a civic duty to the United States. Nao Takasugi, an NJASRC placement counselor, explained students' responsibilities as "returnees": "This is just a means to an end and in this way it is hoped that their contacts will be not only with students interested in going to college but also with the community at-large and thus they would have greater opportunity for helping families make their decisions on relocation. Your sweat and labor will not be rewarded in terms of money but rather by a lasting satisfaction in your heart that you will have had an integral part in helping them wisely resettle in outside American communities."[11] As "ambassadors of goodwill," students in the relocation movement satisfied the NJASRC's goal to assimilate Japanese Americans through education and physical dispersal while dispelling negative myths about the Japanese Americans.

PARENTAL INFLUENCES

Students had dual responsibilities to the NJASRC and to parents who expected them to attain a higher education and fulfill civic and community duties. Despite the traditional Japanese American family structure based on a rigid patriarchy adopted from Japan, many parents of the women interviewed for this study had little gender bias regarding education and actually expected their daughters to attend college.[12] However, this idea of sending a daughter to college was not the cultural norm. In fact, prior to the incarceration, Nisei women were well educated and competitive with their male counterparts only up to the high school level. According to Thomas James, financial constraints and the patriarchal Japanese family system prohibited many Nisei daughters who would have been eligible from attending college. James points out that many women were working to put their brothers through college instead of pursuing their own education.[13] Yet some Japanese American parents thought that becoming a part of the educated elite would provide what Eileen Tamura refers to as "an avenue to middle class" and the "American dream," an essential means to climb the ladder of socioeconomic success in the United States for both men and women.[14] Not only did these parents have a new outlook on their daughters' education, but many had themselves led extraordinary lives.

Nisei women students were particularly influenced by mothers who were both better educated and more independent than most Japanese immigrant women of their generation. Parallel to Stacey Hirose's observations in her study on Nisei Women's Auxiliary Corps, the first-generation Japanese American Issei mothers of female students were independent and in many cases served as the family breadwinners.[15] The Nisei women exposed to their free-thinking, well-educated mothers were apparently less likely to become stifled by the patriarchal family structure that hindered so many Japanese American women. For example, Rhoda Nishimura Iyoya, who attended Vassar College, described her mother as "a woman ahead of her time." Nishimura explained that her ideas "were not typically first-generation Japanese."[16] Contrary to many Issei women who worked in and around the home, Nishimura's mother ventured beyond domestic work and became one of the first women hired by the Mitsubishi Corporation, at the age of twenty-one. After immigrating to San Francisco, she continued to work outside the home as a Salvation Army officer, again leading an uncharacteristically public life for an Issei woman. Another Nisei woman, Esther Torii Suzuki, acknowledges in her memoir that her mother was "the first feminist to cross my path."[17]

Not only were the Issei women educated in many of these families, but several Nisei women attending college came from families in which both their mother and father balanced a life of work and civic and community duties. Such Issei parents expected their sons and daughters to do likewise. For instance, Kei Hiraoka Nagamori graduated from a six-year college in Japan and immigrated to America to help establish the Jane Couch Home, a shelter in Los Angeles for abandoned and abused Japanese picture brides and their children. In the mid-1920s, she also fought to keep two Japanese schools in California open after legislation was passed in California requiring all teachers to pass a written English exam.[18] Because she was one of the few Issei women who could speak English, she was able to pass the test and continue teaching. Yet it is clear that such women were expected to shoulder what Evelyn Nakano Glenn refers to as the "double burden" of having to participate in wage labor and the domestic sphere.[19] While actively participating in the Japanese American community, Kei also raised her daughter Toshiko Nagamori Ito. In addition to caring for their families, many Issei mothers took part in civic and community life, and the legacy of balancing three lives was passed down to the Nisei generation, as exemplified by Kei Nagamori.

Many fathers of Nisei women also influenced their decision to go to college. For example, Masuo Yasui acted as a liaison between European American orchardists in Hood River, Oregon, and Japanese farmworkers. He arranged contracts and loaned the Issei money for down payments on land.[20] A few fathers, such as Michi Yasui's, were able to read and write English. These men were more likely to be exposed to the dominant culture and found that educating their daughters as well as their sons was a social and economic necessity for moving beyond the ethnic enclaves and the agricultural fields for more financial stability and independence.

Wartime arrests and incarceration uprooted both patriarchal structure within the family and the power held by the Japanese American community leaders. As Roger Daniels notes, within the first week of the Pearl Harbor bombings, the FBI detained fifteen hundred Japanese community leaders on the West Coast from their list of allegedly dangerous aliens.[21] Among this first group to be incarcerated was Mr. Kiro Nagano, the president of the Judo Federation, in Los Angeles, and owner of a wholesale produce company. The FBI sweep marked a turning point in many Nisei lives, including that of Kiro's daughter, Momo, who suddenly inherited increased family responsibilities. At the age of sixteen, Momo became responsible for helping her mother settle their business and consolidate all their belongings when they were incarcerated in April 1942.[22]

As both Valerie Matsumoto and Mei Nakano discuss, many Japanese American families experienced fragmentation as opportunities of school, work, and military service became alternatives to incarceration. The Nagano family provides a good example. Momo's eldest brother received security clearance to leave Manzanar and finish his architecture degree. Concurrently, Nagano's younger brother volunteered for the army reserve training program to show his loyalty to America. Meanwhile, Nagano's father was sent to several different concentration camps across the nation and remained separated from his family.[23] When Nagano's brothers departed from camp to pursue life outside, they left her with the filial responsibility of caring for their mother and keeping track of their father's whereabouts.

Thus Nagano temporarily abandoned her own plans of a college education to fulfill her duties as a faithful daughter. As both James and Matsumoto state, for many Nisei women in the camps, relocating was a difficult process tied to family obligations.[24] Nagano's responsibility to her family was firmly rooted in the patriarchal structure of the Japanese American family, and while her brothers had the liberty of pursuing their lives, her plans were deferred. Eventually she was able to reunite her mother and father after months of assembling documentary affidavits in Mr. Nagano's support and attending his hearing in Santa Fe, New Mexico.[25] Momo was then able to free herself to pursue future goals and an education at Wheaton College. The circumstances that Nagano faced in reuniting her parents forced her to take a more active public and political role. Through this process she became more independent and filled the leadership role left to her by her father and brothers by navigating the family during this time of separation.

THE CAMPS AND INDIVIDUAL DETERMINATION

The concentration camp experience often catalyzed a shift in the patriarchal family structure, as was the case of the Nagano family. Nakano and Matsumoto both show that men were no longer the main breadwinners of the family after incarceration. And in some cases Issei men were separated completely from their families in Department of Justice concentration camps. Some women were thus freed from many traditional domestic chores because of the communal setting in the camps and the separation of their families.[26]

Relations between parents and children also changed. The incarceration undermined parental authority thus allowing children more independence and freedom for young Nisei to develop their own interests and goals. Many young women continued to take the traditional path of getting married and becoming a wife, or in some cases felt obligated to take care of younger siblings or elderly parents inside the concentration camps. Nevertheless, the reconfiguration of the family structure in the concentration camps prompted a new social standing that gave some young single Nisei women the confidence and courage to venture on to college.[27]

The WRA, the NJASRC, families, and communities expected the chosen students to be goodwill ambassadors through their daily interactions with mainstream America and their more formal speaking engagements. In comparison to the segregated male troops of the 442nd Regimental Combat Team and even the Japanese Americans who left the camps to work in the wartime factories and fields, these students were able to have more daily contact and interaction with European Americans and were able to partic100ipate on fairly equal ground compared to most Japanese Americans who were forced into segregation. Through this daily, more intimate contact, the Nisei women became ambassadors.

The first of these daily interactions began as soon as they stepped past the barbed-wire fence to travel from the concentration camps to the college campuses. Like the soldiers of the 442nd Combat Team and the wartime workers who left the concentration camps, most of the students took the bus and train to their destinations, receiving their first look at America from the "outside" since incarceration. For many, their first taste of freedom was made bitter by long, arduous, and uncomfortable trips. For example, Hiromi Matsumoto's trip from Gila River Relocation Center in Arizona to Mount Holyoke College in western Massachusetts involved a four-day trip by train and bus.[28] Often students traveled alone and encountered uncomfortable situations when sharing a car with U.S. soldiers and other hostile passengers. For instance, in August 1942, while Masaye Nagao Nakamura traveled from Heart Mountain, Colorado, to Park University in Missouri, the train conductor spat on her as she handed him her ticket.[29] The psychological impact of this event had been so traumatic and scarred Masaye so deeply that she buried this story for nearly fifty years. Nagao's recollection of this incident is a reminder that although the Nisei students left the camps and were able to obtain an education, racism still plagued the country and left deep psychological scars.

As Monica Sone recounts in her memoir *Nisei Daughter,* Japanese Americans leaving the camps were cautious and intimidated by the possibility of racism that lingered outside the camps. Sone recalls leaving for Wendell College in Indiana: "In the beginning I worried a great deal about people's reactions to me. Before I left Camp Minidoka, I had been warned over and over again that once I was outside, I must behave as inconspicuously as possible so as not to offend the sensitive public eye."[30] However, for Sone and most Nisei students, their relationships with European American peers and professors were, in contrast, friendly and casual.

STUDENT LIFE

Although many Nisei women anticipated some hostility on the "outside," for the most part the colleges that they attended were liberal and sympathetic to the Nisei's difficult position, embracing the students and helping them to feel a part of their community. Considering the NJASRC's careful selection of colleges willing to welcome Japanese American students during such wartime uncertainty and distrust, it is not surprising that the Nisei students were well received. Not only was this controlled situation for the benefit and well-being of the Nisei students, but it also proved to be beneficial for the Nisei's mission as cultural representatives. At most schools the number of Nisei students never exceeded five, and so the Japanese Americans on campus never presented a significant physical presence. Furthermore, the Nisei women's positive interactions with their European American peers and faculty served dual functions: The Nisei were able to dispel the anti-Japanese propaganda that stigmatized the Japanese American community, and European Americans were able to show the Nisei their commitment and desire to help. Although the formation of these friendships was no doubt genuine, the Nisei students were nevertheless always reminded of their role as representatives of the Japanese American community.

The women recalled many of their European American peers being quite accepting and helpful. For example, Shizuko Itagaki recalled being graciously received by European American students at Simpson College, a Methodist-affiliated institution in Iowa. On the weekends, Itagaki did her laundry at a European American friend's house in Des Moines, and on a few occasions she came home with freshly baked cookies, too. Itagaki was so touched by this kindness that she wrote to her family in camp about this encounter. Unbeknownst to Itagaki, her father sent the family a wood carving that he had made in camp to reciprocate their kindness toward his daughter. This incident served as a symbol of hope to the Itagaki family that the outside world was not as hostile as some had expected. Furthermore, this hope is precisely what the NJASRC had wished to instill in order to help ease anxieties of resettlement once the camps were closed.[31]

Unlike members of other Nisei groups that left the camps for work or military service, the Nisei students were often invited to the homes of white peers for holidays and vacations, which provided for further opportunities to interact and spread goodwill to their European peers and their families. As Esther Torii Suzuki states in her memoir, "Survival would not have been possible without many thoughtful student friends."[32]

Because the camps were distant from the colleges and because visiting required a permit, many of the Nisei spent their vacations on campus or in the area where they attended school. In such intimate settings the women students also acted as representatives of their incarcerated and "suspect" community. For example, Margaret Yokota Matsunaga, while on vacation from Oberlin College, accompanied a Russian Jewish classmate home to New York City because she could not be with her own family in the Heart Mountain Relocation Center. To help keep Yokota's spirits up, the Jewish friend bought Margaret a Christmas tree and made sure she attended church on Christmas.[33] Yokota's experience represents not only a friendly gesture, but also a genuine attempt to be sensitive and respectful to ethnic and cultural differences during a time of heightened racism and xenophobia.

Although the stories above give evidence to the NJASRC's success at finding welcoming colleges for the Nisei students to attend, the NJASRC had little control over the hostile sentiment toward Japanese Americans in the local towns surrounding the colleges. For example, Park University president William Lindsay warned Masaye Nagao that the townspeople were not pleased with the Japanese American students' arrival and that threats of lynching had even been made. He demanded that she be accompanied into town by her roommate at all times. Nagao recalled: "It was really like having an invisible fence around. If I can't go wherever I want to go by myself, it is like camp."[34] Other students recall similar situations, including Mary Takao Yoshida. In her memoir, she remembers being assigned a senior student to be her "bodyguard" when she entered Texas Wesleyan College, an experience she found extremely uncomfortable.[35]

Although the Nisei students did encounter some hostility in their local towns, only two actual incidents have been recorded in the history of the Nisei student relocation movement. Both incidents, known as the "Battle of Parksville" and the "Retreat from Moscow," revolved around protest from the townspeople. The Battle of Parksville involved a group of residents from Platte County, Missouri, who tried to prevent seven Nisei students from attending Park College. The Retreat from Moscow occurred at the University of Idaho, where six Nisei students were denied admission after arrangements had been made with the university and after security clearance had been obtained. In both cases, the Nisei students were eventually allowed to attend the universities.[36] As James discusses, most of the opposition that the Nisei students faced came from the townspeople living near the colleges, or what he refers to as "local protest," which promoted the government propaganda of Japanese Americans as the "enemy" committing acts of espionage.[37]

AMBASSADORS TO THE COMMUNITY

The Nisei students were encouraged by NJASRC to make public appearances in their college towns to speak about the Japanese American concentration camp experience to local religious and community organizations. For Nisei women, these speeches offered an opportunity to participate in the public sphere, and more than half of the women interviewed for this project reported delivering such speeches. For example, Masaye Nagao recalled giving speeches to local church groups in Kansas City. For many of the students, presenting these talks proved to be extremely difficult. Nagao believed that there was a real need for European Americans to be educated about Japanese Americans and the concentration camps. She said, "These people didn't look on us as Americans. They looked on us as Japanese, as the enemy. No matter how much you said 'We're Americans,' they just didn't accept that. You had to be blue-eyed, blonde, white to be American."[38]

Although audiences were for the most part accepting and responsive, on a few occasions, students occasionally encountered ignorant and even hostile audience members. Nagao recalled one incident in which a church member from the audience announced, "You should feel fortunate that we put you in camps where you were protected." Although she was angered, Nagao disregarded the comment and dismissed the woman as being unable to distinguish Japanese Americans from the "enemy." From then on, Nagao was diplomatic and careful "not to antagonize them too much." Such negative comments put the Nisei students in compromising situations where they had to restrain themselves from showing their outrage in order to continue being goodwill ambassadors.

Some Nisei students, such as Setsuko Matsunaga Nishi, had been trained, award-winning orators in high school. Matsunaga suspects that her oratory skills caught the attention of the NJASRC, helping her be chosen. Matsunaga spoke to various organizations from the Lions Club to churches and high schools, more than three hundred speeches in the two short years that she was at Washington University.[39] Matsunaga's speeches at first prompted a visit from FBI agents who were investigating a complaint that "there was a Jap who's making speeches and propagandizing." Matsunaga reminded them that she had been released from the Santa Anita Assembly Center with clearance from four federal agencies and asked them to come hear her speeches to alleviate their concern over the content. This incident clearly reflects the irony of the Nisei women's role on campus and in the local community. Many colleges had expected that women would be unassuming and cause less suspicion, but Nisei women were leading much more public lives and being more civically active than colleges had anticipated.

Representing Japanese Americans in places where Asians had never been before was a heavy social responsibility for students like Matsunaga and

Nagao. They knew that the Japanese American collective image depended on their success in reaching out to the communities on and surrounding their campuses, but speaking took a great deal of time from their studies. Gladys Ishida Stone recalled that when leaving camp in Amache, Colorado, for Washington University she was "glad to be released from camp, but felt a tremendous burden to do well, not only for myself, but to be a good representative of Japanese Americans." She explained the pressure of her multiple responsibilities: "It was a very hectic period of my life; I did not have the luxury of getting homesick!"[40] Many students had to carefully balance their responsibilities in order to remain dedicated to their own studies while also educating others in order to fulfill their duties to both the Japanese American community and to mainstream society.

Because of the wartime hysteria and dominant society's perception of the Japanese Americans as a "sneaky, dirty" enemy, proving loyalty consumed many Nisei. They wanted to distinguish themselves from their immigrant parents' generation and to prove their patriotism. Nisei men had the option of serving in the U.S. Army. Since few Nisei women entered military service, the incentive to prove their loyalty to America through their presence on a college campus was attractive.[41] They also undertook various tasks to prove their loyalty, which further complicated their lives on college campuses. Many students viewed their role as ambassadors as a form of service to the nation's war effort. Yasuko Takagi,[42] a patriotic student attending school in Denver, Colorado, wrote, "I am indeed fortunate to be one of the first groups to leave the centers for the purpose of education. I will not overlook my opportunity and responsibility which rests upon me. I am here for a purpose and I shall accomplish my task and shall always endeavor to do my best. My high American ideals shall remain with me and I shall do everything in my power to serve this country and help in any way possible and re-prove my true loyalty to the Stars and Stripes."[43] As evidenced in this excerpt, Takagi recognized her responsibility to the Japanese American community as she left the concentration camp for college. It is also clear, particularly in the last three lines, that she views her role as a Nisei college student to be no different from that of a soldier in the 442nd. This super-patriotism is a direct result of incarceration and is a response to the misperception of Japanese Americans as the enemy.

Although for women the student relocation movement was one way to escape the camps and prove their loyalty to America, there were inherent problems with their role. Even the word "ambassador" connotes a sense of foreignness, an individual who represents one country to another. Being labeled an "ambassador" negated the Nisei's status as American citizens. Although many European Americans assumed the Nisei were foreigners, the second-generation Japanese American students worked to counter this misperception. Hattie Kawahara was chosen by *Mademoiselle* magazine to write an article on Japan for its August 1944 issue. Knowing nothing about her assigned writing topic, she wrote a piece titled "I Am an American": "We may look Japanese but in our hearts and thinking we belong to the country of our birth. We know no other life except that which we have had here in America. Thus after Pearl Harbor, the evacuation of all persons of Japanese ancestry from the West Coast to inland relocation centers, regardless of citizenship, came as a great blow to our security and hopes; but we never lost faith in the country which is our home."[44] Kawahara was critical of America's decision to intern the Japanese Americans, yet she hesitated to completely denounce the government's actions for fear of being labeled disloyal and un-American. Her writing reflects the Nisei dilemma of choosing between loyalty to the U.S. government and the principles of democracy, the dilemma all Japanese Americans above the age of seventeen grappled with in answering questions twenty-seven and twenty-eight of the loyalty questionnaire.[45]

Kawahara's article, Takagi's response to her role as a student representative, and the numerous speeches that the Nisei students gave were all components of their mission to gain visibility and dispel the wartime propaganda about Japanese Americans. These women tenaciously sought not only to be seen, but also to be heard in order to secure a new place for themselves and their families. The ways in which the Nisei women students actively sought visibility was exceptional for Asian American women of this time period.

NISEI STUDENTS AS DOMESTIC WORKERS

In addition to the Nisei students' roles as student and representative, they also faced economic responsibilities. Although the NJASRC helped to solicit financial aid from both the participating colleges and religious organizations, most of the students still had to find an additional source of income to pay for their living expenses. In most cases, their parents were no longer in the financial position to support their children's education because of the economic loss they suffered at the time of evacuation and because of the low wages paid in the concentration camps, which ranged between eight and sixteen dollars a month.[46] Unfortunately, work for women students was limited to the domestic sphere despite wartime shifts in the labor market.

American women during World War II were encouraged by the government and media to work in the factories, replacing the men who had gone off to war.[47] By 1944, in many cities, women working in the factories outnumbered the sum total of women working in the whole labor force in 1940.[48] Yet while Rosie the Riveter was off earning good wages in defense work, someone had to tend to the domestic chores, and college students were hired as domestic workers to fill the void. Housecleaning and baby-sitting remained one of the few viable jobs available to help women earn room and board while attending school. For Nisei women, this type of work provided needed income and yet another venue to "spread the good-will."

Although some Nisei women had clerical jobs on campus, most opted to become "school girls" because of the flexible hours and the incentive of room and board.[49] As Evelyn Nakano Glenn mentions, for many school girls, this was their first experience working in a European American home.[50] Although they had helped their mothers with the household chores for years, they had to learn how to cook European American food and clean house to the satisfaction of their employers. For example, Ida Nakashima Schneck, having grown up with no electricity in a farming community in Livingston, California, had to be taught by her European American employer how to do domestic chores, including using the vacuum cleaner.[51]

For the Nisei students, domestic work as school girls restricted their spare time, confining them to a schedule that left barely any time for leisure. The experience of Katsumi Hirooka Kunitsugu, who was a journalism student at the University of Wisconsin, is typical. In exchange for room and board, Hirooka washed dishes and diapers and did light housework for Dr. Mowry, an allergy specialist, and his family. Hirooka recalled: "Being a school girl, the hours that I wasn't at the university I was mainly working at this home. So I really didn't have much free time except on the weekends."[52] Like Hirooka, other women found little time for themselves after completing their studies, work, and ambassadorial responsibilities. Their college experience often did not extend beyond these three roles.

In some cases, the school girls were not only employees of these families, but also became an important part of the family unit. In Tomoe Murata Arai's case, her employment as a school girl for a Coast Guard family before the war changed the course of her life and helped her move from Hawaii to the mainland. However, when the war broke out, she was placed under house arrest and was unable to return home to Hawaii, where Japanese Americans were not typically interned. With the help of her adopted mainland family, Murata secured admission to Connecticut College to finish her degree.[53] In Murata's case, her work as a domestic led her to the East Coast and eventually to reenter college.

Although the school girls' experiences differed depending on their treatment by employers and also by the type of work they did in the home, the students did not report any ill treatment, nor did they complain about being overworked. Perhaps this difference can be attributed to the difference between full-time and part-time domestic work. In most cases, my interviewees went to school during the day and did the household chores and cooking in the evenings.

The Nisei women accepted jobs as house girls in order to obtain a higher education and have a better future than their mothers, who were for the most part domestic and field workers. However, as William Chafe concludes, the women's sphere grew dramatically during the war period, yet the traditional role of women and domesticity remained the same.[54] Glenn also echoes this statement in reference to the Nisei women's broadened horizon, which subsequently shrank during the postwar period.[55] Like many women in the wartime defense industries who were forced back into the home when the war ended, many of the women interviewed for this project – even though most of them finished their degrees and sometimes graduate work – interrupted their careers to become wives and mothers.[56]

AFTER COLLEGE

Nisei women continued to face challenges – of balancing careers, raising families, and pursuing civic and community responsibilities – after graduation. Most of those college graduates interviewed became housewives until their children were grown and then pursued their careers. For example, Shizuko Itagaki returned to college to receive her teaching credentials after the youngest of her four children started elementary school, and soon became a special education teacher in California. She recalled: "It took some time to realize, gee, this is my job and that I'm something besides a mom and a wife."[57] Similarly, Michi Yasui Ando raised six children and then returned to the University of Denver for her degree in education. She spent three decades teaching in the Denver public school system, dedicated to promoting cross-cultural understanding in the classroom.[58]

However, during the immediate postwar era, despite the fact that they were well educated and highly qualified, many of the Nisei women faced both race and gender discrimination in the workforce. Not only did these Nisei women experience what Chafe describes as discrimination against woman in professional employment, but they also experienced postwar racism against Japanese Americans. For example, after Katsumi Hirooka Kunitsugu graduated from the University of Wisconsin with a degree in journalism, she had difficulties finding a job. Commenting on this problem, she said, "I think because being a woman was one thing and being Japanese American was another. I did send out all kinds of letters and all that but received no replies, no encouragement whatsoever. So I came back to Los Angeles."[59] Mainstream presses rejected Katsumi's applications, but fortunately *Crossroads Newspaper,* a Japanese American press, hired her as a columnist.

Similarly, Masaye Nagao Nakamura had worked at Scott Foresman, a textbook publishing company in New York City, and received her master's degree from the Columbia Teachers College, yet the Berkeley School District would not even grant her an interview for a teaching position because of her race. Eventually, in 1949, Nakamura found a teaching position in Oakland, where she became the first Japanese American to teach in that school district.[60] These accounts are typical of the sexism and racism that these educated, experienced women encountered in the job market.

CONCLUSION

Nisei women's wartime experiences, their position as representatives of the Japanese American community, and the knowledge gained through these interactions significantly outweighed what they acquired in the classrooms. As Rhoda Nishimura Iyoya wrote, "I have learned that loyalty to my country does not mean blind obedience to our leaders. Rather, it is my responsibility as a loyal citizen to question such actions. My experience has taught me to examine issues carefully, to define my stand, and then to speak out and be an active, relentless and 'aggressive' agent of reconciliation."[61]

Like Iyoya, other Nisei women who were part of the student relocation movement continued to carry their civic and community responsibilities with them by becoming teachers, lecturers, and philanthropists to ensure that the atrocities of concentration camps in the United States would not reoccur. More than half of the interviewees became educators, perhaps due to the restrictions of the job market for women, yet many of them used education as a means to further their work as representatives and to assist disadvantaged students in inner-city schools. Four of the interviewees also used academia and the college library as a way to disseminate information. A few have worked as "ambassadors" on various levels of banking, research, and medicine. Others became involved in their local Japanese American communities, both in their careers and as volunteers working with issues of redress and reparations, cultural retention, and politics.

In the late 1980s, some of the former colleges established the Nisei Student Relocation Commemorative (NSRC) Fund. The NSRC Fund, spearheaded by Nisei Nobu Hibino, who attended Boston University during wartime, creates annual scholarships for college-bound Southeast Asian American students across the nation.[62] All of these women have followed in the footsteps of their parents as leaders and free-thinking, independent women, and all have contributed to the Japanese American collectivity as they have continued to be among the most visible group of Nisei women.

Yet the history of these women and their postwar achievements have been overshadowed by the well-documented history of the Nisei male soldiers who fought in World War II. Similar to the decorated 442nd RCT, who fought the double battle for America and their community's civil rights, the Nisei students were representing Japanese Americans at home, preparing the nation for the resettlement of thousands of Japanese Americans who were being released. The Nisei women played a large part in this "ambassadorial" effort not only through their excellent progress in academics, but also through their public speeches and interactions with employers, faculty, classmates, and others they encountered. These women were acting as representatives between the camps and colleges, much like the 442nd RCT, yet they were expected to lead the life of a typical American college student – studying, working for room and board, and participating in campus activities.

As the history of the young Japanese American male soldiers has shown, the experience of Japanese Americans' removal to concentration camps reaches far beyond the confines of the camps themselves and does not end with the closing of the camps. The resettlement period, in which Japanese American women took a great lead, is a crucial part of this history that is often overlooked. Within this missing link of Japanese American history lie the stories of the Nisei student relocation movement. The Nisei women's stories captured in this chapter show that although these women were given freedom for their education, they were not freed from the psychological and historical effects of this mass incarceration. Still bound by the wartime racism and the sexism of the times, these women worked with the limited freedom that they had acquired to successfully fill the roles and responsibilities as working students and representatives of the Japanese American community.

MICHI YASUI ANDO was attending University of Oregon when her education was interrupted by the war. Her father was a merchant and farm owner in Hood River, Oregon, in the prewar period. Her mother was interned at the Tule Lake Relocation Center, and her father was in a maximum security camp in Missoula, Montana. Instead of evacuating with her family, Ando went straight to Colorado and enrolled at the University of Denver in 1942. She later received an M.A. in education at the University of Denver. She is a retired teacher, living in Denver.

TOMOE MURATA ARAI was born and raised in Kona, Hawaii. Her parents and grandmother worked on the coffee plantations. At the age of seventeen, Arai came to the mainland as a house girl/baby-sitter. When Pearl Harbor was attacked, Arai was living in Connecticut and she was put under house arrest because of her Japanese ancestry. The family that she worked for then helped her get admitted to Connecticut College. Neither she nor her parents were incarcerated in the concentration camps; however, her experiences as a Japanese American woman on a college campus during wartime are still important to this study. Arai has retired from her position as a librarian at the City University of New York.

HIROMI MATSUMOTO DYE attended the University of California, Berkeley, until the war broke out. She then enrolled at Mount Holyoke College in March of 1943 and majored in mathematics and zoology. She also did graduate work in physiological psychology at Cornell University and in mathematics and engineering at UCLA. Her family owned an orchard in Winters, California, before being interned at the Gila River Relocation Center, Arizona. Dye, now retired in Los Angeles, dedicated thirty-three years to work at Planning Research Corporation, where she became vice president, the highest ranking position on its professional staff.

SHIZUKO ITAGAKI (PSEUDONYM) attended Simpson College, in Iowa, and completed her degree at the University of California, Los Angeles. The Itagaki family was from the small Japanese farming community in Livingston, California. She and her family were interned at the Amache Relocation Center, Colorado. Itagaki, retired in South Pasadena, California, spent twenty years of her life as a special education teacher.

TOSHIKO NAGAMORI ITO was raised in the Los Angeles area. Her mother worked in a Methodist home for battered and abandoned picture brides and their children. Ito's father tried to open the Kato Silk Company in Los Angeles and later sold insurance. After finishing high school by correspondence from the Santa Anita Assembly Center, Ito attended National College in Kansas City, Missouri. She finished her degree at Chapman College with a major in sociology and later attended Immaculate Heart College for a certificate in education. She is now a retired schoolteacher living in Laguna Hills, California.

RHODA NISHIMURA IYOYA attended Vassar College. Rhoda's father was a Methodist minister in Berkeley, California. She and her family were incarcerated at the Topaz Relocation Center, in Utah. Now a retired schoolteacher, she travels nationwide to give leadership seminars to women of color in the National Methodist Church. Iyoya lives in Pasadena, California.

KATSUMI HIROOKA KUNITSUGU attended the University of Wisconsin. Kunitsugu's father was in the wholesale produce business in Los Angles before the war. She and her family were interned at the Heart Mountain Relocation Center in Wyoming. Kunitsugu has held several jobs as a journalist. She is currently the executive secretary of the Japanese American Cultural and Community Center in Los Angeles, California.

MARGARET YOKOTA MATSUNAGA] was originally from Los Angeles, where both her mother and father taught at St. Mary's Episcopal Church Japanese School. She and her family were incarcerated in the Heart Mountain Relocation Center in Wyoming. From there, she attended Oberlin College to study music education. She is a retired public school teacher living in Littleton, Colorado.

FUMIKO MOCHIZUKI attended McFierson College in Kansas during the war. Mochizuki's parents were farmers in central California before they were incarcerated at the Rohwer Relocation Center in Arkansas. She is a retired schoolteacher living in Los Angeles.

JUNE SUZUKI MOCHIZUKI attended Colorado State University, Greeley, and Colorado State University, Fort Collins. Mochizuki's parents were farmers in the San Joaquin Valley, California, and were later interned at the Amache Camp in Granada, Colorado. She worked at Western University as a counselor for twenty years.

MOMO NAGANO attended Wheaton College in Norton, Massachusetts. Nagano's father owned a produce company in Los Angeles. She and her mother and brothers were interned at the Manzanar Relocation Center in California. Her father was moved from several Department of Justice concentration camps. She has recently retired from her position as an administrative assistant at the Japanese American Cultural and Community Center; however, she regards herself primarily as a weaver.

MASAYE NAGAONAKAMURA was born in Hilo, Hawaii, and moved to Seattle, Washington, as an infant. She was attending UCLA when World War II began. She was then incarcerated at the Heart Mountain Relocation Center in Wyoming. In August 1942, she began attending Park University in Parksville, Missouri. She is now a retired elementary school teacher, living in Orinda, California.

SETSUKO MATSUNAGA NISHI grew up in Los Angeles, where her father was a real estate broker. She attended the University of Southern California before the war, hoping to major in music. However, she was required to transfer to Washington University in St. Louis, Missouri, in order to continue her education. Nishi and her younger sister, who attend Rockford College, were among the first to be relocated from Santa Anita Assembly Center. Once at Washington University, Nishi changed her major and received a degree in sociology. Later, Nishi received her Ph.D. from the University of Chicago. She is a professor of sociology at Brooklyn College in the graduate school of the City University of New York. Nishi's research focuses on American race relations.

IDA NAKASHIMA SCHNECK was raised in a Japanese farming community in Livingston, California, before she and her family were interned in the Amache Relocation Center in Colorado. Before the war, Schneck attended Modesto Junior College. From Amache, she transferred to Parsons College in Fairfield, Iowa. She went on to get her medical degree from the Women's Medical College in Pennsylvania and is now a retired pediatrician and is actively involved with the University of Colorado Medical School in Denver.

EMI SASAKI (PSEUDONYM) attended the University of California, Berkeley, until Executive Order 9066, when she was sent to the Tanforan Assembly Center. Her mother owned a candy store in San Jose, California, prior to the evacuation. In September 1942, Sasaki transferred to Washington University at St. Louis, Missouri. She is a retired librarian from Columbia University in New York City.

TAKEKO WAKIJI attended Pasadena City College before World War II. She and her family were incarcerated at the Gila River Relocation Center. In October 1944 she moved to New York City and enrolled at Hunter College as a junior transfer, graduating in economics and accounting. Wakiji is first vice president at the Amalgamated Bank in New York City.

NOTES

1. I use both the woman's maiden and married name on first reference; thereafter I refer to her by her maiden name because that was how she was identified during her college years.

2. Japanese American World War II terminology is problematic. Although the U.S. government's creation of euphemisms was common, I will use the government's terms only when they are used as official names, for instance, Gila River Relocation Center or Santa Anita Assembly Center. When I refer to the camps in general, I have chosen to call them concentration camps, which should not be confused with the Nazi death camps.

3. Sheryl McCarthy, "Exposed: America's World War II Concentration Camps," *Mount Holyoke Alumnae Quarterly* (fall 1997): 22–23.

4. From 1942, when the first four hundred students left for college, to the end of the Nisei student relocation movement in 1945, the total percentage of Nisei women attending college increased by 7.3 percent (Robert W. O'Brien, *The College Nisei* [Palo Alto CA: Pacific Books, 1949], 131). Robert O'Brien was a professor at the University of Washington during World War II and was influential in the student relocation movement. His generous investment of time and energy in the NJASRC, the nongovernmental agency that assisted the Nisei in their college admission processes, influenced his narrative of the Council and the students' experiences. O'Brien paints a bright and hopeful picture of the student relocation and presents only the NJASRC's successes and the students' positive experiences. He uses his book, *The*

College Nisei, essentially to commend the Council for its outstanding service. *The College Nisei* is also problematic in that O'Brien wrote it in 1949, only four years after the end of the war. O'Brien's historical survey of the student relocation and the Council are accurate, but his sociological observations and accounts of the Nisei college experience are outdated and were clearly made before ethnic cultures were appreciated and accepted as a part of the American experience. Because O'Brien's book was a public relations piece and published soon after the war, *The College Nisei* becomes a valuable primary, rather than a secondary, resource for this study.

5. O'Brien, *The College Nisei*, 111.

6. O'Brien, *The College Nisei*, 65.

7. Original name has been changed in compliance with the rules at the Hoover Library and Archives, Hoover Institution on War, Revolution, and Peace, Stanford University, Palo Alto CA, Thomas Bodine Collection, file 7.14. The official files of the NJASRC are housed at the Hoover Library and Archives.

8. O'Brien, *The College Nisei*, 63–64.

9. O'Brien, *The College Nisei*, 90–91.

10. Thomas James, *Exile Within: The Schooling of Japanese American 1942–1945* (Cambridge: Harvard University Press, 1987), 127–28.

11. Letter, June 5, 1945, Japanese American Student Relocation Council Collection, box 43, Esther Takei folder, Hoover Library.

12. See Ruth Benedict, *The Chrysanthemum and the Sword: Patterns of Japanese Culture* (Boston: Houghton Mifflin, 1989), 48–49; Harry H. L. Kitano, *Generations and Identity: The Japanese American* (Needham Heights MA: Ginn Press, 1993), 118–21; and Sylvia Junko Yanagisako, *Transforming the Past: Tradition and Kinship Among Japanese Americans* (Stanford CA: Stanford University Press, 1985), 97–102.

13. James, *Exile Within*, 72.

14. Eileen H. Tamura, *Americanization, Acculturation, and Ethnic Identity: The Nisei Generation in Hawaii* (Urbana: University of Illinois Press, 1994), 91–124. See also Shotaro Frank Miyamoto, *Social Solidarity Among the Japanese in Seattle* (Seattle: University of Washington Press, 1939), 104–10; and Koji Shimada, "Education, Assimilation and Acculturation: A Case Study of a Japanese-American Community in New Jersey" (Ph.D. diss., Temple University, 1974), 68–92.

15. Stacey Hirose, "Japanese American Women and the Women's Army Corps, 1935–1950" (master's thesis, University of California, Los Angeles, 1994), 9.

16. Rhoda Nishimura Iyoya, interview by author, Pasadena, California, November 25, 1996.

17. Esther Torii Suzuki, "Esther Torii Suzuki," in *Reflections: Memoirs of Japanese American Women in Minnesota*, ed. John Nobuya Tsuchida (Covina CA: Pacific Asia Press, 1994), 94–95.

18. See Yuji Ichioka, *The Issei: The World of the First Generation Japanese Immigrants, 1885–1924* (New York: The Free Press, 1988), 207–9.

19. Evelyn Nakano Glenn, "The Dialectics of Wage Work: Japanese American Women and Domestic Service, 1905–1940," in *Labor Immigration Under Capitalism: Asian Immigrant Workers in the United States Before World War II*, ed. Lucie Cheng and Edna Bonacich (Berkeley: University of California Press, 1984), 470–514.

20. Lauren Kessler, *Stubborn Twig: Three Generations in the Life of a Japanese American Family* (New York: Random House, 1993), 75–76, 298.

21. Roger Daniels, *Prisoners without Trial: Japanese Americans in World War II* (New York: Hill and Wang, 1993), 26.

22. Momo Nagano, interview by author, Los Angeles, July 20, 1995.

23. Nagano was arrested and taken to the Jefferson Boulevard Police Department and then moved to the Terminal Island Penitentiary. From there he was moved around from several detention camps – Fort Missoula, Montana; Fort Sil, Oklahoma; Camp Robinson, Oklahoma; and Santa Fe Internment Camp, New Mexico. These internment camps were administrated by the Department of Justice, not the War Relocation Authority. From December 7, 1941, to March 9, 1942, the Immigration and Naturalization Service (INS) held over four thousand Japanese Americans in custody at Fort Missoula, Montana, and Fort Lincoln, North Dakota. Eventually the U.S. Department of Justice had nine permanent and eighteen temporary internment camps. These camps were under wartime censorship and even today little information is known about them (Michi Weglyn, *Years of Infamy: The Untold Story of America's Concentration Camps* [New York: William Morrow, 1976], 176). See also John J. Culley, "The Santa Fe Internment Camp and the Justice Department Program for Enemy Aliens," in *Japanese Americans, from Relocation to Redress*, ed. Roger Daniels et al. (Salt Lake City: University of Utah Press, 1986), 57–71.

24. Valerie Matsumoto, "Japanese American Women During World War II," in *Unequal Sisters: A Multicultural Reader in U.S. Women's History*, ed. Ellen Carol DuBois and Vicki L. Ruiz (New York: Routledge, 1994), 443; and James, *Exile Within*, 72.

25. Nagano, interview.

26. Mei Nakano, *Japanese American Women: Three Generations 1890–1990* (Berkeley: Mina Press Publishing, 1990), 146–48; and Matsumoto, "Japanese American Women During World War II," 438–42.

27. See Matsumoto, 447–48; Weglyn, *Years of Infamy*, 81–83; and Paul Spickard, *Japanese Americans: The Formation and Transformations of an Ethnic Group* (New York: Twayne Publishers, 1996), 110–12.

28. Hiromi Matsumoto Dye, interview by author, Brentwood, California, June 14, 1995.

29. Masaye Nagao Nakamura, interview by author, Orinda, California, June 21, 1997.

30. Monica Itoi Sone, *Nisei Daughter* (Seattle: University of Washington Press, 1953), 219–20.

31. Shizuko Itagaki, interview by author, South Pasadena, California, August 21, 1995.

32. Suzuki, "Esther Torii Suzuki," 106.

33. Margaret Yokota Matsunaga, interview by author, Littleton, Colorado, January 7, 1998.

34. Masaye Nagao Nakamura, interview.

35. Mary Takao Yoshida, "Mary Takao Yoshida," in Tsuchida, *Reflections,* 201.

36. O'Brien, *The College Nisei,* 87.

37. James, *Exile Within,* 122.

38. Nakamura, interview.

39. Setsuko Matsunaga Nishi, interview by author, New York, New York, September 9, 1997.

40. Gladys Ishida Stone, "Gladys Ishida Stone," in Tsuchida, *Reflections,* 335.

41. Approximately eighty Nisei women participated in the WAC (Hirose, "Japanese American Women and the Women's Army Corps," 17).

42. Name has been changed in compliance with the rules at the Hoover Library.

43. Thomas Bodine files, 7.8, no. 6681, Hoover Library.

44. Hattie Kawahara, "I Am an American," *Mademoiselle,* August 1944, Mount Holyoke College Archives, Hattie Kawahara file.

45. Commission on Wartime Relocation and Internment of Civilians, *Personal Justice Denied: Report of the Commission on Wartime Relocation and Internment of Civilians* (Washington DC: Civil Liberties Public Education Fund, 1997; Seattle: University of Washington Press, 1997), 136–40.

46. Commission on Wartime Relocation, *Personal Justice Denied,* 117–33.

47. See William Henry Chafe, *The American Woman: Her Changing Social, Economic, and Political Roles, 1920–1970* (New York: Oxford University Press, 1972), 135–50; and D'Ann Campbell, *Women at War with America: Private Lives in a Patriotic Era* (Cambridge: Harvard University Press, 1984), 103–37.

48. Chafe, *The American Woman,* 139.

49. According to Evelyn Nakano Glenn, the role of the school girl dates back to Japan, where domestic work was thought to be an appropriate job for young, single women to receive domestic training for marriage (Evelyn Nakano Glenn, *Issei, Nisei, War Bride: Three Generations of Japanese American Women in Domestic Service* [Philadelphia: Temple University Press, 1986], 124–27). In the case of the Nisei school girls, it may have been seen as a way to assimilate women into "good

American housewives." However, the Nisei school girl may also be associated with the Japanese school boy who provided domestic labor in exchange for room and board while attending school. Ichioka, *The Issei*, 22–28.

50. Glenn, *Issei, Nisei, War Bride*, 125–26.

51. Ida Nakashima Schneck, interview by author, Aurora, Colorado, January 7, 1998.

52. Katsumi Hirooka Kunitsugu, interview by author, Los Angeles, April 22, 1998.

53. Tomoe Murata Arai, interview by author, New York, New York, August 31, 1997. Although Murata was not incarcerated, she faced situations similar to those of the other women in this study in terms of gender, race, and nationalism. Murata was the only Japanese American at Connecticut College. She recalled being mistaken for a mulatto, because many of the students had never seen an Asian face before. She did have a few friends in the concentration camps; they sent her camp newsletters and printed materials to use in writing a paper on the camps for a composition class.

54. Chafe, *The American Woman*, 188.

55. Glenn, *Issei, Nisei, War Bride*, 128.

56. Chafe, *The American Woman*, 174–75.

57. Itagaki, interview.

58. Kessler, *Stubborn Twig*, 264.

59. Kunitsugu, interview.

60. Glenn, *Issei, Nisei, War Bride*, 112.

61. Rhoda Iyoya, "Japanese American in Topaz Relocation Center," in *No Longer Silent: World Wide Memories of the Children of World War II*, ed. C. Leroy Anderson and Joanne Anderson (Missoula MT: Pictorial Histories Publishing, 1995), 275.

62. See Leslie A. Ito's prologue in Gary Okihiro, *Against Racism: Japanese American Students and World War II* (Seattle: University of Washington, 1999).

Frontiers 21:3 (2000): 1–24.

Like a Bamboo

Representations of a Japanese War Bride

DEBBIE STORRS

My mother, Yoshiko, searched her English vocabulary for a way to describe how she felt after almost thirty years of marriage to my recently deceased father, a retired U.S. serviceman. She helped me visualize the difficulties she experienced in her life: "It hasn't been easy sometimes. My life feels like a bamboo, you know there's a lot of skin, like layers? I feel like every time, all the layers are being peeled away and I've got nothing left. That's the way I feel. Like a bamboo, you know what I mean, right?" I wasn't sure but nodded anyway, digesting her description of my father peeling away her life energy. Misinterpreting my silence, she assumed I didn't understand her use of the bamboo and searched for a more culturally familiar food object. Drawing quickly on a pad, she sketched an artichoke and explained, "You know, the vegetable you like, that's an artichoke, right? Yeah, he makes me feel just like that. You take one leaf out at a time." She mimicked the act of pulling an artichoke leaf out, one by one, and scraping the flesh from the leaf by one's teeth. I shuddered at the imagery. She continued: "Pretty soon I feel like I have nothing left. Pretty soon even my soul is sometimes taken out. The bamboo is the same thing. One skin goes over another skin goes over another skin. That's what it's like."

My mother's use of the bamboo as a metaphor for her life experience struck me as capturing the duality of oppression and resilience in her. The Japanese make resourceful use of bamboo for household items, including broom handles, walking canes, painting brushes, and weaving material.[1] My mother was referring to the sheaths bamboo sheds that are used for wrapping food and making sandals, among other items. The shedding of the bamboo is like the stripping of my mother's sense of self, often to the depths of her soul, that is a common theme in my mother's life stories. Yet bamboo and its sheaths are valuable and strong; its strength and flexibility explains its many uses and value. Like the strength of the bamboo, my mother's sense of self is strong and autonomous, even as the harsh realities of life test its resilience. In this chapter I explore the dynamics between the agency and American and Japanese cultural "frames," or ideologies, that have shaped my mother's subjectivity.

My decision to collect my mother's life stories grew from my dissatisfaction with the research on war brides and interracial marriages. In the research literature I found that even when women's voices were central in the form of stories, they were not analyzed; often they were entirely absent from studies of international marriages. My mother's interest in sharing her life stories derived from her motherly duty to help her daughter as well as from her hope that her stories would prevent other women from experiencing similar adversities.

My focus on my mother's own agency is informed by feminist theorists who challenge the common views of women as passive by highlighting women's acts of resistance within systems of oppression.[2] Given women's multiple positions within social relations and systems of inequality, the crucial task for feminists is to describe and explain women's subjectivities as shaped by complex processes of compliance and resistance, choice and constraint, strength and weakness.[3] My mother's location in gender, race, class, and nationalist social relations in the post–World War II era shaped and developed her sense of self. This chapter focuses on how this historically contingent mix of social relations shaped my mother's responses and her sense of self.

METHODOLOGY

Feminist and other scholars have emphasized how people construct the self partially through stories.[4] For example, Keya Ganguly speaks of identities as "fabrications . . . both invented and constructed" through narratives.[5] Narrators construct a sense of self, for others and themselves, through the telling of stories based on selective memory and the organization of particular life events. This construction can itself be viewed as a form of agency as individuals craft and share their life stories. Furthermore, the crafting of one's self through narrative is a collaborative process extended by the researcher who analyzes, organizes, and presents a narrator's stories. In other words, narratives are two-way constitutive relationships between the narrator and the researcher.[6]

When the relationship between narrator and researcher is an intimate one, the account produces benefits from even more concentrated coordination, making the account more plausible and the identities created more salient.[7] My mother's stories were told to me, her daughter, and our relationship framed her stories. Indeed, the life stories I collected can best be described as exchanges, or dialogues, between the two of us, and because of our mother – daughter relationship, our conversations were immediately personal and intimate. However, as Judith Stacey notes, "The greater the apparent mutuality of the researcher/researched relationship, the greater is the danger."[8] Family members may reveal intimate details of their lives with each other that they would not reveal to other researchers. Although I made it clear to my mother that my interest extended beyond simply understanding her life, our flowing conversations felt like personal moments of disclosure that made it all too easy to forget that there was a research agenda beyond the sharing between mother and daughter.

Our relationship also shaped the nature of her narrative in other ways. Feminist researchers question and problematize issues of authority and ownership, which I found complicated by my relationship with my mother. As much as feminist researchers attempt to collaborate with subjects, ultimately there is a power imbalance. As noted by Stacey, self-reflexivity on the part of the researcher fails to eliminate the inherently unequal relations between researchers and narrators.[9] In our situation, my mother's authority as parent often superceded the authority that most researchers have over subjects. Yet, while my mother had significant authority in the life story collection process, the final decision making concerning editing, interpretation, and publishing was mine. I found no clear or simple solution to these problems. I decided to be explicit about my role in the construction of my mother's narrative and to encourage my mother to participate in each step of the research process, but my encouragement was initially met with resistance.

Upon reflection, I now realize this resistance was due to the structural constraints that prevented her involvement. For example, my mother's refusal to possess a copy of the transcribed interviews reflected the lack of privacy she experienced while my father was alive. Her fear that he would discover them limited her early involvement beyond sharing her narratives. Even after his death, the structural constraints of her life continued to pose a barrier to her fuller participation in the research process. The period immediately following my father's death was one of difficult adjustment for my mother, both psychologically and financially. Even though she had more freedom in her personal life, she was faced with the financial and emotional hardships that many widows face. These hardships consumed much of her time. Today, several years after my father's death, my mother's life has become more manageable, and as a result she has participated much more in the production of this chapter. She read a draft of the manuscript, provided photographs to accompany the text, and requested several changes and clarifications. While her collaboration has increased, it would be misleading to characterize our roles as equal. One continuing limitation to her full collaboration is language. Even though my mother speaks English fluently, she experiences some difficulty reading and writing English. The writing style of the manuscript posed something of a barrier to her full participation. This was evident in the way she read the manuscript, skipping over sections that were difficult for her to understand, focusing instead on the sections in which her stories were central. Upon reflection, the decision to interview my mother in my native language, English, rather than hers, Japanese, is a reflection of the power imbalance between researcher and narrator. Aware of the potential for exploitation even with my mother's consent, I console myself that the research can be of value to others.

Furthermore, the nature of my mother and father's relationship, coupled with my position as daughter, significantly influenced the collection of my mother's life stories. My mother's emphasis on my father as the dominating force in her life was a significant component of her narrative. During the collection of her stories, my role as daughter merged with other roles I have played in our relationship as well as with my role as researcher. Because we shared many common experiences as women living within a traditional patriarchal family and social system, she often viewed and treated me as her ally. I felt like a friend and confidant when she disclosed her realization that her marriage was not what she had hoped for: "I realized and I knew after I came to America, not even two years later, I had made a big mistake. This marriage is gonna be a big mistake." At other times, she spoke to me as the daughter of the man she had married, periodically reassuring me that his inability to be a good husband did not necessarily mean that he was not a good father: "He was a good father though, he always has been. Especially when you were little. He was always so proud of you kids." On more than one occasion, my mother apologized for sharing her negative feelings concerning my father: "I dislike him more and more and I know

I'm talking about your father. I'm sorry." At one point, she worried that her disclosures would threaten family solidarity: "I know some day you'll be mad at me, but that's the way I feel." While our shared status as women shaped the way she framed her narrative in terms of gender domination, our intertwined roles as mother and daughter prevented her from fully exposing the limitations of her husband and my father. Thus, although our familial relationship facilitated her candidness, it also shaped the boundaries of what was permissible to share.

At the time of our interviews, my father was alive. My father was deeply suspicious about my interest in my mother's life. I concluded that his concern was due to his fear about what my mother would reveal and how that knowledge might alter my perception of him. My mother, on the other hand, was both flattered and excited by my interest in her life. I arranged to have my mother visit me for a week, which allowed us to have long hours of private discussions. Amid the sounds and smell of cooking she freely shared stories of her childhood, adolescence, and marriage. After the week of intense dialogue and sharing, she returned home. Seeking more information, I arranged several weekend visits at my parents' home to continue our dialogue. I found it more difficult to talk privately with my mother at her home, particularly given my father's suspicions. My mother was clearly less free to share her stories in her home, often pausing to determine whether we were actually speaking in private. Although it was more difficult to find significant amounts of time to speak privately, we managed to find an hour here and there without the interference of other family members. Our conversations were often emotionally draining, and it was difficult to move from our emotionally intense conversations to interacting with other family members. Eventually I collected about twenty-four hours of taped conversations with my mother.

To analyze the data I collected, I used the concept of narrative frames. "Narrative frames," or "models of intelligibility," assist members within a culture to organize and construct meaning through their life stories. Narrative frames include larger political-cultural conditions, including gender and racial ideologies, that can also constrain a subject's self-understanding.[10] Popular and social scientific representations reflect and maintain such dominant cultural ideologies, affixing and restricting meaning for individuals.[11] In particular, the popular post–World War II image of Japanese women represented by Bill Hume's character, Babysan, and social scientific research on Asian war brides and interracial marriages set norms and expectations over which women like my mother had little control.[12] While my mother's

identity was shaped and constrained by these representations, she also countered these narrative frames. American and Japanese cultural ideologies of
gender, race, and class limited the range of options available to my mother
and forced her to make decisions that she later regretted, but at the same
time my mother's agency in resisting these norms took multiple forms,
including anger, resistance, and endurance, as this chapter will show.

MY MOTHER'S NARRATIVE FRAME: "LIKE A BAMBOO:
A LIFE OF KURO"

Teresa Williams cautions scholars about generalizations concerning war
brides because of the diversity of their experiences,[13] yet common patterns
emerge from the structural forces that facilitate and mediate interracial and
international relations. Women married U.S. servicemen for a variety of
personal and psychological reasons, but the fact that many did so during
the postwar era suggests social, economic, and historical factors played a
role in these seemingly personal decisions. Changes in immigration law, the
elimination of miscegenation laws, and U.S. military occupation throughout Asia facilitated marriages between Asian women and U.S. servicemen.[14]

In many ways, my mother's experience is typical of that of thousands of
Japanese women who married American servicemen in the aftermath of
war.[15] As a young woman, she met, dated, and eventually married a U.S.
serviceman who, unbeknownst to her at the time, came from a working-
class family.[16] The dating and marriage met with strong objections from
many members of her family; however, encouraged by her natural father to
legitimize the perceived illicit relationship, she wed my father in 1958 at a
Buddhist temple. Two years later they repeated their vows at the American
Embassy immediately before their departure from Japan. Once she made
the decision to marry an American GI, her adoptive parents shunned and
later disowned her. None of her family members attended either of these
ceremonies.

My mother was born in 1935, the fourth youngest daughter of her biological parents. She was adopted at age two by her mother's married but
childless sister. According to my mother, this was an act of love on the
part of her biological parents. In Japan, as in the United States, femininity is often associated with fertility. My mother's stories of Japan suggest
that, not unlike the United States, a woman's inability to bear children is
stigmatized. The adoption arrangement alleviated this stigma and allowed
for continued relations between my mother and her birth parents and sib-

lings. My mother's discussion of the adoption and her knowledge of this relationship indicated that there was no stigma attached to adoption itself, at least within her family. In fact, my mother recalled stories of her early childhood with delight and described them as the happiest years of her life, despite the hardships of the war and her adoption. Because of the mothers' kinship relations and because of the conditions of war, she spent significant amounts of time with both her biological and adoptive families. As a child, she referred to her biological mother and father as "aunt" and "uncle," but she recalled always knowing their true relationship. I remember being surprised by this information concerning her adoption because I had known only one *bachan,* one grandmother, my mother's biological mother. This curious omission and recent revelation of family history points to the constructive and discursive display of self that is constantly changing.

My mother's stories of adoption and later rejection set a foundation of liminality in her life stories: as a child she transcended family boundaries but never felt like a full member of either her biological or adopted families. My mother's sense of not belonging, of being distant from both her land and family, physically and emotionally, both begins and ends her narrative. This liminal place, of being but not belonging in both her home and host countries, is linked to her marriage to an American. One evening I sat at my parents' dining room table with my mother across from my father and brother, who were engaged in a discussion in which I had little interest. My mother and I had just completed several hours of interviewing. Silently, she handed me a Japanese–English dictionary and pointed to the word *kuro:* "hardships; trials; difficulties, adversity; trouble; to undergo hardships; to have a hard time of it; to contend with difficulties; to struggle with adversity; the grim realities of life." Later, in private, I asked her why she had brought this word to my attention and she simply explained, "That's my life; that's what he has done to me."

It would be far too easy to interpret my mother's personal relationship with my father as the only force that impeded her autonomy and sense of self. While his role in shaping her experience is at the forefront of her narrative, the primacy of her husband in her life is premised on cultural models of gender and the family. In both Japan and the United States, particularly in the time period in which my mother came of age, women's primary roles were wife and mother. The primary mission of women even today in traditional Japanese culture is to marry and have children.[17]

My mother's stories emphasize her difficulties within her marriage, but to interpret them simply as a story of gender domination and resistance within a patriarchal family structure without taking racism and nationalism in account would fail to capture her subject position as a transnational woman: her narrative is replete with tales of difficulties that emerge from the larger cultural frames of race and nationality. The stripping away of self described at the opening of this chapter emerges from the dynamic interplay between cultural ideologies, subjective experiences, and representations larger than the experience of a single individual.

U.S. NARRATIVE FRAME: BABYSAN

War and postwar activities during three Asian wars shaped U.S. military servicemen's view of Asian women. U.S. servicemen came to view Japanese, Korean, and Indo-Chinese women as "exotic war booty,"[18] a view that was reinforced through Western cultural images in film and print of the Japanese women as "exotic, erotic creatures able to please men in special ways."[19] While sexualized, Japanese women were also viewed as desirable because of their alleged passivity, uncomplaining nature, and willingness to sacrifice themselves to the needs of men.[20] This dual characterization – sexually exotic and passive – is well captured in the character Babysan, a popular image of Japanese women published in military newsletters and whose origin is directly tied to military conflict and occupation. Babysan and similar cultural icons of Japanese women likely influenced my father's perception of my mother. Babysan was drawn by cartoonist Bill Hume, an American serviceman stationed in Japan whose work was published in military newspapers and newsletters.[21] After his discharge, Hume wrote and published *Babysan's World: The Hume'n Slant on Japan.* The title, a play on his last name and allegedly an attempt to help U.S. soldiers view Japanese women with humanity, reveals the exoticization of Japanese women through the use of the word "slant" with the accompanying picture of a well-endowed young Japanese woman with slanted eyes. Hume explains his purpose in writing *Babysan's World:* "This collection is not a textbook on Japan or Japanese custom and tradition . . . these are just a few of the attempts to produce cartoons for the entertainment of the man in uniform in the far east. Many of the comments are excerpts from letters written back to the States, and many of the cartoons already have seen print. Their publication in 'The Oppaman' has given a few servicemen some chuckles – and if you can find a laugh herein or appreciate the charm of the Japanese (Girl – Need I say it) – my mission has been accomplished!"[22] Despite Hume's claims early in the book that Babysan is not a cultural lesson on the Japanese, it is replete with cultural tidbits of information ranging from the Japanese custom of removing shoes before entering one's home to mini language lessons on common and helpful Japanese phrases. Hume's work focuses on the Japanese woman, and one piece of cultural advice he offers to servicemen is identifying the difference between a Japanese geisha and a prostitute. Hume adamantly states that "a Geisha is not a prostitute," followed by a warning of sorts: "Highly respected. Well educated. Proficient in the fine arts like music, dancing, art, social graces, dress, and sometimes intricate customs and ceremonies of her country. Moral beyond reproach!"[23]

Japanese women who interacted with U.S. servicemen were defined not as "nightclub" women or geishas but as ordinary Japanese "girls," interested in American servicemen and American culture. Evidence of their interest lies in the popularity of Western-style dress, although "even the most 'westernized' Japanese girl maintains a complete reverence for the kimono, whether she ever wears it or not."[24] Because of their great interest in Western clothing, one of the greatest gifts a serviceman can give to "his" Babysan is a Sears or Montgomery Ward catalog, which "she'll use . . . as a guide to the latest styles and improvements!"[25] It seems to follow that because Japanese "girls" are fascinated with American clothing, their only real interest in American servicemen is in the material goods that they have to offer. Hume warns his readers, "A serviceman soon discovers that to some girls the best boyfriend is the one who has the most cash. He is then 'ichi-ban' – number one!"[26] Materialistic motives aside, the Japanese "girl" is noted for her politeness, charm, patience, and domestic inclinations.

While Hume speaks directly to these qualities, the images that accompany the text provide a paradoxical representation of the Japanese woman. Sketched in short, see-through American-style dresses, the Babysan character provides the male viewer with the contradictory package of sexuality, childlike naïveté, and passivity. A sketch of a Japanese woman whose breasts are revealed through her sheer shirt as she walks through the streets is accompanied by the following text: "Here I've got two guys standing on a street – they're quite happy and very interested in something. To build a cartoon around them we start figuring – what would make them so interested and happy at the same time? Naturally – a neat and shapely Japanese girl . . . and even more so if it was summer! In warm weather in a small town it isn't too uncommon to observe gals that wear sheer blouses – and not a thing under them except the gals themselves. So let's do a cartoon that is no

Yoshiko Nabeoka as a young single woman, posing in a traditional Japanese kimono, at age seventeen.

exaggeration but a fact. Ain't it fun? The fact, I mean."[27] The written passages describing various cultural practices consistently refer to women's bodies and faces: the Babysan character is a young, curvaceous woman with dark shoulder-length hair, typically flipped up, and slanted eyes. While Hume's cartoons construct Japanese women as culturally and physically different, their difference and contradictory sensuality and naïveté are their appeal.

JAPANESE NARRATIVE FRAMES: GIFT GIVING, *PAN PAN* GIRLS,
AND MARRIAGE

Through the life stories of my mother, I had heard of Babysan long before I discovered Hume's cartoons. After the end of World War II my mother lived in the city of Osaka with her adoptive parents, who owned and ran a hotel and bar. U.S. servicemen in the Korean War routinely took leave in Japan, and the hotel served as a popular recreational site. One of my mother's earliest memories of American servicemen was of those who stayed at her family's hotel, where they would bring prostitutes. She recalled: "They used to call me Babysan, Babysan. And they used to give me chewing gum and chocolate and all that stuff. I was about fourteen."

Material offerings from American servicemen might be viewed simply as an act of goodwill and friendliness. However, when combined with references to my mother as Babysan, they reveal the power of Hume's representation: all Japanese women, even adolescent girls, became Babysan in the eyes of military men.

The practice of U.S. servicemen extending gifts in anticipation and in exchange for the affections of Japanese women was evident in my parents' first date. In retelling the story, my mother reveals the complex cultural and personal reasons for her decision to date a U.S. serviceman despite her family's negative reactions. Their first meeting occurred at the orphanage where her adoptive mother volunteered. My father and his squadron had been asked to volunteer at the orphanage's Christmas party. The church recruited six young women, including my mother and her older sister, to serve as hostesses. Because she could speak little English, my mother never directly spoke to her future husband that day. Instead, another young woman who spoke English informed her that one of the Americans had asked if she could date. She was filled with both apprehension and delight. On the one hand, she knew that her family would not approve of her dating an American, yet Americans intrigued her. She explained to her friend that she was unable to date because she did not have the right clothing:

I wanted to go, but I didn't have any clothes. All I had was my school uniform. It wasn't good enough to go out with an American guy. And my friend said, "No problem, I will help you." So I went to her house with my school uniform on and she let me use a real plain white dress with small polka dots on it. She didn't have any shoes to go with it so she let me use these ugly sandals. I waited for him. He came down and it happened to be raining. And when I saw him I chickened out because I was afraid for my mother's sake. I had seen those GIs come to the hotel with all the prostitutes, they were not good girls. But I wanted to go out. And he was cute, too. He was skinny, tall, dark hair, and had beautiful eyes. So anyway, he came down and I chickened out and started to think I should not do this. In my mind I wanted to go out but something inside me really told me I should not. And then all of my troubles came out of this.

While offering the clothing dilemma to her friend as an excuse not to date this American, the real issue facing my mother was her family's response given the common practice of U.S. servicemen soliciting prostitutes. Like others in her culture, my mother assumed that only "bad girls" dated American servicemen. This narrative frame reduced all interracial relations between Japanese women and American servicemen to prostitution. Her excitement and attraction to her future husband was checked by her ominous premonition that should she date him, her life would be full of troubles. This early story sets up the framing of her life story as a life of hardship. Trying to find a way to escape her commitment for the date, she explained, through her interpreter friend, that she must cancel the date due to the weather: "I chickened out and told my friend that I didn't have an umbrella and it was raining. I didn't want to go. And he said, 'No problem,' and he left. Then, I'll never forget this, he came back with cheap white rain shoes, rubber ones. And a plastic umbrella. And he also brought a small brown sack. Inside the sack was Jergen's skin lotion, instant coffee, and one lipstick. So I couldn't refuse him anymore." This example reveals the contradictions between American and Japanese narrative frames. According to Hume, Japanese – and Japanese women in particular – are materialistic and so American servicemen should protect their resources from greedy women. For the Japanese, the presentation of *omiyage*, or gifts, must be accepted and returned with something of value.[28] My mother's decision to go on the date was tied to the meanings she associated with the reception of such gifts. For her, my father's behavior and the gifts he presented created a sense of obligation. The unwritten social rule to reciprocate gift giving prevented her from rejecting his request for a date.

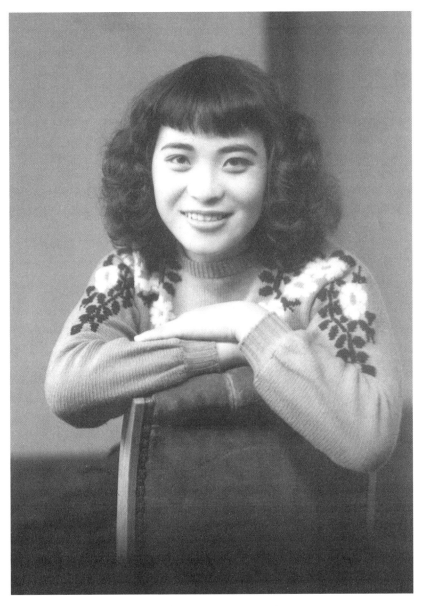

Yoshiko Nabeoka in Western dress, at age nineteen, in Japan.

Like the Japanese narrative frame about gift giving, the Japanese characterization of U.S. servicemen and Japanese women's relationships as illicit forced her to marry an American as a way of legitimizing their relationship. Once her family discovered her frequent outings with an American serviceman, she was informed that she was no longer allowed to engage in the relationship. She continued to see her future husband in secret, although her sister often reported their encounters to her adoptive mother. Finally, my mother was sent to the country to visit her biological mother and father during spring vacation in an attempt to discourage the relationship. There, she met with the same reaction. Her biological parents were worried and displeased: "My real mother was angry with me and said that my adopted mom couldn't handle me anymore. And my dad asked me what the hell was going on. And I told him I met a guy and I liked him. And they thought I was doing something bad. They said, 'What are you planning on doing?' I said, 'I'm going to marry him.' He hadn't even asked me but I just said that." The announcement of their marriage failed to console her biological mother, who was concerned about the shame such a union would bring to her family. The small, rural town where her biological family resided had very little direct contact with Americans. With the war fresh in their minds, their daughter's decision to marry an American was akin to marrying the enemy. Her father's response, on the other hand, reveals how such a marriage was preferred over what others might perceive as illicit activities: "My dad said, 'Well it doesn't make a difference if [he is] American or Japanese. As long as she's happy and she loves him. She should marry. Besides, if you stop her, she'll end up working as a bar girl or as a cabaret dancer.' That's what my dad said."

Illicit activities referred to sexual relations outside of marriage as well as prostitution. The organized prostitution conducted under Japan's Ministry of Health and Welfare facilitated the characterization of the relationships between servicemen and Japanese women as prostitution.[29] Called *pan pan* girls, women who could not find employment in the aftermath of the war were often left with no employment options except official prostitution. Paradoxically, women were required to register as prostitutes and, in doing so, forfeited any possibility of marriage to an American GI.[30] Thus, my mother's biological father supported the marriage not because he embraced such unions, but because he wanted to avoid the public perception of his daughter as a pan pan girl. Her adoptive parents failed to see marriage as a solution. They simply informed her that she would not be able to continue to date an American, and they attempted to limit her activities.

The cultural framing of my mother's relationship as potentially illicit and the resulting shame, combined with her desire to continue to see her future husband, led to her decision to leave her family home. She moved into her older sister's house, and her biological father encouraged her to marry quickly. In less than six months, my parents were married without the presence of her family: "None of my family was there. And so we got married. I met him in February and we married in July. That fast. I really didn't know him that much. I thought I liked him, but I never did love him." Thus the marriage was joined not on the basis of love, but in response to the narrative frames of her culture. Rejecting the characterization of their relationship as an illicit sexual one required her to legitimize it with a legal bond, regardless of the lack of emotional intimacy.

An additional factor that heightened her family's negative response to her marriage to a U.S. serviceman was her rejection of an arranged marriage. Historically Japanese marriages were arranged with the assistance of the *nakodo,* or go-between, particularly with individuals living in distant districts. While this practice was diminishing even during my mother's youth, most families still mediated marriage decisions.[31] In my mother's case, her adoptive family attempted to arrange a marriage with her second cousin assisted by a paid go-between: "A nakodo would help to have people get married because they would check on how long they went to school, what kind of family, how many kids, what the family has, what the parents do, all that kind of stuff they check into. And the families have to be a pretty close, they have to match mostly. They have to be a good family. And my adopted parents, they told me in my future I was going to marry my second cousin because they had a lot of property and money and stuff, and they didn't want to give it to a stranger and wanted to keep it in the family. So they made me wear my kimono and I went with my family to a restaurant to meet him and his family. And I told them later, 'no way.' " Her family's attempt to arrange a marriage to restrict the loss of family resources reveals how women's sexual and domestic autonomy was limited. While all cultures are concerned about regulating sexuality in some fashion, generally sexual prescriptions are heavily placed on women. As Avtar Brah notes, "Women occupy a central place in processes of signification embedded in racism and nationalism."[32] Women become symbols and guardians of race, nation, and class through their ability to bear children and their cultural responsibility to nurture them. My mother's relationship to an American serviceman violated racial, national, and class boundaries, shaping her consciousness.

NARRATIVE FRAMES OF RACE AND NATIONALISM: THE *SEN'SOO HANAYOME*

My mother's marriage to a U.S. serviceman cast her into a group, the *sen'soo hanayome,* or war bride, that came under the scrutiny of social scientists. Scientific inquiry concerning this growing cohort reflected, rationalized, and legitimized racial ideologies. Even before the growth of the war-bride cohort, science had characterized interracial unions negatively, based on ideologies of racial difference and purity. Beginning in the nineteenth century, scientists developed racial taxonomies, hierarchically arranging and differentiating racial groups according to presumed biological, physical, psychological, and intellectual capacities.[33] Early scientific views that races were separate species produced beliefs that racial mixing would lead to morally and physically inferior racial types.[34] In addition, the perceived threat to white supremacy that might occur as racial boundaries were blurred produced a negative response to interracial marriages. Given these beliefs, a number of practices were established to limit such unions, including laws, direct violence, and general social condemnation.

Despite these practices, relations between U.S. servicemen and Asian women flourished in the context of military occupation. Attempts to legitimize these relationships were difficult because many state laws prohibited interracial marriage, and U.S. immigration policies prevented servicemen from taking a Japanese wife and dependents to the United States. However, changes in immigration law in 1946 made it easier for U.S. servicemen to marry their Japanese fiancées.[35] As the number of Asian war brides increased, social scientists identified interracial, international marriages as appropriate topics of study.

The narrative frames of race and nationalism shaped the content of social science research on Asian war brides. At least two distinct emphases can be identified in the social science research on Asian and American interracial unions and Asian war-bride research. The first emphasis concerns the pathologizing of such unions or the identifying as psychologically inferior individuals who participate in interracial unions. For example, Bok-Lim C. Kim negatively characterizes interracial marriages as emotionally strained and conflicted, leading to severe personal disorientation for women.[36] Other researchers focus on the character of individuals who participate in interracial union, implying that their emotional deficiencies lead them to seek interracial unions, which in turn explains the instability of such relationships. For example, Paul Spickard cites the research of George A. Devos, who assumed Japanese women involved in interracial unions were psychologically unbalanced. Not surprisingly, Devos characterized his subjects as "rebellious . . . overtly passive . . . subtly controlling . . . masochistic, . . . and passive-aggressive."[37] Researchers also attempted to identify common traits of American men who engage in interracial unions. Early research characterized men who married Japanese women as working class or lower middle class, estranged from their own families, and "loners."[38] More contemporary research on the mail-order bride business, which has many parallels to the war-bride phenomenon, reveals an interesting contrast. Venny Villapando notes that the profile of men who participate as consumers in this business have higher than average income, are college educated, have experienced difficult divorces or previous engagements, and have come of age before the rise of the feminist movement.[39] While these cohorts of men differ in their social class, the research reveals a common incentive of securing a subordinate female companion. The implication by researchers that American men who seek an Asian wife have unusual personality characteristics suggests that these men significantly differ from American men who do not seek such partners. Such research gives the impression that American men who are not involved in interracial unions, particularly with Japanese women, are not domineering or sexist. Generally, this first group of studies assumes that the problems in these relationships arise from the interracial nature or from the psychological deficiencies of individuals who participate in them.

A second theme in the literature contradicts the negative characterization of interracial marriage by highlighting the stability and favorable outcomes of such unions.[40] Yet, even as these studies emphasize marital stability and content, these studies reflect the larger patriarchal and racist cultural frames. For example, Anselm Strauss cites women's careers and mobility aspirations as universal marital strains. According to Strauss, marital strain occurs less in interracial marriage because Japanese wives, protected from the consumption patterns of American wives, do not make great economic demands on their husbands and are not as career minded as American-born women.[41] This characterization of Japanese women reflects and reinforces racial and gender stereotypes about Japanese women as docile, passive, and domestic. Studies that emphasize the stability of interracial unions between Japanese women and American men ultimately attribute the stability to a commitment to patriarchal gender norms without any critical analysis of whether such unions can be characterized as favorable to both men and women.

While a close analysis of the literature on interracial marriage is beyond the scope of this chapter, this brief review illustrates that the social scientific research on war brides and their marriages reflects larger cultural frames of race, nationalism, and patriarchy. Patriarchal assumptions about women's roles in the family often go unquestioned by researchers, and racist and nationalistic concerns about racial purity and patriotism frame interracial and international unions as problems to be understood and corrected.

While social scientists negatively characterized interracial marriages, similar concerns focused on the progeny of such marriages – mixed-race children. Early social scientists characterize such persons as physically, morally, and mentally inferior. Similar to the depiction of the mulatto as "tragic" in American fiction, the mulatto or mixed-race person was considered "marginal" by social scientists.[42] Mixed-race individuals were characterized as psychologically and social inferior, a result of the identity confusion and rejection that they experienced from monoracial groups and society at large.[43] Like the research on interracial marriage, the contemporary research on racially mixed individuals is split between studies that emphasize the psychological stability of mixed-race children and those that emphasize the identity confusion of mixed-race children.

At the time they exchanged vows, my parents' marriage was illegal in many states in the United States. Again, the illegality was based on the American narrative frame concerning racial purity and white supremacy. Japan had a similar narrative frame. Given this context, their marriage was met by both extended families and societies with disapproval. In addition to the sanctions on their interracial marriage, my parents experienced the rejection of their mixed-race children.[44] My mother found the disapproval most difficult to bear when it came from her Japanese family and American in-laws. Following her marriage and relocation to the United States, my mother, sister, and I lived with my father's extended family while he was on active duty. In addition to living with daily insults about her food preferences and other cultural practices, deeper insults concerning her children troubled my mother:

We had to live with our in-laws in Colorado. And every time I used to cook my rice, his brother-in-law didn't like the rice smell and would call my rice maggots. It was so insulting, and I used to cry every time he said that. I finally left there after your aunt called you guys "damn half-breeds." I didn't understand what that meant until one day her neighbor in the next trailer asked me why I was staying there. She said, "Don't you have anywhere else to go?" I said, "No." She said, "Call your husband's other brother in Wyoming." She told me that they had no right to call my children half-breeds, and I had no business staying there. And she told me what half-breed meant. She explained it by talking about dogs mixing together. And I started shaking, and I cried and that night I called his other brother in Wyoming and told him to come get me.

Her story of how my siblings and I were called half-breed reveals the American concern over racial purity and the distaste toward those who blur racial boundaries, even within the family.

While Americans and American scholars were concerned with the issue of maintaining racial boundaries and purity, the same could be said of the Japanese. The Japanese have historically viewed non-Japanese as intrinsically different and inferior peoples. While the Japanese hierarchically evaluated black and white outsiders with a preference for whites, both shared the common status of being *gaijin*, or outside persons.[45] My mother's characterization of her family of origin's perception of Americans captured this difference: "Americans to them were different. They had different eyes and white skin. To us, they were so much like strangers. And especially in Ishikawa, where most people had never really seen an American except in the newspaper or in pictures." In the perception of the Japanese, the fundamental difference between themselves and the non-Japanese shapes their ambivalence toward and, at times, outright rejection of interracial marriages.

While the Japanese and American narrative frames concern racial purity, nationalistic tendencies also stigmatized international marriages. The realities of war and subsequent defeat of the Japanese understandably led to heightened Japanese hostility toward international relationships with Americans. When the war started, my mother was living in the city of Osaka with her adoptive family, but she was sent back to the country to live with her biological family because it was assumed rural areas would not be as ravaged by war as the larger urban areas. She remembered the rations and bombings from her childhood:

We had a *bokugo* [bomb shelter] in our backyard. We had a big hole and over the top was a roof that was made of wood, . . . and so when we were bombed, we went down there and didn't come out. A siren would come on and that would tell us when an airplane was in the air. Sometimes we were in school and the airplanes would come and everybody had to hurry and run home. I took a shortcut from school and crossed the river to my backyard. Even in Ishikawa we would see the B-29s. . . . I'll never forget it. They would just come down at us. . . . We had a lot of rows of cherry blossoms and I used to stand there and cry. I was so scared my legs were frozen and I didn't think I could run. You could see and hear the airplanes coming down, coming down. And you could actually see the man sitting in the plane. They would come down and you would hear ba-ba-ba-ba [sounds of machine gun firing] and then they'd go back up.

Her family's daily life was also altered by the absence of her biological father, who served in the war. In fact, her family believed that her father had actually died in the war after a long period of time with no word from him: "After the war was over my father didn't come back. We didn't hear from him for a long time. We thought he was dead already and we even had a funeral. Then, two years later, he came home. He had gotten hurt, and they had put him in the hospital. The Americans had taken over, and they had been taking care of him in a different hospital, and that's why we hadn't heard from him. After he had gotten well enough, they sent him home. And I remember that day. I was doing something in the house and I heard my mother scream. And I turned around and in the entryway there he was, standing there, like a ghost." Although alive, her father had suffered the loss of an arm and leg in the war. Given the recent memory and aftermath of war, it comes as no surprise that my mother's family did not embrace her decision to marry an American. "When I married him I guess I was the black sheep of the family because I married an American. And nobody in my whole town had married an American, and a lot of them had never even seen American people. And here I had to marry one. And I think my mother thought more of the family rather than me. She thought more about the shame I brought on my family. Naturally, there were a lot of hard feelings about Americans after the war was over." The social stigma of interracial and international marriage was experienced by the whole family. While her family initially rejected the marriage, the legacy of state-sanctioned prostitution posed an equally shameful interpretation of their relationship. In her family's eyes, the best resolution would be an end to contact of any kind with U.S. servicemen. Unable to impose this, however, the family was left with two potentially shameful situations – the perception of illicit relations or marriage. As neither option was acceptable, and failing to dissuade their daughter from marrying an American, the family responded with rejection. My mother recognized this through her characterization of herself as the "black sheep" of the family although, over time, the ostracizing she experienced from her natural family waned.

The narrative frames that each culture provided my mother limited her actions and propelled her into a marriage of discontent. Babysan, the sen' soo hanayome, and my mother's narratives are all representations of

Japanese women within cultural frames. Frames of race, gender, and nationality limited my mother's sense of self and maintained relations of domination, although not without being contested. It is to the agency of my mother, who resisted this domination, that I now turn.

At the basis of collective norms are narrative frames, composed of ideologies and representations that facilitate individual conformity. The Japanese phrase *shikata ga nai*, or "it can't be helped," indicates cultural norms over which one has little control.[46] In my mother's life, the cultural representation of the pan pan girl and the association of servicemen with prostitution had the potential to shape her as such. To escape this representation, she was left with little choice but to marry. However, her story about refusing to marry her second cousin in an arranged marriage, despite cultural norms, illustrates her independence and individuality. This same autonomy reemerges in her life in the United States as she struggled against the representation of herself as a subordinate female outsider. Later in her narrative she wondered what her life might have been like had she married the man whom her family had chosen: did her decision to resist the arranged marriage and later to marry as a compromise between shame and autonomy destine her to a life of suffering?

This notion of suffering in part stems from shikata ga nai: failing to follow cultural norms and social conventions led to a life of little choice but endurance of suffering. But endurance itself is a form of agency that, when recognized as such, helps to reveal a more complex representation of women's lives. Through her endurance of the suffering partially imposed by shikata ga nai and the decisions she made in response to representations of Japanese women, my mother, like countless other women, illustrates the twin modalities of self-construction that incorporates both cultural forces and individual autonomy.

CLASS AND MOBILITY: THE JAPANESE NARRATIVE FRAME OF
AMERICAN WEALTH

In the context of still-strained family relations, my mother left her home country and followed my father with great expectations about her new home in America. Her expectation of American wealth and prosperity grew from a Japanese narrative frame shaped by the larger sociopolitical context of defeat and military occupation. One of my mother's early disappointments in life in America, influenced by this narrative frame, was her perception of socioeconomic decline in her marriage. Despite her expectations of the wealth of Americans, her experience in this new land was of downward mobility and hardships: "I had no idea he came from such a low-class family. I was so disappointed because I thought America was going to be like what I saw in the movies. I thought all Americans were rich. I thought all of them were. I never dreamed it was this bad." Like countless other immigrants, my mother idealized America as a land of wealth and opportunity. The moment she arrived she discovered her error: "We flew from Japan to Alameda, California, and then took a bus to Wyoming. Boy, I thought America was just like I had seen in the movies. But he took me to a terrible place, Wyoming. It was all country. There was nothing but mountains and dirt. I was so disappointed. I came from a lot better family. I thought I should have known better. When I married him he had nothing but a uniform. He had one shirt and one pair of jeans. That's all he had, but I didn't realize that then he was that poor. I felt so cheated." While some of her childhood had been spent in the more rural town of Ishikawa, my mother spent considerable amounts of time in the large city of Osaka. Her adoptive parents were fairly wealthy business owners who provided her with amenities and unusual educational privileges. She, unlike many young women of her era, completed high school and attended a two-year business college. Her biological family, with whom she spent summers and vacations, owned their own business and significant amounts of land. Using her own mother's educational background as a measuring rod for her family's social class, she stated, "My real mother came from a real good family. And especially to think she was born in 1895. She was a schoolteacher until she was fifty-two or so, and then she retired. But she went to school to become a high school teacher. And they had to have a lot of money to send a woman to school, they had to be of real high class." The contrast between her privileged life in Japan and her new life of poverty in the United States encouraged feelings of betrayal. At some level, the betrayal was her own. Failing to follow cultural expectations in Japan had resulted in a difficult life in the United States. My mother explained that she had no one to blame but herself, for she made the decision to marry my father; yet even as she took responsibility for her early decision, she seemed aware that she was left with little choice. At another level she felt betrayed by her culture and her family of origin. Her decision to marry an American led to her ostracism from both her biological and adoptive families, at least early in the marriage. Her decision to stay in the marriage was in part due to the requirements imposed on her by her female family members. Her biological mother had been adamant that she should not marry an American and cautioned her about the finality of the decision: "My mother said, 'It's your choice to marry.' My mother said, 'If you marry you can come and visit home. But if you cry, and if something happens between you and your husband, my entryway is too high for you to climb back into.' That's what my mother said. I always remember that. She said, 'It's your choice to marry like this so you have to work it out.' " Letters from her mother during her early marriage reminded her that her decision to marry was something she must endure and live with. Coming home to visit was permissible, but coming home to stay was not an option. Divorce was uncommon and shameful, and in many ways she had permanently tarnished her family name and was thus condemned to live out her fate. In her narrative, her marriage to my father was the source of her troubles, but the marriage itself was something she was unable to stop or escape.

IKIGAI: NARRATIVE FRAMES OF MARRIAGE, FAMILY, AND WORK

Another disappointment in my mother's life was her disappointed expectations of marriage. My mother characterized her marriage as a union dominated by patriarchal control that restricted her autonomy. The reality of her married life contrasts sharply with the narrative frame of marriage in Japan. Despite Western images of the Japanese subordinate wife, my mother constructs a woman's wifely role as one of importance with significant financial power in terms of decision making: "In Japan the husband brings his paycheck home in an envelope to the wife. One of the wife's responsibilities is to pay the bills, save whatever they can, but the wife gives the husband so much money a week. . . . That's what a dutiful wife is. But never in my case. He gives me money, but just enough to pay bills." Throughout her narrative, my mother described how her own personal experience of marriage failed to meet her cultural expectations. My father maintained tight control over finances and, in her mind, she was prevented from fulfilling the role of a dutiful wife. Her expectation that a husband be a good provider was something that my father never quite fulfilled, which required her to work in a variety of jobs typical of many immigrant women. While some scholars argue that Japanese women identify family and children as their dominant *ikigai,* or "that which most makes one's life seem worth living," for many immigrant women work and family become merged, with the result that their roles both as mothers and workers shape their sense of self and life meaning.[47]

This was the case for my mother. Not only did she prove herself to white America through her diligence and hard work, she provided amenities for her own children that she had personally experienced as a child and that she desired for her own family. Through her pain and suffering she partially closed the gap in status between her life in Japan and her life in America.

My mother's stories reveal how her experience as worker is intricately tied to her family role and how both are framed by the class contrast in her home and host cultures. For my mother, work allowed her to reject white America's characterization of her as a foreigner, provided her an opportunity to fulfill her motherly duties, and gave her the means to minimize the class disparity she experienced. Yet her work and ability to provide for her family failed to bring her full autonomy because of the gendered and racialized nature of the work in which she was engaged. Like countless other female immigrant workers, my mother's inability to speak fluent English limited the kinds of jobs she was able to acquire. One of my mother's first paid jobs was as a factory worker in an electronics plant in California. She was conscious of anti-immigrant sentiment and the often contradictory stereotypes that immigrants were lazy and took jobs away from Americans. Underpaid and overworked, my mother attempted to counter negative narrative frames associated with immigrants by working faster:

I looked in the paper and saw an advertisement for a factory. There were a lot of international people in Alameda, and I went there for an interview, and they hired me too. I spoke very little English but they showed me what I had to do. In about two or three months they saw how fast my hands worked, I kept working faster and faster. There was a Filipino girl who worked real fast too. But I was faster than she was. I did twice as much work as other people. I would use a tweezers and you would have to put a real skinny wire in the right place. I did that for eight hours a day. But it took me six hours to do what other people did in eight hours. They said they never saw a woman working so fast. In six months they put me in a job to inspect other people's work. I'd look through a microscope and see the work that they did. Oh, my eyes hurt and felt funny. Every forty-five minutes you got to rest your eyes because it was such hard work.

While her work ethic countered the stereotype of the lazy immigrant, it reinforced the specific stereotypes of Asian immigrant women as docile, diligent, and skilled with their hands and led her to compete with other immigrant women on the factory line rather than to find solace with them. Ultimately, she expressed an inability to escape the multiple immigrant frames in the public sphere, even though she was a U.S. citizen.

After years of working in manufacturing occupations, my mother decided to teach a Japanese art form, Bunka embroidery, in her home. Her clientele were mostly older, wealthy white women who, according to her, "had nothing else to do." While some of her students took only a few classes from her, a larger group of women remained her students for as long as ten to fifteen years.

The lure of the classes for the students was not the art of Japanese embroidery as much as it was the chance to socialize. The daily classes served as a sort of therapy session where women could come and talk about their private problems. My mother played the role of host, teacher, and counselor. Because of these roles, she never disclosed her life of troubles to her students and, according to her, they never asked. She mused about how her students often thought of her as their best friend, particularly given the unreciprocated nature of their relationship. While she did become close to a few of her students, the teaching was an economic relationship, and the classes she taught served these ends well. My mother described the economic benefits of teaching: "I had morning classes, afternoon and evening classes. Three classes a day. Monday to Sunday, seven days a week! We used that money and put it all in the house to fix the downstairs. But your father never tells anyone that. Every time money came in we fixed the house. Like the front yard. I used my money and used the excuse that this was his Father's Day present. That cost me a lot to hire people and plant trees, the concrete, the walkway. I did a lot of things like that to make a better house."

Despite the economic constraints placed on her by my father's social class and patriarchal ideals, my mother constructs herself as an important asset to the family's well-being through her paid labor. Through her sacrifices and suffering our family escaped some of the poverty she experienced early on in the marriage. The theme of supporting her family through her suffering also becomes evident in the way she acquired land for her family. My mother explains how one day a car she was riding in was hit by a school bus that had run a red light. She was taken to the hospital and stayed for two days, suffering from a concussion and neck problems. She sued the company and settled for a small monetary amount, which she used to buy vacant lots of land in a nearby developing town.

Beyond the world of work, she found little respite in the private realm of the family, either in her marriage or in her relations with her husband's family. Although forced to work with white clients, she protected her sense of self by overcompensating at work and by avoiding as much contact with whites as possible. However, she was often unable to avoid her white in-laws. In the following story, she recounts her early stay with relatives in Wyoming while her husband was on active duty: "We had to stay with your father's brother and sister-in-law. It was worse than living with strangers. They managed a gas station and a café, and she made me waitress, wash dishes, and work as a maid for no pay. They said they wouldn't pay me because they were charging me to stay with them, for gas money, and for groceries. I tried to be nice and tried to have them like and accept me because I was Japanese. So I tried to help more. If I would have stayed in Japan, nothing like that would have happened. Never. I would not have suffered any of these kinds of things."

My mother's stories about herself in America, already shadowed in shame by her marriage to an American, focus on producing a life to be proud of despite the hardships imposed on her. Stories of reducing shame in her life are at the root of her construction of self as a diligent worker, a good mother, and a dutiful wife. Even the experience of birth becomes a site of potential agency allowing her to differentiate herself from American women who, in her view, shamefully cried in pain: "Even when I had a baby I didn't scream. American people scream and cuss when they have babies. Not me. I never made any noise. All I would say was 'ta, ta, ta, ta.' People couldn't hear me. I wouldn't scream because to scream would be shameful. You should not, you bear your own kid, why should you cuss and yell? Oh, the American women would cuss their husband and scream. They scared me! All I did was to say 'ta, ta, ta, ta' really fast. And you know what the doctor told me? He said, 'I think you would feel better if you yelled like the rest of the women.' I never did. He said, 'You are the strongest one here. You are the bravest woman.' And I didn't believe in having a shot either."

Despite the hardships and troubles she experienced in her life, my mother was not simply a victim of cultural narrative frames; at times, however, she shared stories of resignation. Like earlier Japanese immigrants, her narrative was peppered with a sense of shikata ga nai.[48] In the story above she argued that one not only endure the pain of childbirth, but expect it. Likewise, in her larger narrative, women must expect pain because of their subordinate position within patriarchal society. Her acceptance of such cultural norms resulted in resignation that one's life will be full of hardships.

Yet she endured. Through her stories, my mother revealed in multiple ways her agency in responding to oppressive narrative frames. She discussed her subjective experience as a life of *kuro,* or a life of hardships, rather than one of *gaman,* which, according to Harry H. Kitano, is an important Japanese experience referring to endurance and perserverance.[49] To gaman is to do one's best in times of frustration and adversity; to gaman is not to take aggressive or retaliatory action against one's misfortunes. While gaman does not mean passivity, it does refer to the suppression of one's anger and emotion. Contrary to the concept of gaman, my mother's narrative reveals emotions and displays anger. She was angry at her home country and her family who cast her into the lot of the pan pan girls, and she was angry at her host country for its unreceptive welcome. She spoke of both at length. At times, she directed anger toward those who created difficulties in her life; at other times she was prevented from expressing anger and thus contended with her hardships by elevating herself above others by doing more than what was expected.

My mother expressed her anger in subtle and explicit ways. A key target for her anger was her husband, who remained, for her, the ultimate source of her life of troubles. But, given her dependency on him and her lack of options, she retaliated and acted out her anger through actions such as buying "gifts" for her husband that in reality were for the benefit of the whole family. At other times her stories revealed a more direct expression of her anger. In the following story she describes how she dealt with difficult students who, in her mind, demanded unreasonable amounts of time and who felt racially superior to her:

Oh, my work was so hard with these women. I had a lot of problems with them because some of them said they couldn't understand my English. They are stupid. Little kids understood me! They are ignorant. A lot of people understood me so why couldn't these women? So I had to sit next to them and take [their hands] and show [them] how to do each stitch. It was kind of hard. But in ten years, I had to kick out two women. All they wanted was to have my full attention, and they kept telling me they didn't understand. I couldn't give them all of it because I had ten people in my class at a time and had to pay attention to each one of them. So finally I got fed up. I told them, "If you don't understand my English, you're wasting your money, you're wasting my time." I said, "Please leave." I did that twice. It took me a long time to say that because it hurt. They made fun of my English, you know, so I did that, I told them to leave.

In this story, my mother explicitly rejected what she perceived as American's disdain for immigrants. Rather than continue to expose herself to what she viewed as demeaning and demanding treatment by her students, she explicitly rejected the relationship, despite the economic ramifications. While she accepted that she has been forced to live a difficult life, she did not acquiesce to it. While she was subject to cultural ideologies, both in her home and host countries, she resisted in subtle and explicit ways.

CONCLUSION

The self is a narrative phenomenon; stories are the means by which we create, in the moment, our particular version and sense of self through both the omission, remembering, and articulation of experiences we offer to others and ourselves. While individuals have significant agency in the construction of their past and of the present, the constitutive nature of personal narrative is constrained by cultural narrative frames. My mother's self-representation was shaped by narrative frames and the larger social structural contexts in which she was embedded.

My mother's construction of self was also constrained by her relationship to me, at once the researcher and daughter, and her role as mother, which at times limited her ability to share her full critique of my father. The constraint emerged as she carefully edited her stories, keeping in mind the possible effect of such stories on family harmony. Furthermore, reading my mother's life stories calls for textual analysis, self-reflection on my part, and, as Ruth Behar advises, an "interpretation of cultural themes as they are creatively constructed by the actor within a particular configuration of social forces and gender and class contexts."[50] In this process researchers shift from listener to storyteller. I have provided in this chapter my reading of my mother's life stories as her construction of self in the shadow of larger dominant cultural representations. This has not been an easy task, as the process has raised a variety of emotional reactions for me pertaining to my extended family, my parents, and their marriage. While I was certainly aware of the troublesome dynamics between my parents, the stories my mother shared with me helped partially to explain and contextualize them. At the same time, this narrative is only a partial explanation of their marriage, my mother's construction. My father's stories were never formally collected.

Shaping the representation of my mother's identity is the gendered, racial, and nationalistic cultural frames she experienced within an interracial and international marriage. The representations of Hume's Babysan and social scientific constructions of the war bride reflect and reinforce patriarchal, racist, and nationalist interests. Like the South Asian Indian women Monisha Das Gupta interviewed, my mother's life stories reveal an attempt to forge her "in-betweenness as a valid, creative cultural space," a space where she forges a sense of self that both incorporates and rejects larger representations of women like herself.[51]

My mother framed her life as one of hardship and endurance, at once accepting her fate within the context of shikata ga nai, yet wondering whether living a life of hardships and enduring her condition was her true destiny. My mother contended that part of her endurance was her suffering of being alone: her adoption as a young child resulted in her distance from her natural family, and this separation was repeated with her marriage to an U.S. serviceman. The distance was not simply from her family but from her culture. She explained, "In Japan they say I was born under the star, maybe that's the way I was born. I was born not to be close to my family or to my country. I'm close, but always so far away." Never quite American, she remained also distant from her homeland. Her husband, while the key antagonist in her narrative, in many ways represented the distance of her host culture at large. Intimate stories of her patriarchal marriage were balanced by stories about the equally destructive racism and sexism she experienced in the private world of the family and in the public world of work. From her transnational perspective she also cast a critical eye on her homeland: pushed into a marriage of difficulties because of the association between U.S. servicemen and prostitution, she was forced to endure because of the shame she had brought to her family. Despite these hardships, she did not portray herself simply as a victim. She elevated herself above the shame that her home and host cultures imposed on her through her ability to endure difficult times. This relationship between agency and domination makes her early use of the bamboo metaphor particularly fitting. While my mother was unable to fully subvert relations of domination, like the bamboo, she was and continues to be resilient.

NOTES

1. Mock Joya, *Things Japanese* (Tokyo: Tokyo News Service, 1960), 391–92.

2. See Dolores Delgado Bernal, "Grassroots Leadership Reconceptualized: Chicana Oral Histories and the 1968 East Los Angeles Blowouts," *Frontiers* 19:2 (1998): 113–42; and Pierette Hondagneu-Sotelo, "Overcoming Patriarchal Constraints: The Reconstruction of Gender Relations Among Mexican Immigrant Women and Men," *Gender & Society* 6:3 (1992): 393–415.

3. Cynthia D. Anderson, "Understanding the Inequality Problematic: From Scholarly Rhetoric to Theoretical Reconstruction," *Gender & Society* 10:6 (1996): 729–46.

4. See Ruth Behar, "Reading the Life Story of a Mexican Marketing Woman," *Feminist Studies* 16:2 (1990): 223–56; Edward Bruner, "Life as Narrative," *Social Research* 54:1 (1987): 11–32; Mark Freeman, "Self as Narrative: The Place of Life History in Studying the Life Span," in *The Self: Definitional and Methodological Issues*, ed.

Thomas M. Brinthaupt and Richard P. Lipka (Albany: SUNY Press, 1992), 15–43; Keya Ganguly, "Migrant Identities: Personal Memory and the Construction of Selfhood," *Cultural Studies* 6:1 (1992): 27–50; George Rosenwald and Richard L. Ochberg, "Introduction: Life Stories, Cultural Politics, and Self-Understanding," in *Storied Lives: The Cultural Politics of Self-Understanding,* ed. George Rosenwald and Richard L. Ochberg (New Haven: Yale University Press, 1992), 1–18; and Deborah Schiffrin, "Narrative as Self-Portrait: Sociolinguistic Constructions of Identity," *Language in Society* 25:2 (1996): 167–203.

5. Ganguly, "Migrant Identities," 30.

6. Schiffrin, "Narrative as Self Portrait," 194.

7. Camilla Stivers, "Reflections on the Role of Personal Narrative in Social Science," *Signs: Journal of Women in Culture and Society* 18:2 (1993): 408–25.

8. Judith Stacey, "Can There Be a Feminist Ethnography?" in *Women's Words: The Feminist Practice of Oral History,* ed. Sherna Berger Gluck and Daphne Patai (New York: Routledge, 1991), 114.

9. Stacey, "Can There Be a Feminist Ethnography?" 114.

10. Rosenwald and Ochberg, "Introduction: Life Stories," 1–2.

11. Gordon Mathews, "The Stuff of Dreams, Fading: Ikigai and 'the Japanese Self,'" *Ethos* 24:4 (1996): 718–47; and Dorothy E. Smith, *Texts, Facts, and Femininity: Exploring the Relations of Ruling* (New York: Routledge, 1990).

12. Bill Hume, *Babysan's World: The Hume'n Slant on Japan* (Tokyo: Charles E. Tuttle, 1954).

13. Teresa Williams, "Marriage between Japanese Women and U.S. Servicemen since WWII," *Amerasia* 17:1 (1991): 135–54.

14. The peak years of marriage between Japanese women and American servicemen were between the late 1950s and the early 1960s. Williams estimates fifty-five thousand to one hundred thousand interracial and intercultural unions at that time ("Marriage between Japanese Women and U.S. Servicemen," 138–39).

15. Michael Thornton, "The Quiet Immigration: Foreign Spouses of U.S. Citizens, 1945–1985," in *Racially Mixed People in America,* ed. Maria P. P. Root (Newbury Park CA: Sage Publications, 1992), 64–76.

16. Bok-Lim C. Kim characterizes men who married Japanese women as working class or lower middle class, estranged from their own families, and "loners" ("Asian Wives of U.S. Servicemen: Women in Shadows," *Amerasia* 4:1 [1977]: 91–115).

17. William R. Nester, "Japanese Women: Still Three Steps Behind," *Women's Studies* 21:4 (1992): 457–79. Kalman D. Applbaum, "Marriage with the Proper Stranger: Arranged Marriage in Metropolitan Japan," *Ethnology* 34:1 (1995): 37–52.

18. Elaine Kim, "Sex Tourism in Asia: A Reflection of Political and Economic Inequality," *Critical Perspectives of Third World America* 1:1 (1983): 214–32.

19. See Paul Spickard, *Mixed Blood: Intermarriage and Ethnic Identity in Twentieth-Century America* (Madison: University of Wisconsin Press, 1989); and Aki Uchida, "The Orientalization of Asian Women in America," *Women's Studies International Forum* 21:2 (1998): 161–75.

20. Spickard, *Mixed Blood,* 39.

21. Hume's work was published in the newspapers *Stars and Stripes, Navy Times,* and *Oppaman.*

22. Hume, *Babysan's World,* 10.

23. Hume, *Babysan's World,* 22.

24. Hume, *Babysan's World,* 32.

25. Hume, *Babysan's World,* 108.

26. Hume, *Babysan's World,* 34.

27. Hume, *Babysan's World,* 90.

28. Joya, *Things Japanese,* 662–63.

29. John Lie, "The State as Pimp: Prostitution and the Patriarchal State in Japan in the 1940s," *The Sociological Quarterly* 38:2 (1997): 251–64.

30. Elfrieda Berthiaume Shukert and Barbara Smith Scibetta, *War Brides of World War II* (New York: Penguin Books, 1989), 185–95.

31. About a fourth of all contemporary marriages in Japan are still arranged. In "Marriage with the Proper Stranger," Applbaum describes a new form of go-betweens, *pro nakodo,* that is a modification of an old tradition. The key difference is that modern nakodos tend to be less familiar with families before the actual marriage arrangement procedures, have less contact with the couple after marriage, and typically consist of a two-person team.

32. Avtar Brah, "Re-framing Europe: En-gendered Racisms, Ethnicities, and Nationalisms in Contemporary Western Europe," *Feminist Review* 45:9 (1993): 9–29.

33. See Audrey Smedley, *Race in North America: Origin and Evolution of a Worldview* (Boulder CO: Westerview Press, 1993); and George W. Stocking, Jr., "The Dark-Skinned Savage: The Image of Primitive Man in Evolutionary Anthropology," in *Race, Culture, and Evolution: Essays in the History of Anthropology*, ed. George W. Stocking, Jr. (New York: The Free Press, 1968), 110–32. Both Smedley and Stocking reveal the assumptions underlying racial taxonomies, including that human groups differed from one another in kind rather than type; that biological and physical characteristics were linked to cultural, moral, physical, and intellectual abilities; and that, due to these differences, races could be scientifically and objectively ranked.

34. Stocking, "The Dark-Skinned Savage," 110–32.

35. See Williams, "Marriage between Japanese Women and U.S. Servicemen," 135–54; for a discussion of immigration law changes, 142–43.

36. See Kim, "Asian Wives of U.S. Servicemen," 91–115.

37. George A. Devos, as cited in Spickard, *Mixed Blood,* 127.

38. For a review of studies, see Kim, "Asian Wives of U.S. Servicemen," 103–7.

39. Venny Villapando, "The Business of Selling Mail-Order Brides," in *Making Waves: An Anthology of Writings by and about Asian American Women,* ed. Asian Women United of California (Boston: Beacon Press, 1989), 318–26.

40. See, for example, Gerald J. Schnepp and Agnes Masako Yui, "Cultural and Marital Adjustment of Japanese War Brides," *American Journal of Sociology* 61:1 (1955): 48–50; and Anselm Strauss, "Strain and Harmony in American-Japanese War-Bride Marriages," *Marriage and Family Living* 61:1 (1954): 99–106.

41. Strauss goes so far as to argue that "Japanese brides do not aspire to much, occupationally speaking, but they do require 'steadiness' from their husband in terms of occupation and status" ("Strain and Harmony," 104).

42. For a brief review of images of mixed-race people in literature, see Michelle Motoyoshi, "The Experience of Mixed Race People: Some Thoughts and Theories," *Journal of Ethnic Studies* 18:2 (1990): 77–93; and Cynthia L. Nakashima, "An Invisible Monster: The Creation and Denial of Mixed-Race People in America," in Root, *Racially Mixed People in America,* 162–78.

43. For example, in his book *The Marginal Man: A Study in Personality and Culture Conflict* (New York: Russell & Russell, 1937), Everett Stonequist identifies cultural factors that psychologically impair mixed-race individuals.

44. For the long history and scientific rationale for rejecting mixed-race children, see Stocking, "The Dark-Skinned Savage," 110–32.

45. Spickard, *Mixed Blood,* 42–44.

46. Mathews, "The Stuff of Dreams," 718.

47. Mathews, "The Stuff of Dreams," 721.

48. Ronald Takaki, *Strangers from a Different Shore: A History of Asian Americans* (New York: Penguin Books, 1989), 211.

49. Harry H. Kitano, *Japanese Americans: The Evolution of a Subculture* (Englewood Cliffs NJ: Prentice-Hall, 1976), 109.

50. Behar, "Reading the Life Story of a Mexican Marketing Woman," 227.

51. Monisha Das Gupta, "What Is Indian about You? A Gendered, Transnational Approach to Ethnicity," *Gender & Society* 11:5 (1997): 588.

Frontiers 21:1/2 (2000): 194–224.

What is Winning Anyway?

Redefining Veteran: A Vietnamese American Woman's Experiences in War and Peace

SUZAN RUTH TRAVIS-ROBYNS

I was wounded by your shrapnel.
I'm the one you gave your life for.
I'm the one who stole your wallet.
I'm the one you sometimes didn't pay for the night.

I'm the one you took your anger out on.
I'm the one you came to for comfort.
I'm the one you sometimes called Lisa or Brenda . . .

I'm the one who held you when you were afraid . . .
I'm the one you thought had no feelings, but I do . . .

I'm the one who didn't hold it against you.
I'm the one you probably don't remember,
But I remember you.
I'm the one who is part of you
And you are part of me.

Not one second goes by in my life that I do not speak to you in my heart.
That I do not think of you silently in my heart,
And thank you for your deaths so that I can be here.
I'm the one who wants you to be happy and satisfied.

Because I'm alive and I can feel.

Nguyen Ngoc Xuan, "My Letter to the Wall–November 1989"

The poem above was written by Nguyen Ngoc Xuan, a Vietnamese American woman and a veteran of the Vietnam War. Xuan was born in 1954 as the French were defeated in the First Indochina War, but her defining life experiences occurred during the Second Indochina War against the United States and afterward, following her arrival in the United States in 1974 and her marriage to a U.S. Air Force pilot.[1] Women like Xuan are typically left out of the rapidly growing literature on the Vietnam War because they are neither policy makers nor veterans by the conventional definintion.[2] But by expanding the definition of veteran and examining the war's real battlefields, it becomes clear that the victims of the Vietnam War's violence are as much veterans of the war as the soldiers who fought it. Xuan's story demonstrates that she is, in fact, a veteran and that any understanding of the war must include the experiences of Vietnamese women, both civilians and combatants.

Although she has never been a combatant herself, surviving the violence of others has been a central theme of Xuan's life from the beginning. An act of violence – her mother's rape – created her life. Xuan grew up the seventh child in a family of ten with five brothers and four sisters, raised by an adoptive father and her mother, who is ethnic Chinese. The family lived in ChoLon, the Chinese district of Saigon, South Vietnam, now called Ho Chi Minh City. Xuan's adoptive father did not want his wife to carry Xuan to term because she was the product of a rape, and as she grew up, her father often beat her; he thought she was too independent, and the fact that she sullenly endured being beaten, instead of crying out for mercy like her other siblings did, seemed to fuel his rage. Beating children and wives was common practice and considered a family matter. In traditional Vietnam, education was reserved for boys, and Xuan and her sisters received no formal education. Instead, she began selling food in the Saigon marketplace alone when she was eight; at fourteen she became a prostitute for American soldiers because it paid so much better than her market work. The money she earned helped put her brothers through school and fed and clothed her family. Xuan later married a U.S. Air Force pilot, who also beat her. She said that she learned early that "when somebody is not happy with you, it means you are not good enough. . . . You keep making people mad at you, and they have to punish you."

In some respects, Xuan's experiences parallel those of U.S. veterans: the war became the defining experience of her life, and having lived the first twenty years of her life in a perpetual state of war, she has had difficulty adjusting to life in peacetime and still struggles with post-traumatic stress disorder (PTSD).[3] Xuan was wounded by shrapnel, was forced to make life and death decisions for herself and others, trusted only her mother and siblings, and often could not distinguish communists from government supporters. People she thought were loyal to the South Vietnamese government – neighbors, coworkers, even her adoptive father – turned out to be communists.

But many of Xuan's experiences are in marked contrast to those of U.S. veterans. She did not shoot an M-16, conduct bombing raids, or drop canisters of napalm and Agent Orange; she ran from them. Xuan did not fight for an ideology or a boundary; she fought to keep her family of origin and her children alive. When she came to the United States, Xuan was not coming home; she had no country at peace to go home to. Instead, she faced an even more severe survival test than she had in war-torn Vietnam: life as a battered wife and as a mother separated from her oldest son.[4] Moreover, while most studies on Vietnamese Americans have focused on Vietnamese communities, Xuan came to the United States before the first wave of Vietnamese immigrants began arriving in 1975.[5] So besides living the life of an abused war bride, she was also alone, isolated from family and community. In this respect, Xuan has more in common with other Asian war brides than with any of the subsequent waves of Vietnamese immigrants.[6]

Against all this violence, however, Xuan has survived. She survived the blows of her husband as well as three suicide attempts and, against all odds, was reunited with her eldest son. She has made four trips back to her homeland since 1989 and has worked hard to integrate American and Vietnamese culture. Her experiences are filtered through both Eastern and Western perspectives, for she has created a cultural milieu that includes aspects of both.[7] Having divorced her first husband, Xuan remarried in 1993; her second husband is also a veteran, a man who had been seriously injured in a rice paddy in South Vietnam. She now has three grown sons and works as a seamstress in Portland, Oregon.[8]

This chapter is based on oral history interviews conducted with Xuan in 1994. The interviews were prompted by a conviction that it is important that the voices of Vietnamese American women be heard. Xuan's story is not unique. The war was fought in population centers, and a true civilian in the sense of someone who did not directly experience the war can scarcely be found. One-fourth of the South Vietnamese citizenry became refugees as the warring factions turned their homes into battlefields.[9] My purpose is to discuss how the wartime and postwar experiences of one Vietnamese American woman can add to our understanding about women who survive war, thereby challenging our definition of who becomes war veterans.[10]

Historians and journalists often claim that the experiences of women are left out of war literature because they lack relevance. But to understand the true nature of the Vietnam War, one must understand the experiences of Vietnamese women. For centuries, the Vietnamese have battled to maintain their independence against their giant neighbor to the north, China. Women have filled defensive combat roles in every one of the nation's wars, beginning as far back as the Trung Sisters, who in 939 A.D. led an army that expelled the Chinese from Vietnam and who are celebrated as national heroes. Any reference to Vietnamese history worth reading includes information on the Trung Sisters.[11] The tradition of women warriors continued during the war against the United States when women comprised fully half of the fighting forces of the Southern Communists.[12] Women are not used in offensive operations, such as the 1978 invasion of Cambodia, but only in defense of the homeland; still, their direct participation in war reflects both the historical desperation and determination of the Vietnamese to maintain their independence against great odds.

Nguyen Ngoc Xuan was not one of Vietnam's extraordinary women warriors, and she compares herself disfavorably to the celebrated women warriors of Vietnam's past. Like many South Vietnamese, Xuan did not identify with any of the four factions in the war: the Americans; the South Vietnamese government and the Army of the Republic of Vietnam (ARVN); the North Vietnamese government and the North Vietnamese Army (NVA); or the Southern indigenous Communists, the National Liberation Front, known by their enemies as the Viet Cong. Xuan represents the millions of South Vietnamese who walked the tightrope of survival and chose to focus on staying alive rather than taking sides in the conflict.[13]

The nonaligned South Vietnamese were called the "Third Force" by the Americans who mobilized considerable resources to rally them to the South Vietnamese flag.[14] The majority of these people were illiterate and unaware of the machinations of the war's four factions except when violence was targeted at them by one of the armies involved. The people caught in the middle suffered through retribution from all sides. There were economic and philosophical reasons for the disinterest of the Third Force. First, when the war began, 5 percent of the population of South Vietnam lived off the backs of the other 95 percent, who were peasants on the economic periphery.[15] In order to survive, every household member, including children, had to take part in long days of backbreaking labor. Thus, for considerable numbers, the luxury of political involvement was not open to them. Second, philosophically, most Vietnamese believed in following whichever side was in concert with the will of heaven. Vietnamese culture taught that there was only one truth and only one true way.[16] The way to determine which side followed the will of heaven was to see which side was winning. It took the communists, first as the Viet Minh and later as the National Liberation Front, decades of studied diligence to overcome this attitude, and their success in this arena was far from complete. This mind-set created an "ethic of accommodation" and was the reason that many South Vietnamese changed sides several times during the war.[17] Like millions of others, Xuan, her mother, and her siblings did not care who won, as long as the war ended. To this day, Xuan does not like to take sides: when she attended her son's football games, she cheered for whichever side was winning.

Being nonaligned with any of the four factions did not mean, however, that the war was not part of daily life. Dead bodies lying in the street or floating downriver were the concrete evidence of war that still haunts Xuan. A river that ran behind her house in ChoLon sometimes carried those dead bodies. She recalled: "I see dead body float by my house all the time, blow up like balloon. . . . And sometimes the body got caught underneath the house. . . . You get a stick down and you poke the body, push it out so it float away. Sometimes I smell that same smell. . . . The smell is not in my nose, it's in my brain, my memory. There's no way, you don't know whose husband, you don't know whose daughter, whose father, it's just a body that float by your house."

Xuan said that when she asked her mother about the war, her mother would reply, " 'Go carry the water or go boil the rice.' It more useful than telling you what going on because what can you do about it? . . . She didn't care because you don't know who your neighbor is. If you shoot off your mouth, you can get in trouble. So you don't tell – even your kids . . . I didn't know which side to choose. My [adoptive] father was against me, he didn't care about me, other than to beat me up. My mother loved me too much to tell me what to do, so I had no direction. I just did whatever I thought was necessary to survive."[18]

Xuan's family illustrates the internecine quality of the war. In South Vietnam, as in the United States, the war divided families, and the often-heard

American complaint that Vietnamese who were friends during the day shot at American troops at night is particularly poignant with Xuan.[19] One of Xuan's brothers fought and died in the service of the South Vietnamese ARVN, while Xuan's adoptive father was most likely a communist insurgent. Although her adoptive father worked for the South Vietnamese government in the Interior Department, before each communist offensive in their area he stocked the house with extra food and told his family where the safe areas would be in case of an attack. He was able to cross communist, American, and South Vietnamese lines to check on his family after battles, yet he was not present during the attacks. The evidence of his communist ties is strengthened by the fact that he arranged for his oldest son to be kidnapped and taken to serve in the North Vietnamese Army. This was done without the knowledge of Xuan's mother, the son himself, or any of the other children in the family. When the son escaped and returned to ChoLon in the black pajamas he had been given to wear, Xuan's mother felt forced to turn him in to South Vietnamese authorities to avoid endangering the rest of her family. Yet despite her suspicions, Xuan never once heard her adoptive father make a pro-communist statement to his family, and she believes that knowledge of his double-agent status would have endangered them.

Surrounded on all sides, as were the American soldiers, Xuan had difficulty telling enemy from friend and trusted no one. As she ran from her burning home during the Tet Offensive of 1968, she discovered that there were communists among her neighbors. They were dressed in the traditional black pajamas of the National Liberation Front and carried Chinese-issued AK-47s. Two years later, in 1970, Xuan found out that a woman she worked with was a communist informant. This discovery came at the hands of South Vietnamese soldiers who tortured Xuan's coworker in an adjoining room for fourteen hours while Xuan was forced to listen. Pressed for information, Xuan finally told her interrogators in exasperation: "You might as well torture me too because I don't know what you want to know. If I knew what you wanted to hear, I would tell it to you." Xuan was released.

Xuan could not read, and at first she took official statements about American actions at face value. After her family's home was leveled by American bombs, however, she began to see each of the four factions as an implacable enemy. During the war, U.S. soldiers fought for a noncommunist South Vietnam. But Xuan, her mother, and siblings did not have a preference in the battles they ran from. They only wanted the fighting to end. Xuan wondered, "What is winning anyway? Somebody dies, somebody gets killed.

When people are being killed, there can be no winning. . . . Please, just make peace so I can take care of my family, and I don't care which one of you win, you can have it."

Xuan became a refugee during the Tet Offensive of 1968, which was a major simultaneous surprise attack on the urban areas of South Vietnam launched during the cease-fire for Tet, the lunar new year celebration that is the Vietnamese equivalent of Christmas and New Year's. The Communist National Liberation Front and NVA hit five major cities, one hundred provincial and district capitals, and fifty hamlets. Once American troops recovered, many communists trapped in Saigon took refuge in ChoLon, the Chinese district where Xuan's family lived, and Xuan's home was destroyed by the American counteroffensive.[20]

A few days before the Tet Offensive began, Xuan's adoptive father began to prepare his family. Xuan remembers that he instructed them: "Tie your ID card on your belly, so people know who you are, that you're not a VC (Viet Cong), so you won't get into trouble. . . . Prepare your survival bag to take with you. He told us different areas that we could go to hide." The night the Tet Offensive began, Xuan and her brother and sister were returning home from a movie: "Halfway home, we started to hear guns shooting. We thought it was fireworks, no big deal. But we heard gunshots and it's funny that during New Year, you hear fireworks all the time. It's kind of a celebration. Inside of you, you feel a celebration. But this particular time, when we heard that, something is not right in my heart. My instincts said, 'Get the kids, walk faster, let's go home.' I don't know why." When Xuan and her siblings arrived at home, the neighborhood streets were silent, with families huddling together in their homes. In the middle of the night, helicopters and jets were overhead. "Everything shook and when the fire shoots down, you wonder who is shooting you," Xuan recalled. "Is that American or North Vietnamese?[21] You still don't know who is shooting at you, but it will burn up your house anyway. We would never think Americans would do that because no, America is supposed to be here to look out for you, take care of you, right? You don't think they would burn up your house. That's why a lot of people went with the Viet Cong in the neighborhood because Americans said one thing, Americans did the other thing."

Xuan's family ran from the bombs and survived – but now their possessions were limited to the clothes they were wearing. The family did not have even a bowl to eat rice from. Xuan said, "Everything we have turned to ashes. . . . After that, my perception of life is that anything is possible now – you cannot always be in control." The family joined the stream of people running from the fighting, becoming part of a great human wave that eventually displaced one-fourth of the South Vietnamese citizenry.[22] Xuan said that in desperation she ran in the direction of the greatest number of people. She said she reasoned: "Everyone's going that way; it must be safe." The expression "going with the flow" can instantly take Xuan back mentally to her days as a refugee. For the next six weeks, Xuan and her family slept anywhere they could find a place. When it seemed safe, they returned to ChoLon and created a house of cardboard on the ruins of their former home. Xuan's mother washed their clothes at night and hung them out to dry. The family slept naked, covered with dirty newspapers as makeshift blankets.

But a few months later, in May 1968, the bombs came again as the communists began another offensive on Saigon and other American strongholds in the South.[23] Once again, the family was endangered by the fighting they wanted no part of. Xuan's mother then moved her family to Vung Tau, a coastal city about fifty miles southeast of Saigon that had been a resort during the French occupation. Xuan's mother selected the site because it had been a safe area for civilians throughout Vietnam's war-torn history. The Americans had a massive base camp there, one of ten major port facilities.[24] Xuan again started working at the market, but she quickly learned that she could make more money selling candy at the beach and picking the pockets of American soldiers.

Xuan's adoptive father, who had mistresses most of his married life, did not move with the family.[25] He rented an apartment in Saigon, where he lived with his latest mistress. After paying his Saigon expenses, there was little of his twenty-five-dollars-a-month government salary left, most of which was quickly eaten up by South Vietnam's spiraling inflation. The responsibility of feeding and clothing the family fell to fourteen-year-old Xuan. She became a prostitute at one of the bars that ringed the American base at Vung Tau because she could earn one hundred dollars a month – four times what her adoptive father made as a government employee.[26] Agriculture had been strong in the South before the American war, but with so many peasants forced off the land, the Southern economy depended on providing services to the Americans. Women could find gainful employment most easily in the cities by becoming prostitutes.[27]

Xuan became pregnant twice while she was working as a prostitute. When she was seventeen, she met a soft-spoken South Vietnamese soldier in a bar. She stopped working in order to spend all her time with the man, Huynh

Van Toan, and the couple soon discovered that they were in love. She was pregnant with their first child – a son named Quang – when Toan was killed in battle. Although the two were not married, Xuan thinks of Toan as her first husband: "When they came and told me the news about my first husband, I could feel the baby kicking inside me. I had to survive – I had to go on for the baby." Xuan said that in war, grieving is a luxury: "I cannot feel sorry for myself, there thousands of women in my town go through the same thing. You not alone, everybody suffer and even sometime you cry, you be ashamed to cry because you not the only one who hurt. . . . Everyone is suffering, and if you cry, you discourage people from going on."[28]

Xuan left her son with relatives and went back to work as a prostitute. Not wanting to bring shame to her family, she told them that she earned her money in South Vietnam's thriving black market. Xuan said many of the other young women who worked as prostitutes were teenage refugees who were the sole support of their families. It was common, she said, for many of them to leave home looking as though they were going to the market and then go to a bar and change into street clothes. She said the women helped each other; when one of them was short of money for her family one week, the others would pitch in. Xuan's own family did not find out she was a prostitute until she became pregnant at age nineteen by the American Air Force pilot whom she later followed to the United States and married.

The money Xuan earned as a prostitute went to support her family and even to bribe the government into not conscripting one of her brothers into the South Vietnamese army. Xuan's sacrifice kept her brother out of harm's way: "Up North, they don't have a choice, they have to go [into the army]. But down South, if I have money, I can pay [to avoid conscription]. And I'm ashamed to admit it, I have to pay so my brother don't go . . . because my older brother have wife and have kids. If he go and he die, nobody take care of his wife and his kids. The government don't take care of his wife and his kids. So, it my loss. It's my sister-in-law's loss, it's my nephew and niece loss, it's my mother's loss, not the government's loss. So why fight? We don't want to fight anyway."

Vietnamese male writers often refer to the centuries-long tradition of prostitution in Vietnam. They point out that through the ages young women have sold their bodies, but not their souls, to support their families. These men claim there is no shame in the profession. But, not surprisingly, real women who have worked as prostitutes paint a different picture. Xuan remembers her days as a prostitute:

I fought my war every night in bed with men. Who talks about my war? Who asks me if I'm hurt or wounded? Nobody asks. Not even the closest person to me, my mother, knows or asks. No one knows, it's just a silent war that I have inside of me. . . . I know a lot of Vietnamese women in this country who are ex-prostitutes, they have the same feeling, but we are still in the closet, we are ashamed, embarrassed. We aren't just criticized by American society but the Vietnamese society too. . . . Even my own people, the Vietnamese community here in the United States, they look down on me because I did something that brought shame to our ancestors. . . . They make me feel that I owe them something, that I destroyed something that they built. And in a way, they are right, but I don't know how to fix it.

With the Trung Sisters' brief victory over the Chinese in 939 A.D., the ideal of women warriors became firmly implanted in Vietnamese culture. Communist women were constantly called on to emulate the fierce women of Vietnamese legend. And Madame Nhu, South Vietnam's de facto first lady from 1955 to 1963, organized a women's militia group on the same principle the communists used to call women to arms.[29] But in families like Xuan's, the instinct for survival was far stronger than an ancient ideal. Nevertheless, when Xuan judges her actions during the war, she compares herself disfavorably to the Vietnamese ideal of warrior women: "I'm so ashamed I feel like I wish I was born in the North. . . . The Northern women gave everything so they could be proud to say, 'We are Vietnamese women.' While the Southern women had a different way of surviving, it damaged our reputation, our culture. . . . But in my heart, I know I didn't do that for a wrong reason. In my heart, I know that if I had to do it all over again, I'd do the same thing because my mother comes first, my family is worth it. But I feel like I am responsible . . . to somehow let American society know that Vietnamese women who did these things, it's not by choice and it's not because we enjoyed it."[30]

When Xuan's adoptive father discovered that she was pregnant with an Amerasian child, he demanded that she get an abortion or put the baby up for adoption. He told her that when the communists took over the South, they would execute the entire family for Xuan's transgression. Xuan refused, and her adoptive father disowned her. One of Xuan's sisters had abandoned her Amerasian child after being similarly confronted by their father.[31] Xuan believes her mother invested her with a strong maternal instinct when she decided to carry Xuan to term, despite the fact that she had been raped, and that this instinct gave her the resolve to disobey her father. Xuan did not tell her three sons she had been a prostitute until 1992. Xuan said they told her: "We're really sorry you had to do that. But you are our mother, we are your sons, it doesn't change the way we feel about you." Xuan said, "That makes me feel like I can go on and be honest because my children accepted me. It's an awful past but I have to have a past in order to have a future."

One of Vietnam's best-loved poets, Nguyen Du (1765–1820), wrote a classic poem, "The Tale of Kieu," that parallels Xuan's life. In it, a young woman sacrifices a life with the man she loves to become a prostitute, the one way she can earn enough money to save her father. The Kieu of legend, like Xuan, was cursed with the twin traits of beauty and talent. This was a great misfortune that meant her name appeared in the Book of the Damned and that she must remain strong while racing "from grief to grief" in order to redeem herself.[32] The poem proclaims: "Kieu had to save her kin, her flesh and blood. / When evil strikes, one bows to circumstance. / When one must weigh and choose between one's love / and filial duty, which will turn the scale?"[33] The answer is a foregone conclusion. Kieu pleads with her father to allow her to sacrifice herself for him. "Sacrifice me alone and save our home: / one flower will fall, but green the tree will stay. Whatever happens, I will bear my lot." In the poem, long-suffering is rewarded. "Requiting love for love, she sold herself / and saved her father. Heaven did take note / . . . She who has purged herself from her past faults / sows future happiness."[34] After fifteen years of prostitution and slavery, Kieu saves her father and is rewarded for her filial loyalty by returning to a life with the man she loves. The poem is more than a piece of literature. It is a moral lesson to young Vietnamese that they must repay the debt owed to parents no matter what the cost, and that they must accept whatever fate heaven has in store for them.[35]

What heaven had in store for the Vietnamese was horrifying. The Vietnamese believe that the soul cannot rest until the body receives a proper burial. But with such a massive loss of life, thousands of bodies were never recovered. It took Xuan twenty-five years and four trips back to Vietnam to locate the burial site of her oldest child's father. Xuan's brother was also killed while serving in the South Vietnamese army, and while the family was able to recover a body, it was burned beyond recognition by Agent Orange. Xuan worries that the body recovered was not that of her brother, that his spirit is still wandering aimlessly, along with the three hundred thousand other Vietnamese soldiers – North and South – who are still missing in action.[36] (This contrasts with 1,750 Americans still listed as missing in action in Vietnam.)[37] Xuan grieves for the two million to three million Vietnamese – soldiers and civilians – who died during the war.[38] "It's not just the soldiers that got killed," she said. "There were so many of us that died under the bomb attacks. There's no way of telling how many people were buried without a grave marker. . . . There are spirits wandering out there somewhere. They have no place to be.

"We don't have such a thing as Red Cross in Vietnam. When a Vietnamese soldier die, the body is left there. When American get wounded or die, you have a chopper to come down . . . take the body home. The Vietnamese people don't have such a way to take the body home. Sometime the [Vietnamese] soldier buried in such a location . . . the bomb destroyed the landmark and you don't know where they buried . . . it happened to us all the time. The American people need to be told that we have suffered too."

THE STRUGGLE FOR SURVIVAL IN THE UNITED STATES

Unlike the Kieu of Vietnamese legend, Xuan's reunion was not cause for celebration but meant a continuation of suffering. The father of Xuan's second child, an air force pilot from Oregon's Willamette Valley, wrote her fervent letters begging her to come to the United States. Xuan put him off for over a year but in 1974 agreed to a visit, bringing with her the couple's Amerasian child, Son. Xuan's mother demanded that she leave her oldest child, Quang, in Vietnam.[39] Xuan did not know when she boarded the plane en route to the United States that eight years would pass before she would see her oldest son and that sixteen years would go by before she would see her home again.

When Xuan arrived in the United States, she was put through a bewildering amount of paperwork and customs regulations. She was illiterate in her own language and had only a rudimentary knowledge of English. One ceremony required her to repeat after a military judge; only later did she discover that that recitation had been her wedding ceremony and that she was now married. She thought that Son would find acceptance in the United States, but she soon discovered that her husband's family believed she was only after the family's money and questioned her son's parentage. "It's not true," Xuan said. "I didn't even know anything about the American dollar, even if they had tried to tell me, I didn't understand that much. What does an acre of land mean to me or a thousand acres? It doesn't mean anything to me, my country is so small."

Xuan cried every day and insisted on going back to Vietnam. Her husband pleaded poverty: there was no money for the ticket home. And then the South Vietnamese government fell. Xuan watched the scenes from Saigon on the television, while her husband yelled at her for packing the wrong socks for him. That night, she took an overdose of pills to quiet the turmoil in her mind. She was rushed to a military hospital and, after a brief stay, released to her husband. He informed her that she was crazy. Xuan would make two more attempts to end her life before ending their relationship.

Xuan's reluctance to come to the United States proved well founded. "Survival in this country was harder than war in Vietnam because that's my land, that's my people, my language, my mom, my brothers," she explained. [40] Xuan had only a perfunctory knowledge of English and no education. She was oceans away from everyone she had known and loved. Raised as a Buddhist, she went to a nearby church for advice, where she was told that accepting Jesus Christ as the son of God would resolve all her problems. She did not know who Jesus Christ was. [41] She joined an air force wives club, whose members immediately ostracized Xuan for asking their ages (she was the youngest) and for eating salad with her hands. In Vietnam, without knowing a person's age, it is difficult to know how to properly address them. When she ate in Vietnam, she ate a lot as fast as possible because she did not know when she might have another meal. When Xuan saw the looks she got when she said she was Vietnamese, she started telling people she was Chinese, Thai, or Filipina.

Xuan underwent a painful adjustment to a wealthy and alien culture. She found the vast disparity in wealth between the United States and Vietnam disturbing. "It's just not fair," she said. "How can there be a God? How can there be a heaven? American kids here, education falls in their lap, food is literally in their mouths, all they need to do is take. And the kids in Vietnam are so poor. And they're not bad kids, they're good kids too. And then where is God and why?" Adjusting to peacetime life has been difficult for Xuan. Her coworkers found her unsympathetic when they complained of minor annoyances. They did not know she had faced life and death decisions under the daily grind of war. "When people complain about little things, like they don't have time to go in to get a manicure done, I ignore it because I saw people die. I saw people starving. So what if you don't have time to do your nails? Nobody is gonna die. So I don't pay attention and to them, I'm not sensitive . . . if I was that sensitive to every little cut, every little manicure appointment, I would die. My way of surviving is to see what is a priority and who needs help first."

The overwhelming problem, however, was that Xuan had left her eldest son behind in Vietnam. From the time the communists took over the country until her son made it to the United States eight years later, Xuan was on the phone every week, trying to find someone who could help her. "I called the State Department every day with my broken language. The State Department does not care about one Vietnamese boy, they have more problems. It's a long, long war for me to get my son over here. . . . But the only thing for me to do is call people, I don't know how to write a letter, I don't know English. So I can only call and when I call, they tell me to write a letter. . . . I only have my voice, and sometimes I don't know how to speak right.

"After the South fell, my husband did not want me to tell other people that I had a son in Vietnam because what is family business stays a family secret. Our side is not supposed to know, so I'm not supposed to tell anybody that I've got a son that's stuck behind." Xuan, however, defied her husband. "It doesn't matter how strong or how powerful you are, you can not make a mother stop loving her own children. . . . There are certain things you can not stop. That's one." Finally, in 1979, Xuan found a glimmer of hope: "One day I heard in the news that the post office was doing a letter exchange [with Vietnam] and I sent a letter to my mom. All along my husband told me that I cannot send a letter home because if I have any contact with a communist country, it will endanger his career with the air force and it will endanger my life and most of all, my family [in Vietnam]."

Xuan secretly sent the letter and received a reply from her mother. Her Vietnamese family began the groundwork that would reunite Quang with his mother. Over her husband's objections, Xuan had gotten a job as a seamstress, and she sent all the money she could spare to Vietnam to bribe officials to let her son leave the country. Xuan's husband had been discharged from the air force and did not work again for several years. During this time Xuan's income also had to cover her family's expenses and child support for her husband's first wife and children. Meanwhile, each week Xuan's brother traveled the fifty miles with Quang from Vung Tau to the French embassy in Saigon to begin the paperwork that would allow Quang to leave Vietnam. Quang and his uncle would arrive in Saigon at 4 A.M. to begin waiting in line. When they did not have money to bribe the Vietnamese officials at the embassy, they sometimes failed even to make it to the front of the line. The family was so poor that Quang sometimes had to stay home from school because he had no clothes to wear.

In 1982, Congress passed the Amerasian Act, which was designed to bring to the United States children fathered by U.S. servicemen in Vietnam, Laos, Cambodia, Thailand, and Korea after 1950 and before October 22, 1982. Amerasians experienced virulent discrimination in these Confucian societies where a child's identity was determined by the father.[42] Only two children left Vietnam on the first flight authorized by the legislation. The second flight had eight children on board, seven Amerasians and one Vietnamese boy. The eighth child was Xuan's son Quang. Although Quang's Vietnamese parentage did not qualify him to leave Vietnam under the Amerasian Act – his father was Vietnamese – against all odds, Xuan's persistent campaign to be reunited with her son had succeeded.

However, on the eve of Quang's scheduled departure, Xuan received a telegram from her mother stating that Vietnamese government officials were demanding another five thousand dollars, or Quang would not be using the ticket Xuan had already purchased. "We all along kept bribing the [Vietnamese] government, and I didn't have any money left to send to Vietnam. . . . I mentioned that to my friends, and they told me they'd loan me the money. It's almost like there's such a thing as a miracle. I didn't even ask them. . . . And so, that's another feather for my wing. I got my independence. I had a job. My son got here, nothing matters anymore. I don't have to do anything my husband tells me to do." Xuan's husband responded to her growing independence by becoming more violent. She divorced her husband in 1985, and then took him back into her home for another seven years. In the intervening years, Xuan continued to support her ex-husband financially, and he continued to beat her.

After Quang's arrival, however, Xuan found that she could no longer suppress the horrors she had been exposed to, and symptoms of PTSD began to emerge: "There's so much anger [in me], and it all came up at the same time. The anger of losing my country, my home, anger because Quang's father was killed in the war, the anger of coming here, trying to survive all over again, the anger of being abused for so many years, the anger of not being heard. And all of the pain I started to feel from what happened to me, it all came up at the same time. It was terrifying." Xuan's nightmares became so intense that she often woke her children in the night and huddled them into the closet to hide from imaginary bomb attacks.

Xuan lost contact with her family in Vietnam after Quang arrived in the United States. Letters to her mother were returned as undeliverable. Her Vietnamese family sent letters to Xuan, but she never received them. Xuan suspects either that her husband destroyed the letters or that the Vietnamese government blocked them, or both. She does not know for certain what happened. In 1989 she helped sponsor Michael Peterson, a veteran from Eugene, Oregon, who was going to Vung Tau, Xuan's hometown, to build a medical clinic.[43] The two struck up a friendship, and while in Vung Tau, Peterson located Xuan's mother and siblings. Five months later Xuan returned to her homeland and reconnected with her family.

A VIET KIEU HOMECOMING[44]

Like most Vietnamese, Xuan had never traveled to areas of Vietnam outside her native region. However, when she returned in 1989 it was as the translator on a documentary film project on Vietnamese and American war widows, and in this capacity, she went into the central and northern regions of the country for the first time.[45] There she began to understand the war and the hardships it created for people in different parts of the country in a way she could not even fathom during the war. While taking a late night train through North Vietnam, Xuan thought about the bombs that had constantly disrupted life in the North during the American war. In Hanoi, she met with a communist official who had fought in the war. "When I first come into Hanoi, I feel guilty for sitting in the same table having tea with this Vietnamese government official, *North Vietnamese government official,*" she recalled. "I feeling bad from sitting there talking to this guy, maybe he the one that kill my [first] husband, maybe he the one that shoot Bob [Evans, her husband today] in the face. I feel very bad. I worry that my husband's spirit just watching over me, resent me. But after ten days, I go crazy. I can't take it anymore. I scream aloud, I say: 'What difference does it make?' He doesn't want to go fight, so the Northern guy doesn't want to go fight, but the government make them, so what difference? If he don't kill them, they kill him . . . what difference?"

On her first trip back to Vietnam, Xuan was disgusted by the denial of Southern sacrifices by the ruling Northerners: "In North Vietnam . . . there so many war memorials. I cannot count on all my fingers and toes how many I saw. And when you go down South, there nothing! And how you gonna teach your children about Vietnam's history? That part of history is very important, even if your enemy, even if it's ugly, that part of history. How can I tell my children and my grandchildren: 'Okay, there civil war in our country and here is the North Vietnamese war memorial, where the South Vietnamese war memorial?' There none to be seen."

On three subsequent trips to Vietnam, Xuan's mission has been two-fold: to reestablish family ties and to find the burial site of Huynh Van Toan, her oldest son's father. In 1996, Xuan was successful in locating Toan's grave. During the war, Toan's family did not know that the South Vietnamese military had buried him in a military cemetery outside of Saigon. With victory, however, the North Vietnamese made destroying the cemeteries of South Vietnamese soldiers a priority, and Toan's family discovered where he was buried when they received notification from the new government in 1975 that the cemetery was going to be destroyed. If the family wanted Toan's remains, they were instructed to travel the fifty miles from Vung Tau to Saigon to get them. Toan's father could not afford to make the trip, and the shame he felt kept him from discussing what happened to his son's remains with Xuan.

But Xuan felt she was on a mission, and she persisted. She recruited a Vietnamese friend to investigate and who offered five dollars to anyone who could find Toan's grave. In a country with a per capita income of less than three hundred dollars a year, five dollars is an attractive sum. The first man to find Toan's grave marker removed it to insure his payment. The North Vietnamese had intended to destroy the entire cemetery, which was platted by years, but for some unknown reason, they had stopped plowing down the graves just before the 1971 section in which Toan was buried. They did, however, desecrate the picture on each grave they left standing.

Xuan paid to replace the grave marker. She brought a Buddhist monk to the site to help lay Toan's soul to rest. The ceremony included bringing a feast to the grave and a model paper house that contained money, furniture, clothes, books, even a motorcycle – all the things Toan would need on his journey into the next lifetime. The ceremony concluded by burning the paper house. It had taken twenty-five years, but Xuan had finally given Toan a proper burial.

CONCLUSION

Xuan still suffers from PTSD. She has used her trips back to Vietnam and this oral history project to deal with the emotional wounds of the war. She said the hostility to her experiences and the disinterest in them complicate the process of healing. Above all, Xuan wants to be heard, to tell about her life during the war, even the parts that she finds shameful. She wants to believe that Americans and Vietnamese can learn from the mistakes of war, that some of those who hear of her experiences will be motivated to work for peace, to question political authorities, to stand firm against the steamroller of war. "There's so much in me to share – from a woman, from a widow – not from a political point of view or from a soldier's point of view," she says. "Our voices haven't been heard yet – if people give us an opportunity we can help prevent war. The people who are most hurt by wars are women and children."

The difficult process of integrating two disparate cultures is a continuing one for Xuan. She is still suspicious of other Vietnamese, reflecting years of isolation from the Vietnamese community in the United States, the fact that she was sometimes ostracized in Vietnam for being ethnic Chinese, and the internecine quality of a war in which she could trust only her mother and siblings. Despite her suspicion of and isolation from other Vietnamese Americans, she hopes one day to permanently relocate to Vietnam. And yet, when she returns to her homeland, she feels something is missing – the presence of American soldiers. American troops were in Vietnam during a formative decade of Xuan's life, and she is more comfortable with American veterans of the war than any other group. "Even to sit beside a Vietnam vet, without having a conversation, I know that he saw the same thing that I saw, it's comforting. . . . I know he smelled the same smell, saw the same fire, heard the same blast of the rocket shooting every night."

Xuan is just one of millions of Vietnamese and hundreds of thousands of U.S. veterans who bear the wounds of war. It is important to allow women's voices – women veterans of the Vietnam War – to be heard. Unlike communist women in North and South Vietnam, Xuan did not fight for a cause; her struggle was for survival itself, both in war-torn Vietnam and in adjusting to America. Her war was as a refugee, as a prostitute for American soldiers, as a battered wife in a foreign country, and as a mother separated from her son. But she is no less a veteran of the war than those on all sides who took up arms. An expanded definition of veteran that includes civilians like Xuan who were battered by all factions in the war reveals the nature of total war, in which no true civilians exist. This aspect of the war can never be gleaned from soldiers' accounts, and a complete understanding of the war is not possible without it. It can only be obtained from Vietnam's Third Force, those people like Xuan who fought to stay alive and found themselves caught between the grips of competing factions. The stories of these civilian-veterans allow one to look clearly at the real outcomes of war – not just in terms of territory won or lost, but in terms of the damage done to the human soul and psyche.

NOTES

1. A word about Vietnamese names: the family name comes first; the given name last. The Vietnamese have only about one hundred surnames. Nguyen is the most common, the American equivalent of Smith.

2. The best source for the experiences of South Vietnamese women are Le Ly Hayslip's books. See Hayslip with Jay Wurts, *When Heaven and Earth Changed Places* (New York: A Plume Book, 1989), and *Child of War, Woman of Peace* (New York: Anchor Books, 1993). Oliver Stone's movie based on both books, *Heaven and Earth* (1993), is also a good source. See also Nguyen Thi Dinh, *No Other Road to Take,* trans. Mai Elliott, Data Paper no. 102 (New York: Cornell University, 1976); Arlene Eisen Bergman, *Women of Viet Nam* (San Francisco: People's Press, 1975); and Arlene Eisen, *Women and Revolution in Viet Nam* (London: Zed Books, 1984.) Dinh was the Southern communists' most famous woman general. Eisen's books are propagandistic, but her access to Vietnamese women and her broad knowledge make the works useful.

3. According to the National Vietnam Veterans Readjustment Study completed in 1988, 30.6 percent of male Vietnam veterans and 26.9 percent of female Vietnam veterans suffered from PTSD at some point in their lives. See Peter Kiang, "About Face: Recognizing Asian and Pacific American Vietnam Veterans in Asian American Studies," *Amerasia* 17:3 (1991): 31. Among Vietnamese Americans, depression was the most common mental health problem, and the onset of the depression was normally delayed. See Paul James Rutledge, *The Vietnamese Experience in America* (Bloomington: Indiana University Press, 1992), 103–4.

4. In addition to the physical separation Xuan's abusive husband enforced on her, the Vietnamese community also distanced itself from Xuan because her marriage to an American was seen by most as making her too Americanized. This separated her from what has helped other Vietnamese Americans to survive: the strength of the ethnic community. See Rutledge, *The Vietnamese Experience in America,* 58.

5. Among the best studies of Vietnamese American communities are Rutledge, *The Vietnamese Experience in America*; James M. Freeman, *Hearts of Sorrow: Vietnamese-American Lives* (Palo Alto: Stanford University Press, 1989); and Nazli Kibria, *Family Tightrope: The Changing Lives of Vietnamese Americans* (Princeton NJ: Princeton University Press, 1993). Kibria's work, which fully includes women, gives the most accurate view of the Vietnamese American community in the United States. Rutledge, by largely ignoring women's experiences, makes inaccurate statements, such as saying most women in Vietnam do not work outside the home, and ignoring educational discrimination against girls in Vietnam and the high incidence of wife abuse (*The Vietnamese Experience in America,* 83, 91, 124).

6. David M. Reimers, *Still the Golden Door: The Third World Comes to America* (New York: Columbia University Press, 1985), 24–25, 173. Although 165,839 Asian war brides came to the United States from 1947 to 1975, only 8,040 of them came from Vietnam. Xuan does not know under what provision she was admitted. Although she most closely fits the profile of a war bride, she did not marry the father of her second child until she arrived in the United States.

7. Like other Vietnamese Americans, Xuan has carefully integrated the best aspects of both cultures. See Rutledge, *The Vietnamese Experience in America*, 60–61, 113, 145–47. War has defined U.S.–Asian relations in this century. This fact, combined with the historic exclusion of Asians from U.S. immigration policy, has complicated Xuan's adjustment to life in the United States. See Kiang, "About Face," 34–35.

8. About six thousand Vietnamese live in Portland, Oregon. Neighboring Clark County, Washington, has a population of three thousand Vietnamese. The Vietnamese American population is one of the lasting legacies of the war. Two of Xuan's children are Amerasian and grew up with their father, but generally only about 2 percent of Amerasians ever live with or even meet their American fathers. See Lorraine Majka, "Vietnamese Amerasians in the United States," *Migration World* 8:1 (1990): 6.

9. George C. Herring, *America's Longest War: The United States and Vietnam 1950–1975*, 2nd ed. (New York: Alfred A. Knopf, 1986), 161; Marilyn B. Young, *The Vietnam Wars 1945–1990* (New York: HarperPerennial, 1990), 177; Francis FitzGerald, *Fire in the Lake: The Vietnamese and the Americans in Vietnam* (Boston: Little, Brown, 1972), 427; and Kibria, *Family Tightrope*, 51. At the beginning of the American war, 15 percent of South Vietnam's population lived in the cities; by the end of the war that number approached 50 percent.

10. The bulk of the interviews were conducted from February to September 1994. The transcript totals more than one hundred pages. Hearing women's voices means listening to women "without being guided by models that restrict our ability to hear," not viewing women as victims, and not only asking about events but also about the meaning women attach to them. See Kathryn Anderson, et al., "Beginning Where We Are: Feminist Methodology in Oral History," *Oral History Review* 15 (1987): 103–27.

11. Stanley Karnow, *Vietnam: A History* (New York: The Viking Press, 1983), 100; Gary R. Hess, *Vietnam and the United States: Origins and Legacy of War* (Boston: Twayne Publishers, 1990), 2; Col. Harry G. Summers, Jr., *Vietnam War Almanac* (New York: Facts on File Publications, 1985), 10; "Vietnam," in *Sisterhood Is Global: The International Women's Movement Anthology*, ed. Robin Morgan (Garden City NJ: Anchor Press–Doubleday, 1984), 725–27; Francois Sully, ed., *We the Vietnamese: Voices from Vietnam* (New York: Praeger Publishers, 1971), 69–71; and Kibria, *Family Tightrope*, 38–39.

12. The author explored this subject in an unpublished work, "Women Warriors: The Role of Women in South Viet Nam's National Liberation Front," graduate seminar paper, University of Oregon, July, 1990. Women were concentrated in village defense units, which consisted of the kind of people who appeared to be friendly during the day and shot at Americans at night.

13. During the war, columnist Flora Lewis wrote, "Americans here talk about the war with passion and bitterness. Few Vietnamese do. They speak with the dull tones of hopelessness, of tragedy beyond response or, anyway, beyond any response but the dogged effort to stay alive." Quoted in FitzGerald, *Fire in the Lake,* 396.

14. Throughout the cold war, "Third Force" was a term used to describe groups that were seen as alternatives to communist leadership. The term was also used in the fall of 1974 to refer to groups developing in the cities who favored a peace settlement. Sandra C. Taylor, "Vietnam War," *The 1995 Grolier Multimedia Encyclopedia,* Version 7.0 (Westlake Village CA: Grolier Electronic Publishing, 1995), 7.

15. Ngo Vinh Long, *Vietnamese Women in Society and Revolution* (Boston: Vietnam Resource Center, 1974), 25; Mai Thu Tu and Le Thi Nham Tuyet, *Women in Viet Nam* (Hanoi: Foreign Languages Publishing House, 1978), 111; Pham Cuong, "In the Liberated Areas," in *South Viet Nam: From the N.F.L. to the Provisional Revolutionary Government, Vietnamese Studies,* 23 (Hanoi: Xunhasaba, 1969), 113; and Kibria, *Family Tightrope,* 51. Hess states that 85 percent of Vietnamese lived in villages during the presidency of Nguyen Dinh Diem, which lasted from 1954 to 1963 (*Vietnam and the United States,* 62). Economics alone cannot explain this situation because students from privileged families also could not choose between the various factions until motivated by the Buddhists, and, even then, their commitment to one political philosophy over another was tenuous (FitzGerald, *Fire in the Lake,* 385).

16. FitzGerald, *Fire in the Lake,* 22.

17. Asked which side he supported in the war in 1963, one peasant told an NLF cadre: "I do not know, for I follow the will of Heaven. If I do what you say, then the Diem side will arrest me; if I say things against you, then you will arrest me, so I would rather carry both burdens on my shoulders and stand in the middle." Likewise, the urban Vietnamese often chose a passive resistance to all sides in the conflict (FitzGerald, *Fire in the Lake,* 25, 386). See also Rutledge, *The Vietnamese Experience in America,* 129.

18. FitzGerald writes that the Vietnamese resented the government but offered no complaints because they felt powerless to change it. Raised to suspect all authorities, the Vietnamese saw government as "instruments of the distant, implacable power of heaven or Fate which they had no means to influence" (*Fire in the Lake,* 163, 168). Kibria also refers to this "deep, historically rooted suspicion of formal government"

(*Family Tightrope,* 26, 124). These assessments certainly describe Xuan's mother's view.

19. In the United States, even the family of the man who had primary responsibility for the war, Secretary of Defense Robert McNamara, was divided by the war. The author's current work in progress is a retrospective on the life of Margaret McNamara, Robert McNamara's late wife. Two of the McNamaras' three children opposed the war their father was prosecuting. Craig McNamara believes his mother privately shared his antiwar sentiments.

20. Young, *The Vietnam Wars,* 217, 220. South Vietnamese figures indicate 6,300 civilians were killed in the Saigon area during Tet, 11,000 were wounded, 206,000 became refugees, and 19,000 homes were destroyed (Herring, *America's Longest War,* 191). Throughout the country, the battles of Tet created one million new refugees (FitzGerald, *Fire in the Lake,* 390, 392–93). U.S. estimates indicate 165,000 civilians died throughout the country during the Tet Offensive.

21. The skies over Vietnam belonged to the Americans. Except for a few MIG aircraft that never left North Vietnamese airspace, the North Vietnamese were limited to defensive antiaircraft weapons. But this statement clearly shows the bewilderment of the millions of illiterate Vietnamese who did not understand what was happening in the war.

22. Young, *The Vietnam Wars,* 220; FitzGerald, *Fire in the Lake,* 427; and Herring, *America's Longest War,* 161. The wholesale creation of refugees was not accidental. General Westmoreland believed that making people refugees was an effective way to keep them from the communists (Richard Critchfield, *The Long Charade: Political Subversion in the Vietnam War* [New York: Harcourt, Brace and World, 1968], 173). The United States had no intention initially of resettling the refugees it was creating (Reimers, *Still the Golden Door,* 173).

23. FitzGerald, *Fire in the Lake,* 395.

24. Summers, *Vietnam War Almanac,* 94–95.

25. Over the years, Xuan's father had a succession of live-in mistresses who slept with him in the main part of the house while his wife and children slept in the back part of the house. This was common practice in war-torn Vietnam and continues today. It occurred less often among communists than noncommunists. Traditional legal codes sanctioned polygamy, which was a mark of status among the wealthy. See Kibria, *Family Tightrope,* 46. During the war, the communists tried to retrain husbands not to beat their wives and to be monogamous. Ho Chi Minh, the president of North Vietnam, gave the equality of women great weight. Since the end of the war, these issues have been left up to the eleven million members of Vietnam's Women's Union.

26. Gail Paradise Kelly, "To Become an American Woman: Education and Sex Role Socialization of the Vietnamese Immigrant Woman," in *Unequal Sisters: A Multicultural Reader in U.S. Women's History,* ed. Vicki Ruiz and Ellen DuBois, 2nd ed. (New York: Routledge, 1994), 498. Kelly shows how forced urbanization left women with few economic choices. The surest way to gainful employment was by providing services to Americans, including prostitution. By 1975, half a million South Vietnamese women were prostitutes (Kibria, *Family Tightrope,* 57, 63).

27. FitzGerald, *Fire in the Lake,* 427.

28. This quote is remarkable for its similarity to a quote from Nguyen Thi Dinh, the Southern communists' most famous woman general. She lost her husband in the First Indochina War against the French and states in her memoirs that she wept secretly at night to keep from discouraging other communist insurgents.

29. Demonstrating her delusions of grandeur, Madame Nhu even claimed to be the modern embodiment of the Trung Sisters (Karnow, *Vietnam: A History,* 265–66). For the influence of Vietnamese legends on women, see the prologue in Hayslip, *When Heaven and Earth Changed Places.*

30. Xuan explains, "Up North, I feel sorry, not only the men were forced to fight, the women too. And they have it really bad. . . . There no way you can compare pain or measure suffering, but I think the Northern people have it worse than the South people." Nevertheless, the South Vietnamese lost five times as many civilians during the war as the North Vietnamese. See Summers, *Vietnam War Almanac,* 112; and Young, *The Vietnam Wars,* 280. Herring notes that from 1965 to 1967, the United States dropped twice the tonnage of bombs on the South that were dropped on the North (*America's Longest War,* 151).

31. Fearing retribution from the communists and seeking to assuage their shame, many Vietnamese women abandoned their Amerasian children, as evidenced by the adult Amerasians who still live on the streets in Vietnam. They are all treated like the children of prostitutes. See Majka, "Vietnamese Amerasians," 5–6; and Kibria, *Family Tightrope,* 117. When Le Ly Hayslip gave birth to an Amerasian child, the midwife told her, "Better give him away or kill him and your shame will be washed away" (Oliver Stone, *Heaven and Earth,* 1993).

32. Nguyen, "The Tale of Kieu," in *Of Quiet Courage: Poems from Viet Nam,* ed. J. Chagnon and D. Luce (Washington DC: Indochina Mobile Education Project, 1974), 9, 12.

33. Nguyen, "The Tale of Kieu," 7.

34. Nguyen, "The Tale of Kieu," 8.

35. Nguyen, "The Tale of Kieu," 7–12.

36. Number based on research by Stephen Graw, professor of sociology at Cornell

University's Southeast Asia Project. With approximately one million communist deaths – North and South – and 220,000 ARVN deaths, and given the hardship to the Vietnamese in retrieving their war dead, 300,000 is a reasonable estimate.

37. Hess, *Vietnam and the United States,* 160. There are 2,387 MIAS in all of In-dochina. Hess points out that the MIA numbers for the Vietnam War reflect only 4 percent of those known to be killed as compared to 20 percent in World War II and 15 percent in the Korean War. He writes, "The Department of Defense has discounted the reports of Americans being seen in Vietnam and considers all but one of the MIAS to be legally dead. The exception is maintained for the symbolic reason of demonstrating official interest in forcing a Vietnamese accounting for the MIAS."

38. Casualty rates for the Vietnam War are controversial, impossible to verify, and vary greatly. Summers gives estimates on the low end with 666,000 NVA dead, 223,748 ARVN dead (a standard and reliable figure), 300,000 South Vietnamese civilians dead, and 65,000 North Vietnamese civilians dead. The Vietnamese government's figures are on the high end: 1.1 million communists dead (this includes NLF fighters), and two million civilian deaths. Two to three million is a reasonable figure for Vietnam. This does not include the Laotian deaths or the millions lost during the bloodbath in Cambodia, both of which were intimately tied to U.S. actions in Vietnam.

39. In covering the Vancouver, Washington, Vietnamese community for *The Columbian* newspaper, I have heard this story of grandparents insisting that grand-children be left behind many times. Extended families are the norm in Vietnam (Kibria, *Family Tightrope,* 61).

40. Kibria, a sociologist, challenges the patronizing assumption that migration to the United States improves the status of Third World women: "Women in the midst of such social changes may actually lose their traditional sources of support and power" (*Family Tightrope,* 19). Susan Brownmiller, for example, adopted such a tone in assuming that Vietnamese women with a two-thousand-year-warrior tradition needed Western feminist classics to empower themselves. See Susan Brownmiller, "Women of Vietnam," *The Nation,* July 18, 1994, 82.

41. Like many other Vietnamese who come to the United States practicing Bud-dhism and ancestor worship, Xuan familiarized herself with Christianity and found that she preferred her native religion. See Rutledge, *The Vietnamese Experience in America,* 53–54.

42. The Amerasian provision was part of a detailed and multifaceted immigration law. The United States Code (1982; reprint, Washington DC: The U.S. Government Printing Office, 1988), 8:1154, 71–72; Suzan Ruth Travis, "Son of U.S. Soldier Was Born an Outcast," *The Columbian* (Vancouver WA), April 30, 1995, 1, 3; Rutledge, *The Vietnamese Experience in America,* 132; Jill Bauermeister, "Amerasians in Amer-

ica," *America,* Nov. 27, 1982, 147, 331–33; Majka, "Vietnamese Amerasians," 5; and Reimers, *Still the Golden Door,* 155. Reimers points out that refugees from communist countries are more likely to be admitted to the United States than refugees from right-wing dictatorships.

43. The Huu Nghi Clinic was built during February and March 1989 by the Veterans Viet Nam Restoration Project. The building of the clinic was the first joint U.S. – Vietnamese construction project since the Americans left Vietnam in 1973.

44. Overseas Vietnamese who return to their homeland are called Viet Kieu.

45. Barbara Sonneborn, *Regret to Inform* (New York: New Video Group, 2000), documentary.

Frontiers 18:1 (1997): 145–67.

Cultural Autobiography, Testimonial, and Asian American Transnational Feminist Coalition in the "Comfort Women of World War II" Conference

PAMELA THOMA

> Her words, coiled tightly in my script, tied her spirit to her body and bound her to this life. When they burned, they would travel with her across the waters, free.
>
> *Nora Okja Keller,* Comfort Woman

Bringing together activists, academics, and cultural workers to analyze and discuss the structural causes of Japanese military sexual slavery, the "Comfort Women of World War II: Legacy and Lessons" conference illuminated the pervasive presence of multinational capitalism and the ways in which it implicates nation-states and also responded to and intervened in multinational operations that attempt to control women, particularly in militarized and colonizing situations.[1] Through this illumination, response, and intervention, the conference explicitly participated in transnational feminist activism, but I argue in this chapter that the conference was indebted more specifically to an Asian American transnational feminism.[2] In contrast to other women of color feminisms in the United States, Asian American feminisms – whether locally, nationally, or internationally organized – have sometimes gone unrecognized and have been undertheorized by activists and scholars in the fields of Asian American studies and feminist studies alike.[3] Although there are sometimes conscious and complex reasons for this paucity, which I will briefly address below, the conference offers an opportunity to recognize and analyze Asian American transnational feminist cultural activism. By providing a forum for Asian American cultural texts, the conference presented the politics of this feminism and constitutes an autobiographical text of Asian American transnational feminism. As a cultural autobiography of the coalition politics of Asian American transnational feminism, the conference created as well as critiqued postmodernity by producing a text that establishes an alternative community to modernist nationalisms.[4]

TRANSNATIONAL FEMINISMS

Transnational feminisms are those various comparative forms of feminist practices and alliances that oppose particular and global versions of economic and cultural hegemony and seek social change for women in different locations.[5] They are indebted to politicized postmodernisms in their critique of modern nationalist, capitalist, and patriarchal projects, and to postcolonial studies in their critique of Western cultural imperialism and their emphasis on the contributions of postcolonial cultures in the formation of a heterogeneous postmodernity. More specifically, transnational feminisms incorporate feminist and postmodern concepts of multiple subjectivity to collaboratively investigate the limitations of nationalist communities and to elaborate alternative communities. I consider the various practices and products of transnational feminisms to be forms of resistance to the hegemonic policies of nation-states that promote and protect multinational capital for the growth of their economies. As Inderpal Grewal and Caren Kaplan write in the introduction to their important volume *Scattered Hegemonies: Postmodernity and Transnational Feminist Practices,* transnational feminisms "articulate the relationship of gender to scattered hegemonies such as global economic structures, patriarchal nationalisms, 'authentic' forms of tradition, local structures of domination, and legal-juridical oppression on multiple levels." The collaborative nature of transnational feminisms works "to compare multiple, overlapping, and discrete oppressions rather than to construct a theory of hegemonic oppression under a unified category of gender," which the authors contrast to the failed notion of "global feminism." Global feminism, as many critics have pointed out, "has elided the diversity of women's agency in favor of a universalized Western model of women's liberation that celebrates individuality and modernity."[6] Elsewhere, Kaplan writes that transnational feminism is "an anti-racist and anti-imperialist feminism": "[It] must articulate differences in power and location as accurately as possible. It must also find intersections and common ground; but they will not be utopian or necessarily comfortable alliances. New terms are needed to express the possibilities for links and affiliations, as well as differences among women who inhabit different locations. Transnational feminist activism is one possibility. I would argue that this mode of affiliation occurs in many academic and nonacademic contexts and that its histories and present existence often remain to be read."[7] Transnational feminisms are recognizable by their coalitional, antinationalist, antiexploitative politics rather than by their association with a particular group of feminists defined by class, race, ethnicity, nationality, or some other monolithic category. At the same time, transnational feminist activism may be included on the agendas of groups or individuals who primarily identify themselves in ways other than as transnational feminists.

Asian American women participating in various organizations and alliances and producing cultural texts often demonstrate transnational feminist politics, but their work is frequently not recognized as either transnational or feminist for a variety of reasons: feminist critics tend to overlook Asian American discourse, Asian American women do not want to identify with racist feminism, and there has been strong pressure to unify Asian American discourse. While the Asian American movement, combined with the other social protest movements of the 1960s and early 1970s, led to more public awareness of Asian Americans, the population of Asian Americans relative to other ethnic and racial minorities often leads to their absence in research and scholarship. Feminist studies are no exception to this pattern of neglect and omission. It is also important to recognize that an insidious racial hierarchy and paradigm persist, even in some of the most racially conscious feminist research; studies of African American women are often mistakenly presented as studies of all women of color or even the "real" women of color in the United States. In some cases, Asian American women seem to be considered "too close" to whites to be "authentic" female subjects of color. The disregard of Asian American contributions to feminist politics also comes, quite understandably, from within Asian American discourse. As Grewal and Kaplan point out, "Many women who participate in decolonizing efforts both within and outside the United States have rejected the term 'feminism' in favor of 'womanist' or have defined their feminism through class or race or ethnic, religious, or regional struggles."[8]

Beyond Asian American feminist resistance to or skepticism about hegemonic feminisms, there has been and continues to be pressure to create and maintain a unified Asian American culture.[9] When Asian American feminists have critiqued the limitations of an Asian American cultural nationalism that posits an American-born heterosexual male of East Asian ancestry as its authentic subject and creator of cultural tradition, they have often been accused of being disloyal.[10] A newer incarnation of this tension remains in Asian American discourse. Two versions of an essay titled "Women, Immigration, Gender: Asian 'American' Women," by Lisa Lowe, may illustrate how the internal pressures to choose between feminist and ethnic alliances or to eschew feminist critique in Asian American discourse are still negotiated. In the 1997 version appearing in *Making More Waves: New Writing by Asian American Women,* Lowe provocatively theorizes several narratives by Asian American women as part of a linkage that is "crucial to Asian American feminist and women of color politics." However, in the longer 1996 version appearing in her influential book *Immigrant Acts: On Asian American Cultural Politics,* she refers to the narratives under discussion as "Asian American cultural production." In both versions Lowe incisively analyzes these texts as "linked to an emergent political formation, organizing across race, class, and national boundaries, that includes other racialized and immigrant groups as well as women working in, and immigrating from, the neocolonized world" and as "belonging to a new mode of cultural practice that corresponds to the new social formation of globalized capitalism." But while Lowe cites Grewal, Kaplan, Chandra Mohanty, and others who have identified such cultural production as feminist, and while all of the texts Lowe discusses are texts produced by women, she does not clearly theorize the transnationalism of these works by Asian American women as "feminist" in the version appearing in her book. It is clear that Lowe wants to signify a new political collectivity, citing the "reconceptualization of the oppositional narratives of nationalism, Marxism, and feminism" under globalization, and it is also clear that Lowe does not want to reinstall a liberal feminist narrative of emancipation; but, as Lowe acknowledges, U.S. feminists of color have developed "'situated' non-totalizing perspectives on conjoined dominations, as well as the emergence of politicized critiques of those conjunctions." Still, the pressure to maintain a unified Asian American culture (and possible unitary subject) seems ironically to resurface in Lowe's strategically essentialist choice of the ethno-nationalist term of the 1970s movement, "Asian American," for this new type of cultural production when she writes for a general Asian Americanist or cultural studies audience. [11]

I argue that in numerous types of cultural texts and practices produced by Asian American women, and in particular those presented and created at the "Comfort Women of World War II" conference, lie the opportunity to read and to understand collaborative and decidedly feminist practices useful in affecting the world-system of postmodernity. Not to read them as transnational feminist texts is possibly to miss or misread their significant messages about alternative communities. Asian American feminists have a history of international activism that includes involvement in the antiwar movement as well as in the political and social issues of Asian immigrant women and Asian women who retain close connections to nations other than the United States. Moreover, recent activism and cultural production evidence the transnationalism of contemporary Asian American feminism; the "Comfort Women of World War II" conference is one of a rich array of works that needs to be read in radically innovative *and* feminist ways.[12]

AUTOBIOGRAPHY AND TRANSNATIONAL FEMINIST CULTURAL PRODUCTION

The "Comfort Women of World War II" conference is both a transnational feminist and an Asian American text. It involved the efforts of numerous differently affiliated women; it critiqued the imperialist and nationalist politics of the Japanese government that administered military sexual slavery as well as the multinational economics of governments that have instituted similar systems or refused to acknowledge the role of nation-states in the sexual assault of women; and it participated in creating a coalition of feminists who want to abolish such abuses of women in different locations. Providing a history of the coalition politics of Asian American activism around the comfort women issue, the conference is, more specifically, a cultural autobiography of Asian American transnational feminism. It should be placed, however, in the context of a range of transnational feminist autobiographical texts to fully appreciate the various ways different women contribute to critiquing and constructing postmodernity. In her essay "Resisting Autobiography: Out-Law Genres and Transnational Feminist Subjects," Kaplan builds on Jacques Derrida's observations concerning "the law of genre" to designate these types of emerging autobiographies "outlaw" genres and begins the work of identifying and understanding the contributions of feminists in various locations to postmodernity. Kaplan explains that outlaw genres are deeply transnational because they participate in autobiographical discourse in ways that challenge modernist concepts of individual subjectivity, patriarchal nationalism, and multinational capitalism. Though her discussion does not include texts written by Asian American women, they certainly have participated in transnational feminist production, and a review of the characteristics and functions of outlaw genres that Kaplan highlights can help us consider the participation of Asian American women in this mode of cultural production.[13]

While not foreclosing the possibility of additional forms, the types of outlaw genres that Kaplan identifies include prison memoirs, testimonial literature, ethnographic writing, "biomythography," "cultural autobiography," and "regulative psychobiography." Rather than privilege personal explorations of individuals, these alternative versions of autobiography challenge the power relations of the literary production site and marketplace, the specific social and historical context of the autobiographical subject, and the global system of transnational economic production with its gendered division of labor. More specifically, at the level of literary production, outlaw genres destabilize the conventions of genres by deconstructing the individual bourgeois author, by questioning the authority of written expression, and by reasserting the interpretive or critical role of the autobiographical subject and text. The iconoclastic features of outlaw genres also include resistance to imperializing Western feminist autobiography, because as outlaw genres engage the "discourse of situation or the politics of location instead of the discourse of individual authorship," they critique a simple identity politics based on gender. Instead, they explore coalition politics, or what some observers call the politics of difference, to realign the concepts of self and community. Furthermore, outlaw genres provide materialist analyses of asymmetrical local and transnational labor conditions. As "a global project that employs the efforts of many people, rather than the act of a single hand lifting pen to paper or an individual pressing the keys on a keyboard" – one that challenges "the hierarchical structures of patriarchy, capitalism and colonial discourse" – outlaw genres are forms of transnational feminist cultural production.[14]

The implications of outlaw genres as forms of transnational feminist cultural production are potentially revolutionary: they can reveal the socially constructed and therefore mutable modernist concepts of nationalism and individualism; they can help us imagine and construct alternative communities for a changing world; and they can release "the representation and expression of women from different parts of the world" from hegemonic representational traditions. Yet this potential cannot be realized until or unless the critic collaborates *in* the process of producing a text, instead of appropriating the process. In addition, to participate in the revolution of transnational feminist cultural production, the critic must reveal her relation to the author, extend the process of collaboration to the reception of texts, shift "the subject of autobiography from the individual to a more unstable collective unity," and learn to read the differences between outlaw genres to reveal "possible strategic similarities."[15] In other words, the Western feminist critic must be politicized and read in an oppositional

mode, considering texts that are usually overlooked. As a privileged feminist critic located in an academic institution in the United States, I engage
the "Comfort Women of World War II" conference as part of an autobiographical outlaw genre to include texts that are often disregarded – texts
by Asian American women – in the critical practice and understanding of
transnational feminist activism and politics.[16]

TESTIMONIAL AND CULTURAL AUTOBIOGRAPHY IN THE COMFORT WOMEN CONFERENCE

Extending the process of collaboration, shifting the subject of autobiography, and reading the differences between outlaw genres in order to locate
similar strategies for collaborative social change, I examine two individual
texts from the conference that are not only recognizable elements of the
larger Asian American transnational feminist cultural autobiography of the
conference, but that are also discrete hybrid autobiographical texts or outlaw genres themselves: Kim Yoon-Sim's "Testimony" in the second session
of the conference, which I analyze as modified testimonial narrative, and
Christine Choy's 1996 film *In the Name of the Emperor,* which I read as a
cognate testimonial and cultural autobiography.[17]

    The session in which Kim Yoon-Sim's "Testimony" was scheduled was en-
titled "Roundtable Discussion: Testimony from the Frontline," though it was
not precisely a discussion since it soon became clear that, while collaborative,
the testimonial situation demands a listener as well as a speaking subject.
The session began with a short video produced by the Washington Coalition
for Comfort Women Issues (wccw) and a few introductory comments from
Dongwoo Lee Ham, the president of wccw, but the focus of the session was
Kim Yoon-Sim's testimonial. From the moment she began, it was apparent that retelling her story was psychologically difficult and painful. Kim
Yoon-Sim's testimony, uttered slowly and punctuated with sobbing pauses,
recalled the circumstances of her abduction from her village by Japanese
soldiers, the journey that led to her enslavement in China, the conditions of
the two comfort stations Kim Yoon-Sim survived, her eventual escape and
return to Korea, and the difficult life – what she called the "hidden life" –
she lived after the war. In startling detail but with few words and nearly no
adjectives, Kim Yoon-Sim relayed her thoughts as a fourteen-year-old girl,
the specific physical trauma and health problems she endured, and, most
vividly, the strength and dignity of her life. Her testimonial was a courageous
act of bearing witness, and the audience took on the role of listener without

responding in a discussion. Although one could understand the reticence of the audience as a lack of participation or as a failure to engage with Kim Yoon-Sim, I understand it as part of the conference's recognition that listening is a necessary and participatory aspect of testimonial narrative.[18]

John Beverley describes testimonial as "a literature of personal witness and involvement," and testimonial narrative is usually thought of as a written text that is "elicited or transcribed and edited by another person."[19] Although the life story Kim Yoon-Sim presented at the conference did not follow this written convention, I read it as testimonial primarily because of the characteristic first-person oral account that initiates testimonial narratives. In addition, Norma Field advises that "we need to be prepared to extend our imagination to fragmentary testimonies, to barely distinguishable testimonies," and even "to testimonies that never reach us because their utterers perished first and because their locus, in terms of political geography, didn't matter enough."[20] Kim Yoon-Sim's narrative is a moving personal account of the horrific events and the courageous struggle of her life, and the orality of the text does not render it any less a testimonial.

The oral status of Kim Yoon-Sim's narrative is, in fact, the very element that makes it radically transnational and feminist. Testimonial narrative involves collaborative work across cultural divides where the politics of production and reception as well as other power relations can impinge on the relationship between the speaking subject and the recorder or editor and between the speaking subject and the audience – that is, between women in different locations.[21] In contrast, the collaborative process of Kim Yoon-Sim's testimonial included steps to guard against the appropriation of the text by elite feminists. The organizers of the conference (the "editors") presented the original moment of testimony and immediate interpretation to a diverse audience open to the public without charge rather than producing a translated and transcribed (read "carefully edited") version of it for a paying audience or readership.[22] This refusal to commodify the testimonial text stands in contrast to the many sensationalist journalists who have gone to great lengths to search for and pay former comfort women for their stories. The democratic and egalitarian aspect of the production of testimonial, in which "any life so narrated can have a kind of representational value," was in this case extended to its reception so that the voice of the speaker was no longer disembodied, aestheticized, and commercialized – although I certainly acknowledge that academic conferences and essays participate in the extraction of another layer of value or commodification.[23] Furthermore, by seating the interpreter next to Kim Yoon-Sim and making the relations in testimonial visible to the audience, the conference organizers avoided what Kaplan describes as "the documentary 'truth-value' of the category of 'oral history' by highlighting the relationship between the 'editor' or 'facilitator' and 'subject' or 'speaker.' "[24] The drawback of this compromise was that Kim Yoon-Sim's testimonial was in clear danger of becoming a spectacle since local and university media attempted to record the testimonial as an "event."[25] Despite the pitfalls, however, the decision to open up Kim Yoon-Sim's testimonial to more "editors" and "readers," without obfuscating the mediation and translation and without directly commodifying the text, resists both the alienating and exploitative forces of multinational capitalism and the subordinating and hierarchical forces of patriarchal knowledge production that transnational feminist practices struggle against.

Kim Yoon-Sim's narrative additionally shares with testimonial a connection to a specific collectivity that has been or is oppressed and is attempting to build support for its struggle.[26] Though it is, as Kim Yoon-Sim aptly said, "such an unthinkable thing," her personal story speaks to the similar stories of the more than two hundred thousand women forced into sexual slavery by the Japanese military, and it supports these women's demands for accountability. Before beginning the narrative account, Kim Yoon-Sim clarified the purpose of her testimony, stating that the former comfort women's "stories are all the same, though they looked different"; that "their painful stories are not for sale" (money was not the goal); and that the "number of women is small and getting smaller, we must act now before it is too late." These prefatory statements indicate that her testimony is primarily concerned with the "collective situation in which the narrator lives," and that she "speaks for, or in the name of, a community or group."[27] Kim Yoon-Sim's testimonial, combined with the other texts composing the conference, made it evident that she speaks for the former comfort women and a coalition of transnational feminists (Korean, Japanese, Filipina, and Asian American) who want the Japanese to take both moral and legal responsibility for the military sexual slavery they officially instituted and operated.

The collective voice of the testimonial is complicated, however, by the fact that the conference devoted much of its attention to Korean women without thoroughly acknowledging its partial focus.[28] While some elements of the conference emphasized that women of other nations were abducted and assaulted by the Japanese system, most notably Yuki Tanaka's presentation and Choy's film *In the Name of the Emperor,* the conference was cosponsored by the Korean-oriented wccw and The Korea Society, and the specialty of one of the conference organizers is Korean studies. The result was an emphasis on Korean women that elided the heterogeneity of the community of comfort women. Though obviously not intended by the organizers of the conference, the absence of Filipinas and Filipina Americans in particular, because they have also been politically active in exposing the comfort women system, somewhat weakened the collaborative and transnational message of the conference.[29] As Robert Carr points out, the testifying subject is often taken as a representative: "Although it has become standard operating procedure to assume an easy metonymic relation between the subject of testimonial and the ethnic group from which she or he comes, such closure on difference within the group celebrates the elite reader's ignorance as the group is conversely constituted as infinite duplicates of the 'original' subject presented in . . . the testimonial."[30] Carr here discusses how reading the subject of testimonial as representative and without carefully regarding the testifying subject's positionality in terms of social class and gender can foreclose the reader's understanding of differences within the ethnic group of the testifying subject and thus can encourage the elite reader's ignorance of an entire ethnic group. However, reading representativeness in the subject of testimonial also risks an erasure of differences within the collective itself. The dangers of representative reception practices are then considerable since understanding differences in nationality, ethnicity, and racial identity, as well as in social class, sexuality, and age provides political illlumination for transnational feminist alliance in testimonial dialogue. Indeed, the diversity of women who were assaulted in the comfort women system is crucial to understanding how nationalism, patriarchy, and capitalism combine in militarized sexual slavery, but the range of women involved in the system was not underscored in the conference. There are probably several ways this homogenizing effect could have been avoided, the most obvious but surely the most difficult of which would have been to include additional testifying subjects, creating a polyphonic testimonial similar to Sistren and Honor Ford-Smith's *Lionheart Gal: Life Stories of Jamaican Women.* Other more feasible measures might have been to include an activist from the Filipina branch of the movement, such as Indai Sajor, Nelia Sancho, Ninotchka Rosca, or Sheila Coronel, in one of the sessions, or even to further narrow the title of the conference to safeguard against representativeness.[31]

As testimonial that is presented orally to a large and diverse group of listeners in a public forum, Kim Yoon-Sim's "Testimony" constitutes an indeterminate and modified narrative that foregrounds its accessibility and its difference from the cultural and aestheticized forms of bourgeois literary discourse. In an analysis of the representations of Japanese military sexual slavery in Japanese and Korean nationalized school textbooks, Hyun Sook Kim writes that we should also read the testimonies of former comfort women as countermemory to official written history: "The women are challenging us to question the received 'truths' about imperialism, colonialism, nationalism, and gender oppression and patriarchy and to revise the narratives of national history through which we have come to understand our collective present."[32] Testimonial literature typically begins as a first-person oral narrative that is then transcribed and translated, operations that challenge the authority accorded the written word and the primacy of the individual author.[33] These challenges are extended and expanded by Kim Yoon-Sim's testimonial and indicate the extent to which the conference as well as individual presentations are part of a feminism that concentrates on resisting multinational capitalism and creating transnational communities.

Choy's *In the Name of the Emperor*, another component of the transnational feminist cultural text of the conference, is a fifty-two-minute documentary film exploring the Japanese rape of thousands of women in Nanjing, China, in 1937 and its connection to the systemization of military sexual slavery by the Japanese.[34] Choy explained in her discussion following the screening that she originally intended to focus the film on Nanjing and its residents. However, once Choy arrived in China to begin her project, she was not allowed to travel to Nanjing and was prohibited from filming and interviewing even in Shanghai, where sexual slavery by the Japanese began as early as 1932. While the film contains footage of the rape of Nanjing, most of the documentary records interviews with Japanese veterans of the war and citizens on the streets of contemporary Japan. Choy calls her decision to interview Japanese an "aesthetic of emergency," but the interviews of the veterans, which operate more like confessions, present compelling dimensions of testimonial narrative. Additionally, Choy understands the film in terms of her own participation as director and producer and sees it as a "living witness statement of a survivor," again suggesting that the film is a type of testimonial narrative.[35]

Testimonies from both Choy and the veterans appear in *In the Name of the Emperor*, a layering that makes visible possible variations of the form. Although I am not suggesting a similarity between the community of former comfort women as an oppressed group that seeks accountability and the community of Japanese veterans who committed war crimes, Choy's film seems to allow space for both groups as part of the subject of testimonial. As Field has recently theorized, any meaningful apology to former comfort women must include remorse and testimony, and "testimony involves both victims and apologizers. It entails reciprocity." The confessional polyphonic testimony of the veterans also emphasizes comments Beverley makes about testimonial, including his point that testimonial can come from "the political right . . . [if it] signifies the need for a general social change."[36] Several of the veterans interviewed directly state or imply their desire to prevent the atrocities from happening in the future, and the interviews provide a model for legal testimony, providing evidence that the crimes were committed and that the Japanese military had a sexual slavery system. The confession of veterans has played a significant role, in fact, in the struggle to elicit and verify the claims of former comfort women, since governments and the international community (including, until very recently, the United Nations) have been reluctant to admit to the system and take responsibility, and individuals understandably fear the stigmatization and pain they face in coming forward.

Another aspect of the film that makes use of an interesting though problematic feature of testimonial narrative is that Choy places the viewer in the position of a jury member in a courtroom. Watching *In the Name of the Emperor,* the audience is not only given the responsibility of determining the sincerity of the veterans and confronted with the question of the individual accountability of soldiers in committing crimes that were based upon orders from superiors or institutionalized military practices, but is also asked to consider the place of sexual violence in military aggression.[37] As in several of her previous films, Choy's text engages the viewers' sense of ethics and justice, and the texts are constructed as testimonials, even if the testifying subjects are not all speaking as part of an oppressed community. While it seems simple enough to judge the veterans and the sexual slavery system, transnational feminists may find this construction of the viewer/reader as the arbiter of justice for testimonial problematic given the typically troubled dynamic of the First World viewer/reader of the subaltern or Third World woman's testimony; in the case of *In the Name of the Emperor,* the politics of this arrangement are doubly fraught since the film appears to maintain the position of the subaltern female subject as an Other who does not speak and may not be heard in the film.[38] But when we also consider the film Choy's testimonial, or a "statement of a survivor," she is roughly analogous to the testifying, speaking subject in her role as director and the audience is called upon to hear her narrative and respond in alliance. Like the transcriber in traditional testimonial, the camera lens is a level of mediation through which Choy's first-person perspective is filtered, and the cinematographic visual organization of the film correlates to the written word, another level

of mediation. In both the film and the printed testimonial, the final product also usually goes through an editorial process. Alluding to and partly
confirming her role in the testimonial function of the film, Choy said in her
presentation at the conference that she wanted to provide an "alternative,
new historical view" of the rape of Nanjing, to redefine "global, especially
Asian Pacific, history," and to seek change from people.

Here the testimonial crosses over into another outlaw genre of autobiography because Choy was not a direct witness of the events she recounts.
More exactly, *In the Name of the Emperor* is also Choy's personal cultural
autobiography since it is simultaneously an individual life story and a cultural history. Choy declared the personal nature of the film when, after the
screening, she identified herself as a Korean Chinese Russian American and
said, "All my films deal with my personal experience." She then linked her
personal history and the social history explored in the film with several
comments such as, "Internal conflict is created by external pressure." Using
Bernice Johnson Reagon's notion of cultural autobiography, Kaplan states
that it is a form that "works to construct both the 'safe' places and the border areas of coalition politics where diversity operates in crisis conditions to
forge powerful temporary alliances." Choy's original plan to return to one
of her cultural "homes" in China and re-present the story of the Japanese
attack of Nanjing was an effort to connect her personal life to a cultural
community and history. Though Choy would not cherish this moment of
her cultural community's history, like bell hooks, she uses life writing to do
the hard work of "sharing experiences," to preserve a cultural community
and to construct a cultural "home."[39]

The need to place her personal identity within a larger historical frame
also seems to have influenced Choy's decision to interview Japanese veterans, a move that constitutes a "border area of coalition politics where
diversity operates in crisis."[40] While Choy stated that "history comes from
many points of view," we can only imagine how hard it must have been to
interview the very men who brutalized those she saw as members of her
community. But Choy must have felt an imperative to connect herself to
that historical moment. As Reagon's now famous statement acknowledges,
"You don't go into coalition because you just *like* it"; rather, "the only reason
you would consider trying to team up with somebody who could possibly
kill you, is because that's the only way you can figure you can stay alive." This
description of coalition politics seems accurately to represent at least one of
the reasons for the collaboration of Choy, a self-described Asian American
who is culturally connected to and working on the comfort women case,

and the Japanese veterans interviewed in her film. Another reason for this coalition certainly includes the long-term change in international human rights that transnational feminists are seeking in working toward Japanese accountability for the military sexual slavery in the Pacific War. Regardless of the reasons, when she said that we "have to collaborate with equality," Choy reiterated Reagon's reminder that in coalition you have to allow people to "name themselves" and deal with them from that perspective. *In the Name of the Emperor* is a cultural autobiography in which Choy's personal history, to use Kaplan's terms, connects an "individual with [a] particular communit[y] at [a] given historical juncture."[41]

THE COMFORT WOMEN CONFERENCE AS CULTURAL AUTOBIOGRAPHY

So far I have argued that the "Comfort Women of World War II" conference is part of an Asian American transnational feminism and that the types of cultural production deployed in at least two presentations in the conference are Asian American transnational feminist autobiographies: testimonial and cultural autobiography. Next, I would like to consider how the conference as a whole was a cultural autobiography of Asian American transnational feminism. Kaplan provides some guidance in beginning such an endeavor, for she encourages critics to think about texts in alternative ways and to expand what they think of as "texts": "An oppositional relationship to writing and to genres such as autobiography requires the difficult embrace of unfamiliar narrative strategies as well as the validating insertion of your own familiar modes of expression and your own systems of signification. The histories of coalitions – their dynamism and their difficulties – can be charted as cultural autobiographies of communities in crisis and resistance. The struggle *in* writing remains to be read and recognized by literary criticism. First, it is necessary to read the narratives of coalition politics as cultural autobiographies."[42] Following this lead, possible narrative texts of coalition politics that can be read as cultural autobiography include those written personal histories that also tell the story of a movement or collaborative struggle, such as Mary Crow Dog's *Lakota Woman;* collections that demonstrate the collaboration of the coalition politics they narrate such as Cherríe Moraga and Gloria Anzaldúa's *This Bridge Called My Back;* film and video productions that visualize the histories of struggles or movements, such as Pratibha Parmar's *Warrior Marks;* performative groups that enact and describe coalition politics, such as Sweet Honey in the Rock; academic and political conferences that elaborate and/or elicit coalition politics, such as the 1982 "Scholar and the Feminist IX" conference at Barnard College; and even possibly legal proceedings such as the Anita Hill/Clarence Thomas hearings, or the recent testimonies of South Africans documenting the crimes of apartheid. While this is obviously not an exhaustive list and these are not all examples of cultural autobiographies of transnational feminist coalition politics, they should give us some idea of the kinds of texts that can be read as autobiographies of collaborative struggle.[43]

To analyze the narrative strategies of the collective form of cultural auto-biography one can start by way of analogy to the personal form of cultural autobiography that both creates a safe place of coalition politics and explores a border space or "contact zone" of coalition politics. Though these two features of cultural autobiography might seem to be contradictory, they echo Reagon's point that one has to have both a "home" and live and work in a world with others.[44] Coalition politics draws on the empowerment of identity politics but demands that that empowerment be used to form temporary alliances around differences. A safe place for Asian American transnational feminist political culture was consciously constructed by the organizers of the conference, who created a supportive environment for naming and articulating the sexualized nature of aggression under modern patriarchy generally, the sexual violence of imperialistic war typically, and the racist, sexual enslavement of former comfort women specifically.[45] The conference was organized in an inclusive manner, and the safe environment as well as the contact zone were described at the conference website:

"The Comfort Women of World War II: Historical Legacy and Lessons" will be an interdisciplinary event with wide appeal to faculty, students, and the public. It will use a variety of media and approaches to address an issue that is both historically significant and politically current and that is having a tremendous impact upon relations among Asian nations and within Asian-American communities. Its particular relevance, of course, will be to the lives of women, who are often the victims of sexual violence in war and whose experiences are rarely talked about. Although World War II has been the focus of much scholarly attention, perhaps no suffering from that war has been so invisible, at least until recently, as that of the women of Korea, China, Malaysia, Indonesia, the Philipines [sic], and even Japan itself, who were forced into sexual slavery by the Japanese imperial army and who are still seeking official governmental compensation and apologies.

"The Comfort Women of World War II" will bring together scholars and activists from the DC area, New York, Australia, and Asia, to consider this controversial subject in its many theoretical and pragmatic dimensions. Using historical, political, feminist, and legal perspectives, the participants will both illuminate the past and facilitate greater understanding in the future. Among the speakers will be Asian-American women makers of documentary films; representatives from human rights organizations, cultural societies, and advocacy groups; and faculty members from both Georgetown University and American University.[46]

Beyond deliberately structuring the conference as an inclusive space open to the public and involving activists, academics, legal and political professionals, and students, the organizers set up and promoted awareness of exhibits and screenings of works by Asian and Asian American women that deal with the comfort women issue in various ways. For example, wccw's *Comfort Women* exhibit of photographs and documents, Taeko Tomiyama's artwork, and Miran Kim's paintings were displayed in the Intercultural Center of Georgetown University, where the conference was held; a description of and information on Mona Higuchi's *Bamboo Echoes,* a multimedia installation "Dedicated to the Comfort Women" at the Isabella Stewart Gardner Museum in Boston, was distributed; and the films of wccw, Choy, Byun Young-ju, Diana Lee and Grace Lee, and Hye Jung Park and J. T. Takagi were all shown.[47] As the above discussion should illustrate, Kim Yoon-Sim's testimony was central in creating a safe place since her testimony named unequivocally the crimes of Japanese military sexual slavery and therefore modeled a discussion of sexual violence. The conference clearly created a safe place for the diverse collaborative efforts of Asian American transnational feminists involved in coalition politics.

In addition to constructing a safe place, cultural autobiography also mines the border area or contact zone of coalition politics where diversity can operate in tension. The contact zone of the conference for Asian American transnational feminism was located in discussions of whether the comfort women system was unique to Japan, indicated something particular about Japanese culture, or needed to be addressed for the sake of the future of the Japanese state. In short, the volatile aspects of the coalition work involved loyalties to cultural and political nationalisms, which are ultimately challenged by the very foundations of transnational feminisms. At risk in such discussions was, on the one extreme, a type of cultural relativism that may have excused the criminal behavior of individuals and the Japanese government and, at the other extreme, a racism that could be used to rationalize all kinds of structures and global hierarchies of nations, including the atomic bombing of Japan by the United States. Rather than avoiding these obviously contentious issues, the conference organizers actually provoked or planned a space where the diversity of the coalition would operate in tension. Specifically, every speaker in the first session of the conference, as well as the keynote address by Mrs. Mutusko Miki, wife of Takeo Miki, former prime minister of Japan, addressed the role of nationalism in creating the system and the role of the nation-state in taking responsibility for the system. Anticipating and even encouraging the difficult work of coalition politics, the conference organizers arranged for a text in which the struggle of Asian American transnational feminism could be recognized and read.

That the discourse of nationalism occupies the border or contact zone of Asian American transnational feminist coalition politics should not be surprising if we recall the politics of transnational feminisms discussed at the beginning of this chapter, the legacy of feminist critique in Asian American discourse, and Reagon's observations about the relationship between cultural nationalism, identity politics, and coalition politics: "Of course the problem with the experiment [of identity politics] is that there ain't nobody in there but folk like you, which by implication means you wouldn't know what to do if you were running [the world] with all of the other people who are out there in the world. Now that's nationalism. I mean it's nurturing, but it is also nationalism. At a certain stage nationalism is crucial to people if you are to ever impact as a group in your own interest. Nationalism at another point becomes reactionary because it is totally inadequate for surviving in the world with many peoples."[48] Coalition can be defined as the "cooperative activities of people and groups with different points of view," and the different points of view or assumptions about nationalisms and national identity were the site of tension – the border area or contact zone – for the coalition active around the comfort women issue and explored in the cultural autobiography of Asian American transnational feminism.[49] Connected to an earlier period of interrogation into the limitations of cultural nationalism, the transnational feminism of Asian American women rigorously insists on a critique of the modernist forms of nationalism still holding currency in postmodernity.

Finally, the conference reveals possible characteristics of the collective form of cultural autobiography that are not necessarily present in the personal form of cultural autobiography: sharing a historical narrative and creating a bibliographic and documentary record. In several ways, the conference organizers provided fragmented bits of information that, taken together, presented a narrative delineating, though not in precise chronological order or with a sense of unity, the activism around the comfort women issue as a coalition involving Asian American transnational feminism. For example, everyone was provided with a folder containing the program agenda, a chronology of dates and events on comfort women issues, descriptions of the exhibits associated with the conference, a photocopy of a *Time* magazine article, and information on the wccw. Other materials made available included the United Nations Commission on Human Rights report on the issue of military sexual slavery in wartime, Yuki Tanaka's book *Hidden Horrors: Japanese War Crimes in World War II,* and wccw's video. In addition, the conference was structured so that there were no overlapping or simultaneous presentations, which clearly contributed to a sense of shared cultural history.

The first session of the conference contributed to the sense of a common historical text because it carefully set out the terms of the discourse of the transnational feminist coalition. Margaret Stetz began the session with the presentation "Wartime Sexual Violence against Women: A Feminist Response," which helped to set the tone for both the session and the conference. She described the long history of military sexual slavery, outlined the effects transnational feminist analysis has had in the activism around the comfort women system, and summarized how feminists have worked in various national locations and across national borders. Dai Sil Kim-Gibson's presentation, "Slaves of Sex: Comfort Women in World War II," provided a critique of the Japanese nation-state's role in institutionalizing the assault and colonization of women, pointing out that schools were pressured to provide girls for the Imperial army. Kim-Gibson's analysis of the ideological state apparatuses used to institute military sexual slavery suggested that other nation-states are complicit in disguising what happened: She described, for example, the Smithsonian Institute's Enola Gay exhibit (1995) as one that "buried Japan as a brutal aggressor" in World War II. A representative from Human Rights Watch extended Kim-Gibson's analysis by summarizing how the comfort women system should be approached from an international human rights perspective that forces nation-states to take responsibility and denies their ultimate power to claim authority over women. Tanaka's presentation, "Why 'Comfort Women?' " also analyzed the relationship between nationalism, patriarchy, and colonialism. Ending the session, Chris Simpson discussed the differences and similarities between mass rape and sexual slavery, which hinge on the nation-state's involvement in and maintenance of violence against women.[50] In short, the conference's structure ensured that those attending the conference would have a certain amount of shared information and be familiar with the discourse of Asian American transnational feminist coalition politics.

The "Comfort Women of World War II" conference included and was itself an Asian American transnational feminist text that illustrated the practices theorized by Grewal and Kaplan. In it and through it Asian American feminists worked in collaboration "to compare multiple, overlapping and discrete oppressions rather than to construct a theory of hegemonic oppression under a unified category of gender," and to "articulate the relationship of gender to scattered hegemonies such as global economic structures, patriarchal nationalisms, 'authentic' forms of tradition, local structures of domination, and legal-juridical oppression on multiple levels."[51] Further, the conference articulated a history of Asian American transnational feminism working toward the creation of new forms of community in postmodernity. Reading the conference as Asian American transnational feminist cultural production illuminates alternative modes of expression and narrative strategies that not only will help feminists identify decolonizing signification for women in different locations but will also help feminists recognize, understand, and practice coalition politics more readily.

Feminist politics needs the sophisticated theorization of coalition that contemporary Asian American transnational feminism often practices. Asian American feminism and the narratives that accompany it, such as the "Comfort Women of World War II" conference, are perhaps the ideal sites from which to learn about transnational coalitions, for they are built upon a conscious and critical construction of political community as coalition. The important work on panethnic coalition by Yen Le Espiritu and Sau-ling Cynthia Wong, for example, is widely understood in Asian American and other areas of ethnic studies, and feminist studies would benefit from further and careful attention to this background on coalition. At the same time, Asian American feminist discourse would benefit from situating itself more consistently in relation to feminist thought and politics. Too often the complicated gender and sexual politics within Asian American studies seem to fragment or dismiss Asian American feminism, defining it as assimilationist or as simply part of a racist liberal feminism, or subsuming it within an undifferentiated women of color feminist politics.[52] Asian American feminist politics is arguably a part of the vanguard of transnational feminist coalition, so building on this work is a promising project to which feminists committed to antiracism and anti-imperialism may look for instruction and inspiration.

NOTES

1. The conference, held at Georgetown University, September 30 to October 2, 1996, was organized by Bonnie Oh and Margaret Stetz and was cosponsored by Georgetown University, the Washington Coalition for Comfort Women Issues (WCCW), and The Korea Society. My analysis of the conference is informed by research in my book manuscript, "Asian American Women's Writing: Theorizing Transnationalism." I argue in it that Asian American women's writing theorizes a transnationalism that resists singular and static nationalist affiliation, resulting in cultural production that represents and can itself create alternative communities. My analysis of the conference is deeply indebted to the work of Caren Kaplan, who has been theorizing "transnational feminism" since at least the early 1990s. See especially Caren Kaplan, "Resisting Autobiography: Out-Law Genres and Transnational Feminist Subjects," in *De/Colonizing the Subject: The Politics of Gender in Women's Autobiography,* ed. Sidonie Smith and Julia Watson (Minneapolis: University of Minnesota Press, 1992), 115–38. Although I acknowledge the uneasy relationship many have with the term "Asian American," in this chapter I use it rather than "Asian Pacific American" because the conflation of indigenous peoples of Hawaii and other Pacific islands with people who are themselves immigrants or whose ancestors were immigrants to the United States seems to risk erasure of radically different histories, subjectivities, and politics. For a discussion of problematic terminology such as "comfort women," see Chin Sung Chung, "The Origin and Development of the Military Sexual Slavery Problem in Imperial Japan," *Positions* 5:1 (1997): 220–22.

2. Activism around the issue of Japanese military sexual slavery has largely involved the local and national organizations of women from Korea, the Philippines, and Japan. For an overview of individuals and national organizations, particularly in Korea, and international coalitions active in the movement to make Japan take responsibility for its military sexual slavery in the Pacific War, see Chung, "Origin and Development," 239–43. For an interesting discussion of Japanese hegemony in disseminating information about military sexual slavery, see Hyunah Yang, "Revisiting the Issue of Korean 'Military Comfort Women': The Question of Truth and Positionality," *Positions* 5:1 (1997): 54–57. For details of activism in the Philippines, see George Hicks, *The Comfort Women: Japan's Brutal Regime of Enforced Prostitution in the Second World War* (New York: W. W. Norton, 1995), 237–75, especially 242–45; Hyun Sook Kim, "History and Memory: The 'Comfort Women' Controversy," *Positions* 5:1 (1997): 94–96; and Yuki Tanaka, "Introduction," in Maria Rosa Henson's *Comfort Woman: A Filipina's Story of Prostitution and Slavery under the Japanese Military* (New York: Rowman & Littlefield, 1999), ix–xxi.

3. Feminists often mention, for example, work by Paula Gunn Allen, Gloria

Anzaldúa, Patricia Hill Collins, bell hooks, and Cherríe Moraga when thinking of U.S. women of color feminisms, and perhaps work by Gayatri Chakravorty Spivak or Chandra Talpade Mohanty when thinking of Third World feminisms. The contributions made by Asian American feminists, however, are more often than not disregarded. See Esther Ngan-ling Chow, "The Feminist Movement: Where Are All the Asian American Women?" in *Making Waves: An Anthology of Writings by and about Asian American Women,* ed. Asian American Women United of California (Boston: Beacon Press, 1989), 362–77; and Mitsuye Yamada, "Asian Pacific American Women and Feminism," in *This Bridge Called My Back: Writings by Radical Women of Color,* ed. Cherríe Moraga and Gloria Anzaldúa (New York: Kitchen Table: Women of Color Press, 1983), 71–75. Two important recent works in Asian American feminist critique make major contributions toward filling the gap that omissions in women studies and resistance within Asian American studies have combined to create: Sonia Shah, ed., *Dragon Ladies: Asian American Feminists Breathe Fire* (Boston: South End Press, 1997); and Rachel Lee, *The Americas of Asian American Literature: Gendered Fictions of Nation and Transition* (Princeton NJ: Princeton University Press, 1999).

4. I follow Benedict Anderson here to suggest that not only print culture but also other types of texts in postmodernity participate in imagining and constructing communities, especially those communities that do not rely upon patriarchal nationalisms. See Benedict Anderson, *Imagined Communities: Reflections on the Origin and Spread of Nationalism* (London: Verso, 1983).

5. Use of the term "transnational" is contested. Sometimes "transcultural" is also used to describe postmodern but resistant flows of culture. For three different discussions of the term "transnational," see Arif Dirlik, "The Postcolonial Aura: Third World Criticism in the Age of Capitalism," *Critical Inquiry* 20 (1994): 328–56; Caren Kaplan, "'A World Without Boundaries': The Body Shop's Trans/national Geographics," *Social Text* 43 (1995): 45–66; and Aihwa Ong, "Introduction: Flexible Citizenship: The Cultural Logics of Transnationality," in *Flexible Citizenship: The Cultural Logics of Transnationality* (Durham NC: Duke University Press, 1998), 1–26. The early formulation of transnational feminisms in the United States came from those who recognized that feminism could be as imperialist as other modernist projects. Gayatri Chakravorty Spivak's work, such as the essays collected in *In Other Worlds: Essays in Cultural Politics* (New York: Methuen, 1987), has been catalytic since the mid-1980s. Cynthia Enloe's *Bananas, Beaches, and Bases: Making Feminist Sense of International Politics* (Berkeley: University of California Press, 1989) points out that women and feminists have been complicit in colonization; Chandra Talpade Mohanty, Ann Russo, and Lourdes Torres's edited collection of essays, *Third World Women and the Politics of Feminism* (Bloomington: Indiana University Press, 1991),

has also been extremely influential in rethinking the challenges of collaboration between feminists in different locations.

6. Inderpal Grewal and Caren Kaplan, "Introduction: Transnational Feminist Practices and Questions of Postmodernity," in *Scattered Hegemonies: Postmodernity and Transnational Feminist Practices,* ed. Inderpal Grewal and Caren Kaplan (Minneapolis: University of Minnesota Press, 1994), 17–18.

7. Kaplan, "Resisting Autobiography," 116.

8. Grewal and Kaplan, "Transnational Feminist Practices and Questions of Postmodernity," 17. See also Sonia Shah, "Presenting the Blue Goddess: Toward a National, Pan-Asian Feminist Agenda," in *The State of Asian America: Activism and Resistance in the 1990s,* ed. Karin Aguilar-San Juan (Boston: South End Press, 1993), 147–58; and William Wei, *The Asian American Movement: A Social History* (Philadelphia: Temple University Press, 1993), for their discussions of the origins of the Asian American women's movement.

9. For a discussion of this pressure in relation to Asian American independent filmmaking, see Renee Tajima, "Moving the Image: Asian American Independent Filmmaking, 1970–1990," in *Moving the Image: Independent Asian Pacific American Media Arts,* ed. Russell Leong (Los Angeles: UCLA Asian American Studies Center, 1992), 11. For a discussion in the realm of literary studies, see King-Kok Cheung, "The Woman Warrior versus the Chinaman Pacific: Must a Chinese American Critic Choose between Feminism and Heroism?" in *Maxine Hong Kingston's The Woman Warrior: A Casebook,* ed. Sau-ling Cynthia Wong (New York: Oxford University Press, 1999), 113–33. See Yen Le Espiritu, *Asian American Panethnicity: Bridging Institutions and Identities* (Philadelphia: Temple University Press, 1992), 1–52, for a discussion of the panethnicity of Asian American politics and identity and the first usage of the term "Asian American."

10. See Cheung, "The Woman Warrior versus the Chinaman Pacific"; Elaine Kim, "'Such Opposite Creatures': Men and Women in Asian American Literature," *Michigan Quarterly Review* (winter 1990): 68–93; Lisa Lowe, "Heterogeneity, Hybridity, Multiplicity: Marking Asian American Differences," *Diaspora* 1:1 (1991): 24–44; and Sau-ling Cynthia Wong, *Reading Asian American Literature: From Necessity to Extravagance* (Princeton: Princeton University Press, 1993), for analyses of the Frank Chin/Maxine Hong Kingston debate and tensions about feminist critique between Asian American women and men.

11. Lisa Lowe, "Work, Immigration, Gender: Asian 'American' Women," in *Making More Waves: New Writing by Asian American Women,* ed. Elaine H. Kim, Lilia V. Villanueva, and Asian Women United of California (Boston: Beacon Press, 1997), 273, and "Work, Immigration, Gender: Asian 'American' Women," in *Immigrant Acts: On Asian American Cultural Politics* (Durham NC: Duke University Press, 1996),

158, 165. Echoing Kaplan's essay "Resisting Autobiography," Lowe's reading "seeks to understand Asian American cultural production critically and broadly to interpret the interconnections between testimony, personal narrative, oral history, literature, film, visual arts, and other cultural forms as sites through which subject, community, and struggle are signified and mediated" (*Immigrant Acts,* 157). Lowe's negotiation of the unifying forces in Asian American studies is ironic because her critical intervention in the field characteristically challenges homogenizing paradigms in Asian American studies. For a critical review of *Immigrant Acts,* see Viet Thanh Nguyen, "Asian America and American Studies: Aliens, Citizens, and Cultural Work," *American Quarterly* 50:3 (1998): 626–35.

12. Women of various Asian American ethnic subgroups were certainly involved in international issues before the 1960s, but it may be anachronistic to call this activism "Asian American," since the term was not in currency until the late 1960s. For a basic discussion of the international perspective of the early Asian American movement, the antiwar movement, and Asian American women's engagement with Marxist ideology, see Wei, *The Asian American Movement,* 22–30, 37–43, and 72–81.

13. Kaplan, "Resisting Autobiography," 116–19. Kaplan points out that the six types of outlaw genres that she reviews are not "a comprehensive list or complete map of global literary production that refers to the 'autobiographical' tradition" but simply indicate "a variety of reading and writing strategies in operation as the law of genre intersects with contemporary postcolonial, transnational conditions" (119). For discussion of how literary conventions of genre contain and enable hybrid autobiographical texts, see Jacques Derrida, "The Law of Genre," *Critical Inquiry* 7 (1981): 55–81; and Laura Marcus, "The Law of Genre," in *Auto/Biographical Discourse: Theory, Criticism, Practice* (New York: Manchester University Press, 1994), 229–72.

14. Kaplan, "Resisting Autobiography," 119–22, 135. "The essential categories of autobiography," according to Kaplan, "especially as adopted by Western feminism in the last twenty years – the revelation of individuality, the chronological unfolding of a life, reflections and confessions, the recovery and assertion of suppressed identity – are utilized, reworked and even abandoned" (122).

15. Kaplan, "Resisting Autobiography," 136, 122, 134, 125. See also Caren Kaplan, "The Politics of Location as a Transnational Feminist Critical Practice," in Grewal and Kaplan, *Scattered Hegemonies,* 137–52.

16. There are numerous autobiographical texts by Asian American women that can be examined as possible outlaw genres. Recent publications that represent Asian American immigrant subjects might be the most obvious candidates for inclusion in autobiographical versions of transnational feminist cultural production. See, for example, Le Ly Hayslip with Jay Wurts, *When Heaven and Earth Changed Places: A Vietnamese Woman's Journey from War to Peace* (New York: Plume, 1990); Elaine H.

Kim and Eui-Young Yu, eds., *East to America: Korean American Life Stories* (New York: New Press, 1996); and Sucheng Chan, ed., *Hmong Means Free: Life in Laos and America* (Philadelphia: Temple University Press, 1994). For discussion of Hayslip's work in a transnational frame, see Viet Thanh Nguyen, "Representing Reconciliation: Le Ly Hayslip and the Victimized Body," *Positions* 5:2 (1997): 605–41; and Leslie Bow, "Le Ly Hayslip's Bad (Girl) Karma: Sexuality, National Allegory, and the Politics of Neutrality," *Prose Studies* 17:1 (1994): 141–60. A considerable body of superior critical work on Asian American women's autobiography exists, and much of it considers the innovative or hybrid nature of certain texts. On Theresa Hak Kyung Cha's *Dictée* (Berkeley: Third Woman Press, 1995), see the excellent set of essays by Laura Hyun Yi Kang, Elaine Kim, Lisa Lowe, and Shelly Wong in *Writing Self, Writing Nation: A Collection of Essays on Dictée by Theresa Hak Kyung Cha,* ed. Elaine Kim and Norma Alarcón (Berkeley: Third Woman Press, 1994). On Maxine Hone Kingston's *The Woman Warrior: Memoirs of a Girlhood Among Ghosts* (New York: Vintage, 1976), see, for example, Sau-ling Cynthia Wong, "Autobiography as Guided Chinatown Tour," in *Multicultural Autobiography: American Lives,* ed. James Robert Payne (Knoxville: University of Tennessee Press, 1996), 248–79; and Lee Quinby, "The Subject of Memoirs: *The Woman Warrior*'s Technology of Ideographic Selfhood," in Smith and Watson, *De/Colonizing the Subject,* 297–320. For analysis of Monica Sone's *Nisei Daughter* (Seattle: University of Washington Press, 1979), see Lisa Lowe, "Canon, Institutionalization, Identity: Contradictions for Asian American Studies," in *The Ethnic Canon: Histories, Institutions, and Interventions,* ed. David Palumbo-Liu (Minneapolis: University of Minnesota Press, 1995), 48–68. For consideration of Meena Alexander's *Fault Lines* (New York: The Feminist Press, 1993), see Samir Dayal, "Min(d)ing the Gap: South Asian Americans and Diaspora," in *A Part, Yet Apart: South Asians in Asian America,* ed. Lavina Dhingra Shankar and Rajini Srikanth (Philadelphia: Temple University Press, 1998), 235–65. For a reading of Jade Snow Wong's *Fifth Chinese Daughter* (New York: Harper, 1945) as autobiography, see Anne E. Goldman, "'I Yam What I Yam': Cooking, Culture, and Colonialism," in Smith and Watson, *De/Colonizing the Subject,* 169–95.

17. Kim Yoon-Sim, "Testimony," presented at the "Comfort Women of World War II: Legacy and Lessons" conference, Georgetown University, Washington, DC, September 30, 1996; and Christine Choy, dir., *In the Name of the Emperor* (Filmmakers Library, 1996).

18. For a discussion of testimony as dialogic in nature, see Norma Field, "War and Apology: Japan, Asia, the Fiftieth, and After," *Positions* 5:1 (1997): 1–49.

19. John Beverley, "The Margin at the Center: On *Testimonio* (Testimonial Narrative)," in Smith and Watson, *De/Colonizing the Subject,* 94. Beverley remarks that his definition should be considered "at best provisional, and at worst repressive"

because testimonial is "by nature a protean and demotic form not yet subject to legislation by a normative literary establishment" (93).

20. Field, "War and Apology," 36.

21. See Robert Carr, "Crossing the First World/Third World Divides: Testimonial, Transnational Feminisms, and the Postmodern Condition," in Grewal and Kaplan, *Scattered Hegemonies,* 153–72. Carr is critical of Beverley's aestheticization of testimonial and justifiably concerned with the appropriation and commodification of testimonials; he notes that Rigoberta Menchú's *I, Rigoberta Menchú: An Indian Woman in Guatemala,* ed. Elizabeth Burgos-Debray, trans. Ann Wright (London: Verso, 1984) offers a possible compromise to the problem of the consumption of testimonial in the global marketplace. In particular, Carr supports a suggestion that audio tapes of Menchú's testimonial be produced rather than the translated, transcribed, printed text. For a critical discussion of the relation between the narrator/informant and the recorder/inquisitor/scribe in testimonial, see Doris Sommer, "No Secrets: Rigoberta's Guarded Truth," *Women's Studies* 20:1 (1991): 51–72.

22. There was no registration fee or fees of any kind for the conference. The testimony was mediated through an interpreter, Sangmie Choi Schellstede, vice president of wccw and a U.S. government interpreter.

23. Beverley, "The Margin at the Center," 96; and Kaplan, "Resisting Autobiography," 125. For discussion of the problem of commodification, see also Carr, "Crossing the First World/Third World Divides"; Field, "War and Apology"; and Dai Sil Kim-Gibson, "They Are Our Grandmas," *Positions* 5:1 (1997): 255–74.

24. Kaplan, "Resisting Autobiography," 123.

25. The presence of the media is a complicated issue since, as Beverly points out, part of the purpose of testimonial is to heighten awareness of a particular group's oppression or struggle. The wccw is a nonprofit, nonpartisan, education organization based in the Washington DC area and run by "volunteers of every nationality and diverse points of view." According to the information given out at the conference, media attention has been on the wccw agenda since its inception. The efforts to heighten awareness have no doubt played a major role in the fight for accountability. Moreover, the value that results from the kind of exposure wccw desires should be distinguished from that extracted from testimonials by First World academics, discussed by Carr, and certainly from the kind of value extracted by journalists who pay women for their stories. See Field, "War and Apology," 26–27.

26. According to Beverley, the "situation of the narration in *testimonio* has to involve an urgency to communicate, a problem of repression, poverty, subalternity, imprisonment, struggle for survival, implicated in the act of narration itself" ("The Margin at the Center," 94). See also Kim, "History and Memory," for a discussion of the collective and political nature of former comfort women's stories.

27. Beverley, "The Margin at the Center," 95.

28. Researchers estimate that of the more than two hundred thousand women exploited by the comfort women system, 80 percent to 90 percent were Korean, although Burmese, Chinese, Dutch, Filipina, Indonesian, Japanese, Malaysian, Manchurian, Taiwanese, Thai, and Vietnamese women were also victimized. See Chung, "Origin and Development," 227–32; Yuki Tanaka, *Hidden Horrors: Japanese War Crimes in World War II* (Boulder CO: Westview Press, 1996), 99; and Yang, "Revisiting the Issue of Korean 'Military Comfort Women,'" 57.

29. Filipinas and Filipina Americans have been very active in the collective international organization Gabriela and in the Task Force on Filipino Comfort Women. See Sheila Coronel and Ninotcka Rosca, "For the Boys: Filipinas Expose Years of Sexual Slavery by the U.S. and Japan," *Ms.*, November/December 1993, 10–15; Hicks, *The Comfort Women*, 242–45; and Tanaka, "Introduction."

30. Carr, "Crossing the First World/Third World Divides," 157.

31. I recognize the difficulty of arranging for several former comfort women to speak at the same place and time. See Beverley's discussion of polyphonic testimonial ("The Margin at the Center," 96) as well as Carr's discussion of Sistren and Honor Ford-Smith's *Lionheart Gal: Life Stories of Jamaican Women* (London: Women's Press, 1986) in "Crossing the First World/Third World Divides," 163–66.

32. Kim, "History and Memory," 102.

33. Beverley, "The Margin at the Center," 97.

34. For details on the establishment of "comfort stations," see Chung, "Origin and Development," 223–24; Hicks, *The Comfort Women*, 45–65; and Tanaka, *Hidden Horrors*, 79–109.

35. Christine Choy, remarks prior to and following the screening of *In the Name of the Emperor*, "Comfort Women of World War II: Legacy and Lessons" conference, Georgetown University, Washington DC, September 30, 1996.

36. Field, "War and Apology," 34; Beverley, "The Margin at the Center," 103. Beverley also points out that testimonial "has been important in maintaining and developing the practice of international human rights and solidarity movements" (99).

37. Some of Choy's other films also assign the viewer this juridical function, including Christine Choy, dir., *Who Killed Vicent Chin?* (Filmmakers Library, 1988); and Christine Choy and Dai Sil Kim-Gibson, dirs., *Sa-I-Gu: From Korean Women's Perspectives* (Cross Current Media, 1993). In *Who Killed Vincent Chin?* Choy reviews the case of a Chinese American man beaten to death by disgruntled auto workers in Detroit; *Sa-I-Gu* deals with the interethnic conflicts following the Rodney King verdict.

38. For a discussion of the erasure of the subaltern female subject between com-

peting discourses, see Gayatri Chakravorty Spivak, "Can the Subaltern Speak?" in *Marxism and the Interpretation of Culture,* ed. Cary Nelson and Lawrence Grossberg (Urbana: University of Illinois Press, 1988), 271–313.

39. Kaplan, "Resisting Autobiography," 132. See bell hooks, "Writing Autobiography," in her *Talking Back: Thinking Feminist, Thinking Black* (Boston: South End Press, 1989), 155–56; and Kaplan's discussion of hooks's essay in "Resisting Autobiography," 130–32.

40. Kaplan, "Resisting Autobiography," 132.

41. Bernice Johnson Reagon, "Coalition Politics: Turning the Century," in *Home Girls: A Black Feminist Anthology,* ed. Barbara Smith (New York: Kitchen Table: Women of Color Press, 1983), 357, 367; and Kaplan, "Resisting Autobiography," 132.

42. Kaplan, "Resisting Autobiography," 132.

43. Mary Crow Dog and Richard Erdoes, *Lakota Woman* (New York: Grove Weidenfeld, 1990); and Pratibha Parmar, dir., *Warrior Marks* (Women Make Movies, 1993). Other texts that fit this category include Ché Guevara, *Reminiscences of the Cuban Revolutionary War,* trans. Victoria Ortiz (New York: Monthly Review Press, 1968); Audre Lorde, *Zami: A New Spelling of My Name* (Freedom CA: Crossing Press, 1982); Frank Chin et al., eds., *Aiiieeeee!: An Anthology of Asian American Writers* (Washington DC: Howard University Press, 1974); Asian Women United of California, *Making Waves;* Luis Puenzo, dir., *The Official Story* (Almi Pictures, 1986); Pratibha Parmar, dir., *A Place of Rage* (Women Make Movies, 1991); Luis Valdez's *Teatro Campesino;* Spiderwoman Theater; and the 1995 NGOs and Fourth World Conference for Women in Beijing. Just as the Comfort Women of World War II conference is not limited to a cultural autobiography of Asian American transnational feminism, these examples may also participate in more than one discourse of resistance.

44. See Reagon, "Coalition Politics," 356–61. For a discussion of the contact zone, community, and the classroom, see also Mary Louise Pratt, "Arts of the Contact Zone," in *Ways of Reading: An Anthology for Writers,* ed. David Bartholomae and Anthony Petrosky (Boston: Bedford Books, 1993).

45. For an analysis of the racism of Japanese military sexual slavery, see Yang, "Revisiting the Issue of Korean 'Military Comfort Women,' " 60–66; and Kim, "History and Memory," 87–89.

46. The "Comfort Women of World War II: Historical Legacy and Lessons," http://www.georgetown.edu/faculty/stetzm/women.html.

47. The various screenings included *Comfort Women,* by WCCW; *In the Name of the Emperor,* by Christine Choy; *Murmuring,* by Byun Young-ja; *Camp Arirang,* by Diana Lee and Grace Lee; and *The Women Outside,* by Hye Jung Park and J. T. Takagi.

48. Reagon, "Coalition Politics," 358.

49. Kaplan, "Resisting Autobiography," 132.

50. All of these presentations and discussions took place on September 30, 1996. For a detailed discussion of the U.S. role in the erasure of Japanese responsibility for the suffering of non-Japanese Asians, see Field, "War and Apology."

51. Grewal and Kaplan, "Transnational Feminist Practices and Questions of Postmodernity," 17.

52. For a discussion of how Asian American sexual politics is exaggerated in the popular imagination, see Cheun, "The Woman Warrior versus the Chinaman Pacific," 116. See also Espiritu, *Asian American Panethnicity*; and Wong, *Reading Asian American Literature*.

Frontiers 21:1/2 (2000): 29–54.

The Cost of Caring

The Social Reproductive Labor of Filipina Live-in Home Health Caregivers

CHARLENE TUNG

The movement of peoples across national borders is not a new phenomenon, but with the recent upsurge in discussions about transnationalism and globalization along with increasingly strict immigration laws and efforts to enforce borders, it is a phenomenon that needs to be addressed. While the growth of multinational corporations, such as U.S. corporations in Mexico and other so-called developing countries, including the Philippines, is evidence of a more free circulation of goods and commodities, increasingly restrictive immigration policies are evidence of a less open circulation of people. People are welcomed into countries, are border-crossers, only insofar as they meet the need for "cheap labor" and at the same time produce no strain on the resources of the "host" country. As a result, not only are such migrant workers overlooked by policy makers (governmental and nonprofits), but also by the wider public, leaving their lives and especially the benefits of their work invisible. The inevitable result is that the public overlooks the people, increasingly women, who live and work at the center of the debates. This chapter examines one specific group of these migrant workers: Filipina domestic workers in southern California employed as live-in home health caregivers for the elderly.

While Filipina/o[1] registered nurses (RNs) are highly visible, having been trained and recruited specifically for service in Canada and the United States, many researchers and community activists alike are unaware of the burgeoning numbers of Filipina non-RNs who provide elderly care. While the Filipina women migrant workers to the United States are not under contract as they are in certain Middle Eastern, East Asian, and European nations, they endure similar hardships and living conditions. Filipina migrant domestic workers in the United States care for homes and children, but they are even more likely to care for the terminally ill and the elderly. These caregivers, mainly women, assume not only the companionate and light medical care of elderly persons but also the housekeeping, including cooking and grocery shopping.

The labor of transnational migrant Filipinas lacks visibility within academic circles for a number of reasons ranging from the tendency of the international development literature to overlook women's outmigration as a response to developing nations' globalization strategies, to an unreflective foregrounding of the work of male migrants, to assumptions that Filipina migration to the United States must be primarily composed of the migration of professional nurses.[2] Filipina live-in elderly caregivers, to use the term the women use to describe themselves, especially face such multiple challenges to their visibility.[3]

The invisibility of Filipina transmigrant live-in elderly caregivers is fueled additionally by the nature of the work itself. The labor of Filipina women and the subsequent benefits afforded to U.S. elderly citizens remain invisible not only because the women are often undocumented migrant workers, but also because the work they engage in takes place within the confines of private homes, as part of the informal economy, and squarely within the world of the most invisible U.S. population aside from children: the elderly. Furthermore, they are involved in what is stereotypically considered "women's work," or that which is built upon women's "natural" inclination toward caring and relational thinking. Feminist scholars have worked to redefine this "natural" inclination as labor, specifically as social reproductive labor, or what Evelyn Nakano Glenn defines as the "array of activities and relationships involved in maintaining people both on a daily basis and intergenerationally."[4]

The goal of this chapter is to begin to address the invisibility of these women by sharing the social reproductive labor that shapes their lives.[5] I focus on this labor to highlight both the enduring nature of women's roles as social reproductive laborers in this era of globalization and the continuing undervaluation of this labor. The emotional and physical labor of Filipina migrants caring for the elderly in southern California is as clear a testament to the enduring ideology of a woman's place in this transnational age as it is a testament to women's strength of will to provide for their families.

I begin with a short overview of why we ought to pay some attention to these Filipina caregivers for the elderly and then present a typical profile of who these women are. Next, in order to set the background for their work and life experiences, I briefly touch on the gendered and ethnic-racial division of labor in the United States. Third, I introduce several women and their daily work lives as they engage in physical and emotional labor both as mothers from afar and as caregivers locally. And finally I suggest that an inherently uneven power dynamic exists between employer and employee not simply on the basis of race, ethnicity, migration, and class, as might be expected, but as a result of the emotional labor invested. The Filipina caregivers, in some ways, contribute to their own disempowerment through the offering up of their emotional labor, willingly subverting their own wages and working conditions under certain circumstances.

WHY STUDY FILIPINA LIVE-IN ELDERLY CAREGIVERS?

At least four reasons underlie the larger project upon which this chapter is based. I share them below in order to briefly provide the background for the Filipina migrants' placement in U.S. society:

1. The demand for caregivers of the elderly in the United States is going to increase in the coming decade. Hospitals, reacting in part to rising insurance costs, are quick to release patients who then turn increasingly to in-home care. In addition, demographic projections indicate that an estimated 17 percent of the population will be over the age of sixty-five by the year 2020. Furthermore, the number of elderly persons requiring in-home care is projected to increase from 2.5 million in 1984 to 6.5 million by the year 2025.[6] In California alone the number of people over the age of sixty-five, almost five million now, is expected to double by 2020. The number of older elderly – those over the age of eighty-five – is expected to quadruple.[7] The California Employment Development Division estimates that nurses aides and home health aides will be the fastest growing occupations into the next decade. These trends form a growing demand and a stable economic niche for Filipinas, particularly in California.

2. While Filipina/o Americans total more than 1.4 million and are estimated to become the largest Asian American population in the year 2000 (as well as the second largest immigrant group behind Mexicans), there has been a dearth of research on their lives. The latest figures show that 52 percent of all U.S. Filipinos reside in California.[8] While over 80 percent of Filipinas/os in the United States are foreign-born immigrants and over 60 percent are women, little is known about how these immigrant women are faring.

3. Filipina women workers have largely been overlooked in the research

and in public policy considerations because of the false impression that Filipinas/os (and Asian Americans in general) are middle- and upper-class professionals and that Filipinas, in particular, are professional nurses.

4. Filipina elderly caregivers in the United States are part of the over six million overseas Filipina/o transmigrant workers, both contracted and not, who support the Philippine government and its forty-billion-dollar debt by sending back at least three billion dollars per year.[9] At least 60 percent of these overseas workers are women.[10]

WHO ARE FILIPINA ELDERLY CAREGIVERS?

Given that there are as yet no published studies on Filipina live-in elderly caregivers, what I share is from my research as well as estimates from Los Angeles Filipina/o community workers and from the workers themselves. Records have not been kept, for example, of how many Filipinas are working in convalescent, board and care, or nursing homes. Live-in workers, those who live with their patients, even more easily escape detection. This is not by accident, because many are undocumented, having overstayed either visitor or work visas. One caregiver estimated that in the Los Angeles area at least three-fourths of the caregivers for the elderly were Filipinas. This view is supported anecdotally by community members, Filipina/o social service agencies, and Filipina/o-owned board and care facilities. Informal interviews with Filipina health care workers reveal an extensive network of Filipinas who do in-home elderly care work. In fact, jobs are often obtained through such social networks.[11] For example, a Filipina registered nurse working in a hospital may know of a patient about to be discharged, then tell a caregiver friend, who contacts the patient directly.

Precise numbers of live-in Filipina elderly caregivers are difficult to come by. As part of the informal economy these "unaffiliated providers," as feminist sociologists Emily Abel and Margaret Nelson have called them, are difficult to track.[12] And the reasons are clear. These live-in caregivers often provide care "off the books" or "under the table." While it may be possible to survey the number of licensed board and care facilities or home health care agencies providing such services, such studies have not yet been conducted to my knowledge; furthermore, even if such figures were available they would likely provide only a glimpse into the extent of the work. Second, as Abel and Nelson point out, "many unaffiliated providers may offer more than a single service to an employer," making census designations inaccurate. For example, live-in caregivers frequently provide a combination of medical, companionate, and housekeeping services such as gardening, cleaning, and cooking.[13]

The following description is a composite of a live-in worker drawn from the interviews I conducted:

Marie, 38, arrived in the United States in 1990, leaving her two children in the Philippines. She was not trained as a nurse prior to her arrival in the States, but rather earned her B.A. degree in business. In the United States, she has held seven caregiver positions since 1990 with salaries ranging from five dollars an hour for a forty-hour workweek in a convalescent home, where she was responsible for ten to twelve patients, to three dollars an hour working six days per week, on-call twenty-four hours a day, in a private home. When she worked in a convalescent home, she had to take another job on weekends, usually providing relief for a Filipina live-in caregiver who was taking her day off. For this, Marie would earn an additional fifty dollars. She sends back to the Philippines over 75 percent of her pay. In her current job as a live-in caregiver, Marie is guaranteed no overtime pay, breaks, or vacation. She has no health insurance of any kind. Thus, ironically, she provides health care but has none herself. She plans on staying at least another five years in order to finance her youngest child through high school. When she left the Philippines in 1990, her youngest was six years old. The next time Marie will see her, she will be a young woman of eighteen. She has missed her oldest child's high school graduation and marriage as well as the birth of her first grandchild.

It is within and under these conditions that Marie and women like her must provide care for the elderly.

A WOMAN'S PLACE

Feminist scholars in a range of fields have long written about the false dichotomy between the public realm (marked as masculine) and the private realm (marked as feminine). Women were "naturally" supposed to remain in the private realm, providing care for children, spouse, and the elderly free of charge. Men were just as "naturally" supposed to work outside the home, providing for the family financially. This doctrine of separate spheres, which took hold in the latter part of the eighteenth century, was upheld through legal structures as well. For example, in the 1872 Supreme Court case *Bradwell v. Illinois,* Justice Bradley stated with certainty that the "paramount destiny and mission of women are to fulfill the noble and benign offices of wife and mother."[14]

While this decision is widely dismissed today, and the majority of women and mothers (both white and of color) in the United States are employed outside the home, its ideology remains strong, both nationally and transnationally. Most women continue to work the "second shift" upon arriving home, taking charge of the household upkeep, child care arrangements, and elderly care.[15] Those who are more affluent may hire transmigrant women to cover those responsibilities as paid domestic workers. The separate sphere ideology and its corresponding reality make recognition of domestic work *as work* difficult. It constructs domestic work, insofar as it is acknowledged at all, as women's work and trivializes the work as "natural" and unskilled – devaluing not only the work, but the worker as well.[16]

Furthermore, domestic work, both paid and unpaid, is racialized.[17] Historically as well as in the present, women of color have served as domestic workers in the United States.[18] Depending on class and geographic region, the cult of domesticity was rarely a reality for U.S women of color.[19] According to Glenn, paid domestic workers "were not expected or allowed to be full-time mothers; nor did circumstances allow them even to harbor the illusion."[20] In this way, not only was women of color's *labor* devalued but also their worth as mothers. In the case of live-in elderly care, more privileged white women benefit directly from the labor of less privileged women, usually women of color.[21] As Glenn points out, the concept of mothering and caregiving as "universally women's work disguises the fact that it is further subdivided so that different aspects of caring labor are assigned to different groups of women. . . . *Often the women who perform these services are mothers themselves; yet they are forced to neglect their own children and families to take care of other women's children or elderly parents.*"[22] Here Glenn draws attention to the fact that women of color, who are disproportionately found in the lower echelons of health care as nurses aides and caregivers, are sacrificing their own personal reproductive labor (in the sense of mothering and taking care of their own children or elderly parents) for the sake of other, more affluent, women here in the United States.

As providers of care for the elderly, Filipinas find their work and worth defined within these parameters. Paid caregiving is a stark illustration of the place held by women of color within the U.S. political economy. This social reproductive labor, Glenn notes, includes "activities such as purchasing household goods, preparing and serving food, laundering and repairing clothing, maintaining furnishing and appliances, socializing children, *providing care and emotional support for adults, and maintaining kin and community ties.*"[23] This definition fully encompasses the myriad of duties that make up the elderly caregiver's life. Those are the activities – paid, unpaid, and underpaid – that Filipina live-in caregivers are involved in on a daily basis, both as mothers from afar and in their work lives as caregivers for the elderly.

MOTHERING FROM AFAR

I'm all excited about my trip and looking forward to hugging and kissing and being with my children once again. I can't help having these BIG questions in my head, how we're all gonna react again toward each other after having been separate for so long. We all sounded good together in all our long distance phone conversations, but would it be as warm and loving when we will be face to face this time? Will I be a strict or lenient or tolerant mom in their presence? Will I bore them or will they me? Will I make it out over there financially?

[Having a new caregiver] is going to be very difficult for [my patient] and the new caregiver as well. . . . I feel sad for [my patient] because I know she's going to have a hard time [when I leave]. She'll miss me, and, of course, I'll miss her. And, too, I feel bad for the family. They're going to feel unsure about [my] replacement.[24]

These excerpts are from the correspondence and interview of a caregiver prior to a permanent return to the Philippines after a seven-year absence from her five school-aged children. She was a live-in caregiver throughout most of her time in the United States. The remarks above illustrate the breadth of emotional labor involved in caregiving, particularly while the women negotiate lives both in the United States and the Philippines.

The mental image of Filipinas leaving their children, spouses, and families behind to care for others around the world is a powerful one. Leaving one's own children goes against popular notions in this country of what it means to be a "good mother." One caregiver remarked, "To see us working like this, [Americans] would always say, 'how could you stand that? How could you leave your children and work straight like that?' They never can understand."

Similar to the Latina immigrant/migrant mothers in other studies,[25] the Filipinas in my study, rather than viewing mothering from afar as incompatible with traditional notions of motherhood, saw themselves as merely extending their family obligations by raising their families' living standard. That is, from their viewpoint, they were better mothers for being better able to provide financially for their families. Almost without exception, the live-in workers interviewed explained their presence in the United States in reference to their roles as providers for their families.[26] They were in the

United States in order to earn enough money to fund their children through high school or, for some, college in the Philippines.

The necessity of mothering from afar, not unexpectedly, presented difficulties for the women. One woman, whose two children were four and ten when she left them in the care of her parents, said, "It's worth it, you know, because I can give [them] whatever [they] like. Not really everything, because I'm not there, but I can send them to good schools. I can buy them what they like. . . . I miss their growing up. But what can I do? I sacrifice." Another woman, a mother of five, said, "You always have that guilty feeling. You know you're supposed to be there, beside them. But then, you cannot. . . . You know you need the money, so you just have to work very hard." For the women I spoke to, securing a future for their children by being able to provide for them financially far outweighed any belief that quality mothering was necessarily achieved only by living with their young children.

The women I interviewed used several strategies for maintaining contact with their children and families. A visit to the Philippines was not an option any of the women in this study pursued; release time was difficult to secure and the plane fare out of reach for most women. In the intervening five- to ten-year absences, packages and phone calls were the most common methods the women used to maintain ties to their children. Because as live-in caregivers they were provided room and board, the women sent, on average, well over 75 percent of their pay home. As alternatives to the U.S. and Philippine postal services, money was usually sent back through foreign exchanges, while care packages were often sent through particular shipping companies that cater to Filipina/o Americans. Alternatively, for those caregivers who were more closely linked with a larger Filipina/o community in the United States, smaller gifts and money were hand carried by other hometown members returning to the Philippines for a visit.

Women maintained their mothering most often through phone calls, though a few chose to write letters. One caregiver related, "I don't know, actually, the life of my kids. That's the problem of Filipinas living here. We don't know if they will tell us the truth of the matter." So the women would call not only to speak to their children, but also to other family members, usually mothers or sisters, in order to match stories. With their children, the women focused their phone calls on providing advice and encouragement about schooling. All the women maintained weekly contact, even more when they initially arrived. Consequently, their phone bills were enormous, ranging from $150 to $400 per month. While this may sound counterproductive to their stated goal of saving money to send home, it is a cost they were more than willing to incur. The phone calls, as far as the women in this study were concerned, were not an optional expense; they were necessary in order to mother their children.

And while the term mothering is generally thought to refer only to women's relationships with their children, it also accurately describes what occurs between women and the elderly. As one live-in caregiver explained, "I've been in this job for two and a half years and, as far as I'm concerned, it's all a matter of common sense. I mean, I've [brought up] four kids. And taking care of young children or sick people . . . if you're sensible enough, if you meet problems along the way, you use your 'common sense.'" Following this caregiver's lead in connecting mothering and caring for the elderly, I now turn to illustrating in more detail how caring and emotional labor is central to Filipinas' lives as caregivers to the elderly, for while physical labor and daily work hours can be quantified and easily detailed, it is the emotional labor and investment that is much more difficult to identify and measure.

CARING FOR THE ELDERLY

The extraction, manipulation, and use of emotional labor is commonplace in women's work generally, but especially in the so-called caring professions.[27] In Arlie Russell Hochschild's research on flight attendants and other women service workers, she found that "emotional labor," or an "emotional style of service," was provided by women in exchange for wages.[28] Borrowing from Hochschild's work, I define "emotional labor" as the conscious or unconscious induction and suppression of feelings in order to fulfill the psychological, physical, or monetary needs of both the workers and employers. For the Filipina caregivers in this study, it was the emotional labor required and freely (in more ways than one) given that distinguished them from other domestic workers. Prior researchers have found that most women domestic workers resist attempts by employers to make them feel like "one of the family."[29] Rather than feeling closer to their employers, most women feel that they are being emotionally manipulated. However, this was not so for Filipina live-in caregivers who expressed no reluctance to being made "part of the family." In fact, the Filipina workers took the lead on this, repeatedly expressing, "I treat her as if she's my mother" and "We treat them as our own. . . . It's not just care, we give them love."

As an elderly person's sole companion, Filipina live-in caregivers are called upon to provide far more than light medical service or cooking and cleaning skills; they must provide caring as well. As Abel and Nelson emphasize, caregiving involves "love as well as labor, 'caring for' while 'caring about.'"[30] In an effort to make Filipina caregivers' emotional and physical work more visible, these next sections set out to take us through a typical day for a live-in caregiver with a mobile patient free of dementia, and then for a caregiver with a bedridden patient suffering from dementia. I conclude by suggesting several ways in which the level of emotional labor these women expended inadvertently contributed to the undervaluing of their own labor.

"YOU HAVE TO UNDERSTAND THIS KIND OF JOB, YOU'RE LIKE A CAGED WORKER"

The everyday lives of caregivers for the elderly are filled with both medical and mundane activities such as administering medicines, treating bedsores, bathing patients, helping patients brush their teeth, and watching TV; for those with healthier patients, daily activities may include trips to churches and synagogues, community senior centers, and trips to the area pool and Jacuzzi. The activities and the tempo of the days are primarily patient driven. The lives of the caregivers, it will become clear, are acutely tied to their patients – physically and emotionally.

Companionate Care: Terry

Terry has spent almost every day for the past two years with her patient, Esther. When I first met the two of them Esther was ninety years old and very active. She was able to walk with a cane on her own and dress and bathe herself, for example. The two went on walks almost every day and made it a point to leave the house together for some reason: to see a movie, do the grocery shopping, or visit the senior center in town. Although active, Esther still required assistance. As Terry explained the situation when she began working for Esther following Esther's hospital stay, "If she were left to her own resources, she wouldn't make it. If she has to cook, she [wouldn't] remember to turn the stove off. And it would be dangerous for her. She could trip or have boiling water there and burn herself." Consequently, Terry did the cooking and cleaning, assisted in physical therapy, administered pills, and, as she put it, "I exercise Esther's mind." She did this by asking Esther what they had done "this morning" and "yesterday," as well as about Esther's childhood experiences. Theirs was one of the more companionable relationships I came across, owing in large part to Esther's ability to converse and move about. She was able to clearly articulate her appreciation to Terry. On her part, Terry said she cared for Esther very much as she would care for her own mother.

Beyond the medication dispensing, physical therapy, and personal care duties, in situations where patients are relatively clear thinking and mobile, keeping them company is indeed central to the job. Serving as companions is also what can be one of the most demanding aspects of the job, for live-in caregivers in particular. I learned that living with Esther meant that things ran on a logic all their own, or rather, all the patient's own.

August 12, 1997. After a morning being interviewed, Terry invites me to stay for lunch. Terry prefers I stay with Esther while she makes us egg salad, Spam, and tomato sandwiches on toast with a slice of kosher dill pickle on the side. While Terry prepares the food, I go into the living room where Esther is seated at a folding card table set up next to the picture window overlooking the constant traffic filtering off Santa Monica Boulevard.

Esther beckons me over with a wave of her hand and announces firmly, "We're going to play cards – you and I. You'll play cards with me." And so I sit across from her and, from my vantage point, watch the upside-down cards as she teaches me how to play solitaire. She seems to want my help, but I am worried that I will not give her enough time to find the appropriate cards to place. Happily for me, she seems to be genuinely pleased when I help her find a card – after she has given up. For the most part, her game seems to match my vague memories of how solitaire is played. She "won," she announces after a while. Then I shuffle, as that seems to be my job: "Shuffle them real good now, real good." She tells me to play my own game. I lay the cards out in her direction so that she can view them right-side-up, but she stops me, so I switch them around. From this upside-down view, she proceeds firmly to direct me verbally as I put each card down. It becomes clear she does not remember how to lay the cards out (or is understandably confused from her viewpoint), but she neither admits this nor allows me to re-place the cards. We continue on as if nothing were wrong, and it becomes a mock game because nothing makes sense, at least not to me. The cards are laid out incorrectly from the beginning: Instead of a single row of seven cards, I end up with two rows of three and four cards respectively. And instead of finishing the setup with the top card on each pile faceup, we end up with some cards up and some down. There is no rhyme or reason for her telling me "no!" or "yes, take that one!" or "put the cards here!" or "no, not there!" I am a bit taken aback at first and even intimidated by the exasperation in her raised voice as I try vainly to place cards according to her logic. But then I realize I should just play along, because I am pretty sure Esther is just as confused at that point. By the end of "my" game, I have four rows of cards laid out and a pile of both overturned and faceup cards – in no particular order. Esther looks down at the cards, and then announces firmly, "That's it. You lost. It's my turn to shuffle."

We all ate in the living room that day, Terry perched on the edge of the sofa back facing us, and Esther and I seated across from each other at the little card table. Esther continually urged, "Eat more!", "Eat your sandwich!", "Eat your pickle!" Despite my assurances that I was, smiling as I picked up the pickle, she demonstrated what she meant, saying, "Eat your pickle like this, with your sandwich," as she took one bite of her sandwich and, holding the slice of pickle in her other hand, one bite of pickle. I laughed and obliged her. But owing to Esther's short-term memory loss, the whole scene repeated itself minutes later. Not being used to this, I was not capable of finding a way out of this holding pattern. I looked a bit helplessly at Terry as the scenario began for yet a third time. Terry interrupted by asking Esther other questions – how she liked the food, what they did yesterday, what would she like to do later – skillfully showing me how she managed to keep herself from listening repeatedly to the same conversation, while at the same time "exercising" her patient's mind.

This compassion is particularly necessary in providing live-in care because it is difficult for the caregiver to negotiate space and time away from the patient. The available strategies depend once again on the condition of the patient. Terry used a strategy shared by many caregivers whose patients were mobile. When she felt she was "getting too irritated," she would try to take some time away from her patient, or take her patient and herself away from the house: "I just get out of her way until I could be OK again. Because it's difficult. . . . I just get out of her way. I just do something else. I don't go near her. Because sometimes I might snap at her and [that would] hurt her. So I just stay out of the way. Or maybe we would go out. That's the best solution because when we're out there, I have to be alert. Everything, her movements and everything so she doesn't fall, so she [can] walk safely. And on her part, she's entertained by the different environment." For live-in workers, the need to provide each other space is obvious. As Terry pointed out, going outside the home worked well because it distracted both her and her patient from whatever tensions existed in the house/workplace. However, this strategy depends entirely on the patient's ability to leave the house. The deterioration of her patient's health and ability to walk would signal the closing of this particular avenue of tension release for the caregiver, and at the same time increase the tension in the relationship.

Twenty-Four-Hour Care: Olivia and Leticia

The caregiving situation of Olivia and Leticia was very different from that of Terry because the condition of their patient required a different intensity of care. Olivia and Leticia were not typical in the sense that they lived together with a single patient, but they *were* typical of the women in this study in terms of the schedule they kept for a patient in poor condition, as well as in terms of their commitment and level of care displayed. They worked together to care for an eighty-nine-year-old elderly man, Maury, who was suffering from the last stages of Alzheimer's disease. Maury had been their patient for four years.

June 19, 1997, 6:30 P.M. Olivia and I sit in the living room. Leticia and Maury are just to our left seated in the dining room, Maury in his wheelchair and Leticia to his right facing him. Maury's mouth is slightly slack, his face devoid of any expression. His body hangs slightly forward at the waist, while Leticia coaxes him quietly to eat from the spoon she holds in front of his mouth. Little by little, as the hour passes, he finishes a small bowl of what looks to be oatmeal. As Olivia and I talk, Leticia chimes in; Olivia turns to Leticia for reassurance, and the two complete each other's sentences. They also keep up an almost constant chatter with Maury, who, in this stage of his illness, cannot manage more than a grunt or two in response.

Although Leticia and Olivia both lived with Maury, Leticia had a second job working days as a caregiver for a woman in the same apartment complex. She still helped Olivia with Maury's care, however. Before she headed off to work at nine in the morning, Leticia assisted Olivia in making breakfast and moving Maury into the dining area. She returned once in the afternoon to help Olivia move Maury back to the bedroom for a nap, and again after dinner to move Maury from the bed to the dining area once again. She and Olivia shared duties for the rest of the evening and throughout the night. As Olivia said, "We wake up four times a night, Leticia and I, to visit Maury in the room – to check Maury. So we also are very tired."

Despite the fact that Maury recognized little, if anything, was barely able to speak or communicate, and was unable to eat or otherwise care for himself, Olivia and Leticia continued to extend enormous love and care toward this man, their "employer." For example, Olivia stated that while Maury sat in the afternoon she continued to talk to him "so that his mind will work": "As long as he can be active. . . . Sometimes he's very groggy. . . . His brain is not working that much. There's times when he's happy you know. But there's times when he just wants to sleep all the time. That's why, if he's very talkative one day, oh, we're happy [laughing]. . . . Although he's not answering us [clearly], and his answer is not . . . to the question you ask him, it's OK." Illustrating that they identify strongly with their patient, Olivia concluded that "the hardest thing" is "seeing him not doing well" because "it's as if we are also sick."

A housebound patient such as Maury, in need of constant vigilance, obviously ties the caregiver to the house as well. As Olivia put it, "It's really hard because whenever you want to go someplace, you cannot do it, you know, because of him." Barely pausing, she finished, however, "But it's all right. It's all right." Touching on the emotional costs, she said, "You know, because we took [care of] him for so many years, we cannot leave him at this time because we care for him very much. We don't stay for the pay. We could get more elsewhere. He's a very nice man. . . . That's why we really do our very best." These comments together with Olivia's admission that she subverted her own wages clearly express how the emotional labor invested into the work results in economic consequences. It is this topic – the cost of caring – with which I conclude this chapter.

THE COST OF CARING

Because caring is frequently considered by both men and women to be the "natural" duty of women, it is often not perceived as labor, emotional or otherwise, with the result that issues of power are overlooked. At first glance, owing to the frail mental and physical condition of many patients, it may appear that the caregivers hold a great deal of power over the elderly in this work relationship. For example, the caregivers literally control not only how and when medication will be dispensed, but also what will be worn or eaten and when, and what kinds of activities will fill the day. Some caregivers have complete control over monthly allowances as well. However, this is not a complete picture. Power within a caring work relationship plays itself out in a variety of ways. For instance, in the case of immigrant Filipina caregivers an asymmetry exists in the relationship in that the patient holds advantages of class, race, ethnicity, immigration status, and sometimes gender. However, my focus here is not on those structural conditions, but rather on the infusion of caring into the employer – employee work relationship, a circumstance that I suggest *most* complicates the locus of power.

The primary reason that all the women in this study were living and working in the United States was a desire to better provide for their children and parents back in the Philippines. Yet, ironically, by providing care for the elderly, many of the women forfeited higher wages. As one woman explained, "Sometimes the amount of the pay doesn't matter too much so long as I am comfortable with the way they treat me." It is, in effect, the caregiver's ability to treat patients as they would treat their own parents that discourages them from insisting on any workplace rights such as raises; at the same time it is this attitude that makes them highly effective and sought-after caregivers. Thus, even while it contributes to a high level of patient care, infusing caring into the paid caregiving relationship is to the detriment of the women, shifting power away from them and resulting in poor working and living conditions. For the purposes of this chapter, I touch on a couple of the more tangible and measurable power shifts – time off and wages.

Wages

The live-in caregivers' wages, in all cases, were below the minimum hourly wages required by law and were, perhaps more subjectively, not commensurate with the care given. For example, in the case of Olivia and Leticia, who were jointly caring for Maury seven days a week, Olivia was the only one receiving payment of eighty dollars a day, which the two women generally split equally. Yet they were involved in providing care close to twenty-four hours a day, consistently checking on Maury every two hours throughout the night. The women thus earned a combined income of $3.33 per hour, or $1.65 per person.[31] While an eighty dollar daily wage, or $560.00 per week, may sound adequate at first, when the hourly wage is calculated, it is appallingly low.[32]

The tendency to accept a salary below the minimum wage is especially obvious in those cases in which the caregiver has been with the patient over the course of a number of years. Paradoxically, it is precisely these caregivers who are most deserving of raises on the basis of the changing and more demanding emotional and physical tasks required as they see their patients through physical deterioration. For example, the team of Leticia and Olivia were initially hired to care for an elderly man who, at that time, suffered only mild dementia. Maury was able to feed and dress himself, walk, control his bodily functions, and carry on lively conversations. Over the course of four years suffering from Alzheimer's disease, he became increasingly unable to do any of these things. However, while the women's tasks changed over time, their wages did not adequately change to reflect the increased tasks and mental and emotional labor. Neither the women nor their employers drew attention to this.

A quick comparison between the hourly wage paid to home health agencies to send a nurse's aide as a reliever illustrates how underpaid the Filipina live-in caregivers are. I'll share an admittedly extreme example: Maria is a caregiver for an elderly man who has a trachea tube that needs to be suctioned every two hours. A certified nurse's assistant (CNA), Maria makes seventy dollars a day after taxes, or approximately $2.10 per hour. However, when she takes a day off, her patient must hire replacement licensed professional nurses (LPNs) from a home health agency at the rate of $31.50 per hour for eight-hour shifts, thereby spending $756.00 in a twenty-four-hour period.[33] Compare that to the seventy dollars a day paid to Maria and it is clear that, despite the fact that the replacements are LPNs, Maria is severely underpaid – and quite a "deal" for her employer.

Many of the caregivers readily acknowledged that they could earn more elsewhere, even as live-ins.[34] But if their patients treated them with respect, it virtually guaranteed their willingness to remain in their jobs, despite the low pay. As one woman asserted, "I could earn $120 per day if I really decide to get another patient. . . . As a matter of fact, I already [gave] them my resignation and they did not want me to go." One factor in her decision to stay was the "unknown" of finding a new patient. As she put it, "I am not sure what kind of patient I will have next time." Another commented, "This one is nice, treats me well. I don't know if I will be so lucky next time." But more often than not, the explanations belied an underlying emotional commitment to their employers-patients. As one succinctly stated, "They are so good. I just can't leave them, you see?" In this last instance, the "them" she refers to is not only her ninety-year-old patient, but also her patient's seventy-five-year-old daughter. Not only were the women driven to stay for their own comfort level and emotional connection with their patients, but also in the interest of the patients' families. These nonmonetary factors held them back from asserting themselves. This reluctance to ask for higher pay extended, not surprisingly, into other work negotiations as well.

Time Off

Time off was a rarity among the live-in caregivers in this study, who averaged only two days off per month. However, even when they are given days off, the women generally did not take them for a variety of reasons. The following three categories, in combination, explain some of the reasons behind their refusals to take time off: their own financial necessity; their concern for their patients' health, happiness, and financial situation; and the difficulty in finding replacement caregivers.

Surprisingly, the women's own financial need was not the most common explanation for not taking time off. Nevertheless, it was always of some concern. Since they were paid in daily wages, a weekend off amounted to a loss of approximately $160 in possible salary on average. In those instances in which their employer insisted on a five-day workweek – either for monetary reasons or because family members were available to cover – the caregivers frequently took reliever jobs of their own rather than lose the possible salary to be made on a weekend.

While the women generally did not let concern for their patients entirely control their decisions regarding time off, it remained a factor that also served to keep them tied to their employers. All the women noted that they worried about their patients when they took time off. The intensity of the worry varied by the patients' physical conditions and whom they found as relievers. One caregiver expressed the sentiment of most: "I worry . . . unless I really trust the one I left her with." This commitment to their patients resulted in their rushing home and in constantly thinking about their patients' welfare, even when they were "off." Olivia said, "We are trying to go home early so we can put Maury in the bed. And that's hard. You are always rushing to go home because you always think about him. Wherever you are, you always think [of] Maury. If one of us is here, no problem – because we know everything [about him]. But if we call somebody to relieve us, that's a problem."

Some of the Filipina caregivers placed not only their patients' physical or emotional needs before their own but also their patients' *financial* needs. This is ironic given that those patients who can afford twenty-four-hour in-home care, even at such paltry hourly wages, are generally financially solvent.[35] Caregivers were particularly concerned when an agency was called upon to find a reliever, as agency costs to the employer were commonly twenty to thirty dollars more per day. The women were all aware of the additional financial cost to their patients and thus tended to take the responsibility of finding their own relievers and for no fee at all.

While there are few skilled jobs in which workers are obligated to find their own replacements, in most cases these caregivers took responsibility for finding their own relievers, usually relying on social networks. This process served as a vehicle for "training" newer Filipina caregivers and also provided needed income to these newer arrivals. However, it also contributed to time-off dilemmas. For example, in relying on social networks, geographic location was a determining factor. Those caregivers living in Orange County faced much more difficulty in finding Filipinas to cover for them than did those who lived in Los Angeles. The women often noted that their friends did not drive; hence transportation to the patients' homes had to be managed and arranged as well. Taking all the above into consideration, one caregiver summed up, "It takes a lot of work and planning to take a day off!" For some, it was simply too much trouble.

Further, many expressed disappointment and resentment at the level of care provided by their relievers. Upon returning from a day off, caregivers were often subjected to a litany of complaints from their patients – sometimes unfounded or simply due to their patients' feeling of abandonment, sometimes with good reason. For example, one caregiver who tried to maintain regular weekends off related that her patient "is not happy with her reliever because she told me that her reliever has a temper. She does not know when [the reliever] will be nice and when she will be mean." Faced both with the responsibility of finding relievers and with the guilt for leaving their patients with less than adequate care, many caregivers choose simply not to take days off.

Interestingly, it was on the topic of relievers that the women seemed to realize most strongly the discrepancy between the care they provided and their pay. Some expressed misgivings at having to pay their relievers their eighty dollars per day – knowing that the relievers did far less than they did during a single day. For example, one caregiver related her patient's report that the reliever would just sit and watch TV all day with the patient, rather than do any cleaning, take the patient outside for walks, or even chat. Such reports influenced the caregivers to forego their time off rather than leave their patients with less than ideal care.

What I have shared above are just a few indicators of the extent of the financial and emotional costs of providing care to the elderly. By treating their patients-employers as they would their own parents, Filipina elderly caregivers have, in effect, inadvertently contributed to their own disempowerment. The emotional labor invested serves in many cases to shift the financial power away from the caregivers. At the same time, clearly it is the extent of the emotional labor invested that brings about such effective services to elderly patients.

Before closing, I want to note that I realize I run the risk of portraying these women as either victims or as selfless martyrs. They are neither. To leave it at that would be to ignore the fact that the emotional and physical labor they engage in is what enables them to have job security, food, a roof over their heads, and, of course, income to send home. As numerous caregivers revealed, the level of care they provide is in part strategic. That is, poor care contributes to the quicker death of their patients, which in turn results in loss not only of income but also of housing. Furthermore, all the women in this study expressed a strong belief and satisfaction that their compassion was the most positive contribution they made to their patients' health. The women also expressed satisfaction in living on their own and in providing for their children financially – independently of their husbands or ex-husbands in the Philippines. Thus while their worth is financially underappreciated by their employers and themselves, they certainly stand to gain and experience growth in other ways.

Filipina elderly caregivers seemed most empowered and confident of their authority when it came to caring for their patients; this confidence and authority, however, did not extend to asserting their rights as workers who provide that care. In this regard, they are no different from the rest of us in valuing women's social reproductive and emotional labor. We may instinctively recognize its worth and value in our everyday lives – whether as friends or partners, as caregivers for elderly or children, or as mothers – but we are hard-pressed to demand any kind of payment for it. The social reproductive labor provided by Filipina migrant workers, not only here in the United States but in countries worldwide, underscores the enduring condition of women's work – both its value and its undervaluement – even in our supposed "new global order" and age of transnational movement and commodities. Some things never change.

NOTES

1. Though perhaps uncommon and cumbersome to those not used to the spelling, the usage of Filipina/o is used in order to most clearly introduce and ensure gender inclusiveness.

2. The arrival of these Filipinas to the United States as mothers attempting to provide for their families back in the Philippines comes about through the confluence of numerous political economic factors. The increasing demand in the United States for health care for the elderly, coupled with encouragement by IMF-led and Philippine national policies, has encouraged Filipina women to pursue outmigration as the best available option. See, for example, Rosalinda Pineda-Ofreneo, *The*

Philippine Debt and Poverty (Oxford: Oxfam, 1991), for a more detailed examination of the debt crisis in the Philippines and the Philippine government's response.

3. I use the term "elderly caregivers" to refer to those with little or no offical health care training. When the women had certification as nursing assistants, they used the term CNA (certified nursing assistants). I use the term "home health care worker" interchangeably with "elderly caregiver." Although I do not use the phrase in this manner, "home health care workers" may typically encompass a full range of workers, from registered nurses (RNS) down to CNAS. For more detailed explanations of the nursing industry hierarchy, see Evelyn Nakano Glenn, "From Servitude to Service Work: Historical Continuities in the Racial Division of Paid Reproductive Labor," *Signs: Journal of Women in Culture and Society* 18:1 (1992): 1–43; Nona Glazer, *Women's Paid and Unpaid Labor: The Work Transfer in Health Care and Retailing* (Philadelphia: Temple University Press, 1993); and Timothy Diamond, *Making Gray Gold: Narratives of Nursing Home Care* (Chicago: University of Chicago Press, 1992).

4. Glenn, "From Servitude to Service Work," 1.

5. This chapter arises out of my dissertation work in which I collected data over a period of a year and a half, through twenty oral histories, in-depth interviews, and participant-observation. Participant-observation involved living and working with half of the caregivers for several days. I did not go through any nurse's aide/caregiver training and become an elderly caregiver myself. The early stages of fieldwork involved working in Los Angeles, California, with various immigrant rights community organizations, eventually helping to found a Filipina/o nonprofit workers' center.

6. Grace Kovar, Gerry Hendershot, and Evelyn Mathis, "Older People in the United States Who Receive Help with Basic Activities of Daily Living," *American Journal of Public Health* 79:6 (1989): 778–79.

7. California Department of Finance figures, population projections, 1993, available online at http://www.def.ca.gov/html/demograph/repndat.htm#projections.

8. For example, 92 percent of Filipinas/os in Los Angeles County are foreign born. Filipinas/os make up 67 percent of the city of Carson, 44 percent of Covina, and 24 percent of Cerritos (Paul Ong and Tania Azores, "Asian Immigrants in Los Angeles: Diversity and Divisions," in *The New Asian Immigration in Los Angeles and Global Restructuring,* ed. Paul Ong, Edna Bonacich, and Lucie Cheng [Philadelphia: Temple University Press, 1994], 121).

9. Some estimates on the amount of money sent back to the Philippines by Filipina elderly caregivers range as high as seven million dollars. See, for example, Dean Alegado, "The Labor Export Industry and Post – 1986 Philippine Economic Development," paper presented at the Third European Conference on Philippine

Studies, Institute for Research on Southeast Asia of the National Centre for Scientific Research, University of Provence, April 27–29, 1997.

10. Elizabeth C. Eviota, *The Political Economy of Gender: Women and the Sexual Division of Labour in the Philippines* (London: Zed Books, 1992), 142–44.

11. The other most common route is through job placement agencies that specialize in domestic help or home health care.

12. Emily K. Abel and Margaret K. Nelson, "Circles of Care: An Introductory Essay," in *Circles of Care: Work and Identity in Women's Lives,* ed. Emily K. Abel and Margaret K. Nelson (Albany: State University of New York Press, 1990), 17.

13. Abel and Nelson, "Circles of Care," 17.

14. In this case, Myra Bradwell, a married Illinois woman, sued the state for the right to admission to the bar. She was denied this right in an opinion that presented a "separate spheres" argument, relegating women to the home and maintaining that men's rightful sphere was in the public (*Bradwell v. Illinois,* 83 U.S. 130 [1872]).

15. See, for example, Arlie Hochschild with Anne Machung, *The Second Shift* (New York: Avon Books, 1989). For an in-depth study of daughters who serve as caregivers for their mothers and fathers, see Emily Abel's *Who Cares for the Elderly?: Public Policy and the Experiences of Adult Daughters* (Philadelphia: Temple University Press, 1991).

16. Shellee Colen, "'Just a Little Respect': West Indian Domestic Workers in New York City," in *Muchachas No More: Household Workers in Latin America and the Caribbean,* ed. Elsa Chaney and Mary Garcia Castro (Philadelphia: Temple University Press, 1988), 171–96.

17. See, for example, Mary Romero's extensive work on Chicana/Latina domestic workers in Colorado, *Maid in the U.S.A.* (New York: Routledge, 1992); Colen's work on West Indian domestics in New York City, "'Just a Little Respect'"; and Evelyn Nakano Glenn's work on Japanese American women domestic workers, *Issei, Nisei, War Bride: Three Generations of Japanese American Women in Domestic Service* (Philadelphia: Temple University Press, 1986).

18. See, for example, Bonnie Thornton Dill, "'Making Your Job Good Yourself': Domestic Service and the Construction of Personal Dignity," in *Women and the Politics of Empowerment,* ed. Sandra Morgen and Ann Bookman (Philadelphia: Temple University Press, 1987); Glenn's *Issei, Nisei, War Bride;* and Romero's *Maid in the U.S.A.* Research also includes discussions on white (largely Irish immigrant women from the late 1800s to the early 1900s in the Northeast) and black domestic workers, particularly between the Civil War and World War II. See, for example, David M. Katzman's *Seven Days a Week: Women and Domestic Service in Industrializing America* (New York: Oxford University Press, 1978), which notably utilizes the available writings of domestic workers of the period. Quite a few of the women who wrote

about their experiences had some college experience and thus were not, as he notes, typical; however, their "middle-class sensibilities . . . shed brilliant light upon the shadows which hid much of servants' lives" (6). Live-in domestics, most prevalent before wwii, were usually single African American and Japanese Americans (with the exception of Chinese men from the late 1800s until approximately the 1920s). For the Nisei (second-generation Japanese Americans), the position was considered the middle stage between a woman's father's home and that of her husband's – a training stage to prepare for running a household.

19. Today, geography often determines which women of color are to be found within domestic work. For housekeeping in the West and Southwest, the field is dominated by Chicanas/Latinas. For child care and house care in the East, West Caribbean women predominate. For elderly care in California, especially live-in work, Filipinas predominate.

20. Evelyn Nakano Glenn, "Social Constructions of Mothering: A Thematic Overview," in *Mothering: Ideology, Experience, and Agency,* ed. Evelyn Nakano Glenn, Grace Chang, and Linda Rennie Forcey (New York: Routledge, 1993), 5–6.

21. Two points are worth following up. First, this class and racial division is most predominantly the case with live-in home health care workers. It is less often the situation, for example, for county home health care workers who work predominantly within low-income communities. Second, this debate highlights ongoing discussions in feminism, illustrating that middle-class women's increased opportunities and choices directly impact working-class women. The hiring of housekeepers, child care workers, and elderly care workers is a result of more privileged women being able to afford this kind of service. This occurs not only in private household work, but also in our corporate and professional offices. The successful woman professor, lawyer, or administrator also relies on mostly (if not entirely) female clerical support. That being said, however, feminist scholars entrenched in debates on equality and difference among women might note who is once again absent: men rarely enter into the picture or discussions. We tend to look at the racial and class division and the consequent impact upon women, overlooking the lack of contribution by husbands or sons. Research on elderly care in particular shows this gender division of labor to be acute. So while the racial division among women exists and deserves attention, a more productive public and academic discussion might be to consider the gender division in service and caring work as a whole.

22. Glenn, "Social Construction of Mothering," 7, emphasis added.

23. Glenn, "From Servitude to Service Work," 1, emphasis added.

24. Correspondence from caregiver to researcher, September 7, 1997; and personal interview with caregiver.

25. Colen, " 'Just a Little Respect' "; Romero, *Maid in the U.S.A.;* Denise Segura,

"Working at Motherhood: Chicana and Mexicana Immigrant Mothers and Employment," in Glenn, Chang, and Forcey, *Mothering,* 211–36; Pierrette Hondagneu-Sotelo and Ernestine Avila, "'I'm Here, but I'm There': The Meanings of Latina Transnational Motherhood," *Gender & Society* 11:5 (1997): 548–70.

26. The next most common explanation involved the desire to leave abusive or unfulfilling marriages – a topic for another work.

27. See, for example, Arlie Russell Hochschild, *The Managed Heart: Commercialization of Human Feeling* (Berkeley: University of California Press, 1983); and Abel, *Who Cares for the Elderly?* Child care workers, like elderly care workers, expend much emotional labor. They are hired to care for or mother other individuals. Success on the job relies in large part on their ability to be compassionate and caring, yet maintain a degree of professional distance.

28. Hochschild, *The Managed Heart,* 240.

29. See for example, Colen, "'Just a Little Respect'"; Glenn, *Issei, Nisei, War Bride;* and Mary Romero, "Sisterhood and Domestic Service: Race, Class, and Gender in the Mistress-Maid Relationship," *Humanity and Society* 12:4 (1988): 318–46.

30. Abel and Nelson, "Circles of Care," 4.

31. Leticia, however, also earned $7.50 per hour as a caregiver in her other day job.

32. These computations do not include taxes. Taxes were taken out for those working through agencies. Most women, even if employed directly by the employer, declared their own taxes at year end.

33. According to the agency, the trachea tube necessitates that a licensed professional nurse be sent in Marie's stead – even though Marie, a CNA, learned to do it herself after she was hired. Note that the $31.50 hourly rate includes whatever percentage the agency takes. In addition, the agency that placed Marie over four years ago continues to charge her patients a twenty-dollar placement fee every day for as long as she is employed there.

34. However, despite hearing this often from the women in this study, only one out of twenty women I interviewed and worked with earned over ninety dollars a day.

35. The employers (patients) were financially stable, if not wealthy, in comparison to the caregivers. I want to acknowledge, however, that there still remained the possibility of the patient "outliving" his or her finances.

Asian American Women's Studies Courses

A Look Back at Our Beginnings

JUDY CHU

It has been over a decade since I first team-taught the Asian American women's course at UCLA. I was still a student, as were many of the other members of the team. Together we struggled to obtain materials that were nonexistent, develop an analysis where there previously was none, and perform as leaders even though we had not done so before.

This was in 1973, three years after the first Asian women's seminar was conducted at the University of California at Berkeley, and one year after the first one had been offered at UCLA. Since then, there have been a number of Asian American women's classes taught, mostly in the western region of the United States. In the meantime, I had obtained my doctorate, and upon graduation reflected on the fact that this course had been the most meaningful class in which I had participated; thus, I continued to teach the Asian American women's course at UCLA. Since then, Asian women's studies has matured, along with those teaching it. The history of this course is a case study in the conflict inherent in the struggle to change entrenched social roles.

As did many of the programs of the 1960s, Asian American women's studies grew out of the desire to overturn oppressive roles. Asian Americans were deeply affected by the civil rights and antiwar movements. Both were powerful struggles, awakening an ethnic group that had been taught not to "rock the boat." Asian Americans found the antiwar movement a way of dealing with the increased racial hostility in America that the Vietnam War had engendered; the civil rights movement gave Asians the inspiration to discover their identity and community. Thus, in the late sixties, young Asian

Americans left behind the derogatory term, "oriental," started community service programs, formed political groups, established and wrote for their own newspapers, and fought for ethnic studies classes at their universities.

However, as much enthusiasm and energy as was poured into this new direction, Asian American women increasingly found that they were not part of the decision-making processes. Not only were their contributions not recognized in mainstream society, but they were also excluded from holding power in the movement that held equality as an ideal. There were several reasons for this. There was a feeling among some Asian males, similar to the mood in the black civil rights movement, that their "manhood" had been oppressed for decades and that this discrimination thus gave them the right to dominate Asian women.[1] Second, in attempting to show strength while confronting institutionalized racism, the movement was strongly identified with a ghetto image that was largely "macho" and male. Third, a large part of the civil rights movement emphasized finding oneself and discovering one's ethnic identity within the minority culture, an identity that had been historically denied to minority people by the dominant culture. But, for Asian *women*, much of Asian culture offered only secondary status.

Inevitably, Asian American women found themselves mainly in supportive roles: They served coffee; their speeches were not heard unless a man restated them. Strong, assertive women were labeled "Dragon Ladies," an interesting and contradictory term in a movement trying to erase stereotypes. The frustration women felt can be seen in this poem by Tomi Tanaka titled "from a lotus blossom cunt":

we chronic smilers
asian women
we of the downcast almost eyes
are seeing each other
sisters now, people now
asian women
I'm still with you, brothers
always
but I'm so damned tired
of being body first, head last
wanting to love you when all
you want is a solution to glandular discomfort
that I thought I'd better say my say

> Think about it, brothers
> we are women, we are asian
> we are freeing ourselves
> join us
> try to use us
> and you'll lose us
> Join us. [2]

Asian American women were fighting external barriers, but they also had their own internal struggles. Many Asian women did not feel they had the social skills necessary to be leaders. They had problems feeling confident enough to assert themselves; they had not been trained to deal with the ideological concepts being tossed around at that time. Thus, small groups of Asian women were formed by activists in the early 1970s to talk about these problems: the groups served as important function by providing a safe atmosphere to talk about Asian women as political organizers. It was difficult, however, to find a direction for these groups, as there was no precedent. How much were they to incorporate of the leftist political groups in America, the white feminist movement, or the movement of women in Asia? As some Asian women wrote at the time: "Women in the Asian movement find that those stereotypes are still hovering over their head . . . because the new definition of the Asian woman has not yet evolved, women still find themselves in a limbo."[3]

DEVELOPING THE FIRST COURSES

From such groups came the impetus in the early seventies for the first classes on the Asian American woman's experience that were started at UCLA, Berkeley, and San Francisco State University. At UCLA, the classes were begun through an experimental program and were to be ambitious projects. Among the goals were developing materials on both historical and contemporary aspects of Asian American women; developing a theoretical orientation that would attempt to integrate race, sex, and class contradictions; developing leadership skills among the instructors; and raising the consciousness of students on the issues of culturally based sexism.

The absence of resource materials is reflected in the syllabi of the early classes. Even though the classes were about Asian women in America, a significant portion of the material was on women in Asia, in particular, the social movements for women in China, Vietnam, and Japan. Materials on feudal Asia were easily obtained, as were examples of stereotypes of Asian women in the American media. Thus, a plethora of materials existed on the negative aspects of being an Asian American woman, and whatever new, theoretical material or models that the classes used came largely from the social movements of Asia. These, however, were difficult to translate and apply to the American situation.

The structure of these early classes, incorporating collectivity, consciousness raising, and a community orientation, played an important role in the development of leadership for Asian American women both in and beyond the academic arena. These classes were always collective efforts: Their foundation lay in the belief that learning could occur without the benefit of degrees and titles on the part of the teachers. No one woman had the experiences, academic credentials, or desire to assert herself over others, and this was reflected in the composition of the teaching teams. Although on record the course was taught by graduate students, the actual teaching teams were much more expanded and included students and staff. These women found themselves in groups for the first time, developing a course curriculum in intensive, sometimes painful, efforts to first inform themselves and then determine how to communicate these research findings to others. As one of the first teachers wrote, "As a woman's group, the teaching collective for the Asian woman course began its work with a struggle against the traditional limits of stereotyped 'femininity.' Instructors found the experience of lecturing and speaking out, reading in an analytical and critical way, and assuming responsibilities independently . . . new and bewildering. The group rebelled against individualistic, authoritarian, self-centered approaches to teaching and consciously looked for other alternatives."[4]

On the positive side, the collectivity of these groups provided a safe atmosphere in which to develop leadership skills and analytical thinking on sexism, racism, and classism. However, a consequence of this necessary first step was that these women were teaching concepts that they had yet to fully understand themselves; they were, as one student reported, "The blind leading the blind."

The classes involved personal consciousness raising: The teachers challenged both women and men to examine social roles, and thus the classes were alternately threatening and eye-opening. The classes never had required prerequisites nor did they close enrollment to anyone, though students were usually Asian women. There would be, however, some whites and Asian men enrolled, and, as would occur inevitably in mainstream classes, first the whites would dominate discussion, followed by the Asian men. Asian women would be the last to speak in a class designed for them! A variety of methods were employed to change these dynamics. Classes were broken up into smaller groups of six to ten in which each student was required to take a turn at being a discussion leader, thus giving each person the opportunity to assert herself or himself in a smaller, more comfortable setting.

There were so few Asian women in leadership positions at that time that the women in the teaching collective apparently intimidated some of the students who saw them as "strong women." In reality, as mentioned before, many of the instructors themselves lacked confidence throughout the entire process, and so they had mixed reactions to such labels. This forced them to contemplate what it meant to be considered "strong." Could it mean alienation from the Asian community, which was not accustomed to such women? Or were the women being given a role or label that they really could not fulfill? Ultimately, such attributes were seen as positive, albeit a responsibility.

Though everyday conversation between teacher and student revolved around academic ideas and assignments, the most important activity was a positive redefinition of the Asian American woman. By uncovering the history of Asian American women through oral histories and reinterpretation, students and teachers witnessed her outgrowing her "invisible" status. Asian American mothers came, in fact, to be seen as the backbone of the family, oftentimes compensating for their husbands, who were denigrated by society. To examine such roles, there were seminars such as a panel of Nisei mothers who came to speak about their experiences in the American internment or "concentration" camps during World War II. The speakers reported that it was not only the first time they had been required to speak in front of an audience, but also the first time anybody had asked them about their lives.

By exploring personal histories, students reevaluated the contributions of women in their lives. Relationships with mothers had previously been marked by silence about the past or by memories of mother's insistence that their children "be Asian." But as students persisted, they were able to deepen their understanding of their mothers; as one student wrote in 1971:

 My mother was the center of our family, her strong character dominated most of our young world. Her role as an Asian woman was that of a living "vessel of culture." . . . I try to explain to her not only my opposition to feudal ideas about women but also my growing rebellion against my adopted American values. Sometimes, I think she understands and sympathizes, but when it comes to practice, paradoxically she who has been oppressed so long by feudal values and American exploitation . . . perpetuates these systems by teaching us to accept them. She seems both oppressor and oppressed. [But] when I speak with my mother, I try to understand the importance of the Chinese family in the struggle for survival, that our mothers teach us only what they have learned in fighting to preserve their families.[5]

In order to change such relationships, the Berkeley class had a tea for mothers of students: "It was surprising how interested and open they were. As one mother put it, 'I've sent three children through this university. . . . This is the first time I've been invited by my children to meet a teacher, visit a class, or to talk about what they study.'"[6]

Since the impetus for the class had come from the community, the instructors saw community organizations as integral to the learning process. Students were encouraged to become involved in the community for their class projects. Speakers included Asian women leaders who were active in the community and who proved to be valuable role models as organizers. One class was so devoted to the idea that every week it was held in a different location in the Asian community. Although this was an innovative idea, it was logistically complicated. As an alternative, some classes held optional field trips to such places as Agbayani Village, a Pilipino[7] retirement village in Delano that was built solely through community effort.

DEVELOPING A THEORETICAL ORIENTATION

The most imposing task was deciding on a theoretical orientation in a subject area where little written material and few knowledgeable people existed at the time. And what was to be the main focus on the course – sexism, racism, or class considerations? The impetus for the course came from the frustrations and contradictions that existed between Asian men and women in community organizing, feelings that implied that the course needed to focus on sexism. Yet the basis upon which women were teaching the class at all was their consciousness, as Asian Americans, of racism. A third consideration was examining the role that class contradictions had in determining racial and sexual divisions. This was a much more complex analysis, requiring a sophistication that many of the women had yet to develop.

The confusion was reflected in the only conference on Asian American women's studies classes, held in September, 1974, at UCLA. Eight California colleges were represented by women who discussed their common problems. Although each instructor reported enjoying the collective nature of the classes, problems were occurring because few were willing to be the "leader." Asian women did not lack organizational ability, so this problem did not hurt the basic structure of the class as much as did the lack of political/theoretical cohesion. As one document from the conference states: "Most of us agreed on 'triple oppression,' though this does not necessarily mean the group was united politically. There was a common perspective about the 'problems' but not the 'solutions.' Some groups lean toward a Marxist-Leninist perspective, though none of us had yet developed written or formal principles of political unity. Several groups tried to develop stronger political unity through group study."[8] The difficulties in achieving a theoretical perspective are a result of the contradictions in race, sex, and class status that Asian women face.

Sexism has long historical roots for Asian women, stemming from the feudal ideas perpetuated by Confucianism. The degree of sexism in Asian culture has led to the horrors of bound feet, female infanticide, and domestic slavery in marriage. Such cultural dictates might imply sexism as a main focus on Asian American women, but they did not see this as the main emphasis. The early writings from the Asian women's collective state: "It is the social system, not men, which is the enemy."[9] Although many activist Asian women were strong advocates of women's equality, they would not have aligned themselves with the feminist movement at that time.

This lack of alignment reflected the pervasive role that race had and still has in dividing America. Activist Asian women felt that the predominantly white American feminist movement consistently overlooked issues of race. Such racism took the form of paternalism: Asian women were not taken seriously. Many white women did not even view Asian women as an ethnic minority, and usually saw black women and Chicanas as the only minority women in struggle. One only has to review early feminist books and anthologies to see the absence of Asian American women and their viewpoints. Even though Asian women's classes used anthologies such as *Sisterhood Is Powerful*, the only article on women of Asian descent was on women in China.[10] While some women's groups have since become more conscious of Asian American women, this problem still occurs today. Perhaps white women believed the mainstream view that Asian women were passive and uninterested in feminism. Stories that mainstream America had heard about Confucianism have been so pervasive and so widely accepted that they have excluded deeper interpretations.[11] Some of the differences between Asian women and the feminist movement perhaps also reflected cultural differences. The feminist movement early on addressed issues of sexuality, a subject that was not culturally comfortable for Asian women to discuss. In fact, only recently have the issues of rape, sexual harassment, and lesbianism been addressed by Asian American women.

Racism is and was a more readily recognized problem, however. Students in the Asian women's studies classes have been asked, both in discussion and essay exam questions, which contradiction – race or sex – has more importance for them. They usually answer that it was through racism that they realized inequality existed. Asian American women have long recognized their common experience with Asian American men as victims of racism. Ever since the influx of Chinese immigrants in the 1850s, men had been the object of antimiscegenation laws, anti-immigration laws, and dehumanizing interactions. Racism has had a powerful effect on both Asian men and Asian women.

Yet tension still exists between Asian men and women, much of it directly attributable to the effects of racism. The Asian male has been seen as a sexual threat to white women, especially during the period when immigration of Asian women was barred. But in the 1960s, this changed. The image of the Asian as "model minority" was presented in contrast to the rioting blacks and Chicanos, and the Asian man "disappeared" or became invisible in society's eyes. In the Asian community, males were seen as emasculated: The Asian male image lacked power, strength, sexuality, and charisma. Asian women thus faced a contradiction. Theoretically, Asian women aligned with Asian men, but did the solution to the "emasculation" problem infer the return to sexist roles? Few activist women would advocate such a solution. Tensions have inevitably resulted from this dilemma, and the high outmarriage rate among Asian females is one consequence of this confusion. The general thrust of theories on institutionalized racism still does not address the issues of sex-role development and equitable alternatives, probably because these theories have been promulgated mainly by men.

The ambivalent dynamic between Asian women and men is, furthermore, reflected in the composition of the classes on Asian American Women. Students from other women's studies classes are often surprised by the high proportion of men in the classes – usually about one-third. To Asian women, this is not out of the ordinary, however, considering the commonality of experience felt by Asian women and men, and the strong role played by mothers in Asian men's lives. Yet there are heated arguments within each class on the issue of male-female relations.

As regards contradictions based on class status, much of the thrust of the early courses focused on the issue of class as a determiner of divisions in race and sex. Indeed, statistics show that Asian women bear the brunt of both race and gender discrimination, and are thus subject to class exploitation.[12] In analysis of income differentials, for the same educational levels and seniority, Asian women earn less than white men, Asian men, and white women. This is despite the fact that Asian women are more highly educated than the average American women. In fact, some criticism in the early days of the courses revolved around the fact that the teachers of Asian women's classes tended to be highly educated, ambitious, professional women. This perhaps prevented the students from being able to see the nature of class discrimination and consequently limited their analysis.[13] Looking back, however, perhaps the greater problem stemmed from the fact that class contradictions were seen in a very simplistic way – as being the sole purview of women in blue-collar jobs – rather than including the realization that they existed because of barriers in all strata of American society. It is just as important to understand why Asian women are blocked from upper-level management positions as it is to see why they are overrepresented in waitressing jobs and in garment factories.

RESPONSE BY THE UNIVERSITY ADMINISTRATION

The early classes lacked developed materials, experienced staff, and a definitive theoretical orientation. Add to these problems the sexism and racism inherent in traditional academia, and one can understand that difficulties with the administration would arise. Asian American studies itself was in its infancy; classes had to be offered through other departments or by the Council on Educational Development (CED), an experimental college that sponsored the first Asian women's classes at UCLA. Although these courses enjoyed high enrollments, the administration considered them suspect, and after three years decided not to continue them.

Fortunately, by this time, the Asian American studies program had gained enough stability as a center to determine its own courses, and "Asian American Women" was offered again. However, the classes did change direction after 1975. The emphasis was on gaining legitimacy by hiring instructors with doctorates and by making more structured assignments. Collective teaching teams were no longer used, and TA's were not allowed to teach the courses, but the class was still popular, with a consistently large enrollment and excellent teaching evaluations. The course was integrated into the university curriculum and fulfilled social science requirements as well as a requirement for the women's studies major at UCLA. Speakers and projects related to the community and personal consciousness raising remained an important component of the course. In evaluating the course, one student wrote, "After taking this course, I have become aware of how I am seen as an Asian woman. I am also aware that I can fight back, as I've seen speakers in our class do. Finally, I see my mother in a new light. I used to see her as an ordinary person until I did the oral history on her and discovered [how much] she went through."

The post-1975 changes had many positive effects. The class was institutionalized and thus required less effort than collective training had taken. With a consistent instructor, weaknesses and mistakes in previous classes could be rectified in each succeeding semester. Analysis and materials became more sophisticated, allowing Asians from all backgrounds to feel comfortable. There were trade-offs, however. The unique mixture of backgrounds in the collective teams spawned classes reflective of a broad range of community perspectives, and this teacher training later helped many women go on to excel in a variety of leadership positions. The more structured settings of current classes also have made it more difficult to "experience" the community through direct and creative means.

Yet, institutionalization of the class still does not insure the stability of instruction. The instructors for Asian women's classes are usually on temporary lecture status, rather than on the regular faculty or in a tenure-line situation. Because of the difficulty of obtaining a tenure-track position in an institution dominated by white males such as UCLA, there is no job security. Thus, instructors of these courses look elsewhere for part-time work or permanent employment. Consequently, students do not have as much access to the professor, and research projects on Asian American women are done on a haphazard basis. Offering a class with no stable instruction from semester to semester is tantamount to offering a course on paper only. The class is "on the books," but there is no certainty that it will continue to be offered.

The early Asian women's classes were the agents of change, a role not favored by a university administration devoted to traditional learning. In the minds of the Asian American community, however, the study of Asian American women was important and deserving of a place in the academy. Gathering and generating course materials was a difficult struggle, but it was only through such classes that such development could take place. In fact, the first Asian women's journal, *Asian Women*, came from the papers written for the first class at Berkeley in 1971.

The troubles that these classes experienced mirror some inherent contradictions in the philosophy of higher education. Are university courses to be confined to traditional learning and thinking, the compilation and organization of already established materials? Or can they be divergent, spawning new, creative thought and experiences? The Asian women's classes had to take dramatic steps in confronting entrenched ideas and in developing new ones.

Innovations within Asian women's classes continue to occur, and there are some general questions that women in all areas of women's studies need to address. These courses are changing the self-image of Asians, but how much impact is this change having on the rest of society? How much integration should there be between ethnic women's courses and women's studies? Perhaps women's studies courses could incorporate more materials on Asian American women, but dialogue needs to take place to insure this interaction. On a more theoretical level, each ethnic women's group is understandably developing materials separately, yet comparisons between experiences are necessary and could yield a deeper understanding of the American social system.[14]

Asian women are making many gains. There are now videotapes on the Asian woman's experiences, photographic exhibits chronicling Asian women's history, oral history, research and articles, and even best-selling books.[15] There are national and local organizations for Asian/Pacific women, as well as a variety of conferences and seminars held annually, especially in the western United States.

Our needs, however, are as multiple and pressing as ever. The lack of available services in the community for Asian women continues to be a prominent concern. The problems of newly arrived immigrant and refugee women include everything from wife battering to special health problems to exploitation at the workplace. The assessment of such needs has been carried out by Asian women, some of whom have had the opportunity through these courses to analyze critically the experiences they have taken for granted all their lives. Certainly, the Asian women's classes have been an instrument of change, with or without the university administration's blessing. With greater institutional support, they can be an even more effective agent of change – as they must be as long as race, sex, and class inequality continue to exist in American society.

NOTES

1. Sara Evans, *Personal Politics: The Roots of Women's Liberation in the Civil Rights Movement and the New Left* (New York: Vintage, 1979).

2. Tomi Tanaka, "from a lotus blossom cunt," in *Roots: An Asian American Reader*, ed. Amy Tachiki (Los Angeles: UCLA Asian American Studies Center, 1971), 109. Used with permission.

3. "Asian Women as Leaders," by the Editorial Staff, *Rodan*, April 1971, 1.

4. May Ying Chen, "Teaching a Course on Asian American Women," in *Counterpoint: Perspectives on Asian America*, ed. E. Gee (Los Angeles: UCLA Asian American Studies Center, 1976), 235.

5. Lai Jen, "Oppression and Survival," in *Asian Women* (Berkeley: Asian American Studies Program, University of California, 1971), 24–25.

6. Jen, "Oppression and Survival," 27.

7. I use this spelling deliberately: It is correct, according to Pilipinos, who have no "f" sound in their language. The name *Philippino* was imposed upon them during colonial Spanish rule; now they are redefining themselves.

8. Statewide Conference on Asian American Women Courses, September 7–8, 1974, UCLA Asian American Studies Center, Los Angeles, unpublished conference proceedings.

9. Editorial Staff, "Politics of the Interior," in *Asian Women* (Berkeley: Asian American Studies Program, University of California, 1971), 128.

10. Robin Morgan, ed., *Sisterhood Is Powerful* (New York: Vintage, 1970).

11. Asian women can count among their forebears many women who were activists. Korean American women, for instance, immigrated to escape feudalism in Asia and actively organized against the Japanese invasion of Korea. Asian history is more complex than it appears on its traditional surface: One of the legendary figures in Chinese history is Fa Mu Lan, who, in a twelve-year war against the Tartars, substituted for her father and led an army to victory. Pilipino women have a strong history of matrilinealism prior to feudalism, which can be found today in the matrilineal naming given to Pilipino American children. Japan also had some matrilocal structures prior to feudalism, and according to legend, the goddess Amaterasu began life in Japan with her light.

12. "Selected Statistics on the Status of Asian American Women," *Amerasia Journal* 4 (1977): 133–40.

13. Mayumi Tsutagawa, "The Asian Women's Movement: Superficial Rebellion?" *Asian Resources* (1974): 55–64.

14. For such a discussion see Gloria Joseph and Jill Lewis, *Common Differences: Conflict in Black and White Feminist Perspectives* (New York: Anchor Books, 1981).

15. See, for instance, these resources: Asian Women United, *With Silk Wings: Asian American Women at Work*, Berkeley, 1983, four videotapes; Chinese Historical Society of Southern California, *Linking Our Lives: Chinese American Women in Los Angeles* (Los Angeles, 1984); Akemi Kikumura, *Through Harsh Winters: The Life of a Japanese Immigrant Woman* (Novato CA: Chandler and Sharp, 1981); Maxine Hong Kingston, *The Woman Warrior* (New York: Knopf, 1977); Cathy Song, *Picture Bride* (New Haven: Yale University Press, 1983); Noriko Sawada, "Memoirs of a Japanese Daughter," *Ms.*, April 1980, 68–76, 110.

Frontiers 8:8 (1986): 96–101.

De/Colonizing the Exotic

Teaching "Asian Women" in a U.S. Classroom

PIYA CHATTERJEE

I am into my second month of teaching an upper-division undergraduate course on women from cross-cultural perspectives. I have designed it around Third World women's issues by complicating the categories "Third World" and "feminism." The topic of "Asian women" is presented through introductory debates that cover gender and Islam, political economy and Indian rural women, Chinese women and state communism, and Asian/-American[1] women's immigrant histories within the United States. There are fifty-three women and eight men in this particular class. We have spent three days discussing stereotypes and perceptions about Muslim women, colonial histories, and constructions of "the Orient." I have juxtaposed Leila Ahmed's critique of veiled reductions and Sarah Graham-Brown's writing on the history of orientalism and photography with Yasmina Bouziane's video *Ali Baba: Hollywood and Paris at Its Best.*[2]

A couple of weeks after we have discussed the complex connections between gender, colonialism, and the histories of orientalism, I notice that a woman has brought a friend to class. I am aware of his measured scrutiny. The next day, she hands me a piece of paper, saying it is a gift from him, a portrait. I find a sketch, a calligraphy almost, of a woman's face, long hair, large eyes placed against a faint outline of a mosque, some minarets. I start laughing, aghast at this transparent text of otherness: an imaginative snapshot of pedagogy made into exotic stillness. I ask her if he had attended our earlier discussions on the relationship of gender and orientalist history. She says no.

Many months later I show the sketch to an Indian woman, a friend, who points out that the woman's hands end in long fingernails with teardrops

Portrait sketched by a classroom guest.

that might signify blood. Combined with the minaret-like structure on one corner and the almost medusa-like tresses, the overall impression conveys both desire and danger. The face is almost pretty, the hair graphically curled. The possible signs of a titillating, and bloody, otherness rest on the outer frames of the image.

I have learned from the students in previous classes where I have presented debates about gender and orientalism that my own signature apparel of *shalwar kameez* (tunic and pants) and shawl has been misinterpreted as being "Muslim." The long loose tunic is "read" as tropologically kindred to a veil, "traditional" in a regressive sense.[3] In the first class in which I taught these issues, I introduced the minefields of cultural, racial, and gendered stereotypes through which Asian/-American women must negotiate a sense of place and agency. We explored the important ways in which these negotiations are embedded within community patriarchies that have been recrafted through immigrant experiences and the dominant culture's presumptions of cultural-bound "passivity." Several Asian/-American women in the class began a lively discussion about the stereotypes around Asian women as symbolic beacons of "tradition." Suddenly, a non-Asian woman, who I presumed was "white,"[4] challenged me: "So why is it that you continue to wear the clothes you wear?" While the class discussion was complicating the idea of "tradition" through various readings of Asian women's histories, this particular commentary suggested an unease with what appeared as emblematic of Asian difference: "traditional" clothes and the bodied picturesque. Now, as I ponder the meaning of the drawing, I am again made aware that my choice of clothing is being read *as* a conscious or political "choice."[5]

I am deeply uncomfortable about using my appearance as a pedagogical tool, yet this student's honest, uneasy, and even hostile interrogation of my dress and appearance suggests important scripts about nativism that I try to decenter in the classroom. Assumptions about representative authenticity, animated by embodied signals of "tradition," are reified through visual interpretation. Their effects are potent.

To use one's self as a pedagogical tool goes deeply against the grain of my cultural upbringing. I have memories of growing up in a joint family where we were disciplined gently if we asserted too loudly our personal and private ownership of a certain toy or a comic book. I am also aware that my own unease with generic *desi* ("of the country") interpretations about the open examination of the self is gendered: A desi woman does not frame her own individuality so explicitly, so publicly.[6] Indeed, the lessons taught to women are these: to serve, to learn how to use power through silence, and to stay on the edges of a frame. I am aware that I have not learned these lessons well and have also been permitted some transgressions.

Beginning with the everyday philosophies and rituals of family that stress the collective and the value of public effacement, the exercise of interpreting the self remains a difficult one. Yet, because one's pedagogical location is challenged by other kinds of philosophies, including a liberal extreme individualism in which "choice" is considered both autonomous and unburdened of history – constructing a hybrid self is a matter of ontological, theoretical, and pedagogical importance. Therefore, in the specific instance of inscription, *not to speak* is unwittingly to represent one's presence as a singular "authentic" representation of gendered others in a large cartographic arc that spans North Africa and large areas of West, South, and Southeast Asia.

So despite these contradictions, and because of them, I literally fling the shawl down and speak. It is with discomfort that I do so, and I am relieved when we move into other textual spaces where my own otherness is not so clearly determined by the gaze of my audience. In the first introductory days of teaching, I continue to interpret this gaze and its enigmatic silence as monolithic. I am unprepared for this pedagogy of the spectacle.

Compelled by classroom conversations that reify exoticism, spectacle, and personhood, this chapter examines how pedagogy animates the vectors of power through which women/difference/culture are engaged. Not only do these vectors constitute the substance of the class, they are also activated through the teaching/learning dynamic of pedagogy. At one level, I am interested in teasing out the dialectical connections between the abstract understandings of "culture" through interrogations of various written, visual, and oral texts in which differences are codified. Classroom pedagogy is the medium through which power, agency, and historical practice "out there" are linked to the immediate ontologies of difference within the borders of the classroom.

At another level, I suggest possible realignments around the discourses of difference through pedagogical practice. Discourses of difference within discussions about Asian/-American women suggest larger scripts and histories: the contestation of different definitions of Asian/-American "identity"; the racialization within and between other immigrant and "minority" communities; and the demarcations of class and status. Pedagogy becomes a medium through which these larger scripts are translated into the microcosm of classroom cultures.[7]

The arguments around pedagogy, culture, and difference intersect. I begin by addressing these intersections as part of a process through which I continue to learn what it means to be a teacher in a cultural landscape rife with conflict over who can teach and who can attend classes. The wider politics of location must be made explicit: legislative challenges to affirmative action policy have publicized the debates "on difference," with immediate impact on students and educators within the California public university system where I teach. For example, underscoring issues of diversity in the classroom are questions about immigration and migration and the specific politics of the U.S. – Mexican border that directly affect many of my students. While my reflections on teaching in southern California contain the subjective potency of ethnographic "thick description," they must also be situated in wider political scripts that have profound ramifications on the composition of classrooms and the climate of accepting "pedagogies about difference."

As a teacher who is both an Indian immigrant woman and a "South Asianist," I have had to reflect on my own "alie/nation" and its "dis/connections" to the histories of working-class immigration across the U.S. – Mexico border and the "Asian Pacific" rim. How do I engage the histories of U.S. "identity politics," which have a direct relevance to my students, without jettisoning my own intellectual objective: that is, to introduce them to cultural histories that are ineluctably "foreign" and outside the realms of an immediate Hyphen-American experience. In other words: how can the substance and design of a class cut across the seemingly absolute mapping of a difference "out there" to the variety of hybrid backgrounds "in here" without either appropriating the specificities of U.S. minority/working-class histories *or* diluting the particular histories of dis/connection?

The idea of "the nation," imagined and realized through state power, draws out its discourse around issues of authenticity, citizenship, and "home."[8] The borders of the imagined and actual nation-state draw the line between "foreign" and the "alien," the "First" and the "Third." I gesture toward the power inherent in such a landscape of the political imagination through the use of the slash and hyphen. The marks indicate a conjoining of the discourse of the nation (the slash marks the alien and allegiances not connected to the "American") with the immigrant push-and-pull of assimilation, integration, and "Americanization" (the horizontal plane of the hyphen). Yet, the hyphen appears too smooth a plane for the border-walks between nations and their states of power; the slash punctuates a jaggedness that is appropriate to many experiences of displacement.

Some of my students are children of immigrants who negotiate issues of assimilation and integration. Many are first generation, some are second. They focus on the racial/ethnic, gender, and class politics that define their sense of exclusion and inclusion in the dominant living paradigms of "Americanization." For some, college classrooms have provided a space in which their own on-the-street realities and experiences can be discussed as culture and history worthy of study and engagement. The classroom can be a place within which they can traverse difficult conceptual terrain and articulate their own alignments toward the cultural histories with which they are presented.

Some of these cultural histories gesture to "roots" in uneasy ways. A few South-Asian[9]/-American students have challenged my introduction to Indian women and rural poverty. They argue that such an emphasis reinvests the image of the subcontinent as a site of undifferentiated mass poverty, the land of Mother Teresa. Concurring with the problems of such monolithic assumptions, I ask the class to examine how and why such images are produced. However, I insist that the students confront other reasons, such as their own class and status positions within their "roots" and in the United States, that inform their reluctance to grapple with the ground realities of gender and rural poverty. Thus my interest in examining the other side of the slash, the "foreign," is to highlight the ambivalences of displacement and through that to connect to the varied experiences of dis/identifications of first-, second-, and third-generation immigrant students.

When discussions about cultural histories in which most students have no basic geographic knowledge are met with seeming indifference (or codified into a titillating and dangerous exoticism), my determination to make the "out there" relevant is underscored. When I perceive a lack of curiosity, or even resistance, to the material, I highlight the discourse of the nation, state power, and the assumptions of the "First" and "Third" inhered in these. I suggest that the historical and theoretical perspectives of outside-within cast a sharp and critical lens upon assumptions of authenticity, citizenship, and the politics of hyphenation that can obscure the cartographies of global power within which the United States remains a central player.

Yet if I do not make an attempt to connect (but not conflate) underlying themes of class, colonialism, race, and gender politics, I am doomed to reinscribing "difference" onto a map of the incommensurable, the other fixed in a place too removed for humanizing engagement. The binary of self/other is reinscribed. If learning is to be meaningful, then a dialectical dance between the "out there" and "in here" is imperative. It is a tense and critical process that engages difference through a critique of dominant visions that situate "culture" on static maps of power.

PEDAGOGY/CULTURE AND NO-SAFETY ZONES

As a postcolonial, Third World, feminist teacher, I work with the following basic philosophy: If I am to make what I teach critical and meaningful then my task is to jostle assumptions about what constitutes our perceptions of otherness by not locking them into the distance of the picturesque. The task is not to create a zone of safety within which knowledges of difference can be easily apprehended. Indeed, as I have already suggested, some of their inscriptions do not allow easy abstraction. I am not allowed the safety zone of disembodiment. When a calligraphic portrait is drawn in class, I am aware of how my placement in the picturesque reengages the safety of distance in terms of exoticism and alienation. These are the immediate and historical effects of the colonizing gaze that has linked women and the exotic.

Indeed, if difference is gazed "at" or drawn with pleasure, it suggests a mystification of this desire and its target of consumption. I shared with one class my first experience teaching an introductory Indian anthropology course. On the first day of that course, a student with a rather deadpan look on his face asked me whether I was going to serve tandoori chicken.[10] With the class, I start laughing, aghast but humored at this marking of culinary desire. I have known for some time that somewhat watered-down North Indian cuisine, which passes for "Indian" cuisine, has become for many their first introduction to "Indian" culture. Indeed, the smell of spices and curries has signified South Asian (and not only "Indian") otherness in important ways.[11] Smell, as much as sight, charts the parameters of cultural difference. A house with too much spice will smell "strange" to others. Tasting something mild, but different, is fine. Desire and consumption have to mediate the borders of what is palatable to dominant tastebuds.

Springing off this culinary tale, I warned my class that course material and discussion will not permit an easy consumption of difference, that I will insist that they enter into the frames of the picture, dwell on why the frames are drawn. They may also taste too much chili, too much sour, a little dash of tartness. As for my student who wanted tandoori, I suggested that he cater a delicious feast for the whole class. I was certain that the neighboring Indian restaurant would be delighted to have such good business. But I told him that, while I would be happy to have everyone eat and enjoy, dancing would not be part of the entertainment. No belly dancing, no *bharatanatyam*.[12] My tone was tart.

Though difficult and often angering, I have learned by following bell hooks that being vulnerable about my own sense of alienness in front of my students, and emphasizing that teaching, like learning, is a continuous process, has resulted in conversations that do not seek an easy "resolution" about misunderstandings.[13] Rather, these conversations have carved out a relatively trusting space for engagement about those very differences.

This engagement is mutual, though the dialogue is often tense and always inflected by the terms of institutional power and authority. Mutuality, in other words, is not about equal reciprocity in this instance. Power moves through every vein. It is, however, deeply dialogical.

Pedagogical vulnerability also traverses a jagged and thin line between democratic engagement and a professorial authority that is often delegitimized by inscriptions of gendered otherness.[14] As I have already suggested, when the subject positioning of authority is perceived and interpreted as exotically "other," then the contradictions of "teaching difference" are a more palpable and bodied business. How does a teacher read students' commentaries: as unease with the authority structures of the classroom or as a negative unease, even anger, with bodied difference?

THE "FIELD" IN TIME AND PLACE

I have been teaching undergraduate and graduate courses in the Department of Anthropology since 1995 and in Women's Studies since 1998 at the University of California, Riverside, a public university located an hour east of Los Angeles in a region known as the Inland Empire. The university has a student population of approximately ten thousand, many of whom come from the adjoining areas of San Bernadino, Riverside, and Orange counties. I have spent four years adjusting to this economically and ethnically diverse student body by designing courses around international women's histories and politics. Substance, design, and delivery of these courses on cross-cultural "women and gender issues" have mediated my assumptions about the relevance and significance of this material to my students' lives. Whether informed by economic constraints (e.g., working to pay for tuition and living expenses), familial responsibilities, a commuting culture, or categorical indifference (e.g., a general education requirement), their responses to the pedagogies of "difference" have shaped and transformed my teaching practice.

While graduate seminars in anthropology focus on social theory and postcolonial and feminist ethnographic writing, the undergraduate classes in women's studies are broadly conceived. Though my own research and writing examines gender and political economy in postcolonial India, my undergraduate classes do not privilege my South Asian training.[15] The syllabi are designed to encompass "Third World" women's politics within global frames that include minority and working-class women's histories in the United States. However, a large component of the class juxtaposes rural Indian, Chinese, and Asian American women's histories. Underwriting each examination of Asian women's cultures, whether defined as "feminist" or not, are discussions about political economy, orientalist frames that sexualize and render invisible diverse realities, the general problems with reductive and essentialized framings of "culture," and the specificity of racial and ethnic politics within U.S.-based women's movements. This Asian rubric is framed within and contrasted to other cultural contexts, which include African American, Middle Eastern, and Mexican American/Chicana specificities.

When listed through the women's studies program, women constituted a majority of the class with an average gender breakdown of 95 percent women and 5 percent men. Interesting variations occurred when the course was listed only in anthropology, when men made up 24 percent of the class. Ethnic composition, as with the rest of the campus, has been diverse, with a large number of Asian and Latino/a students and some African American and Native American students. I offer this basic information to sketch, with porous boundaries, an outline of the field. My methodology, following the basic tenets of ethnographic investigation, is a collage of participation and observation embedded within the terms of institutional power. Within the university system, though I may be perceived as an "outsider" (in ways I have already suggested), my authority is institutionally legitimated. Composing the syllabus, grading, creating exams, monitoring attendance, and granting extensions are all exercises of authority that create the terms of distance, acceptance, and, yes, even the measured surveillance of perceived outsideness.

How, then, to narrate these field notes? The subject/objects of my meditations are unaware of these textual reflections. They have participated in this narrative unwittingly. Because my observations span four years, some of the illustrations and my interpretations of events are just that, my own authoritative invocations.[16] As such, *some* of these interpretations lack the next step of the dialogical process within ethnographic translation: how would these "natives" respond to my analysis? Because my own pedagogical musings in class are highly reflexive, many issues (the discomfort of being marked alien in dress, for instance) were discussed in class. Indeed, at the beginning of every class I assign work by Paulo Freire and bell hooks in order to offer my approach to education and classroom cultures.[17] In journals, "think pieces," and group discussions, I encourage immediate responses to class material. Journal entries have often challenged or criticized my choice and presentation of material. That feedback has proved important to subjects taken up in subsequent days – and has even shaped my syllabus in subsequent versions of the class. It is through these critical responses to my teaching that I also cull what I shall call "vectors of unease": perceptions, conflations, and connections with gendered difference.

THE "EXOTIC" AND BEYOND

An introduction to the "Asian" women rubric in the class begins with a discussion around gender, Islam, and orientalism. I ask the class to bracket the term "Orient" for discussions that will encompass South/-East Asian and Asian/-American women's histories. A two-pronged objective is, ideally, set into motion. On one hand, stereotypes of gendered otherness that metaphorically travel to other parts of the globe, such as the belly dancer or geisha, are complicated. On the other hand, postcolonial histories that complicate such enduring tropes of exoticism and its desires are examined. A few weeks later, we enter into discussions about the specific images that "orientalize" Asian women's lives ("lotus flower," docility, passivity) that reconnect these images to orientalisms of gender and sexuality in different parts of the Arab world. I urge the class to reflect on the ways in which these external and internalized perceptions constrain Asian/-American women's involvement in the mainstream women's movement in the United States.[18]

These feedback loops are difficult to negotiate but important if I am not to have the journeys into particular women's experiences turn into a menu of incommensurable differences. The task is not only to navigate and present discourses of difference "out there"; it is also to pose strategically the historical and political linkages of these differences to the immediate articulations of the classroom and to the social contexts within which they are embedded.

International women's movements that have gained momentum in the past decades have argued that practicing the "global" within the "local" and creating a dialectical relationship between the two is at the heart of a strategic humanist project, whether one defines it as "feminist" or not. Pedagogy works as a dialectical link, or bridge, within the class's global/local examinations. As I have already suggested in the introduction, the difference of a global "out there" can be read in disconcertingly embodied ways. Yet, it is through that very site of "otherness" where a pedagogic act of connection might occur.

Let me offer some moments of rupture and illumination that tested the borders of my pedagogy. These were ruptures that taught me, again, the creativity and surprise in all dialogue. They are offered as ethnographic snippets and staged as performance. They are presented here as an amalgam of commentaries that are fragmented, culled from memory, and necessarily partial. As such, the amalgam presents a methodological pastiche shared with more traditional understandings of "fieldwork" where journals and notes constitute an important template for ethnographic and textual analysis. Unlike subjects in other fields who, for the most part, do not and cannot access the final products of text, my students may do so.[19] Indeed, I hope they will.

I do not claim an "exact" representation of dialogue presented here, and because of this, the dialogues are not placed in quotation marks. In order to camouflage identity, I have not marked students in terms of racial/ethnic or gender positions unless they become "identified" through the process of dialogue. No pseudonyms have been given in order to underscore my own marked institutional and authorial power and to protect the identity of students. Because these topics have been discussed in all lower- and upper-division courses, they may have taken place in any of six classes. Ethnographic time and place is purposefully fissured, categorically fluid.

The strategy of scripting the conversations into dramatic form is intended to underscore the performative, partial, and subjective remembrance of my *authori*tative invocations.[20] It is also a strategy through which I can talk back to the peculiar and powerful exoticization of the ethnographic gaze of my class. I am recreating, as faithfully as possible, the narratives from notes and memories of conversations. As the ellipses suggest, these are fragmentary but close renderings of particular moments of conversations in classes. Because I have not used tape recorders for any class discussions, these are representations. They do not claim any absolute representations and are necessarily porous. In the tradition of drama, however, it is the reverberations of bodied and oral effects (rather than individual identity markings) that interest me most. Analogous to other fictions of ethnography, they suggest transcendent and wider political scripts.

DOTS
Act 1. Scene 1. Class #x-1.

PIYA: Okay, folks, today we move to women in India. Let me emphasize the specificity of this territorial and historical location because "India" is hugely diverse, and I want to attend to the question of what "Indian" women we speak of. But before we do this, I want to ask you, when you think of Indian women, what comes to mind immediately? Stereotypes. [Silence] . . . Don't be scared, I have heard them all. Come on.

DIFFERENT VOICES: Poor. Oppressed. Docile. Passive. Dowry-death. Wife-burning.

PIYA: Excellent, you have covered most of them. See the connections with our previous discussions on the veil and Islam. . . . What else? Where do you think these images get generated? . . . [Silence] How about films and movies, media? . . .

STUDENT: I am interested in Indian film. I know there is a big industry there. And the pictures I have seen of Indian women, at least the actresses, is that they are voluptuous, dance around trees, and so I think exotic, erotic first. Those women don't look docile to me. . . .

PIYA: Interesting, this isn't a class about Indian or, indeed, Hindi film, which is what I think you are referring to, [Nods assent] and we could have complicated discussions about ideals of women and sexuality depicted through these films . . . but this exotic, erotic connection as a more "outside" look in is interesting. . . . Can we push that more?

STUDENT: I don't know about other films but what about *Kama Sutra*?[21] Have you seen it? What do you think about it?

PIYA: You go first. What did you think? . . . [Silence] Okay, I guess you don't want to go out on a limb. I had problems with it. I saw it in Calcutta with my sister and we were expecting some powerful statement about women's sexuality, and, well, we felt the plot was weak and there was too much attention paid to incredibly boorish sexual politics of royal men. I read some *Elle* review about how it "liberated" sexuality, . . . but both of us thought it was a hoot, but nothing more than gloss and made for an outside audience. But, worse, I think its power was its beautiful colors and scenes. . . .

STUDENT: Yeah, it was really gorgeous. All those fabrics. Do all Indian women dress like that?

PIYA: [irritated] No, no. This is the major problem I had with it. That it re-invested women's sexuality through the picturesque . . . the erotic, exotic connection, . . . and this is why folks here lap it up. This is a problem. What "Indian" women are we looking at – women within a certain depiction of royalty. . . .

STUDENT: [puzzled tone] You know, I have been listening to this and I am confused because I have a whole other view about Indian women. . . .

This erotic, exotic stuff does not fit. . . . I have always thought actually that Indian women are mean old hags with dots on their heads. . . . They wear long gowns like you are wearing, and they stare at you meanly. . . . They dominate the men around them. [There is a pause, a few loud gasps, some students look at Piya nervously. One or two look angry]

PIYA: [taking a deep breath] Hookkkkaaay. Wow. Okay, let me think about this. [Pause] You make an interesting remark. And you should be aware that it is loaded. First, let me ask you why you make such generalizations? Do you know any "Indian" women, and from what did you draw your perception of them as "mean old hags with dots on their heads"?

STUDENT: [nervously] Oh, mmaaan. You are not getting how I meant that, I meant that they are strong women. . . . you know, dominating. . . .

PIYA: Oh, no, I think I get what you are saying. I also asked for your opinion. But I will not deny that I am really affected by what you have said. I really am interested in how folks create their perceptions and generalizations . . . so I am asking you again, what happened to make you conclude that all Indian women are . . . ?

STUDENT: Okay, I remember one day when I was at the park with my young daughter and I saw these old women, I think they were from India. Anyway, they were wearing like the thing you wear, you know the long thing, and they had dots on their heads. I remember they were loud and they stared at me meanly.

PIYA: Right, . . . there are lots of things going here, . . . [Pause] but let me begin by noting the way you moved from a specific and strange encounter to a pretty massive generalization. . . .

STUDENT: [more embarrassed than defensive] But I have said I did not mean it like you are taking it. . . .

PIYA: Perhaps, but what you have to deal with, and what we have to deal with, is this: What are the effects of what we say and what we think of others who are "different" from us? What is initially striking about your comment is this: You see something, the dots, the long gown. Immediately, you notice the way they are looking at you. . . . It is all together. . . . But what is it that you see that you mark as somehow negative? I mean, "dots on the head" and "mean old hags" kinda go together. . . .

STUDENT: Did I really say mean old hags? [Others nod in assent]

PIYA: [in rushed speech, visibly upset] I throw out a general question to everyone because I don't want to keep you on some hot seat, though I think we really need to address this commentary more specifically. But here is a general thought. I guess I am really a foreigner in so many ways, but part of being foreign is that I can ask about things in other ways. . . . So since you know more about being here than I do, at least most of you, can I ask you this because it puzzles me? Help me out. Teach me about the United States.

Why is it that difference is seen as threatening in the U.S.? This is a big paradox for me because look at this class, look at all the diversity here, and I think, how terrific. I mean you see someone with a dot on their head, or a thing in their nose [I emphatically point at my nose] . . . . Why don't we go and ask people about their dots – in a respectful way, of course? . . . We are different from each other, but why the taboo, why the negative? Why don't we, you, engage the difference. . . .

[Silence] . . . . Okay, I want us to reflect on what happened in this comment, and I would like to come back to it because it is very complicated. . . . [Turning to student] Look, I appreciate the fact you were honest, but this is hard, and I want to attend to this over the next few days. But to all of you, I want you to think about difference, about how and why and through what specific moments you/we create our images of other people who are not the same as us. And I would like to end by saying that about ten years ago a series of anti-Indian hate crimes occurred in New Jersey – aimed at Indian immigrants. One of the gangs that was later indicted for crimes, which ranged from firebombs in letterboxes to murder, was called the Dotbusters.[22] I want you think about that. Dotbusters.

Act 1. Scene 2. Class #x-2.

PIYA: Right, I wanted to say a few things before we move into a more grounded examination of Indian women's lives [Looking around for the student who had made dot comment] Okay, where is he? He has not come to class. Hmmm. I wanted to thank him for having the guts to say what he did because I asked for opinions. And I want to make clear that this is the kind of stuff that needs to be talked about, but it is really hard. This is what I learned. [Pause] My response to what he said was very felt, and even angry. Did you guys read it as angry? [Several nervous nods] Yup, I probably was, but I was also trying to process the levels of the commentary; it was hard. Remember bell hooks and pedagogy? Well this was a really obvious moment of vulnerability. But I don't want him, or you, to walk away, weirded-out by this. Talking about any of this is hard because we are all involved, whatever fence of "identity" we sit on. Working through how we form our perceptions takes a lot of guts, and that is the point. None of this is a given, any of these categories: they are lived. This is why it is hard to abstract – but we must if we are to understand that the effects of what we think or say do have a lot of ramifications. We are responsible for our words. Does anyone want to say anything? [Long silence] Okay, I guess not. Let us move on. If anyone knows him, please tell him to come to class.

Scene 3. After Class #x-5.

STUDENT: [nervously] Hi. Um. . . . Can I talk to you?

PIYA: Aha. So you are back. . . . Good. Yeah, let's walk, I am heading to my office.

STUDENT: [smiling, nervous] You aren't going to beat me up, are you?

PIYA: Do I look like I am? I was sorry you did not come to the next class, you know after our discussion. . . . I did say at that point that I appreciated your honesty . . . though, of course, I was very affected by it, but then I have been thinking. . . .

STUDENT: I really did not say "mean old hags," . . . did I? I asked someone else, and she said I did. I didn't even realize I said it. . . . That is scary. . . .

PIYA: Yeah, you did say it. But I guess I was more interested in the whole thing, the dots, first, and "the mean old hags" . . . and where you began to think about "Indian" women. . . . The park thing . . . what was that about?

STUDENT: I have daughter whose mother is Hispanic, and I take her out. So I was sitting there, and these women were there. Man, were they bossy and loud! And they glared at me, which is what I remembered. . . .

PIYA: Okay, so think about that, . . . why did their "bossiness" and loudness make them "mean" and "hags"? . . .

STUDENT: But what I meant was that they were strong. . . .

PIYA: Come *on!* Don't tell me that "mean old hags" is not negative. . . . Okay, your notion of their strength was that it made them mean, and old, and haggish.

STUDENT: Jeez. You are tough. I don't have trouble with strong women. My mother was strong. My girlfriend was strong. Why would it be a problem?

PIYA: Yup . . . okay, but lots of things about gender . . . . [With awkwardness] Now I am curious about the way they looked at you, also why they become "mean," . . . right? I am wondering about that because they did something that made you respond in a defensive way. . . . What was this meanness? . . .

STUDENT: Reasons? I don't know. You mean because I am black? I am not sure. Maybe. . . .

CLASSTALK
Act 2. Scene 1. Class #y-1.

PIYA: Right, today's readings are about "class." They were good readings, and I hope we can bounce off them in our discussion. So what are the subtle ways in which we make quick judgements about people's backgrounds, read "economic" background and status perhaps in ways that we don't even register consciously? . . .

STUDENT: Like in *Pretty Woman* where she did not know how to use the silverware in the fancy restaurant. . . .

STUDENT: The way people talk . . . accents. . . .

PIYA: Yeah, great. Accents. Who has seen *My Fair Lady*? [Lots of hands raised] So what is going on with accents, pretty obvious, huh? . . . Her becoming a lady means changing her cockney accent. . . . What about here? How do we read accents?

STUDENT: Well, English accents are considered "classy" – they sound so smart. . . .

PIYA: Really? But as *My Fair Lady* points out – which British accents? . . .

STUDENT: Yours. You have an English accent.

PIYA: Does it "sound" British to you? I have been told, in India, that it is very "Amerrrican." Other folks tell me it sounds Danish. . . . So what do you assume about my class. . . .

STUDENT: There is something about being really educated that you pick up, and it sounds "classy," like you come from a well-to-do family and all that. . . .

PIYA: Interesting. Yes, I have had the privilege of a great education, and I mean "privilege" in the class sense of that, but my immediate family history has lots of things that would surprise you. For one, English is not a comfortable language for my family. Why?

STUDENT: It is not their first language.

PIYA: Right, it is not their mother tongue. They have not adopted it as a mother tongue as I have. What do you think is going on – why I have and they may not have?

STUDENT: Colonialism. British. And your education.

PIYA: Yes, excellent. But there are lots of Indians of my parents' generation who speak English very fluently. But in my family this is not the case, though everyone can understand and speak the language. None of my elders had access to a fancy education, like I did, because of both colonialism and class, though they saved and sacrificed every penny for their children's education. Why? Because my father and uncle were refugees from the Indian Partition of 1947. [I briefly explain Partition] Though they did very well financially, they are utterly self-made and my class contradictions are there.

So if you perceive that my "classy" accent indicates smooth sailing, think again. Think about that article by Bernice Mennis about being Jewish and working-class and what her education does to her relationship to her family.[23] . . . I bet there are a lot of folks here whose mother tongue is not English, and you have struggled with these issues [Nods here and there] . . . So folks, here is the moral of the story: Don't judge an accent by what you hear [Chuckles all around].

Act 2. Scene 2. After Class #y-1.

STUDENT: Piya, I wanted to tell you something really strange. I was remembering it when you were talking about the stuff about your family. I was at a talk that you gave a few years ago. And I remember being really surprised by your presentation because the woman who had organized the talks had said something strange before we went to your lecture. . . . I didn't think it strange then, though I was surprised by your presentation. . . .

PIYA: Uh-huh. What do you mean . . . about me? What for? I was just a guest speaker. . . .

Student: Yeah. She said that you were from India, a princess, from this aristocratic background, and that we should be really careful when we spoke to you.

Piya: [jaw dropping] You are kidding, no, you have got to be kidding! Wow. That is amazing. But she did not know who I was. So I became a princess to the class. Oh, no. Just like that [Snapping fingers] This is too weird. I must say this is very upsetting. No, don't worry, I will never say anything to her, but thank you for letting me know. I guess an "accent," and what else, is judged by its cover. Gotta write about this postcolonial princess stuff. I am getting tired of it. That is what I am going to call it – postcolonial princess. . . .

INTERPRETING THE ACTS AND OTHER THEORETICAL GESTURES

Through the scripts of dots and class, I am aware of how moments of classroom dialogue (in its immediacy), reflection (with friends), and writing (this chapter), offer both the excitement and debilitation involved in opening one's self to situations of unease. When a pedagogic logic of vulnerability is at play, then neither inscription nor rupture should be surprising. The spaces of engagement that they break into are themselves uncharted, creative, and critical. They also pose important questions about the theoretical languages through which we craft our analysis and understanding of racial meaning systems in the United States. Specific (yet conflated) inscriptions of exoticism suggest the vexed politics of South Asian/-American women's experiences. Why, I may be asked, should I interpret such an appreciative interest in gendered otherness (tandoori chicken or a quick sketch) as racially coded?

An analysis of the cultural economies of difference, within which paradigms of "race" history are embedded, demonstrates the mutual inflections of these categories (gender/class/race/ethnicity/sexuality) as lived experience. "Culture" cannot be ossified into distance. It is a constituting and constitutive body of categorical signs. The powerful and important binaries of the black/white paradigm or Pan-Asian theories of connective solidarity are not adequate models for the conflicted cultural and class politics of South Asian/-Americans who may situate themselves,[24] or be situated, in conflict with other "minority" communities including other Asian/-Americans.[25] While these paradigms offer important, necessary, and intersecting moments of history/theory,[26] they do not provide an adequate language for many South Asian/-American women's histories.[27]

In this particular examination of pedagogy within which "exoticism" was to be deconstructed through careful attention to the specificities of histories in Asia and the United States, its bodied reification was stunning. Yet it is the multiple positioning of the gaze that is illuminating. In the first act, the discussion about the erotic/exotic Indian women as a site of *visual* pleasure switched into another register when the women become "mean old hags with dots on their heads." Danger sits on the other side of desire that, medusa-like, might rear a strange head of hair and dots.

In my immediate oral response to the student in the public domain of the classroom, I reined in the first defensive response to what I perceived as a hostile remark. But as my response gained momentum, I spontaneously threw out the reference to the Dotbuster attacks in New Jersey. Somehow, my response caught on to a set of historical events in which the "dot" came to define Indians as "dotheads" and compelled hate crimes against Indian immigrants. More significantly, my identification with the alien otherness marked by a specific comment about the "dot" is apparent when I explicitly marked myself as a "foreigner." While there is certainly no connection between a comment thrown out in a class discussion with events that occurred ten years ago on the other coast, my instinct caught onto a bodied and ideological thread. I knew that the "exotic" had just turned ugly.

Yet, another important index sits within the interpretive moments of the first act. Indeed, the subject position of the student speaker creates an important, and problematic, moment of silence. I have to ask myself, why is it that I could not articulate an adequate analysis of the complex racializations of the commentary, and its history, into the public orality of the classroom? Why could I not push the issues of racial subjecthood – his African American/black positioning and my Indian – into the conversation about the possible racialization of a "mean" gaze upon him? My internal dialogue about such a "failure" opens into other important examinations about "South Asian" racisms vis-à-vis African American/black communities in the United States.[28]

I have much to learn about how to articulate the contested categories of race within the public domain of my U.S. classroom. It is a recognition that is inflected by my position as an Indian immigrant woman whose own racial and class identity is consistently reified and placed against the dominant and binary paradigms of "race" in problematic ways. Indeed, how does a foreign "brown" woman claim the authority to speak *publicly* to an African American man about the possibility of a racist gaze from other "brown" women? And speak also to his own gendered and racial/cultural inscriptions of otherness?

At this point, I am bereft of a language. I know there are no singularities here. There are many paths to the truths of all our alienations. I merely gesture toward their paradoxes: the boxes within the boxes within the boxes. The conversations are ongoing. I am only grateful that the classroom allows these fragmentary, partial, even failed examinations of *shared* woundings.

I come full circle with the second act, where class is accented. Though the first and second acts occur within different times and spaces, the discussion of the film *Kama Sutra* and the last revelation of my alleged background as a princess stages one theater, one play. The exotic is made into a seamless classed object, fixed immutably into some strange visual and accented pastiche of the British Raj gone postcolonial. I dance in these Kafka-esque inscriptions, aware that a certain history is being rewritten as a monolith, a seamless veiling of its own fears of contradiction and disorder.

While this inscription of being what I call a "postcolonial princess" has haunted my immigrant experience, I recognize how inscriptions of class can obscure other forms of marginalization. How could one speak through these other modes of alie/nation, marked by immigrant status and racial/cultural difference, without denying postcolonial privilege? The inscription of a hypervisible royal subjecthood reduces raced scripts of marginalization into monolithic understandings of class power and privilege within global frames. Access to privileged education maintains the elitism of bourgeois postcolonial scholars, such as myself, within the U.S. academy, but the translations of such class experience between "Third" and "First" Worlds also need to be complicated through discussions of race, ethnicity, and nation.

More significantly, the task of complicating "class talk" is urgent in other ways. The specific coming to "voice" about reductive inscriptions is compelled by my need to envision a more collective and coalitional understanding of cultural politics and pedagogies. By writing into the rhetorical, bodied, and contradictory forces of marginalization, I seek a political lexicon that is honest about privilege but does not deny other valences of marginality. Such a lexicon might lead us to a pedagogy that is dialectically connected to the histories of daily life, through and beyond the limits of individuated and specific life experience.

As I reflect on these coupled theaters of dots and privilege, I recognize again how the classroom has allowed me to enter and create the spaces of the possible. I have learned that I, too, could arrive at some "voice" to engage some of the silences resting deep in one particular immigrant experience. What was most significant, however, was that despite the awkwardness and even the lack I felt in these voicings, it was in these classes that I first began to articulate my own confusion about South Asian/-American experience. Indeed, it was through the give and take of orality, which is the gift of classroom pedagogy, that I began to understand more clearly the contours of slash and hyphen, the difficult choreography of being outside/in and inside/out.

HOME BOUND

Then, again, there are the epiphanies less fraught but equally powerful. These are languages of "home" that haunt the postcolonial and im/migrant imagination.[29] A Vietnamese/-American woman comes to me at the end of a class after I have given the final assignment, a research paper or project around gender issues, broadly defined. She is nervous because her facility with English writing and composition is not good. In a couple of journal entries, she has written an evocative narrative about her family's journey to the United States as refugees, or "boat people." I tell her how much I learned from her journals. Could she work these reflections into a larger research project?

"But what about my English?" she responds. I tell her to break into Vietnamese if she has problems with the translation of terms and footnote English meanings at the bottom of the page. Both languages speak this history and its hybridity. I am convinced, reading her effort and sincerity, that the text she will offer will be unique and telling. She hands in thirty pages of a remarkable narrative: poetic, fragmented, but also one that meticulously documents the particularities of her family's history into a wider analysis of Vietnamese immigration into the United States. The project is a peerless tour de force.

The next term, she comes to my office with some sweet spring rolls that her mother has made, offering them to me as a gift. I am struck by this gesture and its familiarity. Her gesture is a certain rendering of Pan-Asian sensibilities about "respect": the offering of food as a gift to a teacher. There are other symbolic economies here: of authority, obeisance, and inclusion. It registers power, but it welcomes me within. I am caught suddenly in a web of something beyond nostalgia. She tells me that the stories of rural Indian women were kindred to her memories of Vietnamese village life. She did not think they would be so similar, so familiar. Neither did I.

It is perhaps a banal, even egregious, gesture to assert one's teaching as the most "rewarding" aspect of one's career and sense of "vocation." Certainly, as a process and an ongoing narrative, it combines the most frustrating and angering experiences with the most positive, uplifting moments – to have had an affirming and positive effect on someone's life, however briefly. Through teaching, I continue to learn, and relearn, the politics of alienation not only as the personal and deeply subjective experience of my *chosen* "exile" and its concomitant loss but also the necessity of placing that alienated subjectivity into a wider relief by connecting it to a broader experience of loss and exclusion that many of my students share. When they don't, and even when they are seemingly indifferent, their apparent stasis compels me to suggest that what is at stake is a psychic and political understanding of others, and othering, in a most significant sense.

Can we reenvision the methodological and theoretical connections between studying "gender and cultural difference" as cultural production and politics within the site of teaching and learning itself? Can reflections on "pedagogy" and classroom practice retool and broaden our understandings of "culture" and "difference" in a larger theoretical sense? In other words, by paying close attention to classroom pedagogies as cultural processes can we glean new insights about our own assumptions about cultural practice "out there" or "in here"? The disciplinary mapping of difference (the cartography of a "field" elsewhere) collapses if these interrogations consider *culture as a pedagogic process.*

As an anthropologist, I am also interested in thinking about pedagogy as a fertile conceptual ground for reimagining ethnographic practice itself. The "field" of investigation is not only "out there" in research sites where cultures are produced (whether they lie within or outside our national borders); it rests also within spaces where we bring alive through oral and visual narratives those stories of otherness familiar and unfamiliar to our own ethnographic "expertise" and experience. Our specifically anthropological pedagogy is, after all, culled from what we have learned from "there." The traditional "field" is also, following the same logic, a pedagogic site where the "natives" are also our teachers.

It is significant that this chapter has traveled with me to North Bengal, India, and the home villages of tea plantation women whom I have known now for eight years. I script its "end" on the border of Bhutan, on a sloping fringe of the Eastern Himalaya. Tomorrow, a *mahila samity* (women's organization) from New Dooars Tea Estate and Debpara Tea Estate will meet with one doctor, a local teacher, and a politician to begin a conversation about tying together income-generating projects with a nongovernmental clinic in which they will be primary decision makers. We have discussed education and health at length in our many talks over hot red tea in the villages. We engage other pedagogies. My role is always that of a student. Only sometimes am I a teacher.

Consider all these narratives as a set of globally connected field notes: an ethnographic site that is both home and not-home, familiar and unfamiliar, and where we, teacher and student alike, straddle the inside/outside borders of power and dance its ineluctable paradoxes.

NOTES

I am grateful to Marian Sciachitano, Linda Vō, and other reviewers for their careful editing. I extend my gratitude to Tatha Banerjee, M. S. Chatterjee, Nigel Hughes, Erla Marteinsdottir, and Parama Roay, who faxed and e-mailed material between Riverside CA, and Calcutta and Banarhat (India). Thanks also to colleagues at the University of California, Riverside's Center for Asian Pacific America (CAPA) for a close reading and vigorous critique of this chapter.

1. I use the slash and hyphen to indicate the important ways in which "Asian"

identity politics in the United States is complicated by various immigrant experiences whose primary alignments reside in a territorially distant "Third World" as well as within the "Third World" politics of being an Asian, minority, and sometimes working-class community in the United States. I add the slash and hyphen to register difficulties of assuming that binary or bifurcated positioning. The slash, in particular, punctuates the disjunctures within the staggered economies of identification. I am indebted to Grace Poore's critical reflections about the contested permeability of the category "South Asian" and its vexed relationship with a certain U.S.-centric Asian American positioning. She notes that "while U.S. acceptance of the identity of 'Asian American' is another victory in the struggle for setting the record straight in U.S. social history, the term, unfortunately, subsumes those of us who are Asian but not American" ("The Language of Identity," in *A Patchwork Shawl: Chronicles of South Asian Women in America,* ed. Shamita Das Dasgupta [New Brunswick NJ: Rutgers University Press, 1998], 25–26).

2. Leila Ahmed, "Western Ethnocentrism and Perceptions of the Veil," *Feminist Studies* 8:3 (1982): 521–34. See Sarah Graham-Brown, *Images of Women: The Portrayal of Women in the Photography of the Middle East, 1860–1950* (New York: Columbia University Press, 1988). Yasmina Bouziane is a Moroccan photographer and filmmaker based in New York. Her work includes multimedia exhibitions, videography, photography, and film and offers trenchant postcolonial and feminist critiques of "orientalist" representation through both archival and contemporary popular "texts." *Ali Baba* is a short video montage of film and media representations of sexuality and gendered otherness in contemporary depictions of the "Middle East."

3. For an interesting ethnographic discussion about how the actual *hijab,* or the practice of veiling, is deployed hybridly and as a sign of resistance within Pakistani immigrant identity-making, see "'We Are Graceful Swans Who Can Also Be Crows': Hybrid Identities of Pakistani Muslim Women," in Dasgupta, *A Patchwork Shawl,* 56–58.

4. I place quotations around the category of "white" to indicate the ways in which my perception of this student's "whiteness" needs to be complicated by a deeper reading of the history of "whiteness" in this country. I want to be alert to the assumptions of my own gaze and categorization. Interestingly, later in the class, this particular student berated me in a journal for "forcing" her to read African American women's histories. An interesting dialogue between us about her interpretation of my "choice" of material as "coercion" and her own unease did take place outside the public domain of the classroom, and though we achieved some understanding about the racial politics of "difference," I was somewhat validated by my intuition that her question of my apparel was a hostile one.

5. I have been informally asked why I "choose" to wear the shalwar kameez,

but this was the first time that such a question was posed within the context of institutional authority. The consciousness of being inscribed does not influence my daily decisions, so this perception of "choice" was instructive.

6. Often used by expatriate and im/migrant South Asians outside South Asia, desi suggests an identity beyond the specificities of regional, religious, and national roots. I use it because it suggests this hybrid subcontinental sensibility rather than the more limiting and hegemonic descriptor of "Indian" for the particular point I am making here about my own postcolonial, immigrant, and transnational (Nigerian, Indian, and North American) subjectivity. At the same time, I also recognize that its very linguistic roots in the North Indian language, Hindi, contains hegemonic effects. Nevertheless, I seize its vernacular destabilizations while recognizing its limits.

7. For an important discussion of pedagogy as a vehicle through which a critical ethnography "of difference" within the U.S. university's paradigms of multiculturalism take place, see Deborah Wong's "Ethnomusicology and Critical Pedagogy as Cultural Work: Reflections on Teaching and Fieldwork," *College Music Symposium* 38 (1998): 80–100.

8. Chandra Mohanty and Biddy Martin, "Feminist Politics: What Has Home Got to Do With It?" in *Feminist Studies/Critical Studies,* ed. Teresa de Lauretis (Bloomington: Indiana University Press, 1986), 191–212.

9. I use this category advisedly, following Grace Poore's detailed discussion about the history of its umbrella-like usage for people from the subcontinent living in the United States. Apart from its possible co-optation by Indians to hegemonize it for contemporary Indian history, it is also problematic for members of a diaspora who have lived in Malaysia, Kenya, and the Caribbean and contend with other frames of race, class, and ethnicity ("The Language of Identity," 22–25).

10. Tandoori chicken is a delicacy of North Indian Mughlai cuisine. It is cooked in a special oven, the *tandoor,* and has a characteristic reddish glaze.

11. Sonia Shah notes, "For me, the experience of 'otherness,' the formative discrimination in my life, has resulted from culturally different (not necessarily racially different) people thinking they were culturally central: thinking that *my* house smelled funny, that *my* mother talked weird, that *my* habits were strange. They were normal; I wasn't" ("Presenting the Blue Goddess: Toward a National Pan-Asian Feminist Agenda," in *Women's Lives: Multicultural Perspectives,* ed. Gwyn Kirk and Margo Okazawa-Rey [Mountain View CA: Mayfield Publishing, 1998], 39).

12. *Bharatanatyam* is a form of classical South Indian dance.

13. bell hooks, "Theory as Liberatory Practice," in *Teaching to Transgress: Education as the Practice of Freedom* (New York: Routledge, 1994), 59–75.

14. Homa Hoofdar subtly and powerfully presents these contradictions of authority and otherness in "Feminist Anthropology and Critical Pedagogy: The An-

thropology of Classrooms' Excluded Voices," in *Radical In<ter>ventions: Identity, Politics, and Difference/s in Educational Praxis,* ed. Suzanne de Castell and Mary Bryson (Albany: State University of New York Press, 1997), 211–32.

15. By "privileging," I mean the following: In textual substance only a couple of days are spent specifically on Indian women; however, orally, I often use that experience and expertise to compare, contrast, and connect with women in very different cultural and national contexts.

16. I will be using this chapter to engage the boundaries of pedagogic dialogue and debate by offering it to subsequent classes for critique and reflection. Responses and reflections from students will be incorporated into another ethnographic staging.

17. Paulo Freire, *Pedagogy of the Oppressed,* trans. Myra Bergman Ramos (New York: Herder and Herder, 1970). See also hooks, *Teaching to Transgress.*

18. Merle Woo, "Letter to Ma," in Kirk and Okazawa-Rey, *Women's Lives,* 64–68.

19. This raises some very important questions around issues of accountability and textual circulation in the production of ethnographic texts. Though many anthropologists have situated their work in circuits of accountability to communities they have studied, a theoretical and pragmatic critique of language, literacy, class, and imperialism (embedded in the discourse of globalization) and its relationship to anthropological *politics* is yet to emerge in the *center* of disciplinary theorizing about ethnographic practice. See Edward Said, "Representing the Colonized: Anthropology's Interlocuters," *Critical Inquiry* 15 (winter 1989): 207–25. In this presentation, my students are located in the structural analog of "natives" of old anthropology, but because this chapter will circulate "here," they will access and critique my authorial invocations.

20. Marianne Paget, "Performing the Text," *Journal of Contemporary Ethnography* 19:1 (1990): 136–55. In using the dramatic form, I am creating an analog to "dance," which Elizabeth Wheatley argues is an expressive form that can subvert the ethnographic gaze ("Dances with Feminists: Truth, Dares and Ethnographic Stares," *Women's Studies International Forum* 17:4 [1994]: 421–23).

21. This is a film by the New York–based Indian filmmaker Mira Nair, equally well known for the popular success of *Salaam Bombay* and *Mississippi Masala.*

22. For a brilliant and insightful analysis of these events, see Deborah Misar, "The Murder of Navroze Mody: Race, Violence, and the Search for Order," *Amerasia Journal* 22:2 (1996): 55–76.

23. Bernice Mennis, "Jewish and Working Class," in *Women: Images and Realities,* ed. Amy Kesselman, Lily McNair, and Nancy Schniedewind (Mountainview CA: Mayfield Publishing), 232–35.

24. Sucheta Mazumdar, "Race and Racism: South Asians in the United States," in *Frontiers of Asian American Studies: Writing, Research, and Commentary,* ed. Gail

M. Nomura et al. (Pullman: Washington State University Press, 1989), 29. See also Amritjit Singh's extended discussion of Indian racism against African Americans, in "African Americans and the New Immigrants," in *Between the Lines: South Asians and Postcoloniality,* ed. Deepika Bahri and Mary Vasudeva (Philadelphia: Temple University Press, 1996).

25. Misar, "The Murder of Navroze Mody," 57. In the specific events of hate crimes in New Jersey, Misar, quoting a *Washington Post* article, notes that another gang who targeted Indians, called the Lost Boys, included "one black, one Jew, several Greeks and Italians, three Filipinos, one half Filipino and half Indian, and several Anglos"(Al Kamen, *Washington Post,* November 16, 1991, A6). Misar argues that this shatters any binary formulations of white/nonwhite and Asian-on-Asian violence (62).

26. See Singh's important discussion of these intersections, in "African Americans and the New Immigrants," 95, 100–101.

27. Shah argues that conjuntures of racisms, placed as bicultural feminisms, must be linked to create solidarity across Asian women's groups. These new craftings, however, must stretch the binary understandings of racial economies of difference ("Presenting the Blue Goddess," 37–42).

28. See Sucheta Mazumdar and Amritjit Singh for the most comprehensive discussions of the feudal and class mythographies that translate into immigrant and bourgeois models of superiority and racism vis-à-vis other minority communities, but in particular, African American/black communities (Mazumdar, "Race and Racism," 25–38; and Singh, "African Americans and the New Immigrants," 98–103).

29. Chandra Talpade Mohanty, "Defining Genealogies: Feminist Reflections on Being South Asian in North America," in Kirk and Okazawa-Rey, *Women's Lives,* 92–97.

Frontiers 21:1/2 (2000): 87–110.

Negotiating Textual Terrain

A Conversation on Critical and Pedagogical Interventions in the Teaching of Ethnic Autobiography

SHELLI B. FOWLER, TIFFANY ANA LÓPEZ, KATE SHANLEY,
CAROLINE CHUNG SIMPSON, AND TRAISE YAMAMOTO

This chapter is the product of an online conversation on a topic that followed a panel presentation at the November 1995 American Studies Association meeting in Pittsburgh. The conversation panel at the ASA convention generated much discussion about the necessity, and inherent difficulty, of negotiating cultural difference(s) in the reading and teaching of ethnic autobiographies. Following the panel presentation last fall, we continued the discussion for a brief time on the Internet.[1] Although the theme for last fall's American Studies Association was "Toward A Common Ground" our discussion at the conference did not focus on, or find, "A Common Ground" (in the uppercase sense of the phrase), nor was it the intention of our panel to do so. Instead, the focus of both the ASA panel and the following discussion was on the rough and rocky terrain that must be carefully negotiated on any path headed toward the celebrating of commonalities: in our view, the exploration of that terrain is a difficult and ongoing task that should appropriately precede the discovery of any common ground to comfortably settle on.

The collective conversation that follows does not attempt to offer definitive answers to the complex issues of appropriate reading strategies and pedagogy for the diverse genre of ethnic autobiographies. It is, instead, a continuation of a dialogue that attempts to articulate some of the central concerns we have, and it is an attempt to broaden the conversation beyond the panelists and audience participants at last year's conference. Likewise, there is no effort here to reach consensus. Each of the participants, Tiffany Ana López, Kate Shanley, Caroline Chung Simpson, Traise Yamamoto, and I, work within the field of ethnic literature, yet each of us brings to the conversation a range of both similar and different concerns. We began this online discussion with two questions raised by audience members at our panel session: first, what connection is there between the reader's "subject position" and her/his ability to "read" strategies of resistance in an American ethnic autobiography and, second, when you are teaching American ethnic autobiographies, or any ethnic literature, do you have any particular classroom strategies that you use for foregrounding the issues raised by the texts? In other words, are there different pedagogical strategies that you use to introduce students to "reading the strategies of resistance" in ethnic literary texts?

Shelli B. Fowler

KATE SHANLEY: Because it is so difficult to generalize a subject position, this question is exceedingly difficult to answer. On the one hand, American Indian tribes vary so widely that an "American Indian" reader is already immersed in multiculturalism. I remember once in graduate school, the professor of a minority literature course turned to me and asked me if I could read the Navajo passage before us. As an Assiniboine, I might be able to read a Lakota, Dakota, or Nakota passage, but Navajo . . . ! On the other hand, American Indians all share a certain history of oppression, being forced to live with U.S. policy and government practice toward indigenous peoples. I do have things to say about the boarding school experiences of Natives, reservation life, general philosophies toward land use and relation to other-than-human beings. Some of that a non-Indian can bring to his or her reading of a particular text, but certainly not all.

In addition to those differences, some texts – *Papago Woman*, for example – need to be analyzed from an academic perspective as well as from a culturally specific context.[2] Ofelia Zepeda, who is herself Tohono O'Odam, would undoubtedly have a different reading of the text than I would have, but we would probably share in our analysis of the text relative to the history of anthropology, Ruth Underhill's generation of scholars, and her place as a woman anthropologist. Similarly, *Lakota Woman* (a book whose story I know because I have lived through that period of time as an Indian) risks being read by a non-Native woman, let's say, for its feminist content alone.[3]

CAROLINE SIMPSON: Encoded in this question is the presumption that conflicting positionalities account for the processes by which the works of ethnic writers are repeatedly misread or flattened. Certainly I agree that every text, be it literary or filmic, is read within a field of social relations that determines readers' strategies of reading. But it might be better to begin by considering less obvious relationships between readers and texts. I sometimes encounter readers of autobiography who, reading from positions of marginality (positions that are often similar to the writer in question) produce a disturbing depoliticization of autobiographical texts. In these cases, the marginalized or minoritized reader holds so tightly to the claim of victimization as the only legitimate grounds for valuing the texts of people of color that she/he becomes an unwitting accomplice to the ghettoization of those texts. The result is a continuation of the worst reductions of multicultural education: the marginalized writer is only "heard" when she speaks in the tones of suffering and pathos. I concentrate on the politics of reading marginalized literature "from the margins" both because it complicates the sometimes essentialist assumptions about the interconnectedness of positionalities of the marginalized reader and writer and because it represents the most troubling sort of misreading. When, in my classroom, a Asian American student reduces the political or ideological complexity of an autobiographical work by an Asian American writer to an expression of perpetual alienation, I recognize that reading is sometimes an act of violence against the self, an act that extends the damage already done to people of color in this country. I think I may call this a sort of misreading because it represents a fundamental denial of the urgency of addressing current institutional and political struggles by restricting our comments and conversations about the works of people of color to the terrain of past suffering.

SHELLI B. FOWLER: I agree with Kate that it is very difficult to adequately define and/or generalize a subject position, and yet I do view it as at least one way to address issues of difference. Likewise, I think Caroline's point is equally important – that misreadings occur when positionality is so narrowly defined that it leads to an entrenched (and unproblematized) emphasis on hearing only the claim of victimization within a marginalized text. I tend to focus on what Michael Awkward refers to as "the politics of positionality" by encouraging readings that negotiate between the extremes of essentialist and antiessentialist definitions of a subject position.[4] Readings that work to acknowledge the complexities and fluidity of identity(ies) are often likely, in my view, to produce more complex analyses of American ethnic autobiographies (or any text, for that matter). Thus, I work to locate a text within the specific historical and cultural moment(s) of its production and, additionally, to attend to the current historical/cultural moment that informs its reception.

TIFFANY LÓPEZ: The relationship between a reader's subject position and his/her ability to read strategies of resistance in American ethnic autobiography is a tenuous one. A typical and essentialist response would be to say that readers of color are able to access the text in ways that white readers cannot. This response is problematic for a number of reasons, not the least being that it risks permanently locating ethnic autobiography on the margins. There is something comforting and powerful about working with a text that seems to clearly reflect one's own subject position. Yet the risk in embracing the notion that one's subject position enhances one's ability to critically read any given text is that it detracts from the ever urgent need to do one's cultural homework. Certain cultural experiences may provide an added point of reference. However, critical reading strategies also demand the application of learned intellectual and rhetorical skills.

Questions of representation have been important to my thoughts about teaching, especially in terms of the role my identity plays in my position as a teacher of ethnic literature. I find that my Latina/o students want to see themselves reflected in the texts we read. For most, it's the first time they have encountered representations of Latinos by Latinos. Yet they also want to see themselves mirrored in me as a Chicana professor on a campus where 25 percent of the student body is Chicana/o, and only a handful of the faculty across disciplines teach Chicana/o texts. My goal has been to get students to see beyond the obvious connections of subject position and more toward how historical and cultural context function as the most integral elements in the reading of texts. Most of all, I want them to see how historical and cultural context is not a final truth as much as the subject of an ongoing conversation.

TRAISE YAMAMOTO: The whole issue of subject positions and their relation to reading autobiography is, I think, always going to be vexed by the question of identity politics. That is, while I agree with Caroline that it is highly problematic for students to restrict their readings to victimization narratives, there are a number of factors at play that can be productively used to further understanding of strategies of resistance and modes of agency. For one, many students of color have never before had the opportunity to read an autobiography written by someone with whom they identify – or are identified with – racially. We should not forget that this can be immensely empowering; if that sense of empowerment seems to be coming from some sort of glorified victim status, the instructor has to proceed very carefully.

A second factor, at least for my students, is that the experience of reading an autobiographical narrative written by someone "like them" is compounded by the novelty of having that text taught by a person of color. Clearly, the potential problems of identity politics – when it is assumed to be a fairly simplistic formulation in which "being" X therefore means A, B, and C – might lead students, in the worst case, to take on a righteous sense of "payback time." But I don't think this is necessarily to be expected. I have not found, in fact, that students of color tend to be the ones to resort to victimization narratives; rather, I have generally found this to be the practice of either conservative white students ("All they do is whine. The past is the past.") or liberal white students ("It's terrible what was done to them. I'm ashamed to be white."). Obviously, not only white students are vulnerable to these sentiments. I have to say, however, that it is most often among white students that I find the kind of misreadings I consider most disturbing.

I think it is helpful to remember that identity politics, when it is understood to be something other than a putative correspondence between A and B, needs not be ahistorical. That is, a tendency to misread, as well as an ability to read "with" a text, is often grounded in experience. For instance: a non-Japanese American is very likely to have little or no knowledge of the internment, and this lack of knowledge often leads to misreadings of not only those Japanese American autobiographies dealing with the internment, but also of Japanese Americans generally. Such readers are unlikely to find anything in these narratives that seriously challenges or undermines the stereotype of Japanese Americans. On the other hand, readers with some knowledge about the internment and the history surrounding it are likely to understand that the authorial stance in, for instance, Monica Sone's *Nisei Daughter* and Yoshiko Uchida's *Desert Exile* is directly related to the historic and social circumstances of the prewar and wartime Japanese American community.[5] Such a reader would presumably be able to walk the fine line between reading these narratives as exemplifying consciousness of an imposed group identity, and grossly overgeneralizing them as accurate portrayals of an entire community.

SHELLI B. FOWLER: Most often, I have found that students do not have much familiarity either with various ways of reading/interpreting literary texts, or with the primary texts on my syllabus. For example, the upper-division introductory African American literature course that I teach every fall semester draws a wide assortment of majors. Some are English majors with, perhaps, some familiarity with some of the literature, but many are nonmajors who are taking the course for one of the university's general education requirements. The nonmajors are less likely to have read any of the works on the syllabus and are also less likely to have had any introduction to literary theory, or ways of reading. I am also likely to have a large majority of (visibly) white students, many of whom are from small towns within the state of Washington. I cannot assume that the students, collectively, will have experience either in critically engaging with literary works or in critically engaging with the complex issues of cultural differences, including racial differences (from either lived or intellectual/academic experience).

Generally, students are somewhat resistant (though mostly passively resistant) to thinking about race or what difference race might make in the reading/interpreting of a literary text. Because I read, and teach, literature within an historical and cultural context (a context that grounds/frames my analyses of race), I find it necessary to discuss the historical/cultural context from which the text emerges and to try to get students to begin thinking critically about race and racial positioning – both historically within U.S. culture as we examine non-contemporary texts and, currently, as we locate ourselves as contemporary readers and interpreters. To that end, I usually begin the course by foregrounding issues of race, racial positioning, and racial representations.

Given the geopolitics of my local situation and institution, it is useful to position/locate myself in relation to the course material as a way to initiate the discussion. I often begin this task by asking students to ponder the following question: does it matter that I am a European American woman teaching an African American literature course? Student responses often run the gamut from expressions of essentialist identity politics ("I thought the professor would be black because this is an African American literature course."), to expressions of anti-identity politics that often tend to efface or avoid the issues of race altogether ("No, books are just books; it doesn't matter who wrote them or who teaches them."), to comments that suggest a weariness regarding the topic of race ("Racism no longer exists, and we're all on a level playing field in college, so it doesn't make any difference at all."). What follows are several class sessions that focus on a range of related topics, from discussions of current "race politics" in the academy to discussions about how inclusive the category of American literature is or is not, to the ways in which naming and categorizing impacts our knowledge and valuing of various "bodies" of information. Students begin to (re)consider that American literature survey courses, for example, are not named "Euro-American Lit. 101" when that, very often, more accurately defines what they have read in the course. My intent here is to facilitate students' awareness/understanding of how the complexities of race, privilege, and power are connected to the production and institutionalization of literature. And I want students to begin to critically engage with the complexities of race, privilege, and power, both historically and in their own contemporary culture. I find that in doing so, I must continually attend to the students' collective *dis*comfort regarding the topics of race, racial positioning, and racism. (That's a topic for discussion in and of itself. . . .) I want to encourage their movement toward struggling with the complexities of racialized difference(s) and, likewise, encourage the use of complex reading strategies that attend to the differences race does (or does not)make, rather than have them avoid the issue completely, or settle for an easy answer (one that often leads to the kind of narrow readings that Caroline discussed earlier).

To move from the generalized foregrounding discussions toward more specific discussions about appropriate reading strategies for African American literature, I usually have the students read a particular Charles Chesnutt short story, "The Passing of Grandison" (1899).[6] The reading of this story (without any prior explication of reading the strategies of resistance) works to illustrate, for many students, the ways that readers often make cultural assumptions as they read narrowly from either their own subject position or from a position that unquestioningly accepts dominant cultural assumptions. It also exemplifies the need for learning to read the strategies of resistance in an ethnic literary text in order to adequately or accurately read or interpret the text. Chesnutt's story directly addresses the reader's potential stereotypical/racist assumptions about the central protagonist in the story. Simultaneously, Chesnutt indirectly teaches the reader (any reader) about the importance of the trickster figure within the African American literary tradition, as he "signifies on" both Colonial Owens in the short story and on any reader who makes the same assumptions as Colonel Owens (that is, any reader who continually reads Grandison's racial positioning in a stereotypical and racist way and who fails to read his subversive access-to-power maneuvers that are clearly celebrated in the short story).

CAROLINE SIMPSON: I think Traise's response addresses the complex politics of reading as a student of color and provides a necessary rejoinder to my concerns about the victimology that sometimes emerges from students' readings. I certainly wouldn't abandon my belief in the usefulness of a certain tactical brand of identity politics, and I would second her point that reading is grounded in experience. My own career as a reader of Asian American autobiographies originated in a politics of identity; that is, in a sense I was riveted by the power of the experience described in this or that book precisely because we (the writer and I) occupied the common territory of Asian in a country where the Asian American is often the most "alien" American.

I was reminded of that fact this year when I was teaching a revolving topics course generally listed as "women writers." It is assumed the focus of this course will vary from quarter to quarter, and in my quarter I focused it as "Asian American Women Writers." The class was composed of predominantly white, middle-class women, at least a third of whom approached me during the first week of class to a) express their anxieties about reading such a "different" cultural type of literature or b) express their surprise of frustration that the course listing – "women writers" – didn't adequately define my course. For these white women, many of them well acquainted with a range of women studies courses, the concept of woman effectively erased the recognition of Asian American women's work and experiences. The few Asian American women in the course were consistently and almost exclusively addressed by their white (and black) classmates only when they were in need of the native informant to define Asian terms or customs, the "tell me about your people's ways so I won't be lost here" sort of question. The dynamics of this course illustrates where at least some of the anxious rejection of all forms of identity politics comes from: the loss of privilege or mastery that used to define the experience of American literature, particularly for the white reader. Certainly some of my students' comments during the first week and their constant positioning of Asian Americans as cultural archives for their own instant edification indicated a fairly high level of anxious maneuvering. They called on all Asians present to deliver the uncomplicated truth of our uniform difference or pain or our struggle against crude racism, never suspecting that their form of tolerance of the exceptional was the more common garden variety form of liberal racism. I shared with Asian American students in the course the experience of negotiating very similar assumptions, requests, categorizations, and frustrations, a fact of Asian American identity that is as undeniable as the differences that separated our individual understandings of those negotiations. None of us, however, left unchallenged any assumption, however subtle, that a recognition of Asian Americans' continuing experience of racism was a license to pathologize and arrest the categories of "Asian American Women." I hope the productive point of that recognition for non–Asian American students was an increased level of self-examination that led to broader material and social critiques rather than collapsing into either white guilt or abject identification.

TIFFANY LÓPEZ: As each of you has already acknowledged in your various responses, our subject position affects the reading strategies that we bring into the classroom. This year I employed two different strategies designed to help students learn how to complicate their readings of Latina/o literatures. Both concern pointing out the problem of expecting one individual to "speak for" an entire culture.

To begin, I ask students how my last name (López) published in the course catalog affects the assumptions they bring to class on the first day. What if my last name were Smith? Certainly, for some, my Spanish surname "legitimates" me as a professor of ethnic literature in a way that would not be necessary if I were teaching, say, a survey course on modern American poetry. My own presence in the classroom further underscores this inquiry. My presumably "authentic" body immediately troubles their reading of the larger body of Latina/o literature, as they assume it to be represented by my person. I am light-skinned, female, and look much younger than my thirty years. I immediately disrupt the expectation that there is a clear and direct correspondence between the professor, the literature, and the students. This helps to focus the class on the literature as an object of discovery and analysis and not just as representative of one's subject position and unquestionable cultural truths.

The second strategy I employed this year was to begin the class with Himilce Nova's *Everything You Need to Know about Latino History*.[7] This text brings the issues of representation and identity politics directly to the forefront. The book is clearly marketed as "speaking for" Latino culture. The book jacket features stereotypical icons of Latino culture, such as a mission, a mariachi player, folklorico dancers, and a cactus. Blurbs on the book explicitly position Novas as a native informant; that is, because she is Cuban, she is "in the know."

Many students became angry with the book's employment of stereotypes and Nova's reductive take on Latino history. Other students, however, who did not know anything about Latino history, found the book extremely informative and did not fully understand why some students would take offense. This text provided an ideal way to begin the course in that it so easily facilitated a discussion of the complexity of representation and cultural authority. The book prompted a dialogue that revealed how *both* Latino and non-Latino students are taught to see an author as speaking for his/her community. At the end of the discussion, the class came together in that they all agreed that issues of representation play a complicated role in the reading of ethnic literature. In this way they (re)defined what it means to be an oppositional and/or resistant reader. Ultimately, resistance means working against what you have been taught.

KATE SHANLEY: One, if not *the* primary problem in teaching American Indian subjects is that of confusing the ethnic/racial experience of being Indian with some vague blood heritage and/or liberal sympathy for Indians. My only solution, however partial, to combat such appropriation is to beat the drum slowly all term about what it means, has meant, and will mean in the twenty-first century to be Indian. I try to do that in several ways: 1) by stressing that tribal identity has always been one specific to a particular region and history, including perhaps urban settings; 2) by pointing out how American mainstream identity shamefully allows for "playing Indian" without self-consciousness; 3) by stressing that cultures change and that technology is not equivalent to "civilization"; and 4) by making it clear to the students that being Indian means knowing the painful realities of dispossession and the legacy of cultural genocidal efforts. Making money as "representative" Indians can be done ethically – Indian scholars, teachers, spiritual leaders, politicians, and lawyers do so all the time – but the world is also full of plastic medicine men and women and other confidence game players. I doubt that any respectable person wants to be seen entirely as representative of either a certain tribal view or a "Pan-Indian" voice, but those of us who are in positions of visibility must accept the reality of our being seen as representative, some of the time at least, and must act accordingly. In general, American individualism as its typically viewed differs significantly from American Indian individualism, however; thus, notable people who are recognized for whatever reason by the mainstream culture may not be as important to their cultural groups as are others who will live on in oral history for some time to come. Some of this may apply to other ethnic groups as well.

SHELLI B. FOWLER: I want to briefly pick up on something that Tiffany mentioned regarding the ways in which students as readers are taught to view a Latina/o author (and, arguably, any ethnic writer) as speaking for her/his community. I agree that it is important to continually complicate the analyses of racial representations. And it is important to facilitate what Traise has referred to as the arduous task of encouraging readings that both negotiate the readers' awareness that ethnic autobiographical narratives exemplify a consciousness of an imposed group identity while simultaneously messing with the readers' tendency to oversimplify and overgeneralize the texts as accurate portrayals of an entire community. One way to begin this task is to briefly encourage students to examine assumptions they've been taught about reading "nonethnic" autobiographies. In other words, most students have been taught that Euro-American autobiographical texts are representative texts that speak for some universal, consensual "American identity." For example, students may well have been taught that a text like Ben Franklin's *Autobiography* speaks about American values and ideals for *all* Americans, that Ben Franklin "speaks for" America (within a particular time frame, anyway). Students are not usually consciously aware, however, that they have been taught to read Franklin's *Autobiography* in that way. It can be a very useful pedagogical strategy, then, to *temporarily* move the students' focus away from the morass of issues of representation(s) within an ethnic autobiography that is being either critiqued or lauded for its representativeness and toward the broader issues of representation of community(ies) within literary autobiographies in general. That is, one of the things I tire of is how often questions of "speaking for" or "to whom" become embattled *only* in the reading of ethnic literature, where race and questions of racial representations seem to spring up for many students for the first time. Racializing whiteness is a necessary and useful reading strategy and is too rarely raised in readings of Euro-American literary autobiographies. It often helps to shift students' critical awareness to assumptions they have made (or have been taught to make) about historical or contemporary Euro-American autobiographies. Such a strategy temporarily moves the burden of individual versus representative identity-making from the ethnic autobiography to the larger genre of autobiography, where it should reside as "a way of reading" for all literary texts. This is, as I mentioned earlier, a *temporary* interjection into the very often fraught discussions of identity construction(s) within ethnic autobiographies. The point is not to elide the issues a particular ethnic autobiography raises; instead, it is a pedagogical strategy that (momentarily, anyway) encourages students to (re)examine the kinds of expectations they may be placing on a ethnic autobiography that they do not equally place on their reading of a Euro-American text. And likewise, it attempts to develop further students' critical reading and analytical thinking about racialized, gendered, (and so on) literary representations in general.

Most of the students in my literature classrooms are not readers who critically examine the literary construction(s) of identity(ies) along the lines of race, gender, class, sexual orientation, age, religion, and physical ability/disability in all the literary texts they read/view. They seem to unthinkingly accept such constructions as relevant topics for courses with race or ethnicity named in the title or course description. As Caroline's white female students' resistance to viewing Asian American women writers as adequately appropriate under the rubric of "women writers" indicates, we need to continually attend to the micro and macro significance of resistant writers and readers. As Tiffany has suggested, teaching reading strategies of resistance for ethnic autobiographies also acknowledges the necessity of encouraging students to engage in the task of working against what they have been taught.

CAROLINE SIMPSON: Having railed against abjection in the reading of ethnic autobiographies, I'm also aware of yet another way to turn this concept of abjection so that, in its insistence on marginality, it represents a revolutionary transformation of, among other things, the sovereignty of the speaking subject. This concept of abjection as dissension, an idea often solely attributed to Julia Kristeva, offers at least another means of reworking some students' attempts to shuttle between finding either a victimization narrative *or* a model minority story when they address Asian American autobiographies. In fact, very often students rely on reading some Asian American texts as success stories to resecure their belief in fundamental Americanism, liberty, truth, and justice for all.

I'm thinking of how in one class I had discussed Mary Paik Lee's *Quiet Odyssey*, the story of Lee's immigration to the United States in the early part of this century and her subsequent economic success.[8] Lee is very careful to emphasize her triumph over obstacles of extreme poverty, racism, and family illness, and in the final pages delivers a statement of nonchalant acceptance that may read as a positive summing up of her life. Because so many students embraced the message, which clearly seems to confirm the Horatio Alger myth, in teaching this book I emphasized group work on those few passages that describe the limitations imposed on Lee as an Asian in America. What happened while students rightly questioned my focus on the "negative stuff" is that I was able to talk about how this seemingly minor preoccupation with say, prejudice, in fact determines much of the structure of the narrative, how Lee uses it both to displace and fulfill our expectations. In short, as a writer she depends on our misrecognition, on our need for her to be *only* quiet, suffering, oriental; she gives us that easily enough and then uses it to mask those points of palpable anger and even sarcasm about citizens with privileges very much like our own as middle class, native born, and, perhaps, white. Bringing out the narrative and ideological function of her ordeal, how Lee "pre-reads" the readers' privilege before they ever open the pages to "read," exposes autobiography as a form that proliferates possibilities from any number of narrative strategies. In this case, my work was caught up in rendering the book much more troubling and challenging for students, who were trying too much to read it as just a story of success.

TRAISE YAMAMOTO: Caroline's analysis of Lee's *Quiet Odyssey* is particularly cogent to the reading of Asian American autobiographies. Lee's strategy of employing a "quiet" surface beneath which she deploys her anger in a critique of white American society is one that can be found in a number of Asian American autobiographical texts. This is particularly true in Asian American autobiographies written prior to 1965. Historical context becomes extremely important in these earlier autobiographies: in the simplest sense, an Asian American could hardly expect his/her book to be published if it were an overt diatribe against white racism. So there's often a certain amount of coding, or hints to, as Caroline calls it, misrecognition.

One strategy to get students to read autobiographies such as Sone's *Nisei Daughter* or Jade Snow Wong's *Fifth Chinese Daughter* in more complicated ways is to ask them what they like about the book (students almost always like these two texts quite a bit).[9] Students will generally identify elements like humor, perseverance, a nongrudging attitude toward racism, and a belief in "American" ideals. I then ask them to entertain the possibility that Sone and Wong purposefully orient their narratives to evoke exactly those reactions, and to think about how those reactions might function as a necessary dimension of Sone's and Wong's textual presentation of self.

To further this line of inquiry, I ask the class to think about what is *not* present in the narratives: overt anger, criticism of white American racism, doubt about the Horatio Alger–type mythos that informs the narrative (especially in Wong's book). Then I point to key passages where these elisions result in awkward ruptures, places where the narrative falters or is somewhat anomalous in relation to the narrative as a whole. How, for instance, is it possible that Wong can claim that "Mills [College] living was democratic living in the truest sense" and then directly follow this statement with her description of Mills Hall: "The building housed over a hundred girls, and its kitchen staff was entirely Chinese, some of them descendants of the first Chinese kitchen help who worked for the founders of the college" (157). What does such a passage tell us about Wong's own positioning in relation to other Chinese Americans? What does it tell us about racial identity and class?

In Sone's *Nisei Daughter*, the strikingly cheerful tone is offset by frequent ruptures in the text, where Sone references feelings of anger and rebellion that are never represented in the text itself. Paying close attention to such instances suggests a very different and conflicted self than that which emerges from the deflections of the surface narrative.

Given all this, however, I think it is extremely important to remain attentive to the difference between reading "under" a text and misreading the text altogether by machinating it in accordance with current critical tendencies. That is, one can, in my opinion, only go so far with Wong's text. One would be hard put, in my opinion, to claim that beneath her assimilationist narrative demeanor Wong is "really" engaging in a radical Third World critique of mainstream white American values.

So here's the question I'd like to put out for consideration: if we can argue for the ways in which these narratives make use of a textual surface that seems to conform to dominant cultural expectations in order to distract readers from the underlying critique, what keeps us from ending up in a kind of textual free-for-all zone? I'm thinking here of the whole "rage for agency" issue – that is, where critics have sometimes been so desperate to recuperate a female character or writer that the critic finds, indeed insists upon, a resistance that may not in fact be there. What if the whole question of subject position dovetails into the question of whether agency and resistance are to be found, and if so *who* is doing the finding? How do we protect ourselves from charges of self-interested, revisionist resistance-mongering?

KATE SHANLEY: An essay I use frequently in class, Walker Percy's *Loss of the Creature*, helps students realize that I want them to explore their own sovereignty.[10] In particular, I want them to move beyond seeing personal sovereignty as choices, such as when to come in at night or whether to drink or do drugs. Last term, a student writing about what personal sovereignty means to him began by talking about slavery as the ultimate loss of sovereignty. I had to work with him to get himself to see that a slave might have more freedom in his or her mind, freedom to see and think for him/herself, than might a rich, co-opted white politician.

Beginning a course with essays such as Walker's helps students get at issues related to agency and radicalism without calling them such. It also foregrounds issues of individualism, how our ideas about it are structured by culture, politics, and gender.

TRAISE YAMAMOTO: In terms of individualism, Kate makes an important point: there are differing kinds of individualism. Too often with Asians, in particular, there is a widespread belief that Asian/Asian Americans don't believe in individuals. Of course, this isn't true. What is true, however, is that how that subject functions vis-à-vis other subjects may diverge quite a bit from American ideologies of individualism. This difference is brought into sharper relief within the context of racism in the United States. So in a lot of Asian American autobiography, for instance, the writer frequently speaks less as "an individual" – assuming that term defines a coherent, self-made, and separate being – and more as a subject constructed by and within his/her community. Often, such subjects write as spokespersons. There is often a didactic purpose to the narrative, a desire to bear witness to the wrongs enacted against, and the survival strategies of, the writer's community. Many Nisei autobiographers explicitly note that they wrote their books so that the internment would not be forgotten and to make readers (read "white readers") aware of "prejudice" (a term much more often invoked than "racism"). In such texts, the details and personal musings of the individual writer take a back seat to the writer's sense of herself as witness, spokesperson, or, in Elaine Kim's phrase, cultural ambassador.

SHELLI B. FOWLER: I want to return for a moment to the topic raised earlier regarding, as I think Traise termed it, "the whole 'rage for agency' issue." The issue of reading strategies of resistance and acknowledging/recognizing authorial agency in doing so is very important. I'm reminded of something Wahneema Lubiano wrote recently in which she asks, "What political work does insistence on a difference, on an identity, do? What political work does staging, performing, foregrounding, articulating, or criticizing recognition of an identity do?" Lubiano critiques the Chicago Cultural Studies Group for leveling the importance of those questions with the generalized assertion that "What do subalterns have in common except somehow they are dominated?" She argues: "Somehow that statement 'all they have in common is domination' empties out the very thing I want to focus on: what it means to be dominated. Domination is complicated and varied. But domination is so successful precisely because it sets the terrain upon which struggle occurs at the same time that it preempts opposition not only by already inhabiting the vectors where we would resist (i.e., by being powerfully in place and ready to appropriate oppositional gestures), but also by having already written the script that we have to argue within and against."[11]

It seems that one way to address the "rage for agency" issue is not to do so on any set terms of a Eurocentric literary critical discourse. In other words, at moments it seems that having to engage in the debate over agency and "*who* is doing the finding" works to keep us from moving forward in examining the complexities of power relations. It is, arguably, often strategic to deflect or ignore questions generated by those on the precultivated terrain of literary analysis (of the Eurocentric variety), questions that are primarily intended, perhaps, as a means of obstruction. The issue of relationships of power – issues of cultural and racial domination and subordination – are inherent to the production of ethnic autobiographies; each racialized autobiographical subject/producer will negotiate different kinds and forms of domination given her/his racial (and gendered, and sexual, and classed) position in U.S. culture. I am more interested in turning the classroom discussion, as I think most of us here have articulated in one way or another, away from generalized commentary about how the reader might just be looking too actively for resistance. It is more productive to move forward with discussions that examine how domination is complicated and varied, and to turn to the specific text in order to explore and explicate the particular ways that issues of domination and subordination are being challenged and reinscribed.

For example, when I teach African American autobiographies and am looking at the slave narrative genre, I often teach Louisa Picquet's narrative after students have worked through Harriet A. Jacobs's *Incidents in the Life of a Slave Girl*.[12] This can highlight some of the complex questions of agency for students because they tend to view Jacobs's narrative as "authored by herself" in ways that Picquet's narrative, *Louisa Picquet, the Octaroon*, makes much more problematic.[13] Picquet's narrative employs an amanuensis, and unlike most of the nineteenth-century narratives, her text follows a question-and-answer format. Students "forget" to recognize, or initially "refuse" to acknowledge/grant, authorial agency to Picquet in the same way that they have just "allowed" Jacobs agency in the construction of a narrative self. Arguably, students more quickly read the ways that Jacobs signifies on a white readership, but they cannot as easily read Picquet's strategic textual resistances because of the format of her narrative. Rather than spending nonproductive debate over the use of autobiographical texts and amanuenses in a general sense, I keep students engaged in the issue of a white male amanuensis and a black female author within the specific context of the slave narrative genre. We examine the specific forms of cultural resistance that emerged from the specific context and history of black/white, female slave/master power relations. Students begin to take their learned awareness of the ways in which African American women exercised agency (for example, through the subversion of domination without the dominating individual always being overtly aware of the subversive strategies employed upon/around him/her) and they begin to (re)examine their assumptions about "control" of textual representations. In other words, with a particular awareness of culturally specific signification the students begin to read the specific passages in which Picquet subverts her amanuensis's direct intentions and simultaneously constructs a different textual self than the amanuensis directly intends. Louisa Picquet's authorial intention, then, becomes not something the students want proved to them, but something they recognize and explore/explicate as they examine the significance of cultural, racialized difference through a critical awareness of how domination and subordination operate in a specific historical moment.

TIFFANY LÓPEZ: In ethnic autobiography, the issue of racial struggle – that anyone writing "as" a person of color inevitably addresses, either overtly or in code – is placed center stage. All individual struggles depicted in the text usually get read as representative of a communal struggle with dominant culture. Here, I'm thinking about Shelli's point about the importance of introducing comparative readings. In what ways are ethnic writers engaging in strategies and modes of address common to autobiographical writing in general, and in what ways/terms can we actually distinguish Cherrìe Moraga from Ben Franklin beyond the obvious? Though the ethnic author may be writing a narrative of struggle to gain a sense of individuality, that struggle, ironically, gets read as representative of a larger cultural struggle. The theme of race is a deceptively convenient marker on the playing field. Interestingly, ethnic writers such as Cecile Pineda, John Rechy, and Montserrat Fontes, who refuse to position race as the central theme of their texts, usually don't get taught as ethnic writers.[14]

Not only do we have to deal with those reading strategies taught by the larger culture, but we also have to work around and through those enforced by other learning environments that also shape the reading of agency and resistance. The pure lecture format, of course, encourages students to believe that there is only one correct response to the text, to turn to the professor as the one with all the answers. How is this also compounded by the notion of the singular speaking subject as representative of an entire culture?

In thinking about Traise's question of *who* is doing the finding, my immediate response is to say those in positions of privilege and power, that is, those controlling dominant modes of production, especially related to visual culture, and those controlling the key modes of production within ethnic communities. However, from the perspective of the students, ultimately, the professor is doing the finding. The professor of color is in a double bind.

The time for carefully working through close readings and using our position of knowing (both book knowledge and lived experience) is undeniably important, especially to the teaching of readings that resist all too common gestures of colonization/ghettoization. Yet how do we do these things in such a way that our pedagogical approach itself reflects the complexities and nuances of the texts? How do we get students to see how all these threads are working at once? How do we separate those threads and then bring them together again? What gets lost and what is gained in the parceling out?

TRAISE YAMAMOTO: I agree with Shelli that it can be incredibly tiresome to continually point out the assumptions about individuality versus representativeness that students often make in relation to Euro-American autobiographies and autobiographies by people of color. And while I also agree that it is important to point out the nonparallel manner in which different autobiographical narratives are read, I think we must be careful not to remedy such problems with equal application of pedagogical techniques (not, mind you, that I think this is what Shelli is suggesting). That is, I have too often seen instructors make the hideous mistake of shifting from applying a Eurocentric reading of autobiography to a text written by a person of color, to a kind of reverse-face, wherein the kinds of readings applicable, say to African American slave narratives are bizarely applied to contemporary autobiographies written by white subjects. While I suppose some version of this practice might potentially be useful as a way to racialize whiteness, sloppily thought-out versions can be extremely problematic, functioning as a kind of textual liberal pluralism in which, in the worst incarnation I can imagine, the majority of autobiographical subjects are joined in a fellowship of shared metaphoric slavery. I think some of us will recognize that what lurks beneath my objections here is a distrust of the ways in which the specificity of raced subjectivities have been appropriated by white subjects, some of whom, without any apparent self-consciousness, suddenly proclaim themselves "mestizas," some reincarnation of a Native American holy person, and/or able to "relate to" the experiences of former slaves.

This perhaps has veered into a whole other territory, but I think that what motivates me here is the sense that we must always and are always walking a fine line (which may be, as Caroline said, often determined by the particular composition of a particular class). In this case, for instance, we must be able both to register objections to the ways in which autobiographical subjects of color are assumed to be representative in a manner that reifies racist "they're all the same" mentalities, as well as acknowledge that many subjects of color do not think of themselves in terms of the isolated individual self, but as subjects inherently part of and comprising of the community. The key, I think, is to keep the issues of history and agency foregrounded. If the history of racism in the United States is manifested by an imposed group identity, it is also true that a chosen sense of intersubjective communality suggests a strategy of agency, survival, and resistance.

SHELLI B. FOWLER: Yes, I very much agree that keeping issues of history and agency foregrounded is crucial and central to avoiding the problematic "slippage" that occurs if students want to move toward an "equal application" remedy instead of wrestling with negotiating historical (and contemporary) issues of power imbalances between and among cultural groups. And yes, I also agree that avoiding the issues of classroom "dis-comfort" altogether by "shifting" to Eurocentric reading strategies of ethnic autobiographies is nonproductive pedagogy. I don't know how often teachers attempt to "apply" reading strategies for ethnic autobiographies to Euro-American autobiographies, since most of the time it seems to me that teachers teaching ethnic and/or Euro-American autobiographies do not have the specific training in the ethnic literary critical field, and too often are teaching a "multicultural literature" course without having read the critical literature produced by scholars in the various ethnic literature fields. In other words, I fear that more often ethnic autobiographies are (mis)read from uninformed/untrained positions that do not attend to the difference that race/ethnicity makes in the production/reception/interpretive reading of an autobiography.

I don't think I understand clearly, Traise, your point about how a critical, strategic (and appropriate) reading of an African American slave narrative can be easily translated into a way of reading any historical or contemporary white-authored autobiography. That is, attending to the particular dynamics of race relations and to the production of slave narratives within their specific historical and cultural moment would not provide a means for explicating a white-authored autobiography in the exact same "reverse-face" way because the dynamics of race and power are not the same. I don't quite get how that is a way to "racialize whiteness" either. In fact, I'd argue that such an attempt would effectively erase the significance of (and ability to critically analyze) whiteness as a racial category altogether.

I very much agree with Traise's assertion that tendencies toward a kind of textual liberal pluralism are highly problematic and ultimately ineffectual in any effort to adequately and accurately read the specificity of raced subjectivities. I do think the demographics of specific classrooms and the subject positions of individual teachers within those classrooms affect, and thus should impact, pedagogical strategies in a variety of ways and contexts, and that choosing an appropriate pedagogical strategy is an always already difficult task. (And I do think discerning the difference between an "appropriate" and an "appropriative" pedagogical strategy is not something that enough teachers of "multicultural lit" courses – teaching texts outside of their scholarly field and/or training – think about often and carefully enough.) I also think Traise's objections to the problematic of white appropriations of the identity of the ethnic "other" (in any wide variety of ways) accurately define the problematics of uninformed and *un*self-reflexive teaching and reading. A useful and productive and progressive analysis of cultural difference(s) has not occurred if a white student, for example, leaves a classroom on, say, African American slave narratives and feels easily able to " 'relate to' the experiences of former slaves." (One of the issues here revolves around what instructors feel authorized to teach and why; what kind of training in the field is or is not required of teachers of ethnic autobiographies; and how to address the continual problem of readings that [unintentional or otherwise] work to appropriate nonwhite textual subjectivities.)

TRAISE YAMAMOTO: My point is that one cannot easily translate, for instance, reading strategies for African American autobiography to white-authored texts. I sat in a seminar once in which an unfortunate analogy was made between the ways in which slave narratives reappropriate certain formal structures as a means of critiquing Christian, democratic ideals, and how many (seemingly generic, read "white") women do something very similar in relation to (a seemingly generic, read "white" patriarchy. It seems to me this is not a rare move at all. Yes, absurd. Inappropriate: absolutely. This racializes whiteness only indirectly, and not in any thoroughgoing or even particularly productive way. It seems ridiculous said this way – and it is – but I've often found that white students/readers don't consciously recognize themselves as white until they realize that they *aren't* African American, Asian American, Chicano/a, or Native American. To this extent *only* does such a move result in a rather dim version of racializing whiteness. Shelli's distinction between "appropriate" and "appropriative" is absolutely key here. In the latter mode, I would argue that very often the white reading subject recognizes his/her raciality for precisely the two seconds before that raciality is disavowed.

CAROLINE SIMPSON: I'd like to address Traise's questions about the politics and impact of reading resistance. It is true that in many circumstances we do not or should not need to find resistance where in fact it doesn't exist. Doing so may miss the opportunity to discuss the most obvious realities, how the avoidance of controversial issues or the muting of political rage in ethnic autobiographies reflects the limitations placed on, or certainly felt by, at least some "raced" writers. But there isn't any easy solution to the questions she raises. The decision of whether or not we should preoccupy ourselves with gleaning resistance in ethnic autobiographies is, I think, clearly guided by the constitution and politics that emerge from the classroom we happen to find ourselves in. While I emphasized moments of Lee's anger or indictments of American ideals in one class, the one I mentioned earlier, in another quarter, with students clinging to a different set of assumptions, I have taken another approach, although not necessarily one diametrically opposed. I also consider the larger pressures of what in the last ten years has been a growing Asian American political and cultural visibility and how the students' and my opinions about our functions in this reemergence affect our readings of each other as well as the text. Tiffany spoke especially well to this complicated dynamic and offered a directive that seems to me the point, perhaps, of this whole conversation: that in the classroom we try to help our students question the grounds for their own readings by constantly being willing to question or shift our own. That means attending to the relationships among reading strategies, experience, and social identity. I have to consider how my contribution as a multiracial Asian American will be taken by Asian American students who are generally not multiracial and, in the worst case, may dismiss my hesitations as the self-loathing of a half-breed; or, by those who are multiracial and may try too frequently to agree with me, and ignore real intellectual differences. Both are avoidances of how our "levels of self-interested revisionist resistance-mongering," as Traise names it, can limit our ability to consider alternatives.

I have to work hard, and sometimes I hate it, to take seriously the reasons why students do not or cannot accept my suggested interpretation of a part of a text. There is a whole range of resistances that may proliferate in any classroom whether or not you focus on the resistant voice of the text. The usefulness of a concentration on resistance must, then, be determined by the immediate classroom dynamics and how it unfolds within the terms of

a much larger cultural debate. I think this is the tension that must be negotiated, and negotiated differently, from quarter to quarter, from semester to
semester.

TIFFANY LÓPEZ: I think I understand Traise's point about how applying reading strategies from ethnic autobiography can be invoked as a way to racialize
texts by white writers. Texts by white authors are seldom read for what they
demonstrate about whiteness as a cultural, or racial, or ethnic category.
As Shelli pointed out in her example of Ben Franklin's text, students are
rarely asked to engage in questions of textual representations of whiteness
when reading Euro-American autobiographies. And, issues of agency and
resistance (albeit different kinds) can be found in forms of autobiographical
writing by white authors. Ethnic writers demonstrate an awareness of white
culture; certainty white writers do the same, though not in like terms. The
question, it seems, is whether or not we can read autobiography by white
writers as precisely about whiteness in ways comparable to how we've come
to think about race and ethnicity in works by Asian American, American
Indian, African American, and Latina/o writers.

   I think applying reading strategies of ethnic autobiography to white texts
is, as has been pointed out, problematic. An uncritical application of reading
strategies adapted from work in ethnic autobiography that are used in an
attempt to map out a reading of whiteness is problematic because whiteness
is, then, too simply defined as "not-like" the racialized "other." Such a move
completely puts under erasure differences in signification – that is, suggesting that whiteness marks subjectivity in a way that Latinidad or blackness
cannot. Though the focus may be on whiteness, the category of "the other"
is invoked as necessary to the defining of whiteness as an ethnic category.
How do we read whiteness on its own terms?

KATE SHANLEY: The reading process *is* an appropriative one to some extent,
as is "cross-cultural understanding," and so forth. It seems to me that what
we seem to be wanting the readers, in this case, students, to do is back
off and learn through understanding "difference," the not-me. Along that
vein, class size makes a world of difference, as does the teaching load of the
instructor. What that means, I think, is that the grounding principles related
to the history of a particular person, textual production, ethnic group, and
regional history and culture give all students in the class a common frame of
reference. Beyond that, as I said earlier, we can teach them something about
the pitfalls of reading from an "outsider's" point of view (stressing, of course,

that an Asian who is not Japanese may not read in the same way as a Japanese American), but generalizing a reader beyond that is difficult. That's where class size and instructor's workload come in. If the teacher has time to know each student, both through the person's writing, in-class discussion, and one-to-one conferences, she/he has a better chance of knowing where the reader/student stands. Even at that, individual differences become evident on course evaluations – where two people will have opposite responses to the classroom dynamics, for example, responding that there was not enough or too much lecturing, or holding differing views about reading material or discussion.

That leads to notions of radicalization in the autobiographical writing and subsequent reading processes. American Indian autobiography "writers" arrive in the classroom considerably mediated; as H. David Brumble III says, over 80 percent of texts that fall in the category of American Indian autobiography have already passed through significant translation (read alteration).[15] My guess is that some American Indian autobiographers enter the process of telling their mediated stories with some understanding that the collaborator/editors will shape the stories to the non-Indian audience; other autobiographers do not realize the extent to which that can and/or will occur. They simply know they want to preserve their knowledge for the next generation. Getting at an accurate sense of the authors' (assuming two) intentions can be difficult, if not impossible. The tricky thing is getting student readers to "hold the question in their minds," something I see as an essential component of American Indian pedagogy. They need to recognize that their understanding will grow over time and that it's respectful, therefore essential, to stop short of judging others, another component of American Indian pedagogy – what I identify (after Carl Rogers) as "unconditional positive regard." For example, if an Indian autobiographer holds the position that her culture is dying and that Indians should embrace Christianity if they hope to survive, we must, as much as we are able, appreciate that point of view from its subject position and its historical groundings. Most of all, we need to learn to wait until we have acquired more information about how a particular person in a particular time could come to feel that way. Given the multicultural nature of survey classes, such understanding may not come for ten years. If, somehow, I can impart basic principles of respect (as stated above), I can be more assured that the student will arrive at understanding (perhaps wisdom) about the knowledge that comes his/her way at some point in the future. In a way, my approach is more modest, perhaps, than what other teachers would do (assuming students will not understand cultural perspectives during the term) and more ambitious (assuming they will change not just the content in their heads but the way their heads work).

In general, I have been trying to evolve a way of teaching that gets students out of the competitive mode – having the correct opinions, feeling they have to have a definitive opinion, to sound-off as smart – and into the communal mode, even silent mode, of letting things soak into their hearts.

CAROLINE SIMPSON: I'm reminded by the direction our conversation has taken just how much teaching ethnic autobiographies requires of us and our students in the way of dancing between very personal fault lines without collapsing into self-indulgence. The membrane between ourselves and these texts seems inevitably so much more permeable, and what I hear in so much of what's been said already is that a significant part of our effort is concentrated on turning that heightened relationship between text and reader to an advantage by constantly keeping ourselves and our students aware of the dangers and benefits of that space. But so far we've concentrated almost solely on how we negotiate the racial politics involved. I wonder how each of us has dealt with the further complications of sexual, gender, class, religious, and academic politics that are more than coincidental to the way we (as teachers and students) approach the reading of racial representation in these texts.

When I discussed Mary Paik Lee's autobiography, for instance, I failed to mention how much her persona is influenced by her early adoption of Christianity, as well as how many of the important lessons of her life are molded into the form of lessons or allegories of Christian charity or faithfulness or fortitude. Much could be made of the significance of this set of ideological beliefs in determining her rhetoric or thinking about what it means to be "Asian American," "woman," "old," or "diasporic." Certainly that Christian ideology influenced the way I read and taught Lee, particularly because I was an "out" lesbian in the classroom, and my students skeptically approached the notion that such a devout, heterosexual Christian could really be arguing anything particularly resistant. Again, an attention to Lee's historical context, to the historical and social force of Christianity in Korean nationalist movements and in the education of the first generations of college-bound women in Korea, is critical. For Lee, as a Korean American woman of a certain generation, who was also heterosexual and from a revered class of scholars, Christianity was inevitably tied to revolutionary political progress for Korean women in particular, something we could never say was true of Christianity as a political ideology (which it always is) in, for example, the Philippines.

How do we examine Lee's work as Asian American feminists then? As diasporic Asians, whose passage was enabled by considerably more economic privilege? As Asians or Asian Americans who reject, based on the fact of their long and continuing imperialist mission, Christian ideologies? I'm thinking not only of Lee's book, although I've talked about it a great deal here, but also the work of Nisei writers. Traise has mentioned and the central, although not always obvious, importance of sexuality in many of their works: *Nisei Daughter* and *Farewell to Manzanar*, to name just a couple. Also, David Mura's (a Sansei's) writing on race and sexuality seems to me absolutely pivotal in its attempts to theorize the sexual effects of racial and racist identifications, what's borne on or through the lived body.[16]

Reading and teaching autobiography can bring us closer, it seems, to an important awareness of how the bodies we teach in and read in, and the bodies we read in the author's work, are constantly confronted with each other. Since these are clearly bodies marked in multiple, political ways (ours, our students', the author's), we must be careful how we gesture toward these bodies when teaching ethnic autobiographies. We don't want to collapse important distinctions or encourage representationalist readings.

TRAISE YAMAMOTO: The awareness of bodies that Caroline speaks of gets right to the heart of how subject positions, the politics of location, and identity politics work in the classroom, as well as in the other work we do. What's involved is a kind of doubled or self-conscious vision, when you have to be aware of how your visible identities are being read. And most often, I want to be aware of those readings because I want to do what I can to subvert them – not simply out of some impulse to prove my own individuality, but because letting those readings go unchallenged has implications on the textual level.

For instance, when I walk into the classroom, it is pretty clear that I am an Asian American woman. That signifies several things to the students who do not yet know my teaching style. For many white students, I am read as either a woman of color who possibly is hostile toward white people, or its diametric opposite: that as an Asian American woman I will be kinder and gentler than non-Asian women of color. For students of color, and particularly for Asian American students, my presence in the classroom means that either I will be "easier" on them or that the classroom will be a safer place than what they are used to. And then sometimes, they are just taken by the novelty of the situation.

I think all of those perceptions need to be disrupted. The problem with not doing so goes back to the potential problematics of (a simplistic) identity politics. Time and time again, non–Asian American students have blamed their inability to understand the material or class discussion on the fact that no one in their family was in an internment camp or an immigrant on Angel Island. I always point out to such students that I have never been in an internment camp either. I often also ask whether she/he thinks that the difficulty with Medieval studies, for example, is that none of us is Medieval (at least not in any literal sense). Of course, my family was interned during the war, so I do know something about it through family stories, and the fact of internment has had direct consequences on my life. But there needs to be clear distinctions made between experience, identity, subjectivity, and ontology. There may be overlap to some extent, but no one should forget that these terms are not synonymous.

TIFFANY LÓPEZ: I'd like to turn to Caroline's question of how to deal with the complications of sexual, gender, class, religious, and academic politics as also affecting our approach to teaching and reading representations of race. Certainly for me as a Chicana, those other identity positions most charge my own sense of subjectivity. Those points have, in many ways, affected me more because they bring to the forefront the illusionary nature of race as a unifying element in the imagining of community. For example, there is no such thing as a singular Latino culture. How, then, are Puerto Ricans, Cubans, Chicanos, et al. to build community?

Cherríe Moraga's work has been at the core of any teaching I've done of Latino or Chicano autobiography.[17] Her discussion of Catholicism is rooted in her being a light-skinned Chicana, not being a native speaker of Spanish, coming into a sense of her lesbianism as a youth, and her awareness that the male is always privileged over the female in Chicano culture. All of these elements complicate readings of Latino identity, especially given that Moraga's sense of Chicana identity comes from her relationship to her mother's – and not her father's – body.

Reading Latino authors has taught me much about Chicano literature because it challenges me to do my cultural homework. I cannot make assumptions that because I am Chicana I will identify with the cultural experiences described by Esmeralda Santiago's *When I Was Puerto Rican*.[18] But I feel that I've certainly learned the most from reading gay and lesbian writers of color. Works by Michael Nava, Achy Obejas, Emma Perez, Teri de la Peña, and Richard Rodriquez demand a much fuller definition of Latina/o culture that takes into account a broad range of shifting subjectivities.[19] Because Latina/o gay and lesbian writers are marginalized within their own communities, they have had to redefine community so that it includes sexuality as productive to the culture's conceptualization of community building. These writers have been paramount to my teaching because they trouble the students' belief in race as the most common frame of reference in the reading of Latina/o autobiography.

KATE SHANLEY: In Caroline's discussion of resistance, I am reminded that a teacher may never see the change she/he has fostered, but she/he can nourish it "in the blind," as it were, by responding with kindness and acceptance, as Caroline suggests, without condoning violence or violation. The worst sort of response, in my opinion, is judgment or condemnation – and that can be subtly delivered. I struggle with this principle, ideal, in my own teaching because I have strong beliefs and opinions and am not always as open or centered as I would like to be. Just as acts of racist and sexist domination are quick solutions to the need for power, certain forms of authority in the classroom are quick solutions to the need to feel centered, in control. Teachers need to find support among their peers and to live within institutions that value pedagogy. (A big subject, I know.)

The issue of being multiracial, while painful on the personal level where people want "the real thing," particularly "real" Indians, is a teachable "moment" in the classroom. The media hype about diversity focuses people's minds on "race" or visible difference at the expense of the complexity of human populations and experiences – we all know that. First, I comfort myself by keeping in mind that my classroom may be the most important place for the complexity of the issue to come out; in that regard, it is a sacred space, one where we accord one another mutual respect and work toward a greater good. As such, our space has the potential of fullness. Sometimes that feels like a hopeless ideal, but I do believe in ideals, however unattainable. And students are full of idealism; they want to know harmony is possible, and I believe they also want to know the full truth about the world. They come to us having been bombarded by violence – perhaps from as close to home as their parents' troubled lives, but certainly in seeing their world as environmentally on the verge of collapse, as rampant with disease, AIDS chiefly, and as politically corrupt. The last place I want them to retreat into is denial; yet how do I offer the spiritual comfort and foster the strength to encourage them to look at things as they are? It's no wonder that some want to say "the past is the past; let's move on."

TRAISE YAMAMOTO: I'm wondering about a teaching strategy and a student strategy that often comes up in the teaching of ethnic literature; that is, the use of analogy. On the one hand, analogues can be powerful tools, a way to structure and forward thinking. I think we have all employed analogies at one time or another in the attempt to begin where students are. But analogies can also be misleading and unproductive. I spoke earlier of instances in which a slack and facile desire to "relate to" a particular experience easily turns into an act of appropriation. Specificity is flattened and differences are elided. Here's an example: in teaching Japanese American autobiographies, at least those written by Niseis, I have frequently come upon the opinion that the internment camps "weren't that bad." If I dig a little, I have found that the basis for this opinion lies in the comparison between the Nazi extermination camps and the concentration camps in the United States. The analogies that some students have made between the two quickly become a comparative racking-up of what's bad, what's worse, and what's worst. I imagine a lot of people would agree that such comparisons are not only beside the point, but are also incredibly disrespectful. The question, then, is how do we use analogy as a pedagogical tool without falling into the many traps therein?

KATE SHANLEY: Awhile back, someone forwarded to me a list of winners of a bad analogy contest. I copied it for my class and we went through a few. They were funny, of course, but provided a neutral way (that is, none of the students had produced them, nor had I) to discuss why they were bad. I always try to talk about how analogies made with Hitler and the Jewish Holocaust are not usually useful, how what a person hopes to capture in a good analogy is perhaps only one comparable aspect, but one that helps us grasp the emotional force of seeing event A (a relatively unknown) as like event B (a relatively known). Of course, students may actually know little about event B as well, but have simply learned a habit of mind – reductive thinking to make something complicated seem more assimilable into a known body of knowledge. I believe the reason for using good and bad analogies alike is to make emotional sense of the world; perhaps addressing the emotion a person is trying to get at (sympathy and/or compassion in the case of a good analogy and comfort/order in the case of bad analogies). If the teacher acts as mediator/facilitator in listing all the things about A and all the things about B, then letting the students collectively ponder them, even until the next class period, often a balanced reasoning will emerge. Best that it emerge from them.

I wrote an article once (as yet unpublished) about how Black Elk and Lame Deer "borrow" the authority of a particular discourse, religious testimony, to pull their readers into their worlds. Once pulled in, the reader can begin to qualify the differences between religious worldviews. We seem to be pulled toward things that are like us. Denise Low's excellent article on Chief Seattle's speech addresses many of the issues we have discussed here, but particularly how Chief Seattle used "common ground" (literally and figuratively) to lure his listeners toward an understanding of how Anglo and Indian worldviews differ relative to land.[20] She also outlines the appropriation of that speech in its various forms and for various purposes since it was originally published (even then, thirty years after the event and twice translated). "Borrowed" authority only works in the hearts/minds of sophisticated thinkers, thinkers who both know what is at stake and how two sides are alike and different.

AN ASIDE: once while visiting New Orleans, a cab driver launched into a diatribe against blacks, I guess expecting sympathy from me for this point of view. I let him dig his hole sufficiently, then told him I am American Indian and take issue with his racial characterizing of social problems. He immediately switched to say he had immense respect and admiration for Indians and, to my surprise, backpedaled a bit on his original position against blacks. He was nonetheless seeing a hierarchy of oppressions. Oddly enough, I had a similar experience with a cab driver in Minot, North Dakota. Recently relocated from New Jersey, the cabbie just launched into a diatribe against Indians; I imagine he was shaping his antiblack sentiments to his new locale. It was a short ride and I only had time to tell him I am American Indian and I did not appreciate his attitude. (I suppose inadvertent "passing" as white can give a person a dubiously privileged view of in-group sentiments, at times.) With analogy making, the goal should be to lessen the distance between an "us" and "them." Perhaps a pedagogical solution to the problem of over-analogizing is to try to remain aware of when it's a distancing enterprise and when it's a genuine attempt to probe an issue for deeper understanding.

The point I am trying to make with the cabbie stories (and I should add, I have had many pleasurable conversations with cab drivers as well) is that often if ethnic minorities aren't lumped together in the same pot, they are played off one another – victims/vipers and exemplars of culture seem to be the extremes. Again, getting at the emotional intent of the speaker seems most appropriate. To show American Indians, for example, to be "multidimensional and fully sentient human beings" (Alfonso Oritz's phrase) requires revealing unsavory aspects of history and culture as well as admirable traits – and all of that takes time.[21] For example, while it's readily apparent that the Navajo were brave to walk the hundreds of miles to and from Fort Sumner and to generate songs about walking in beauty in the process, they also raided their less mobile Pueblo and Apache neighbors; those two things need to be put in the context of all that was happening in the Southwest at that time.

CAROLINE SIMPSON: What is it with cab drivers at academic conventions? I, too, have had a couple of memorable backseat conversations with cab drivers while en route to my next destination. At the 1993 MLA convention in Toronto, a cab driver heard my Southern accent, then saw what he read as my "native people's" face, and asked me where I was from. He literally refused to believe I was Asian American and proceeded to tell me a story about a friend of his who "looks just like you" who's a member of a native Canadian group. Asian American students here in the Pacific Northwest have had similar reactions to my presence on campus as an Asian Americanist, saying on their class evaluations, "When you started talking, you freaked me out!" I cite these seemingly trivial points of the misrecognition of my representative "otherness" because I think they're an everyday example of the problem with the dependence on analogies, particularly with regard to the often manic need to manufacture an understanding of ethnic discourses. (But like the rest of you, I too can't avoid using analogies in the classroom.) I suppose I began my career in the classroom being skeptical of them because they so often seemed to accommodate students' need for a quick handle on the materials under consideration and, obviously, because of my own personal experience of being made to feel analogue-less. But good teaching, that is radical teaching, can't be founded on unexamined feelings of personal alienation, however valid they are. Just because I distrusted analogies did not excuse me from understanding and working with students and colleagues who believed they could produce worthwhile insights.

I try to make sure the analogies I consciously employ will undo students' assumptions about "the them" in question without collapsing too many distinctions. But perhaps it bears recognizing that analogies are predicated on just that, on however momentarily ignoring distinctions in order, as Kate pointed out, to assimilate what I don't know into what I do know and on that basis render an "informed" evaluation. I think, too, that Kate's exercise on the errors and blindnesses built into analogies is critical for students from the outset, especially since so much of the activity of reading autobiographies is focused on the conscious or unconscious relevance, or relationship, of other to self, margins to mainstream. In large measure, we're implicated in the work of breaking down those binaries of identification that underline racist discourse and thinking, so it's much more than the question of to analogize or not to analogize. It's also the question, isn't it, of how much essentialist ideology can I employ against itself? I'm not saying we shouldn't use analogies or that they can't be immensely helpful to complicating students' understandings, just that I want to be clear about the limitations in full sight of the students so we can all use that sense of analogies' limitations to be more self-critical of other "mainstreaming" gestures.

This kind of approach, however, may also make some students feel hesitant to commit to any sort of critique; they feel, and sometimes rightly so, that there's just not enough time to read the book, understand it, *and* take apart what's wrong with all the disciplinary strategies they've been given before. So it's an approach that's bound to frustrate some and empower others. The classroom, it seems to me, is a space of contestation in as much as it is a community of differences that must sometimes be reckoned with without recourse to finding a common ground. What will be the terms of that common ground, anyway? As the teacher I have the power to enforce all articulations of common ground, but there's also the potential that one student may resist another student's understanding of "our commonality."

The issue of common ground was the theme of the 1995 American Studies Association meeting, and at least in my department, that theme generated some debate about the desirability and terms of common ground for many disenfranchised groups. Why the move now, some wondered, to find common ground? It occurs just as ethnic studies, for instance, finds itself attaining some degree of institutional viability. I digress to make this point as a way of concluding that the desire to reconcile otherness with what's familiar (that we've indicated is so troubling about the use of analogies) is also an issue in other ways within the academy. I suspect how we negotiate this issue in the classroom has a lot to do with how (or even if) we confront it at other levels, within our departments, within our fields, at conferences, in our personal relationships, and so on.

TIFFANY LÓPEZ: I have taught Piri Thomas's *Down These Mean Streets* and Luis Rodriquez's *Always Running* in direct dialogue with one another.[22]

Rodriquez says he was inspired to think about cultural oppression in terms beyond race (that is, in terms of class status and urbanization) after reading *Mean Streets.* The text represents two distinct generational responses to conditions of race and class oppression. Though both are Latino men, these writers illustrate the diversity within Latino culture and complicate the defining of Latino identity. Thomas is a black Puerto Rican from the East Coast and Rodriquez is a brown Chicano from the West Coast. Each has a different sense of voice. Thomas makes no excuses for his behaviors, nor does he try to sugarcoat his experiences of violence. In contrast, Rodriguez goes out of his way to explain his actions and to do so with a great sense of looking back.

After the class examined the aspects the texts highlighted for them as readers – issues of assimilation and racial and class oppression – I brought up another, less explicitly focused element that unifies the two texts: violence against women and the male protagonists' struggles with their fathers. We then explored how Latino masculinity in these works emanates from the father-son relationship and directly impacts young Piri's and Chin's treatment of the women in their communities. Close readings around issues of gender and sexuality clearly revealed that the father-son relationship in these works most impacts the ways in which Thomas and Rodriguez saw themselves *first* as men and second as Latino men. There are great differences in the Latino male protagonists' relationships with women in their communities, with white women, and with white men. Gender and race are mutually informative, and struggles with race issues are integrally linked to the struggles with gender issues. In times of crisis, the young male protagonists consistently turn to the privileges of gender and sexuality to overcompensate for the subordinate status they feel concerning their lack of racial privilege.

Our previous course readings of gay and lesbian writers opened up a space for this critique. Perhaps this is a way to address Traise's concerns about analogy. In class discussions, we directly compared these heterosexual male Latino writers to gay and lesbian Latino writers in terms of their approach to working through issues of sexuality as part of clarifying issues of race. However, at the same time, I pointed out one of the differences: that gay and lesbian writers consistently address the issues frankly and consciously, while Thomas and Rodriguez, carrying the unmarked privilege of heterosexual men, do so in a much more veiled fashion. Certainly, at the time, I wasn't thinking about using analogy as a conscious pedagogical strategy.

I agree with Traise that much of the time analogy can be misleading. I think this has a lot to do with the set of assumptions that students bring with them into the classroom. The trick, it seems, is to employ an analogy in such a way that uses likeness as a point of departure, but that simultaneously disrupts the students' expectations that reading "likeness" means a clear and easy mapping of experiences. I disagree with Kate's comment that judgment can be delivered subtly. In this case, it's our job to deliver judgment and to clearly state why such comparisons are problematic and wrong.

This raises a question for me as to how to plan these things so that they do come off as critical interventions. This conversation has been helpful to me because it brings the issues of pedagogy to the forefront in a way that doesn't usually happen outside of conversations in the halls with colleagues who are also wrestling with these questions. Those moments of crisis in the classroom are frustrating because the answers, the planned thinking of how to deliver analogies, for example, for the most part happen outside of the classroom. In the classroom itself it is much different because student responses may completely derail your originally intended direction. So much of our teaching is about being able to "shoot from the hip." Rarely can we thoroughly anticipate before-hand which analogies, interruptions, judgments, or anecdotes will be necessary or helpful to draw upon as critical interventions. Those movements, it seems, draw more upon teaching that emerges from a more unconscious level. It is my hope that conversations such as the one we're having now feed into the unconscious and help develop the conscious ability to negotiate which pedagogical strategy is best to use when. Teaching is a performance in that it is in large part dependent upon one's audience. It requires both rehearsal and the art of improvisation. And, like performance, the role is written into the body. One's subject position is integral and inescapable.

SHELLI B. FOWLER: The use of analogies as a pedagogical strategy for teaching ethnic autobiographies is, as Traise says, a powerful teaching tool as one way to structure and forward thinking. And, simultaneously, as Traise, Kate, Tiffany, and Caroline have suggested, it is also a fraught and problematic strategy, as susceptible to the production of misleading and unproblematic readings of an ethnic autobiography as it is in stimulating complex (re)thinking and (re)readings of ethnic autobiographies. (One cringes, for example, at the ways in which [mis]readings inevitably result from the oversimplified analogies and comparisons that occurred in the seminar Traise attended, mentioned in an earlier response.) One of the ways that an analogy may be of some use, as a *momentary* pedagogical intervention, is as another way to facilitate students' reconsideration of the issues at hand; that is, if and when the classroom becomes a site of entrenched resistance to seeing/reading textual resistances in all their complexities, an analogy may be a useful teaching tool.

In my classrooms, entrenched resistance most often manifests itself in some shape or form as white students' guilt about, or overt rejection of, the complexities of cultural/racial/gendered/sexual/physical/religious in-equities and difference(s). A "moment" of examining a possible point of "likeness" can be a way to shift the general entrenchment. But, as Tiffany points out, the use of analogy must be done with a conscious intent to con-struct a comparison that shows likeness but that at the same time disrupts the students' expectations that a discovered likeness will mean "a clear and easy mapping of experiences."

There is, then, a necessary and unavoidable burden on the teacher who invokes the analogy (or, alternately, to make significantly complex an anal-ogy generated by a student within the class discussion). For example, it is often a difficult task to get students engaged in critical analyses of racial representations within dominant cultural ideologies. I have found that in a classroom with the majority of students having access to large amounts of cultural privilege in, at least, visible ways (in terms of race, gender, physical ability, and so on), it can be helpful to find a useful "teachable moment" that facilitates students' thinking about their own cultural privilege in nonde-fensive ways. Sometimes students with the greatest amounts of unexamined privilege(s) are the most resistant to discussing/recognizing/conceptualizing the notion of unearned cultural privilege. When this resistance surfaces, it can be helpful (though also potentially "dangerous," if the analogy is not negotiated carefully) to find an experience of stereotyping or unfair treat-ment that such a culturally privileged student can conceptualize. Asking the class if they can think of a way in which a white, straight, able-bodied, young, Christian, male may have been – in some historical period in U.S. cultural history – "momentarily" stereotyped or discriminated against on the basis of a perceived identity can create a useful teachable moment. (Un-less, however, one is ready, willing, and able to negotiate a heated discussion of contemporary affirmative action policies in some depth and detail, it is most useful to construct a historical analogy similar to the way Ronald Takaki does in *A Different Mirror*.)[23]

Often students do not have enough of a detailed picture of U.S. labor and economic history to have thought carefully about the ways in which race has been constructed differently in different historical contexts. Providing the basis for an analogy by suggesting that an Irish immigrant might have faced employment and housing discrimination on the basis of what was, through the turn of the century, viewed as an inferior race/religion – whiteness via Irish ethnicity and Catholicism – can work to jolt some students to consider the ways in which unequal distribution of resources are aligned with cultural stereotypes and the creation of racialized "others" via ethnic stratification. It can also provide a space for them to consider how their perceptions of race and religion, for example, have been socially constructed, and how those constructions have shifted over time. The "danger" alluded to above, however, is very present given most students' general desire to equate oppressions as early and as often as possible. The task, then, is to invoke an analogy that seems, on the surface, to be reassuring in its inclusivity, but to follow their all-too-common impulse to efface difference (often phrased with students' claims that "well, then, we're all oppressed") with the probing question of how contemporary constructions of racialized identities have shifted at the end of the twentieth century.

Likewise, for entrenched responses that insist that racism isn't an issue any more and it really is a level playing field, and so on, I often bring a twenty-minute video, *True Colors*, into the classroom. This *Frontline* video, done in 1991 in St. Louis, takes two college-aged men similar in age, physical ability, education, class background, and who are visibly different only in their racial identities, and follows them around St. Louis with a hidden camera. The film repeatedly exposes the numerous ways that race does matter as it documents the two individuals' attempts to secure the same housing, interview for the same job, get service at the same department store counter, and inquire about buying the same car. This very current and contemporary picture of overt and covert racism helps disrupt the (primarily white) students' tendencies to equate all cultural differences (following the difficult task of getting them to recognize and discuss race and racism at all). Again, I often think this kind of use of analogy is best conceived of as a kind of "last resort" within a particular demographic classroom construction that has reached a static entrenchment in its collective discussion of how race and racialized identities and unequal distributions of cultural power are interconnected. Such a strategy is problematic and can work against the teacher's best intentions of engaging students on an affective and intellectual level if the analogy is not carefully negotiated. There is a definite obligation here on the part of the analogy introducer to claim full responsibility for what Kate has called the place where the teacher acts as mediator/facilitator, where she/he must attend to the ways students collectively ponder the particulars of event A and event B.

I think it is an incredibly difficult task to effectively negotiate an analogy, such as the example mentioned above, as a teaching tool that furthers complex analytical critical thinking. Doing so as a planned intervention, to cite Tiffany's phrase, is crucial; otherwise, it is likely to generate more of the very classroom resistances that it is intended to disrupt.

KATE SHANLEY: I agree totally that teaching is like shooting from the hip. Classroom dynamics depend on so many factors, primary among them, the personalities involved. Over the past four years I have been experimenting with a course on personal and cultural sovereignty. The first year was a smashing success – one student even took a year off from school to figure out what his education could/should mean to him. He's back and is much more self-directed in his studies. Others continued to write glowing letters about how much the course meant to them. I use a lot of American Indian autobiography in the class. Subsequent classes have not been as good because of my stresses and the scheduling problems they face. (Too much to go into here.) Besides the performance aspects in general, I also know I cannot always figure out what works well for others, and vice versa; plus a couple of articulate students can stir up the pot, which without them hardly reaches a simmer. All of these indeterminate factors affect the classroom dynamic.

I also agree that meaningful and useful conversations about pedagogy are rarely as field specific as I would like. I try often to make pedagogy an open topic of conversation, particularly in graduate classes, for the express purpose of creating communities of engaged teachers, but also to learn from others what works for them. At Cornell, I serve on the Human Resources Council, which advises the provost on ethnic minority affairs on campus. At a meeting this fall, after I had returned from the American Council on Education conference on "Educating a Third of the Nation," I suggested that the administration makes a commitment to teaching for diversity an imperative in *all* new faculty hires. We'll see what happens with that. If such a pedagogical commitment were institutionally supported, we might be able to hope for more discussion among our colleagues. Just an idea.

On another matter mentioned earlier, I think conversations such as these are valuable because once we are able to clarify for ourselves a "proper" depth and tone to classroom discussions (figuring out how to slip in, around, and out of bad analogies, stereotypes, and disrespectful attitudes, however unwittingly held), we can challenge students with ideas that are above their heads – questions that do not go the way of closing the book on topics when the course ends. I often look around my classroom and imagine the students as future determiners of U.S. policy toward indigenous peoples, imagine them as John Colliers, Andrew Jacksons, Richard Nixons, Elaine Goodales, Charles Eastmans refashioned for the nineties. It's a chilling idea, but I do think many carry attitudes that indicate they have not learned from the mistakes of the past. We do have an obligation, in other words, to get tough with them, too, in terms of teaching the critical thinking skills sometimes painfully acquired.

TRAISE YAMAMOTO: Tiffany's strategy with Rodriguez and Thomas seems to me a really helpful way to address the problematics and potential advantages of analogy as well as the intersecting trajectories of identity. As Caroline pointed out, class, sexuality, religion, and immigration history all disrupt and complicate what can easily turn into an uncritical use of race as *the* informing lens of analysis.

This is enormously important in Asian American autobiography because one of the things that must be continually pointed out is that race and ethnicity are not synonymous. "Asian American" is a political and coalitional term, within which ethnic specificity signifies much more than categories of nomenclature. Again, the issue of analogy is operative: while "Asian American" connotes analogous experiences between and among various communities of Asian ancestry – experiences wrought by the context of U.S. racism and issues of immigration/resettlement – any easy analogies based on these experiences are immediately troubled by historical circumstance, generational concerns, and so on. Thus, a topic of much debate and discussion within Asian American studies is the increasing awareness that the majority of Asian Americans in this country are first-generation immigrants and/or identify as trans- or multinational subjects. Clearly, analogies can only go so far when reading, for instance, Nguyen-Qui Duc's *Where the Ashes Are: The Odyssey of a Vietnamese Family*, Helie Lee's *Still Life with Rice: A Young American Woman Discovers the Life and Legacy of Her Korean Grandmother*, and David Mura's *Turning Japanese: Memoirs of a Sansei.*[24] How far one generalizes these texts into some sense of "Asian American autobiography" must be guided, constrained, and informed by considerations of ethnic and generational differences, gender and sexuality, economics and geography: what, for example, is the significance of the fact that Mura grew up in a largely Jewish suburb in the Midwest, and Lee, born in Korea, was raised in Los Angeles in close contact with the Korean American community?

I want to make a perhaps graceless leap to another issue of autobiography studies that concerns me greatly. I think it is extremely important to ground such a course in a discussion/study of "the autobiography" and "the autobiographical." These terms are played with pretty fast and loose, and this is very problematic given the way in which "ethnic" writing generally is perceived to be always autobiographical. When I teach poetry, students rarely mistake T. S. Eliot for Prufrock or begin with such statements as "When Yeats is dreaming of a Ledean body . . ." But with work by poets of color, I must continually remind students that the speaker in the poem is not necessarily the writer him/herself. One obviously has to tread carefully here in order not to fall into some kind of neo–New Critical, hyperformalist trap, and there are plenty of writers (along any number of identificatory categories) who purposefully collapse the distinction between writer and speaker.

In addition, then, to a very careful discussion of the autobiographical form, there must also be a rigorous inquiry into the use of autobiography by marginalized subjects. Why, in Asian American literature, do we consistently see the autobiography as the vehicle through which different Asian ethnic groups at different times inaugurate their participation in the literary community? At the present moment, when Southeast Asian writers are just beginning to make their presence known, it is again in the realm of autobiography where we are seeing this literary emergence. These issues are paramount to the study of Asian American literature, as well as to the study of the autobiography in American literature generally. Some basic questions are helpful. Students often think these are "easy" questions, but quickly realize that the answers – if in some cases easily derived – push them into complex matters of subjectivity and identity. To whom is the autobiography addressed, and why? What is the narrative arc of the text? What is not addressed in this account? How "personal" is the autobiographer? What is the author's overall tone? Such questions, I have found, are very helpful in getting students to think in textual and formal terms, and away from the kinds of easy assumptions about "Asians" or "Asian women" they may bring to their reading.

KATE SHANLEY: I couldn't agree more about the importance of understanding the difference between "race" and ethnicity. In fact, in many ways people of different "races" from a particular region – say, California or Alaska – may have more in common with each other in terms of cultural attitudes than people of the same "race" have in common with someone of their "racial" group from another part of the country. That is not to say that people of different "racial" backgrounds (but who are from the same region/geography) recognize how alike they are. American Indian as a category is the multicultural collective term that does indeed denote a politic.

Two texts I have taught in an introductory American literature class that highlight the construction of voice in interestingly similar and dissimilar ways are *The Autobiography of Benjamin Franklin* and Charles Johnson's *Oxherding Tale*.[25] While the first is autobiographical, no one doubts that it's masterfully constructed to present Franklin as an American hero, the self-made man, and so on. Johnson's text plays off Franklin's autobiography in amusing and illuminating ways – presented in the first person (like an autobiography but peculiarly and self-consciously anachronistic in its voice/knowledge). Richard Wright's *Black Boy* strikes me as fictionalized in many ways, with the addition of particular themes, such as hunger.[26] The line blurs so readily. Similarly, Ray Young Bear in *Black Eagle Child* presents himself and his life through several characters, by his own admission, making "the author" difficult to locate indeed.[27] And Gerald Vizenor's *Interior Landscapes* seems divided in two, with distinctively different visions, from early and late depictions of his life, ending in an abstraction, even an absence of the author.[28]

I also agree that students tend to see all ethnic writing as autobiographical. In addition, they often refer to women (of all races) and ethnic minority writers by their first names – ever notice that? Can you imagine a class discussion in which we spoke of Hemingway as Ernest?

SHELLI B. FOWLER: As much as many of my responses have focused on interrupting some of the students' resistances to analyzing the difference race makes in their understanding of ethnic autobiographies in a primarily white classroom, I also want to reemphasize how I philosophically conceive of those as "moments" of pedagogical intervention, rather than as the central focus of a class that has ethnic autobiography as the subject matter.

As important as it can be at moments to gently encourage students to work through their unexamined dominant cultural assumptions about a particular subject area in ethnic literature, it is, arguably, more important to continually "push the envelope" of students' critical reading and thinking processes by staying focused on the topic at hand – ethnic autobiographies. Unfortunately, the discipline of literary studies has not yet become sufficiently integrated, and literature is not routinely read with attention to the complex issues of raced subjectivities and racial identities; and most of my students have not been introduced to the primary texts I teach in a course on African American autobiography as part of their required coursework as English majors. Part of my work, then, is to teach these texts without "apology" or "justification/explanation" regarding their legitimacy as texts in the broader field of American literature. If one spends too much time working to facilitate students' "comfortableness" with complex issues of racialized, gendered, classed, sexual, cultural identities, one misses the opportunity to facilitate critical thinking in that *un*comfortable place where we are uncomfortable because we are unfamiliar. It seems that the place(s) where we are temporarily, anyway, *un*comfortable are often the place(s) where we are best able to (re)conceive and explore the problematics of "received wisdom."

TRAISE YAMAMOTO: One of the very interesting developments to come out of the confluence of autobiography theory and the feminist theory articulated by many women of color has been the way that the autobiographical impulse has made its way into fields other than English. But this practice itself needs some careful thought. I'm thinking of the way that the autobiographical gesture is invoked – on something of a regular basis – in recognition of the need for a politics of location. In general, I think this is a positive move. In Dorinne Kondo's book, *Crafting Selves: Power, Gender, and Discourses of Identity in a Japanese Workplace*, the author's own visible identity as Japanese American becomes an important aspect of Kondo's anthropological project.[29] That is, she recognizes the ways in which her own identity as a Japanese American affected the Japanese workers who were the subjects of her study.

There are plenty of other instances where a scholar takes stock of his/her own location in ways that are enormously productive to the project at hand. It's a way of taking responsibility, when it's working at its best.

In its less fortunate incarnations, however, the self-reflexivity of a politics of location devolves into solipsistic autobiographical anecdotes whose relevance is not always apparent, but whose folksy inanity is all too clear. The almost obligatory I-am-this-I'm-from-there litany – however artfully narrativized – seems to me a tiresome exercise whose social cousin is the party monologuer who can't seem to differentiate between what might be of interest to the new acquaintance and what is merely boring. A case in point: a talk that began with the speaker identifying herself in minute detail, listing identity markers from the fact that she was white and an academic to her "identity" as a homeowner and as someone in hoc to the bank. Is it only my own intolerance for such listings that leads me to believe that they are, at least partly, directly responsible for the ways in which we must always deal with the charge that the autobiographical – either in self-identified autobiographical texts or in instances such as Kondo's study – is merely the subjective? I write "merely" there because I have found that whenever a student, or conference-talk audience member, uses the word "subjective," it is almost always derogatorily inflected with an implicit modifying "mere." I might also point out that when brandished irresponsibly, the autobiographical gesture, laboring under the guise of a politics of location, is a mighty convenient way of focusing attention on oneself.

KATE SHANLEY: I'm not sure if I get your point, Traise, about "listing identity markers," but in the American Indian context (and as I have said, 87 percent of what passes as Indian autobiography comes out of the "as told to" tradition), many autobiographers or life-story tellers identify themselves according to tribe, clan, and family markers. I'm thinking particularly about one text, a pictographic autobiography by White Bull, the man who claims to have killed Custer. He writes in Lakota beside each picture he draws, frequently identifying himself as the son of One Bull and nephew to Sitting Bull. Some critics do not accept his work as autobiography, but Hertha Wong has an interesting argument for seeing it as such in her book *Sending My Heart Back across the Years*.[30] I take a position between yeah and nay – his text particularly shows itself to be self-generated, an amalgamation of forms and unmediated by an editor; thus, I take it to be autobiographical. The important reasons why a Lakota person would tell of his or her life are there: an important event, a situation of the self within tribe, clan, and family, a swearing to the truth and offering of possible collaborators (like coup tales), and a use of a native language and somewhat appropriated visual medium.

All of that said, I agree in general (especially given the example you offer) that the reason why the person "declares" him- or herself is the most important thing. Henrietta Whiteman presents her view of history through an autobiographical rendering of her people's (Cheyenne) history, beginning with the creation narrative, in *American Indians and the Problems of History*.[31] Perhaps hers is a supreme example of the interwoven communal and individual identities and subjectivities, if a community can be said to be "of one mind."

TRAISE YAMAMOTO: I think autobiographical studies provides one of the most complex avenues for teaching and thinking about subjectivity and textual identity/ies. As we've all said at different points in this conversation, these issues are all the more complicated by each of our visible and not-visible identities, the various trajectories or – as Caroline put it – fault lines that can both engage and obscure the texts we teach. The expectation to be a native informant is strong. At the same time, many of us also have to acknowledge that our areas of study have resulted in an amount of expertise in fields very close to our own sense of identity. As I've said earlier in this conversation, the easy correspondences that students will often assume between the instructor's identity and the text under discussion must be continually disrupted by the instructor. Perhaps most importantly, students need to be taught how to disrupt and intervene in those assumptions on their own.

I think one has to be very aware at all times of the ways in which such a seemingly personal form, the autobiography, is already vulnerable to mis-readings that decontextualize the individual from the forces of history, economics, sexuality, race, and gender. At the same time, a lot of ethnic autobiographies are taught in such a way as to render the autobiographi-cal subject the site of racial fetishization within his/her own text. That is, race becomes the sole paradigm through which subjectivity is viewed. This suggests a fundamental misunderstanding of the way in which subjectivity is constructed. Race both informs and is informed by numerous vectors of identity that shift and are deployed in relation to particular contexts. This is a crucial point to get across in the teaching of ethnic autobiographies. For instance, while the experiences related in any given Asian American autobiography may represent, to an extent, the experiences of other Asian Americans, it does not follow that the subjectivity of all "like" individuals. As with so many issues related to the teaching of ethnic autobiography, it is a fine line one has to walk.

KATE SHANLEY: As I grow older, I realize how thoroughly my life has been guided by a (here I need a word that sums it up and none will do entirely) fear/anxiety/hope/dismay related to my being invisible to and silenced by other people. Lest I wax autobiographical, let me simply say, I care less about it now than I used to. That helps and hinders my teaching; I walk a fine line. Some terms student evaluations range from, "I felt the teacher knew more than she would share with us," to "the tangents were interesting, though we could have talked more about the book." I think one of the most important issues/questions we face as either radical teachers or teachers who are perceived as "other" is the extent to which we reveal ourselves, use our own personal histories to illuminate particular things in the texts we teach at particular times. I alternately feel it's essential I enter as myself in my teaching and resent that there is a certain demand placed on me that I do – clearly an ambivalence. So many other teachers of other subjects can hide behind the text, the history, the context; I'd like the same option. Then again, to act as though everything we do is *not* political seems abhorrent to me also. It's certainly a day-by-day, situation-by-situation thing. We are back again to the "representative" aspect of identity politics, which is redundant perhaps, but it won't go away.

SHELLI B. FOWLER: I'd like to end by reemphasizing the importance of en-gaging in critically aware, self-reflexive acts of reading and teaching. Traise's concern about the kind of academic posturing that invokes a descriptive identity without any critical consciousness of what is meant by a "politics of location" is an issue that has troubled African American literary studies for some time. Ann duCille's "The Occult of True Black Womanhood: Critical Demeanor and Black Feminist Studies," for example, examines the prob-lematics of racial/gender/class positioning that results in only a superficial gesture toward what should be the very serious consideration and nego-tiation of how racial/gendered/classed/sexual identity(ies) affects the way an individual sees/reads/perceives and makes meaning in the world around him/her.[32] DuCille calls for discussions of "cultural literacy and intellectual competence." within the field of African American literary criticism; she ar-gues that critics and readers of African American literature must recognize and carefully attend to the various ways that cultural difference(s) affect our valuing, or devaluing, of "bodies" of literature.

In other words, simply locating yourself on a cultural identity axis by listing identity markers doesn't do much. Unless there is also the intellec-tual willingness to continually negotiate the complexities of power rela-tions among identity markers, there is no critically conscious, self-reflexive awareness of difference(s) and no real understanding, then, of the politics of location. This conversation has explored some of the numerous ways that the complex intersections of cultural identities make appropriate reading strategies an issue in the teaching of ethnic autobiographies. Arguably, the more unearned cultural privilege one has, the more difficult it seems to be to grasp the significance of inequities and the unequal distribution of cultural power. Progressive pedagogy that acknowledges the importance of the politics of location requires each of us to endlessly examine the ways in which we have more or less access to dominant cultural power, and to continually analyze how that affects our interpretive readings and our pedagogical strategies. In particular, for white academics working in the field of ethnic literature, it means that we must work through and against the ways that racial privilege inevitably works to hinder our understanding of racial difference. I am not arguing here for an essentialism that suggests "you have to *be* it to *know* it." What I am arguing for is an increased critical awareness of the ways the *privilege* of whiteness increases the challenge we who are white face in gaining a critical competence that requires a cultural literacy (or cultural literacies) that is not ours and will never be *ours*. There is, historically (and currently), a tendency for white teachers and readers to move quickly away from the issue of racial difference toward an analysis of gender, or class, or sexual orientation, or other cultural identity markers, in an attempt to forge a seemingly safer common ground. While the intersections of identity differences are central to any complex analysis (as the participants of this conversation have suggested), eliding the difference race makes in order to feel comfortable about what we all might share as women, or gays and lesbians, for example, remains a strong tendency among many white academics. Effacing racial difference in such a move must be avoided because it prohibits an accurate analysis (comparative or otherwise) of gendered, classed, sexual, or any other difference. There is, as Traise has just suggested, a fine line one has to walk in the attempt to wrestle successfully with the complexities of identity issues (of both writer and reader) in reading ethnic autobiographies. It is not usually an easy or comfortable walk, but it is a necessary one.

CAROLINE SIMPSON: Our varied conversations here testify to the rich rewards and the hard questions that each of us has confronted in the teaching of ethnic autobiographies. When addressed as literary, historical, and political articulations, ethnic autobiographies demand that we examine our deepest assumptions about identity and self, as many of us have been pointing out. We have to be vigilant not only about the assumptions we may make about the writers and their works, as somehow "representative" of their various cultural communities, but also about the assumptions we make about our students and each other. So much more seems possible to address by dint of the personal voice, and thus so much more may go awry, particularly if we believe that any one critical perspective will save us. While it is true that focusing solely on race blinds us to other differences, as I have emphasized, it is also true that we need to be clearer about the distinctions between racial identities. And although I, for one, have stressed the need to historicize the issues and experiences that give rise to a particular text, as someone trained by historians, I'm also painfully aware of the failure of historical context to account fully for the experiences and choices of people of color in the Americas. Instead, we must continually develop and employ new and dynamic pedagogical approaches, a process that requires no less than a constant and tactical realignment of our critiques. Because the potential to misread or diminish these works is still so prevalent, and because that potential is still so often unexamined, it is vital that we resist or correct such moves before they become entrenched and, so, closed to inquiry.

TIFFANY LÓPEZ: This conversation has been about the sharing of stories. Forging critical interventions in the teaching of ethnic literature is difficult and sometimes painful work because it requires that we confront not only issues of race but also the factors of racism that encompass the work. In teaching autobiography, I've found that students, in general, feel empowered to bring personal experience into the classroom. Yet when students of color share personal experience, more often than not their stories get read as culturally representative. The risk is that they will be spotlighted as the "native informant." Often, students of color put themselves in this role because it is the first time their subject position is legitimatized. Any teacher of autobiography must keep in mind such risks and be prepared for those moments in which they surface.

While personal experiences can wonderfully supplement classroom discussion, personal experience alone must never be conflated with or substituted for close critical reading strategies. Often in the classroom a perverse sort of liberal racism takes place – what in her work the sociologist Barbara Trepaignier calls "unaware racism" – in which white teachers and students do not push people of color beyond personal experience.[33] Their stories are interpreted as beyond question and beyond critique even though the teaching of autobiography would in and of itself seem to put the "personal" in a critical framework.

When there is no intervention that purposefully directs personal experience toward developing critical reading strategies, a terrible burden is placed on the student of color. Recognizing difference does not mean that difference should go unquestioned. If our job as teachers is to challenge students, then we must remember to challenge *all* students. For it is through the sharing of stories – be they about one's personal life or how one sees a given text – and the resultant critical exchange that students learn to become more pointed and critical thinkers, speakers, and writers.

NOTES

1. The authors of this chapter would like to collectively thank Sue Armitage, who attended the initial conversation panel at the November 1995 American Studies Association conference, and who suggested that we continue the conversation in an article for *Frontiers*. This online conversation was written on the Internet via a listserve; all five of the authors were connected by the listserve, with each of us receiving all of the comments and responding to each other by logging on once a day and engaging in the conversation. This worked to create a feeling of an ongoing conversation with only a small amount of lag time as comments were sent out on the listserve to all five recipients. The authors would also like to thank *Frontiers* editors Patricia Hart and Karen Weathermon for their gentle prodding, endless patience, and helpful editing suggestions.

2. Maria Chona, *Papago Woman*, ed. Ruth Underhill (New York: Holt, Rinehart, and Winston, 1979)

3. Mary Crow Dog and Richard Erdoes, *Lakota Woman* (New York: Grove Weidenfeld, 1990).

4. Michael Awkward, *Negotiating Difference: Race, Gender, and the Politics of Positionality* (Chicago: University of Chicago Press, 1995).

5. Monica Sone, *Nisei Daughter* (1953; reprint, Seattle: University of Washington Press, 1979); and Yoshiko Uchida, *Desert Exile* (1982; reprint, Seattle: University of Washington Press, 1984).

6. Charles Chesnutt, "The Passing of Grandison" (1899), in *The Heath Anthology of American Literature*, vol. 2, ed. Paul Lauter, et al. (Lexington MA: D.C. Heath and Co., 1994), 474–85.

7. Himilce Novas, *Everything You Need to Know about Latino History* (New York: Plume, 1994).

8. Mary Paik Lee, *Quiet Odyssey: A Pioneer Korean Woman in America* (Seattle: University of Washington Press, 1990).

9. Jade Snow Wong, *Fifth Chinese Daughter* (1950; reprint, Seattle: University of Washington Press, 1989).

10. Walker Percy, "Loss of the Creature," in *The Message in the Bottle: How Queer Man Is, How Queer Language Is, and What One Has to Do with the Other* (New York: Farrar, Straus and Giroux, 1975), 46–63.

11. Wahneema Lubiano, "Like Being Mugged by a Metaphor: Multicultural-

ism and State Narratives," in *Mapping Multiculturalism*, ed. Avery F. Gordon and Christopher Newfield (Minneapolis: University of Minnesota Press, 1996), 66.

12. Harriet A. Jacobs, *Incidents in the Life of a Slave Girl; Written by Herself*, ed. Lydia Maria Child, 1861, ed. Jean Fagan Yellin (Cambridge: Harvard University Press, 1987).

13. Louisa Picquet, *Louisa Picquet, The Octaroon: A Tale of Southern Slave Life* (1861), reprinted in *Collected Black Women's Narratives*, ed. Henry Louis Gates, Jr. (New York: Oxford University Press, 1988).

14. Cecile Pineda, *The Love Queen of the Amazon* (Boston: Little, Brown, 1992); John Rechy, *The Miraculous Day of Amalia Gómez* (New York: Arcade, 1991), and *Sexual Outlaw* (New York: Grove Press, 1977); and Montserrat Fontes, *First Confessions* (New York: Norton, 1991).

15. H. David Brumble III, *American Indian Autobiography* (Berkeley: University of California Press, 1988).

16. Jeanne Wakatsuki Houston, *Farewell to Manzanar: A True Story of Japanese American Experience During and After the World War II Internment* (Boston: Houghton Mifflin, 1973); and David Mura, *Where the Body Meets Memory: An Odyssey of Race, Sexuality and Identity* (New York: Anchor Books, 1996).

17. Cherríe Moraga, *Loving in the War Years:* Lo Que Nunca Paso Por Sus Labios (Boston: South End Press, 1983); and Norma Alarcon, Ana Castillo, and Cherríe Moraga, eds., *The Sexuality of Latinas* (Berkeley: Third Woman Press, 1993).

18. Esmeralda Santiago, *When I Was Puerto Rican* (New York: Addison-Wesley, 1993).

19. Michael Nava, *The Hidden Law* (New York: Ballantine Books, 1994); Achy Obejas, *We Came All the Way from Cuba So You Could Dress Like This?* (Pittsburgh: Cleis Press, 1994); Emma Perez, *Gulf Dreams* (Berkeley: Third Woman Press, 1996: Teri de la Peña, *Margins* (Seattle: Seal Press, 1992), and *Latin Satins* (Seattle: Seal Press, 1994); and Richard Rodriguez, *Hunger of Memory* (New York: Bantam, 1982), and *Days of Obligation* (New York: Viking, 1992).

20. Denise Low, "Contemporary Reinvention of Chief Seattle: Variant Texts of Chief Seattle's 1854 Speech," *American Indian Quarterly* (summer 1995): 407–21.

21. Alfonso Ortiz, "Indian/White Relations: A View from the Other Side of the 'Frontier,'" in *Indians in American History*, ed. Frederick F. Hoxie (Wheeling IL: Harlan Davidson, Inc., 1988), 1.

22. Piri Thomas, *Down These Mean Streets* (New York: Vintage, 1991); and Luis Rodriguez, *Always Running: La Vida Loca: Gang Days in L.A.* (New York: Simon & Schuster, 1993).

23. Ronald Takaki, *A Different Mirror: A History of Multicultural America* (Boston: Little, Brown, 1993).

24. Nguyen Qui Duc, *Where the Ashes Are: The Osyssey of a Vietnamese Family* (New York: Addison-Wesley, 1994); Helie Lee, *Still Life with Rice: A Young American Woman Discovers the Life and Legacy of Her Korean Grandmother* (New York: Scribner, 1996); and David Mura, *Turning Japanese: Memoirs of a Sansei* (New York: Atlantic Monthly Press, 1991).

25. Benjamin Franklin, *The Autobiography of Benjamin Franklin* (New York: Collier Books, 1962); and Charles Johnson, *Oxherding Tale* (Bloomington: Indiana University Press, 1982).

26. Richard Wright, *Black Boy: A Record of Childhood and Youth* (New York: Harper and Row, 1966).

27. Ray A. Young Bear, *Black Eagle Child, The Facepaint Narratives* (Iowa City: University of Iowa Press, 1992).

28. Gerald Vizenor, *Interior Landscapes: Autobiographical Myths and Metaphors* (Minneapolis: University of Minnesota Press, 1990).

29. Dorinne K. Kondo, *Crafting Selves: Power, Gender, and Discourses of Identity in a Japanese Workplace* (Chicago: University of Chicago Press, 1990).

30. Hertha Wong, *Sending My Heart Back across the Years: Tradition and Innovation in Native American Autobiography* (New York: Oxford University Press, 1992).

31. Henrietta Whiteman, "White Buffalo Woman," in *The American Indian and the Problem of History*, ed. Calvin Martin (New York: Oxford University Press, 1987), 162–70.

32. Ann duCille, "The Occult of True Black Womanhood: Critical Demeanor and Black Feminist Studies," *Signs* 19:3 (1994): 591–629.

33. Barbara Trepaignier, "Silent Racism in White Women" (Ph.D. diss., University of California at Santa Barbara, 1996), cited with permission.

Frontiers 17:2 (1996):4–49.

Restructuring Identity

The Autobiographical Self of a Japanese American Woman in Lydia Minatoya's Talking to High Monks in the Snow

AKI UCHIDA

I am a woman caught between standards of East and West.
Lydia Minatoya

Identity has always been a problem for Japanese American women, as for other ethnic minorities in the United States. Their history of immigration, their experience with exclusion policies, their incarceration during World War II and the following resettlement, and the stereotype of being a "model minority" all seem to raise questions about their identity in terms of their race, ethnicity, gender, and status as "Americans." The position of U.S.-born Japanese American women is ambiguous both in relation to the prescribed "American" norm – which is white, Christian, middle class, heterosexual, and male – and in relation to the prescribed norm of their family, community, and what is ideologically "Japanese." As daughters and descendants of immigrants, they experience a tension between the forces of cultural "assimilation" and "maintenance" that interact with intergenerational conflicts. They are not quite the same as their white peers, nor as their parents. Often they are caught between the two groups, which are presented as antithetical to each other, implying that they must choose one or the other, that they cannot be one without denying the other. According to Patricia Hill Collins, the Western pattern of "either/or dichotomous thinking," in which people, things, and ideas are categorized "in terms of their difference from one another," forces one to see the world in terms of mutually exclusive categories.[1]

Because identities are also seen, as Dorinne Kondo writes, as "fixed, bounded entities containing some essence or substance, expressed in distinctive attributes,"[2] the "essence" of Japanese American women is seen as reducible to either being a "Japanese woman" or an "American woman." And yet, when they do choose one identity over the other, they are faced with the fact that their choice still marginalizes them; they still must deal both with the consequence that they are simultaneously something else and with the forces of objectification that render those not white, Christian, male, heterosexual, and middle class as the Other.[3] They are caught in a double bind, a no-win situation, unless they opt to take an alternative route of consciously embracing and celebrating their multiplicity and their identity as Japanese American women. This means that they simultaneously resist, critique, and challenge the practices and discourses that marginalize and exclude them for being unclassifiable and anomalous. It involves rejecting the imposition of identity by the dominant culture and creating an identity that is multiple, open, shifting, and at times internally contradictory, shaped by the conjunctions of history, society, and personal relationships, and emergent from the juxtaposition of the conventional and the creative forces of culture. One arena in which this has been done is through writing. Ethnic minority writers have offered a critique of the dominant culture or promoted a new definition of American identity in various genres, including poetry, fiction, drama, and autobiography and memoir; Japanese American women have been no exception.[4]

In this chapter, I discuss how Lydia Minatoya's *Talking to High Monks in the Snow*, a memoir by a third-generation woman, illustrates an attempt to avoid marginalizing notions of identity. Focusing on the ways in which the text disrupts autobiographical conventions, I analyze how the self is constructed as a multiple, shifting, and unfinished process that rejects the traditional notion of a static and unitary identity embedded in the language of dualism and essentialism.[5] As such, her text contributes to the ongoing discourse of resistance by ethnic minorities, albeit in a limited way due to its failure to dismantle the politics of middle-class privilege from which the author benefits.

AUTOBIOGRAPHY AS A SITE OF IDENTITY CONSTRUCTION

Talking to High Monks in the Snow belongs to a literary genre that has been particularly notable in its effort to construct Japanese American women's identity: the memoir and autobiography. Central to these texts is the process of self-creation,[6] which for ethnic minorities involves the reinvention of ethnic identity and ethnicity.[7] Autobiographies as individual stories expressing a unique life are paradoxically also intended to have some utility,[8] based on the assumption that personal stories are generalizable and represent something that is "both more communal and more abstract than the particular life."[9] The significance of creating this identity thus transcends the individual and becomes communal; the individualistic searchings in the autobiographies "turn out to be revelations of traditions, re-collections of disseminated identities."[10]

Because one of the functions of Japanese American autobiographies and memoirs is to create individual identities that simultaneously speak to the identities and experiences of other Japanese Americans, autobiographies also construct the identity and the stories of one's family and community. Two themes regarding family and community occur repeatedly in Japanese American women's autobiographies. The first is the mother – daughter relationship, specifically the interface between the stories of mothers and the stories of daughters.[11] The maternal voice (its presence or absence) occupies a central space in the autobiographical subjects' expression of their self-consciousness as gendered, racial, and ethnic beings. The mother is often presented as a figure that connects the daughter with her Japanese roots.[12] In the context of white hegemony in the United States, however, the mother's embodiment of Japanese-ness can sever the mother – daughter tie.[13] The hegemonic discourse of what it means to be "American" (especially against the backdrop of Japanese American internment during the war) forces the daughter to distance herself from the mother, who reminds her of her "difference," in order to become "assimilated" into the dominant culture.[14] Although usually the mother (and the Japanese-ness represented by her) is eventually reembraced, it is with an ambivalence and a sense of loss that the gap between the daughter's voice and the mother's can never be closed. In their dialogue with their mothers, the autobiographical subjects express a longing that they simultaneously deny and know cannot be satisfied.

The second prevalent theme is the incarceration experience during the war. The psychological effect of the internment camp experience on Japanese Americans has been discussed in depth elsewhere,[15] but one fact related to the present discussion is the number of autobiographies by Japanese Americans after World War II that, according to Ann Rayson, describe "the coming to terms of the author with a split cultural identity whose dichotomy was exacerbated during the camp experience."[16] These Japanese American texts can be read as complementing each other in a larger project that seeks to present the experience of Japanese American women with respect to the historical moment that involved a major shared epiphany: the incarceration. Although the discourse of the camp experience may take on diverse forms, it exists collectively as a legacy to be drawn upon in the creation of Japanese American identity.

However, the genre of memoir and autobiography, which allows communal concerns and interests to be addressed, can also reproduce the essentialistic view of identity that made the identity of Japanese American women problematic in the first place. In the attempt to define what it means to be a Japanese American woman, one can fall into the trap of assuming that there is an "authentic" set of experiences, or "voice," that is essential for one to be defined as a Japanese American woman. The question that needs to be asked is not what the "real" Japanese American identity is, but how identities are resisted, created, and transformed in autobiographical writing, and how this process contributes to the collective discourse of what it means to be Japanese American in the United States. Needed are critiques of, and alternatives to, the notion of a fixed, unitary, essentialistic identity, not a "different" and more "authentic" unitary, essentialistic identity that reproduces marginality and exclusion.

Autobiographical discourse of identity and subjectivity tends to present identity as if it were an entity constant and continuous over time. As a result, readers have tended to see the autobiographical writings of Japanese and other ethnic American women as stories of personal victories of "coming to terms with" or "discovering" who they "really" are after enduring and overcoming racial barriers and difficulties, rather than as critiques of the identity that the dominant culture imposes on them or as the unfinished process of newly creating who they are. Their Japanese American identity tends to be seen as something essential to the self that had always been there but hidden and in need of being found, as if it existed within them prior to their awareness or acceptance. But we must be aware of the force that autobiographical and narrative conventions have in shaping our interpretations and not lose sight of the resistance against the essentialist notion of a single coherent identity in the texts. It is in this sense that Minatoya's memoir becomes an important point of departure from "conventional" autobiographical writing. Her text, while seeming to conform to the conventions of autobiography and the tradition of Japanese American women's autobiography, actually subverts them through her resistance to essentialistic "Japanese American identity" and her crafting of an identity that is multiple, shifting, and self-contradictory.

TALKING TO HIGH MONKS IN THE SNOW: AN ANALYSIS OF THE
CONSTRUCTION OF AN AUTOBIOGRAPHICAL IDENTITY

Minatoya is a *Sansei* (a third-generation Japanese American) born in 1950. She is of a generation of Japanese Americans whose identity has been discussed less frequently, many of the autobiographies by Japanese American women having been written by the previous generation, who directly experienced the internment. Minatoya's text explores the particular ways in which race, ethnicity, and gender as social and historical relationships shape the lives of a postwar generation whose experiences differ from those of the prewar generations. However, it is the narrative features of her text that make it unique among autobiographies written by Japanese American women. Diverging from the conventions of autobiography through her strategies of self-representation and narrative structure, Minatoya offers an alternative way of looking at identity as a complex process challenging the traditional model of a coherent self that fits into a world organized in mutually exclusive categories and dichotomies.

Strategies of Self-Presentation: The Narrator and the Narrated

In an autobiography, the author typically deals with her identity on two levels. She is the subject telling the story through the writing, and she is also the protagonist of the story, the person *about* whom she is writing. Conventionally it is assumed that the writing subject (author) and the subject written about (protagonist) are identical. The author creates an illusion that the narrator/protagonist/"I" *is* the author, that the speaking subject is the writing subject. The chronological, linear order in which the events are presented also helps to sustain this illusion. The author's subjectivity is made invisible to preserve the unitary, continuous existence of the protagonist's ("I") identity as her life is chronicled. In other words, the event of narration is hidden behind the narrated events. Some autobiographical writings, however, do not strictly follow this convention, thus disrupting the text's (and the reader's) construction of a unitary and continuous self and story of the protagonist. For example, Estelle Jelinek has observed that women's autobiographies tend to project a self-image that is multidimensional, fragmented, and unfinished, in a style that tends to be episodic and anecdotal, nonchronological and disjunctive: "They may begin as chronological narratives, since chronology helps give a sense of order and control over one's life. But it is soon superseded – usually unconsciously – by interruptions to that safe progression with anecdotes, even out of order, and all kinds of insertions – letters, articles, even descriptions by others."[17] This is what happens in Minatoya's text, more explicitly and frequently it seems than in most previous autobiographies by Japanese American women, where the authors' more rigorous adherence to the conventions of autobiography leads them to be read more straightforwardly as "quests" for a "real" self.

The extent to which Minatoya's narrative interrupts the linear flow and creates a breach in the singularity of subjectivity may be better understood by first examining a more "conventional" narrative as a basis of comparison. Monica Sone's memoir *Nisei Daughter* was published almost forty years before Minatoya's *Talking to High Monks in the Snow;* Sone is second-generation Japanese American and Minatoya is third generation. However, the two narratives closely resemble each other, both centering around the protagonist's search for her own identity. It is the way in which each narrative projects this process of creating identity that differentiates the two texts.

Sone's narrative clearly follows the convention of preserving a unitary and continuous autobiographical subject. It starts with the narrator/protagonist Kazuko Itoi discovering that she "had Japanese blood" and, much to her chagrin, being sent to a Japanese school where she finds herself switching her personality back and forth like a chameleon. As anti-Japanese feelings heighten in the United States, climaxing after the attack on Pearl Harbor and the resulting evacuation order, she experiences racial discrimination and feelings of ambivalence about being Japanese: "I felt like a despised, pathetic two-headed freak, a Japanese and American, neither of which seemed to be doing me any good."[18] However, by the end of the narrative, she has overcome these negative feelings, announcing to her parents, "I don't resent my Japanese blood anymore. I'm proud of it, in fact, . . . It's really nice to be born into two cultures, like getting a real bargain in life, two for the price of one. . . . I used to feel like a two-headed monstrosity, but now I find that two heads are better than one" (*ND* 236). The autobiography concludes with her statement "The Japanese and the American parts of me were now blended into one" (*ND* 238). The protagonist's identity is constructed in a linear, progressive manner that moves from her awareness of her race as a disruption to her childhood, the irreconcilable duality of her American and Japanese selves, to a resolution that sees her dual identity as a "bargain, two for the price of one." The transformation process is completed: from chaos to order, from a two-headed freak to a blended human being.

This linearity seems to present a sense of completion in the narrative – that Sone has actually "found" (rather than newly created) her "real" self and that the search is over.[19] There is one constant voice, that of the protagonist, that does all the narration; there is a single "I" throughout the text, the author's subjectivity being completely subsumed under the subjectivity of the protagonist. It therefore seems unquestionable that the author, writing about the past, shares the identity with the protagonist. This creates the impression that, since the protagonist's identity seems completed at the end of the narrative, the author's identity also must have been frozen since then. The author's use of her name, however, betrays this continuity. Whereas the protagonist is consistently referred to as Kazuko Itoi, it is as Monica Sone that the author writes the text. The use of different names for the author and the protagonist implies that the singularity of the author and protagonist cannot be assumed, that the identity of the author may differ from the seemingly completed identity of the protagonist. In other words, the identity of Kazuko Itoi was not "finished," the problems with her identity not resolved, as the narrative had projected.[20] However, the sense of completion created by the text's adherence to autobiographical convention undermines this sense of uncompleted identity, weakening the messages of resistance and critique embedded in Sone's text.

In contrast to Sone, Minatoya directly deals with the author – protagonist relationship and the construction of the "I." The narrative does not follow a simple, linear progression. On the surface, the major narrated events are placed in a temporal sequence to capture her "Asian American odyssey," as the subtitle indicates; beginning with her parents' experience, her childhood, and her early career in academia, it continues with her experiences of being fired, traveling to her mother's home in Japan, teaching in Okinawa and China, sojourning in Nepal, and returning to the United States. However, this sequence is constructed as a string of episodes, anecdotes, and vignettes, all loosely connected in the manner of free association. The result is that the narrative seems fragmented rather than following a single, smooth trajectory, and the significance of each fragment to the autobiography as a whole is not explicit. Moreover, the chronological flow is constantly disrupted by flashbacks, flashforwards, and commentaries that reflect the narrator's, rather than the protagonist's, consciousness. Together, these techniques inevitably remind the reader that the autobiography is an event of narration by someone other than the protagonist.

The text begins *in medias res* with Minatoya's mother's stories about Japanese womanhood, with the mother's voice saying, "I believe that the Japanese word for wife literally means honorable person remaining within."[21] The mother's stories reveal the identity of the mother: she is a second-generation Japanese American, educated in Japan, who grew up without her mother, experienced the panic of Pearl Harbor and the trauma of internment, and met her husband in the camp. The dialogue in which the mother's stories are told, on the other hand, reveals the identity of the listening protagonist, Minatoya, as an "American daughter" (4). The dialogue is followed by the author's commentary in a voice that is totally different from the voice of the inquiring child in the previous dialogue: "I am a psychologist. People often ask me, 'How did wartime Relocation affect Japanese Americans?' Relocation was a wall that my mother's music could not scale" (14). Thus, early in the autobiography the author disrupts the narrative flow and the singularity of the "I." She also tells the circumstance of her name, Lydia: "My parents searched for a conventional name. They wanted me to have the full true promise of America" (31). She wryly points out: "Call it denial, but many Japanese Americans never quite understood that the promise of America was not truly meant for them. . . . And so my parents gave me an American name and hoped that I could pass. They nourished me with the American dream: Opportunity, Will, Transformation. . . . My faith was unshakable. I believed" (31, 32, 33). But this faith was only for a brief moment during childhood innocence, as the use of the past tense and her tone of voice reveals; although an American, the American dream did not always apply to her.

Minatoya writes about two episodes in her childhood that reveal her anxiety to belong and be accepted. One is her experience of being a "teacher's pet" and ultimately outgrowing the obsession to win her teacher's approval; another is her fascination with the mother of her best friend in school, a woman who, unlike herself, felt "no need to belong" (40). This episode is followed by a sudden fast-forward: the next thing we know Minatoya is in graduate school, taking psychological tests and psychotherapy as part of her training. She scores high in lying and "faking good" in trying to make an impression (41). However, the therapist's behavior reveals that she has negative feelings toward Minatoya. Later the therapist tells Minatoya that she used to hate the mother of a Japanese diplomatic family in her neighborhood. Minatoya imagines her own mother and her father in the place of the Japanese diplomat: "There they are: clean, honest, and reverent, diligent, docile, and perhaps a little dull. Evoking their neighbors' hate" (42). By association she recalls her Uncle Koji, a No No Boy during the war and an antithesis to her parents: "Some Japanese tried to change" (43). He was declared a menace and sent away; neither her uncle nor her parents fared any better. She also recalls her grandfather, who by the end of the war "had retreated into cranky apathy," having lost everything forever in the incarceration (44). Then the narrative returns to her experience, moving backward in time to her junior high school days: "When I reached junior high school, I wanted to be a beatnik" (44). She recalls her ambivalence with herself among her friends, "pretty blonde girls who rode in convertible sports coupes," who lived in a totally different world: "I wanted *authority*. I was a sidekick to that bevy of beautiful girls, a foil for their fair, statuesque vitality. They were young women: studious, happy, seemingly blessed. I was that terrible painful thing – an adolescent: vacillating, vulnerable, and hostile" (44–45). Her childhood episodes thematically evoke much later memories; the lives of her parents and relatives and her own intersect, transcending the temporal barrier. This thematic connection of stories is privileged over the preservation of a linear narrative and a single protagonist.

Even her childhood self is reconstructed in different ways. For example, flashbacks inserted later in the text when Minatoya is visiting her mother's family in Japan present a dimension of her childhood that is totally different from the one she related earlier. Meeting her relatives, she recalls how an aspect of feudal Japan had been transmitted from her mother to her American girlhood: "And so, I was shaped. In that feudal code, all females were silent and yielding. Even their possessions were accorded more rights. . . . And so, I was haunted. . . . While other children were learning that in America you get what you ask for, I was being henpecked by inanimate objects. While other children were learning to speak their minds, I was locked in a losing struggle for dominance with my clothing, my toys, and my tools" (103). The picture she gives here is rather contradictory to the previous one of her "American" childhood in which she was given an American name so that she could "pass," in which she believed in the American dream. The multiplicity of the self can also be seen in the multiple names the "I" takes in the text. The protagonist is both Yuriko or Yuri-chan, as her family and relatives call her, and Lydia or Lydia-chan as her Japanese friends call her. In China, she is also referred to as Dr. Lydia. She exists in a myriad of relationships and roles and speaks in numerous voices: a daughter, a granddaughter, a student, a teacher, a friend. "I" here is, as Trinh Minh-ha says, "not a unified subject, a fixed identity, or that solid mass covered with layers of superficialities one has gradually to peel off before one can see its true face. 'I' is, itself, *infinite layers.*"[22]

Finally, Minatoya's narrative does not present the self as "finished" or having resolved all the conflicts and confusion at the end. The self-image projected during her sojourn in Asia increasingly becomes one that positively integrates her duality: "I saw my presence as a perfect case of goodness of fit, as a meeting of yin and yang" (162). Yet at the end of her journey, anticipating her return to the United States, she becomes nervous, again losing her achieved comfort with her duality: "Change unnerves me. Behind every opportunity lurks the possibility of my undoing. Was I now Asian? Was I still American? Would I have to choose between the two?" (264). Identity is conceptualized as fragile, possibly "undone," not fixed and given but dynamic and achieved as a process. In this manner, Minatoya frequently violates the autobiographical expectations regarding self-presentation. Throughout the text, the linear progression of the narrated self is constantly disrupted. It is also made impossible for the reader to separate the narrated self and events from the narrating self and the event of narration. Moreover, both the narrated self and the narrating self constantly shift positions and sometimes seem to lack coherence; the voices are reflexive, but fragmented. Both selves are non-unitary, incomplete, unfinished, in the process of continuous construction, and constantly in dialogue with each other.

Construction of the Autobiographical Self: Becoming Japanese American

Despite the multiplicity and fluidity of the "I" and the fragmentation of the narrative, the construction of Minatoya's identity does follow a trajectory that evolves from confusion to comfort with her identity as Japanese American. Like many autobiographies by women of ethnic minority groups, Minatoya's story starts with her own childhood experience of learning and realizing the predicaments of being "different" in a white- and Christian-dominated culture, despite – or precisely because of – her conviction that she is "American." Her anxiety about being different is shaped both by the racism that resulted in the internment of Japanese Americans and by the hegemonic force of culture that renders nonwhites as the Other and outsiders. Her alienation, like that of other ethnic minorities, is a testimony to the paradox and perils of American ethnic identity. It is precisely because she identifies herself as "American" that she ends up not belonging anywhere. "I wanted to belong," she recalls (29); "*My* differences dislocated me, made me simpering and sullen" (40); "I longed to be one thing or another, to blend and belong or to stand at a distance, boiling with racial rage, formidable and feared" (45); and "All of my life I have wondered: Who am I?" (162). She cannot find a place for herself among other Americans, and prior to her sojourn, she rarely identifies with the Japanese either. She does not share the Japanese-ness that she sees in her parents, and she claims that her parents cannot understand or become Americans: "They and their parents before them have come from a crowded land. There, you do not flaunt your individuality. My parents are Japanese. They have no idea of what it means to have a public personality" (42).

She also rejects a simplistic identification with other Japanese Americans and Asian Americans. She recalls an episode in which she is requested to attend a Remembrance Ceremony to commemorate the anniversary of the wartime Japanese Relocation Act. "Can we count on you to be with us?" she is asked. This request evokes a powerful response:

> The "we" is intentional. It implies a duty to my parents, my family, my people. Involuntarily, I recall a scene when I was eight years old: I have returned from school and stand in anger before my mother. "Liar, liar!" I shriek. "You made me look stupid in front of the whole class!" "*Nani*, Yuri-chan? What is it?" asks my mother with concern. "You told me you were sent to camp because America made a mistake. Teacher says no. You were sent because you are a traitor." My mother pulls me close to her, she kisses and soothes my brow. "I am so sorry, Yuri-chan," she says, "for all the sadness like this that you will face." I tear free. "Liar," I sob. "Lousy Jap traitor."
>
> I stop myself. There are things I do not want to remember. (56–57)

She does attend the ceremony, but her account is strangely detached and descriptive. She relates none of her own feelings, emotions, no reference to "I," as if she were there as an outside observer. This mode continues in the episode in which she is attending the first organized gathering of East Coast Asian American women. Her description of a consciousness-raising session is again detached and even cynical, especially when the discussion turns to the topic of Asian American women's experience of often being treated as foreigners:

> "I hate it. It makes me feel like an F.O.B.," wails a college sophomore.
> "F.O.B.?"
> "Fresh off the boat. They act as if I'm one of these new immigrants you see these days."
> No one seems embarrassed by the acronym or by the disdain in her voice. (59)

She ends, "I'm glad I'm not judgmental, like these *other* women, I think with relief" (59). Her alienation from "her people" is evidenced in her voice, and the whole episode emerges as a critique of Asian American women's cliquish and elitist concept of identity.

It is only after she leaves for her sojourn to Asia that Minatoya's Japanese American identity starts to take shape as a connecting, rather than alienating, force. Just before her journey, she recalls a comment by a drama student about acting beginning with action: "It starts with a simple act portraying a simple positive intention. One intention, one action, then another, and another, and gradually you are asserting your vision. Your audience – the people who are around you – can recognize and respond to something solid and authentic" (69). As with most episodic memories in the text, there is no explicit connection made between the insight offered here and the protagonist's assertion that she has "relinquished stability and embraced mobility" in her journey (69). However, it does seem to provide a corner-stone to Minatoya's journey through which she develops her identity and her confidence and comfort in it. It can be used to interpret how identity is conceptualized in her odyssey between Asia and America: identity is formed through the process of conscious action, acting toward what one wants to become, and whether one is "true" to the self is dependent on the action of asserting one's vision.

As Minatoya starts her journey, she reconstructs herself as an immigrant woman arriving in the United States at the turn of the century: "Each lived within a kaleidoscope where familiar shapes lay shattered in shards of color: dazzling, fascinating, infinitely varying. They waited for their worlds to reassemble in understandable patterns, with more hope than faith and with twinges of gladness for the wondrousness of unknowing" (74). She goes to Japan with what she describes as her "immigrant soul" (74). It is here that Minatoya starts "remembering" her own connection to Japan and identi-fying her double vision of "East" and "West," "Japanese" and "American," "Asian" and "American." At the home of her mother's family she newly constructs herself as "a woman caught between standards of East and West" (104). Here she experiences a split within herself in reaction to her relatives: "At first, the American in me grinned. . . . But quickly, the Japanese in me surfaced" (104–5). The flashbacks to her childhood, as noted earlier, also depict different, almost contradictory, dimensions of herself. Instead of the girl anxious to belong in America, she recalls a girl resisting America by "communicating through discordant fruit" (102), which Minatoya now associates with the Japanese. This girl deliberately misspells the name of the high school teacher who attempted to dissuade her from applying to be a foreign exchange student ("The point is to sponsor an *American* kid" [102]). When her boyfriend badmouths her mother ("Your mother is so deferen-tial, so quiet. . . . Women like that drive me crazy" [102]), she scorches his scrambled eggs and hides the sports section of the Sunday paper. Minatoya's different recollection of her past self has direct implications on the way she is reconstructing her identity in this context: a Japanese American not only ready to claim her Japanese-ness but also engaging in acts of resistance. It also underscores her shifting view of identity; even who she was in the past is not fixed, singular, or consistent.

Minatoya returns once to the United States after her visit to her mother's household in Japan. Her identity is already different in her temporary return; she now quite explicitly claims her "Japanese-ness" in America: "I am the daughter who left home, who went away to college, who went away to work. I have been indulged by my family. I can move in the outer world at will and leave *my Japanese spirit* to be nurtured at home" (119, my emphasis). She also adopts the Japanese good-bye ritual of her parents when she leaves her family again for Japan: waving until each is out of the other's sight. As she tells her companion in the car, "It's only a symbolic thing, so that my last memory will be that they are awaiting my return" (120). It is also symbolic in another sense, however; by participating in this ritual she is again claiming her Japanese-ness as a Japanese American.

Upon arriving in Japan for the second time, to teach psychology on a U.S. military base, Minatoya feels at ease with her identity. She stays in a hotel standing in "a border area between America and Japan" (130), and she fits comfortably. "The hotel seems a bit like me," she observes. "Pieces of East, pieces of West forming their own odd integrity. . . . I feel a twinge of pride" (131). The Okinawa base to which she is assigned is also a place that seems like herself. Finding the match between her identity and her surroundings, she feels sure of her identity and relieved of the anxiety she grew up with: "All my life I have wondered: Who am I? But as I lived in Japan, my anxiety eased. I was a Japanese American, teaching cross-cultural psychology, on American bases in the midst of Japan, and the sheer intellectual tidiness of my situation pleased me" (162). For Minatoya, her identity as a Japanese American was not a given but had to be constructed in her odyssey. Her voice has changed; somewhere during her stay in Japan her attitude toward her "marginality" has transformed from ambivalence to celebration. In a conventional narrative, this is where the story ends, at the point where she has "come to terms" with her Japanese American identity. However, this is not the end of the story. Her identity is not an end product, is never finished. This becomes a mere step for her next move outward: "Like a toddler who finds first her footing, and then cannot be contained, I fell love with the world beyond" (162). Thus when asked by her school to teach in China, she accepts without hesitation.

In China, Minatoya's self-awareness takes on a new turn. Through her experience of teaching English and her relationship with her students, she develops a new understanding of what it means for her to be "American" and what she means to them. Although at first she is charmed by her students' eagerness to listen to her stories and the simple details of her life and by the activities they plan to do with her, she gradually realizes, "It was *my* childhood that was being celebrated. It was *my* innocence that was being protected." For the students who experienced the Cultural Revolution, through which everything they had was destroyed and lost, she represented a fairy-tale past, a faith in dreams: "For I was the only one who had experienced a happy childhood. I was the one with so much confidence in the possibility of individual happiness that I had chosen the profession of counseling. And my culture *legitimated* such a profession; America deemed *reasonable* the job of helping people to find meaning and pleasure in their existence. For the Chinese, such a thing was dumbfounding" (180). While she sees directly only the bright side of China, she becomes aware of the darker side and the significance of her presence: "Tacitly and over time, my students and I spun a soothing myth. That our lives were not so different. That their futures would be much like mine" (181). Particularly after the student massacre at Tiananmen Square in 1989, she is less certain of the positive outcomes of their collaborative vision for her students.

Leaving China, Minatoya travels to Nepal. Here she also confirms her identity as being both Japanese and American, an interface between two cultures, by expressing her comfort in being physically at the junction of different cultures, religions, and races: "I, who have always felt discomfort with being in-between, stand in perfect peace in a cobbled crossroad on the roof of the world at the edge of a new year. I stand amidst Christians and Hindus, among Anglo-Saxons and Asians. Perhaps this is why I have come to this place" (212). But again, her identity shifts as she notes some ambivalence with Asia: "I am an American. I have no patience with fatalism, no regard for the gift of forbearance. Often Asia disconcerts me. She has lured me back. She has willed me into the investment of my time and caring. And again and again, she shows me scenes that I am powerless to change" (236). The experience of being American in China and Nepal has altered Minatoya's notion of who she is. Now her voice almost contradicts her earlier voice that asserted her Japanese-ness, almost seeming to regress to her pre-odyssey conviction of herself as an American distinct from being "Asian," breaking the narrative illusion of linear progression in identity.

While she has claimed herself as Japanese and Asian, it is not an absolute, static identification. Rather, her identity is once again seen as being in a constant flux.

Thus, through the odyssey, Minatoya creates her identity embodying multiple elements of Japan, Asia, and America, all of which she claims for herself as Japanese American and Asian American. It is this act of claiming that enables her to be simultaneously Asian and American, on the one hand recognizing herself in Japan and Asia, on the other confirming herself as American. "I am a curious creature," she says (255), being one thing while simultaneously being another, resisting a simple either/or categorization and delimitation. It is this dynamic configuration of identification that she presents as her Japanese American identity.

The Reconstruction of the Maternal Bond

Earlier I noted that the mother – daughter relationship is given a major significance in the narratives of Japanese American women's writings and that the mother figure often represents the Japanese-ness that the daughter has lost or rejected but still longs for. The mother – daughter relationship is intertwined with the daughter's search for her identity. However, a text and/or a reading of a text that simply equates the mother with Japan and Japanese-ness evokes the danger of ascribing an essentialistic identity for the mother, as it assumes that there is something inherently "feminine" or "maternal" about Japan or Japanese culture, that there is something inherently "Japanese" about mothers, and that the identity as "Japanese" for the mothers is fixed and static. It also assumes that the "Japanese mother" is "there" as an essence in the daughter, "waiting" to be reclaimed or recovered. For the daughter's narrative to function as an effective critique of the marginalization of Japanese American identity, it thus needs to problematize the unidimensional and essentializing view of identity for the mother as well. Minatoya's narrative does address this. As with other Japanese American autobiographies, the mother – daughter relationship occupies a central space in Minatoya's narrative; however, here it is the mother's identity as well as the daughter's that is constructed as multiple, fragmented, and contradictory.

On the surface Minatoya, the daughter, may seem to symbolize Americanization, and her mother may seem to symbolize Japan. In this reading, prior to her journey Minatoya can define herself only if she separates from and defines herself in opposition to her mother: "An American daughter, I cannot understand the teachings of my mother's okoto [Japanese harp]. . . .

Direct, assertive, American, I break into my mother's reflection" (4, 5). Her mother's voice sounds like the Japanese voice, telling Japanese stories, interspersed with Japanese words and phrases that both fascinate and repel her. Moreover, Japan evokes the maternal; her grandmother and her aunt, both deceased, feature as salient maternal figures in her mother's stories. Minatoya herself also makes various references to the importance of the mother in Japanese culture: "The Japanese love their mothers: gentle, lovely creatures who listen and soothe, who feed and encourage. . . . To them, the creative force *must* be maternal" (113); and "In Asia, to be taken from your mother's side before the natural separation point of marriage is the most poignant of fates" (127). Finally, Japan (and Asia) itself is constructed in the image of the mother, referred to as "she" and "Motherland" and even performing maternal functions: "Like a mother who kisses her bruised daughter and shoos her back to play, Asia had transformed the ache of my lapsed career" (264). Thus Minatoya's odyssey is, in this reading, a journey to reclaim the "mother," Japan and Asia, for herself; to find motherly acceptance and love in the motherland; and finally to return to America, the "father" country, with a new identity and confidence.

However, despite the surface equation of the maternal with Japan, a closer examination of the narrative construction of the relationship between Minatoya and her mother reveals that the mother's identity is actually as ambiguous, un-Japanese, and contradictory as Minatoya's own. While seeming to represent racial and cultural difference in the United States, Minatoya's mother's Japanese-ness is also constructed as an anomaly; unlike the mother figure in Sone's *Nisei Daughter,* she does not present "the absolute pole of Japanese identity."[23] She is incomplete, not quite belonging in either Japan or the United States. As Minatoya starts her odyssey and her identity reconstruction, the initial distinction between her mother and herself begins to diffuse. As she constructs and claims her Japanese-ness, she also constructs and claims her mother's Japanese American-ness. The tie between herself and her mother is reconstructed not only through the daughter moving closer to the mother, but also through the mother becoming more like the daughter.

While appearing to be an almost stereotypically Japanese woman, Minatoya's mother is simultaneously presented as the antithesis to the same image. There are various places in the narrative where the mother seems to represent anything but a quintessential Japanese woman's spirit. For example, she refuses to give up her work despite her husband's anger: "'My work gives me happiness. . . . I do not care if you speak as Husband,' she said daringly. 'I am a Designer!' " (25). She is also the one who encourages her daughter to "soar" instead of being confined: "Soar as high as you can. Go as fast as you want. *Never* let anyone stop you" (115). It is she who, through her stories, fills the daughter's "timorous soul with flight dreams" (115). Particularly in an episode where Minatoya recalls the trip she took with her mother to Japan, her mother's very "Japanese-ness" is called into question. "The last trip was a disappointment to my mother. I could see it in her eyes. . . . What my mother saw was that she no longer was Japanese. . . . In America, my mother's Japan had frozen," Minatoya observes. "In America she was well aware of her strangeness. In Japan she had hoped for vindication" (192, 193). But, as the daughter, Minatoya confesses: "I liked the fact that my mother seemed out of place. It proved that she was not so Japanese after all. She was more like me. More normal than I had thought" (193).

Minatoya's mother is also incomplete and suffering from a sense of loss in terms of her relationship with her own mother. Minatoya's mother is a woman without a mother, whose ties with her own Japanese mother have been severed. "I was a motherless child," she says, referring to her childhood experience (4). Minatoya's maternal grandmother was a rebel: she fell in love with a Filipino while accompanying her husband in the United States and eventually was divorced in Japan. For her transgression she was sent away; family ties were severed; she was never allowed to see her children again. Early in the text, Minatoya's mother tells a story to her daughter about the time when her mother had taken all her children to a photographer's studio for a formal portrait:

"I was excited and I turned to call my mother's attention to something. She was wiping away tears with her kimono sleeve. I never before had seen her cry and thought, Why in the middle of such a grand adventure?" Okaa-chan pauses. "I suppose that that happened just before Ojii-chan had us sent from her house."

There is a longer pause.

"How I wish I could have a copy of that picture," she says. (7–8)

Minatoya's mother's yearning for the picture represents her inner search for her own mother. The stories that attempt to reconstruct her image, as a parallel endeavor, are incorporated into Minatoya's story of reconstructing ties with her mother. Although Minatoya had never known her grandmother, she attempts to retrieve the connection: "I think about my grandmothers. . . . I too have come to this place because of their best intentions" (155).

The narrative ends on Minatoya's wedding day, symbolically the day that the Japanese believe to be the day of separation of a daughter from her mother. On this day the unknown story of her grandmother is told. Her uncle tells her mother that he learned a "terrible secret" – that their mother had tried to kill them: " 'On a night selected for auspiciousness,' says my uncle, 'Mother mixed rodent poisoning in a gruel of tea and rice. She could not bear separation from us and murder-suicide was considered an honorable act. She placed the gruel on the table and gathered us around her' " (267). The attempt had been thwarted when one of her sons had reached for the bowl and, making a face of disgust, thrust it away, spilling the gruel across the table. Listening to her uncle tell the story, Minatoya pictures her mother as a little girl and reflects: "Her singing mother has carefully plotted her murder" (268). The image of Minatoya's grandmother as a sweet Japanese mother, a heroine, is violently disrupted. It is almost as if the tie between the mother and daughter has been severed again. Her uncle concludes that their mother "saw the spill as divine intervention. Buddha told her to let us go. From that point on, she busied herself with preparations. She stopped weeping and started to plan for our futures" (268). at the price of this revelation, Minatoya's mother's wish is fulfilled: She is given a copy of the portrait mentioned early in the narrative, the photograph for which she had yearned. With the secret revealed, she chooses to accept and reconstruct her own presence over rejection, to reclaim her Japanese mother despite her attempt to kill her. She "proclaims almost fiercely" that today her mother has come to see the joyous wedding day in which she gains a new son.

The maternal bond that is reconstructed, therefore, is between two mother – daughter pairs: between Minatoya and Minatoya's mother, whom the daughter could not identify with earlier in the narrative, and between Minatoya's mother and her mother, whom the daughter grew up without. During Minatoya's odyssey, her identity becomes closer to her mother's, and her mother is recreated through her memories and stories as being more like her. Her mother's "motherlessness" and her search for the photograph are evoked as a parallel to Minatoya's own "motherless" situation in her lone search for identity. The construction of the maternal link is therefore a dialogic process involving the narrator's own attempt to connect with her mother and her mother's attempt to reconnect with her mother. Moreover, the reconstruction of the mother – daughter bond does not represent a simple "recovery" of the daughter's Japanese heritage; instead, both the mother and the daughter are themselves reconstructed as Japanese Americans with dynamic, often contradictory, and fragmented identities.

CONCLUSION

Autobiographies for members of minority and oppressed groups are arenas where identities marginalized in the dominant culture can be explored. Lydia Minatoya's *Talking to High Monks in the Snow* is one text that invites examination of the various ways in which identity is constructed as being fluid, multiple, contradictory, and incomplete, exploring what it means to be a Japanese American woman by refusing to define the self as a static, coherent, unitary entity. Minatoya's text, working around the autobiographical conventions, problematizes the unity and continuity of subjectivity by constructing a narrative that is multivocal and intertextual in its presentation.

However, the text is not without its limitations as an autobiographical writing that sets the political agenda for the empowerment of marginalized groups. Minatoya disrupts the hegemony of the essentialist and static view of identity but does not guide the reader in the direction of collective action for change. As a critique, Minatoya's text is limited in the sense that she does not deal with aspects of her identity that give her power and privilege as a middle-class American. She does not question her entitlement to believe in the "American dream" (even if only to be disillusioned later), to travel and work in countries such as Japan, China, and Nepal, to have the luxury of setting out on an "odyssey," to be able to come and go whenever she pleases, to be changed through encounters with others without the responsibility to change. Indeed, Minatoya's odyssey reads like a travelogue in which the focus is on herself, while the others she encounters are described mostly in terms of the impressions they make on her. Thus, although she realizes that her innocence as a traveler is actually ignorance that she can afford because she is American, she is often unable to see herself or her project of identity construction as capable of bringing about political change (or as being complicit in preserving the status quo). Politics involving the people she encounters are often reduced to pathos, "scenes" that she is powerless to change.

One such scene is that of the starving children begging in Nepal and the American tourists unwilling to see them. Another is that despite Minatoya's confession of her denial and naïveté regarding the lives of her students in China and at the Okinawa base, she still seems reluctant to step out of the bliss her ignorance allows her and acknowledge the realities of the Tiananmen Square incident and the Persian Gulf War: "Much later, after I had returned to America, when my students were sent to the Persian Gulf,

I realized there were things that I had refused to see. Even after China, I stayed blind. I had so wanted to believe that my students would always be carefree, that I could not see they were soldiers. I could not see them in peril. I could not see them at war" (263). Although she is sensitive to the inequality and discrimination that those without power face and empathizes with their humanity, Minatoya's identity is not that of an activist; her stand toward politics is basically the preservation of the status quo. Her text does not present a threat to the ideology where individuals are seen as solely responsible for their success or failure, an ideology from which, despite her disillusionment with the "American dream," she has benefited. This is where her autobiography is limited in its potential for presenting a radical and liberatory vision.

As bell hooks has aptly said in her critique of the contemporary feminist movement, "naming one's personal pain . . . not sufficiently linked to over-all education for critical consciousness of collective political resistance" can easily lead to "misnaming, to the creation of yet another sophisticated level of non- or distorted awareness" or to "even greater estrangement, alienation, isolation, and at times grave despair."[24] Minatoya neither moves beyond naming her pain on issues other than those that concern her own marginal-ity, nor links her problems with identity to a larger system of oppression. Perhaps this is the challenge of autobiography that focuses on individual, rather than sociopolitical, process: Is it possible for a nonactivist's autobi-ography to have a politically emancipatory utility? Is it only by being an activist that one can draw the connection between one's personal search for identity and politics that go beyond one's personal concerns? This is a question that needs to be answered in future studies of autobiography.

That is not to say that Minatoya's autobiography does not make an im-portant contribution to the growing body of literature that, as Lim states, "inscribes as central the experience of Asian American women in a society in which the Asian American is still the model, because invisible, minority."[25] The text offers readings that are not reducible to being yet another account by an "oriental" woman that is expected, in Mitsuye Yamada's words, "to move, charm or entertain, but not to educate in ways that are threatening" to the reader.[26] But the possible readings are not always apparent and given; as readers we are selective, and we "read into" texts certain meanings that serve our own beliefs and agendas. In Minatoya's text I have read the au-tobiographical construction of the self that resists either/or categorization and essentializing. Subversive readings have the potential of creating subversive texts. There still seems to be much space for such readings of the existing literature, just as there is space for the creation of new literature, autobiographical or otherwise, by Japanese American women.

NOTES

1. Patricia Hill Collins, *Black Feminist Thought: Knowledge, Consciousness, and the Politics of Empowerment* (New York: Routledge, 1990), 68.

2. Dorinne K. Kondo, "M. Butterfly: Orientalism, Gender, and a Critique of Essentialist Identity," *Cultural Critique* 16 (fall 1990): 11.

3. See Collins, *Black Feminist Thought*; bell hooks, *Talking Back: Thinking Feminist, Thinking Black* (Boston: South End Press, 1989); Michelle Cliff, "Object into Subject: Some Thoughts on the Work of Black Women Artists," in *Making Face, Making Soul / Haciendo Caras: Creative and Critical Perspectives by Women of Color,* ed. Gloria Anzaldúa (San Francisco: Aunt Lute Foundation Books, 1990), 271–90; and Elizabeth V. Spelman, *Inessential Woman: Problems of Exclusion in Feminist Thought* (Boston: Beacon Press, 1988).

4. For memoirs, see, for example, Monica Sone, *Nisei Daughter* (Boston: Little, Brown, 1953); Yoshiko Uchida, *Desert Exile: The Uprooting of a Japanese American Family* (Seattle: University of Washington Press, 1982); and Jeanne Wakatsuki Houston and James D. Houston, *Farewell to Manzanar* (Boston: Houghton Mifflin, 1973). Shorter works in other genres can be found in the following anthologies: Asian American Studies Center, *Asian Women* (University of California, Los Angeles, 1975); Asian Women United of California, *Making Waves: An Anthology of Writings by and about Asian American Women* (Boston: Beacon Press, 1989); Shirley Geok-lin Lim and Mayumi Tsutakawa, eds., *The Forbidden Stitch: An Asian American Women's Anthology* (Corvallis OR: Calyx Books, 1989); Sylvia Watanabe and Carol Bruchac, eds., *Home to Stay: Asian American Women's Fiction* (Greenfield Center NY: The Greenfield Review Press, 1990); and Mitsuye Yamada and Sarie Sachie Hylkema, eds., *Sowing Ti Leaves: Writings by Multicultural Women* (Irvine CA: Multi Cultural Women Writers Press, 1990).

5. Teresa de Lauretis has stated that the notion of identity as multiple and shifting is emerging in feminist theory and writings of and about subjectivity. As will be seen from my analysis, the identity reconstructed in Minatoya's text is very similar to the concept of the self that de Lauretis sees as emerging in feminist writings. Thus it is interesting, as I will discuss later, to see how Minatoya's text seems to fall short of taking a political and therefore a feminist stance. See Teresa de Lauretis, "Feminist Studies/Critical Studies: Issues, Terms, and Contexts," in *Feminist Studies/Critical Studies,* ed. Teresa de Lauretis (Bloomington: Indiana University Press, 1986), 1–11.

6. This phrase from John Paul Eakin is cited in Estelle C. Jelinek, *The Tradition of Women's Autobiography from Antiquity to the Present* (Boston: Twayne Publishers, 1986), 4.

7. See Michael M. J. Fischer, "Ethnicity and the Post-Modern Arts of Memory," in *Writing Culture: The Poetics and Politics of Ethnography,* ed. James Clifford and George E. Marcus (Berkeley: University of California Press, 1986), 194–233; and Elaine H. Kim, "Defining Asian American Realities through Literature," in *The Nature and Context of Minority Discourse,* ed. Abdul R. JanMohamed and David Lloyd (New York: Oxford University Press, 1990), 146–70. Fischer maintains that ethnic autobiographies expose the conception of ethnicity as reinvented and reinterpreted anew by each generation and each individual through struggle. The creation of a new ethnic identity in autobiographies is a process of "finding a voice or style that does not violate one's several components of identity," which "is an insistence on a pluralist, multidimensional, or multifaceted concept of self" (196). Kim maintains that the most recurrent theme in Asian American literature is the claiming of America for Asian Americans, which means "inventing a new identity, defining ourselves according to the truth instead of a racial fantasy, so that we can be reconciled with one another in order to celebrate our marginality. It is this seeming paradox, the Asian America claim on America, that is the oppositional quality of our discourse" (147). Likewise, Lee Quinby, in her analysis of Kingston's *The Woman Warrior* as a memoir that rejects unitary and continuous subjectivity, uses Michel Foucault, who makes a similar point: in the modern era, which places individuals in "the simultaneous individualization and totalization of modern power structures, . . . maybe the target nowadays is not to discover what we are but to refuse what we are" and "to promote new forms of subjectivity through the refusal of this kind of individuality which has been imposed on us for several centuries" (Michel Foucault, "The Subject and Power," qtd. in Lee Quinby, "The Subject of Memoirs: *The Woman Warrior*'s Technology of Ideographic Selfhood," in *De/Colonizing the Subject: The Politics of Gender in Women's Autobiography,* ed. Sidonie Smith and Julia Watson [Minneapolis: University of Minnesota Press, 1992], 297).

8. This paradox is noted by Margo Culley, "What a Piece of Work Is 'Woman'! An Introduction," in *American Women's Autobiography: Fea(s)ts of Memory,* ed. Margo Culley (Madison: The University of Wisconsin Press, 1992), 3–31.

9. Shirley Geok-lin Lim, "Japanese American Women's Life Stories: Maternality in Monica Sone's *Nisei Daughter* and Joy Kogawa's *Obasan,*" *Feminist Studies* 16:2 (1990): 292.

10. Fischer, "Ethnicity and the Post-Modern Arts of Memory," 198. Moreover, Lim maintains that many minority texts in American literature can be read as allegorical: the private story of an individual Asian American woman can be seen to "project

a political dimension" as it becomes an allegory of the embattled public ethnic identity of Asian American groups in a repressive homogenizing society ("Japanese American Women's Life Stories," 292–93). This echoes Fischer's contention that the autobiographical searches for ethnicity "also turn out to be powerful critiques of several contemporary rhetorics of domination" (198) and Kim's view of Asian American literature's "claim on America" as being an "overarching collective concern, the invention of an American identity" that is "part of our resistance to domination" ("Defining Asian American Realities," 147, 170).

11. This theme is prevalent in literature by American women in general. For further discussions on the mother – daughter relationship in American literature, see Cathy N. Davidson and E. M. Broner, eds., *The Lost Tradition: Mothers and Daughters in Literature* (New York: Frederick Unger, 1980).

12. For example, in both Sone's *Nisei Daughter* and in Uchida's *Desert Exile,* the Japanese poems written by the mothers are embedded in the autobiographical texts. This association of the Japanese culture and race with the mother is also seen in autobiographical fiction such as Joy Kogawa's *Obasan* (Boston: D. R. Godine, 1982). For a detailed analysis of the role of the mother in *Nisei Daughter* and *Obasan,* see Lim, "Japanese American Women's Life Stories."

13. Natalie Rosinsky has pointed out that women writers of racial, ethnic, sexual, and economic minority groups have delineated their apprehension of the social forces that intervene between mother and daughter and that, perhaps because the added oppression of minority group membership exacerbates this often painful relationship, these writers seem particularly aware of its tragic destructiveness. See Natalie Rosinsky, "Mothers and Daughters: Another Minority Group," in Davidson and Broner, *The Lost Tradition,* 280–90.

14. For example, Sone, Uchida, and Houston (significantly all Niseis writing about the camp experience) each describe at least one episode that identically exemplifies this mother – daughter distancing, where the daughter feels chagrined by her mother's Japanese-ness in public, particularly by her odd English and Japanese mannerisms. Lim, in her comparative reading of Sone's *Nisei Daughter* and Kogawa's *Obasan,* argues that Sone's text rejects and eventually silences the racial discourse of the mother ("Japanese American Women's Life Stories").

15. See, for example, David J. O'Brien and Stephen S. Fugita, *The Japanese American Experience* (Bloomington: Indiana University Press, 1991); and Valerie Matsumoto, "Japanese American Women During World War II," in *Frontiers* 8:1 (1984): 6–14, and "Nisei Women and Resettlement During World War II," in Asian Women United of California, *Making Waves,* 115–26.

16. Ann Rayson, "Beneath the Mask: Autobiographies of Japanese-American Women," MELUS 14:1 (1987): 44. Rayson discusses the five major autobiographies

(Mine Okubo, *Citizen 13660*; Monica Sone, *Nisei Daughter*; Jeanne Houston, *Farewell to Manzanar*; Akemi Kikumura, *Through Harsh Winters: The Life of a Japanese Immigrant Woman;* and Yoshiko Uchida, *Desert Exile*) and the way in which each author "seeks to define herself and American culture as a synthesis of opposites, but also as the congruence of similar value sets" (47). For the effect of incarceration on the productivity of autobiographies, see also Mei T. Nakano, *Japanese American Women: Three Generations 1980–1990* (Sebastopol CA: Mina Press Publishing, 1990).

17. Jelinek, *The Tradition of Women's Autobiography*, 187–88.

18. Sone, *Nisei Daughter*, 158–59. Future references to this text will be given parenthetically with the abbreviation ND.

19. This also presents a false sense of "resolved-ness" to the narrative. Becoming able to feel proud of her dual heritage does not right the wrongs inflicted upon her and her family for being Japanese American – the racism, discrimination, and incarceration that forced her to feel cursed, like a "two-headed monstrosity," in the first place. The narrative celebrates her new identity, but the sense of resolution with which the narrative ends undermines the critique of and resistance toward the marginalizing force of the dominant culture that the narrative presents.

20. Therefore, Jelinek's observation that in women's autobiography the authors tend to see themselves as "unfinished" (*The Tradition of Women's Autobiography*, 187) does seem to apply to Monica Sone's autobiography.

21. Lydia Y. Minatoya, *Talking to High Monks in the Snow: An Asian American Odyssey* (New York: Harper Collins, 1992), 3. Future references to this text will appear parenthetically.

22. Trinh T. Minh-ha, *Woman, Native, Other: Writing Postcoloniality and Feminism* (Bloomington: Indiana University Press, 1989), 94.

23. Lim, "Japanese American Women's Life Stories," 295.

24. hooks, *Talking Back,* 32.

25. Lim, "Japanese American Women's Life Stories," 309.

26. Mitsuye Yamada, "Asian Pacific American Women and Feminism," in *This Bridge Called My Back: Writings by Radical Women of Color*, ed. Cherríe Moraga and Gloria Anzaldúa (Watertown MA: Persephone Press, 1981), 71.

Frontiers 19:1 (1998): 124–46.

Remembering "the Nation" through Pageantry

Femininity and the Politics of Vietnamese Womanhood in the Hoa Hau Ao Dai *Contest*

NHI T. LIEU

Much has changed as a result of the Vietnamese migration overseas, but the *ao dai* forever remains the same, like our love for freedom and democracy and our love for the homeland of Vietnam.[1]

> *Nam Loc Nguyen, Vietnamese songwriter and cohost of the 18th Annual* Hoa Hau Ao Dai *Long Beach Pageant.*

Beauty contests may appear frivolous and trivial, but as a cultural practice they stage complex struggles over power and representation. Some feminists have argued that beauty contests are ideological regimes that reinforce dominant constructions of gender and idealized forms of femininity. Yet these organized events are much more complicated than just outright attempts to objectify, control, and commodify women's bodies. Scholars of beauty pageants have begun to bring forth the contradictions inherent in the beauty contest by situating them in multiple systems of culture, struggles for power and control, and discursive fields of practice.[2] While many have located beauty pageants in dominant discourses of nationalism all over the globe, few have addressed the significance of local "ethnic" beauty pageants.[3] What happens when racially and ethnically marginal immigrant communities organize their own local beauty pageants to commemorate their version of "the nation"? Which elements are different and which remain the same? How can we make sense of this need for beauty pageants in immigrant communities, and what do the pageant contestants come to represent?

Despite the increasing accommodation toward multiculturalism and the crowning of nonwhite contestants in American national and state beauty pageants, racist practices remain prevalent in beauty pageants in the United

States. As Sarah Banet-Weiser points out in her study of the Miss America pageant, "The presence of non-white contestants obscures and thus works to erase the racist histories and foundations upon which beauty pageants rest."[4] Moreover, because mainstream pageants tend to reaffirm whiteness and dominant understandings of American citizenship, they can sometimes conflict with cultural goals and beliefs of ethnic and immigrant communities. As such, beauty pageants in general serve different purposes for ethnic and racialized communities in the United States. And though some aspects of "ethnic" beauty pageants replicate larger American national and state pageants, they also simultaneously articulate alternative cultural practices that counter the dominant discourse from which they are excluded.[5] To resolve these exclusionary practices that disqualify Asian women from representing the "nation" by virtue of their race, Vietnamese Americans have organized their own separate beauty pageants to provide alternative spaces in which "ethnic Vietnamese" women have the opportunity to participate and to reign as beauty queens for their ethnic community.[6]

THE PAGEANTRY OF THE *AO DAI*

What distinguishes a Vietnamese American beauty pageant from all other beauty pageants is its incorporation of the traditional Vietnamese dress called the *ao dai* into every pageant.[7] The basic ao dai for women is a long flowing dress worn over long full palazzo pants. Although it varies in style, the formal dress most often worn for competition is a form-fitting tunic that slits into front and back panels from slightly above the natural waistline down to below the knees. The ao dai was originally worn by royalty, but by the early twentieth century it became a fashionable clothing item for the "modern" Vietnamese woman. Because the garment is difficult to work in, middle-class women and adolescent schoolgirls most commonly wore it. Others, including men, only wore ao dai on holidays and special occasions.

   Though the ao dai's familiar mandarin collar and panel designs reveal remarkable Chinese and French influence, the Vietnamese insist that the ao dai is uniquely and authentically Vietnamese. Symbolically, the ao dai invokes nostalgia and timelessness associated with a gendered image of the homeland for which many Vietnamese people throughout the diaspora yearn. Journalist Nguyen Hoang Nam has observed that the meanings associated with the ao dai have "been perpetuated by countless puppy-love, maudlin poems and novels that engraved, for the most part, the traditional Vietnamese concept of female beauty: innocent, frail, chaste, shy, and soft-spoken."[8] The ao dai conjures up romantic images of a Vietnamese past that is pure and untainted by war.

Vietnamese ao dai beauty pageants are one of the most visible examples of Vietnamese immigrants trying to negotiate the process of assimilating into bourgeois American culture while remaining ethnically Vietnamese. These pageants have been permanent fixtures in Vietnamese American festivals and celebrations since the late 1970s. Their cultural origins, however, are not from Vietnam. Rather, they are an invented cultural tradition created by Vietnamese immigrants in the United States.[9] Beauty pageants in Vietnam tend to place emphasis on a woman's physical appearance. Vietnamese American ao dai pageants, however, recognize the "overall beauty" of young women. This includes her public speaking skills, her appearance and gait in ao dai, and most importantly, her ability to retain her ethnic and cultural heritage. Unlike the beauty pageants that take place in Vietnam, Vietnamese Americans celebrate their cultural *difference* as immigrants in a collective effort to preserve "Vietnamese culture and tradition through beauty pageants."[10]

Ao dai beauty pageants are significant not only because they bridge symbols of the past with bodies that represent the future, but also because they work ideologically to evoke an "imagined community" that authenticates the persistence of Vietnamese ethnicity and carves out cultural roles for young Vietnamese women between the ages of eighteen and twenty-six.[11] Ao dai beauty pageants have become ritualized events that dramatize major debates concerning nationalism, ethnicity, gender, sexuality, and other issues Vietnamese Americans and other Vietnamese in the diaspora face. Indeed, they are crucial to the production of new, hybrid gender and ethnic identities. In fact, later, we will see another kind of hybrid beauty, one that is defined through plastic surgery and other postmodern technologies.

CULTURAL POLITICS AND IMAGINING THE HOMELAND

Hundreds of thousands of Vietnamese refugees fled their homeland after the Communist takeover of South Vietnam in 1975. Fearing for their lives and potential persecution from the new government, they left in successive waves with hopes of restarting elsewhere in the world where they would not be threatened.[12] Since 1975, Vietnamese refugees have resettled all over the globe including the United States, France, Australia, Canada, and other refugee-receiving nations. The current population of Vietnamese in diaspora has grown to nearly 1.5 million, and 593,213 of them live in the United

States.[13] As exiled political refugees who lost their land to the Communists, the Vietnamese in diaspora remain vehemently opposed to the new regime in power. Despite the reopening in recent years of Vietnamese borders to commerce and tourism, some overseas Vietnamese refuse to return. This condition of exile has not only strengthened the spirit of nationalism among the overseas population, it has also made the collective memory of the former nation ever more meaningful. The creation of Vietnamese beauty pageants outside the Vietnamese nation, along with the nostalgia they invoke, has enabled the imagining of communities and fostered the growth of nationalism among exiled Vietnamese scattered throughout the diaspora.

Ao dai beauty pageants are not mere diasporic cultural productions created for the purpose of "cultural preservation." Held in large public auditoriums and civic centers, they also provide a forum for overseas Vietnamese to protest the racial politics of dominant American beauty pageants and challenge the limitations the Communist regime placed on cultural practice in Vietnam. When the Vietnamese refugees fled Vietnam, they never completely severed their ties with the existing nation of Vietnam. With relatives in and sentimental memories of Vietnam, the cultural politics between the exile communities are always in dialogue with that of the current nation. Moreover, because these communities are in exile, the imagined nation is both ambiguous and ambivalent in relation to the former nation and the new nation in which they have resettled. Since fleeing Vietnam, overseas Vietnamese have staged countless public protests to criticize what they deem as corrupt and inhumane conduct by the Communist government.[14] At the same time, Vietnamese exiles throughout the world have also voiced their opinions on how the governments of the new nations they have settled in should relate to the Socialist Republic of Vietnam. Formerly barred from returning and presently reluctant to return physically to the homeland, Vietnamese exiles emotionally and metaphysically reconstruct, through cultural celebration and pageantry, the Vietnam they lost. Holding beauty pageants has become one of the most powerful ways for Vietnamese communities to publicly assert feelings of cultural nationalism as well as anti-Communism. Through the beauty pageants, the anti-Communist political voice of the imagined community of Vietnamese in exile is reaffirmed and the existence of communities in the United States and throughout the world is validated.

Organized in both northern and southern California in 1977, the first ao dai pageants were immediate cultural inventions. They were as much a response to the new Vietnamese government's imposition of a dress code on the South Vietnamese as they were an effort to preserve and claim the Vietnamese national dress. When the world of the elites and their "bourgeois decadence" collapsed in Vietnam during the mid-1970s and early 1980s, the status-laden ao dai also lost its position as the official national dress of the Socialist Republic of Vietnam. On men, the ao dai was seen as representing the "old regime."[15] On women, it represented the extravagance and futility associated with capitalist wastefulness. According to fashion freelancer Lan Vu, "the *ao dai* receded into the background, making appearances only at family gatherings and special occasions" after 1975 when "the Communists ordered everyone to wear the basic work outfit of buttoned top and pants."[16] Though the Communist government never made it illegal to wear an ao dai, anyone caught wearing the garment risked surveillance that could even lead to home searches. Vietnamese immigrants remember that the Communist government made it very difficult for anybody to don the ao dai because it drew so much attention. For these reasons, the ao dai became a hidden material object shielded from public display. However, the more the Communist government seized the ao dai, the more overseas Vietnamese insisted on preserving their national dress along with other items of material culture, such as the old South Vietnamese flag, as national symbols of Vietnam. As in the period of decolonization, when the ao dai, according to Van Ngan, became "a symbol of silent opposition to French colonialism," ao dai pageants became a symbol of Vietnamese American protest against the Communist forces that displaced it.[17]

Selecting the ao dai as the national symbol for the "imagined" Vietnam invokes both classed and gendered articulations of nationhood. The ao dai was the official wardrobe of Vietnamese elite men and women. The long and fluid dress accompanied by a pair of lengthy flowing pants not only requires superfluous lengths of cloth to produce, but each dress also requires custom tailoring. As such, the ao dai can be an expensive commodity to own. Working-class men and women could only afford to don the ao dai for special occasions such as weddings, funerals, and holidays. Because Vietnamese immigrants brought the ao dai with them, it continues to make appearances at these same occasions throughout the diaspora. However, significantly more women than men wear ao dai. Throughout its history the ao dai for men remained fairly unchanged in style, and as Vietnamese men adopted Western styles of dress the men's ao dai almost entirely disappeared. Ao dai fashion for women, on the other hand, not only exhibited regional distinctions but also stylistic change over time. In the 1990s, many diasporic Vietnamese communities have witnessed the resurgence of ao dai fashion among younger Vietnamese American women. Though this may indicate that young Vietnamese American women are rediscovering their roots through the ao dai, community beauty pageants may have also contributed to the construction of this classed and gendered expression of ethnic and national identity.

FORMING PARTNERSHIPS THROUGH CULTURAL AND CAPITAL

Originally conceived in the late 1970s both to preserve Vietnamese culture through amateur performance and to raise funds for refugees and orphans, ao dai pageants of the late 1990s have turned into commercial enterprises that rely not only on the sponsorship of professional businesses but also on professional talent to entertain audiences throughout the pageant. As annually organized gala events that claim to "bridge together the uniqueness of the western culture and the diverse cultural richness of the Vietnamese communities," beauty pageants receive sponsorship from numerous small Vietnamese American businesses and organizations as well as larger American private corporations.[18] The size of the pageants often depends on the amount of support organizers can muster from business and commercial sectors. However, many pageants have grown into commercial industries that link communities and various economies at both the local and global levels. Organizers work with ethnic businesses but they also promise to "promote partnerships among the Vietnamese community and America's private corporation[s] or foundation[s]."[19] Some pageants offer "benefit packages" that give sponsors "opportunities to break into the multi-*billion* dollar Vietnamese consumer market by direct marketing of products or services at the actual event."[20] In the 1990s, transnational corporations such as AT&T also seized the opportunity to sponsor Vietnamese pageants as a crucial element for winning the business of Vietnamese worldwide.[21] Transnational corporations particularly profit from conditions of exile and diaspora. Telecommunications companies, for example, strive to close the space/time continuum between overseas Vietnamese and their relatives in the homeland by advertising long distance telephone connections. While the financial contributions made by transnational corporations remain considerably less than those of ethnic businesses, the investment interests in overseas Vietnamese communities speak to the potential significance they will play in the future of transnational capitalism.

The videotaping and mass marketing of Vietnamese beauty pageants by the Vietnamese American entertainment industry reveals the extent to which technology has transformed the preexisting modes of communication in a context of transnationalism and global capitalism.[22] The video entertainment industry has made it possible for all Vietnamese who cannot attend live beauty pageants to enjoy hours of the gala events without having to leave the comfort of their own homes. At a cost of only fifteen to twenty-five dollars, the affordable videos enable working-class Vietnamese who may not be able to afford attendance at a live show to participate in and be a part of the imagined community. The videos not only feature beautiful young Vietnamese women in the pageant but also a variety show featuring famous professional Vietnamese singers performing song and dance routines. Packaged in colorful shrink-wrapped boxed sets and decorated with collaged images of contestants and performers, beauty pageant videos are available for sale in most Vietnamese-owned record stores, and in some areas they can also be bought at local Vietnamese businesses such as small markets.[23] Beauty pageant videos are the perfect vehicle for advertising ethnic businesses as well as transnational corporations because they can reach a wide audience. Though it is difficult to trace the distribution of any given pageant video, it is not impossible to imagine the possibilities of its cultural and political impact, particularly to the Vietnamese in diaspora. Rich in symbolism and imagery, the pageant videos work on multiple levels to stage highly contested meanings of gender, nationalism, ethnicity, and identity among the Vietnamese in exile. In addition, they sell ethnic-specific products and advertise in ways that attract the Vietnamese consumer.

COMMEMORATING MIGRATION THROUGH PAGEANTRY

The rest of this chapter seeks to provide a close reading of a commercially produced video recording of the eighteenth annual ao dai pageant held in Long Beach, California, in 1995. Titled *20 Nam Chiec Ao Dai Vien Su,* or "The Dislocation of the Ao Dai in Faraway Lands," this pageant commemorated the twenty-year anniversary of Vietnamese migration. Organized by college students and alumni of California State University, Long Beach, and sponsored primarily by Vietnamese American business elites of southern California, this ao dai beauty pageant featured a host of prominent Vietnamese American entertainers. The juxtaposition of the variety show and the beauty contest created a highly glamorized spectacle that encouraged community members to attend and contribute funds. What made this pageant unique was the extraordinary use of the ao dai to unearth feelings of nostalgia.

The commemorative ceremonies opened with a performance by Thai

Thanh, a seasoned female performer who has entertained generations of Vietnamese. Standing on an elevated platform behind the contestants, she sang the classical Vietnamese operatic ballad "Hoi Trung Duong," a song about the three main rivers located in the northern, middle, and southern regions that geographically connect the nation of Vietnam. On stage dancing in front of the vocalist were twenty-one young female contestants, wearing three regional styles of dress that symbolically represented the three regions to which the song alludes. Physically, Thai Thanh embodies the maternal past. Revered and respected, she is an allegorical figure who narrates the national history of Vietnam for the future generation of Vietnamese Americans, represented by the contestants as well as younger members of the audience. For the older generation, she tells a familiar tale, conjuring up images of a unified "homeland" and using allegory to induce memory and nostalgia.[24]

In addition to joining three politically and culturally diverse regions into a unified Vietnam, the historical narrative in the song "Hoi Trung Duong" imagines a mythical homeland void of regional, religious, political, and linguistic differences. Preferring to recognize the unified historical Vietnam over the partitioned Vietnam of the Geneva Accords of 1954 and the current Socialist Republic of Vietnam, overseas Vietnamese envision and remember a harmonious nation before the war and before their subsequent displacement. Such nostalgic longings and politically salient representations of the Vietnamese past have become essential themes in Vietnamese American celebrations. Without these recurring images of a mythical and unified homeland, Vietnamese communities throughout the diaspora would not coalesce or attend cultural events such as the ao dai pageant. The pageants are thus produced for overseas communities to consume as well as to learn about new cultural practices of different local Vietnamese American communities.

The ao dai pageants construct a nostalgic nationalism and reaffirm Vietnamese identity. Vietnamese Americans also celebrate regionalism and their ability to accept and embrace historical and regional differences. The pageants work in a way that enables viewers to inhabit multiple subject positions: as members of the imagined nation, as distinct peoples from different regions, and as Vietnamese refugees who left their homeland and resettled elsewhere in the world. In the context of the 1995 Long Beach pageant, this was achieved through the wearing of the ao dai by the contestants; as the contestants danced in the opening act, wearing different regional ao dai, they created the illusion that it was possible to map the bodies and the identities of the young women directly onto the various regions of the Vietnamese nation.[25] Though these efforts to create unity among the Vietnamese signified cooperation amid difference, they also revealed a desire to link diasporic Vietnamese globally. The metaphorical erasure and disavowal of regional and local distinctions, in essence, dramatized the organic wholeness of the "imagined community." Wherever in the world this ao dai beauty pageant video may have traveled, it created the space and spectacle for the Vietnamese in the diaspora to collectively imagine themselves as a united whole.

Central to this vision of collectivity was the displaced ao dai and the diasporic communities that the ao dai symbolized. Rather than focus on the narrative of migration, the beauty pageant charted the historical transformations of the ao dai and its resiliency as a sign of cultural persistence among the Vietnamese in exile. Organizers and contestants from this pageant repeatedly asserted that, in spite of the fashion changes the ao dai has endured, its original form remains the same. Likewise, despite the tumultuous history the Vietnamese has endured, they insisted that their "core cultural values" remain the same. The traditional dress was thus employed as a metaphor to give meaning to the experiences of migration and cultural change among the Vietnamese throughout the diaspora.

THE SPECTACLE OF THE NATION IN THE FEMALE BODY

Ao dai beauty pageants are public rituals dedicated to venerate the endurance of Vietnamese culture. As community rituals, they ensure the continuance of gendered Vietnamese cultural practices. Making the female ao dai central to the ritualistic imaginings of a nostalgic and unified homeland necessitates a discussion about the discourse over the female body and what it represents.[26] While women are often marginalized in politically significant ceremonies, the body chosen to represent symbolically the Vietnamese nation in this civic event is, significantly, a female one. Though the ao dai is the traditional Vietnamese dress for both men and women, Vietnamese American men are not obligated by the community to preserve Vietnamese culture by wearing the ao dai. Vietnamese American women, on the other hand, are *expected* to wear this cultural symbol. A woman's refusal to wear the ao dai can be interpreted as a lack of effort and allegiance to Vietnamese culture; conversely, her willingness to embrace the ao dai becomes a major source of ethnic pride for herself as well as the community at large.

By making the ao dai the quintessential symbol of Vietnamese culture and the main focus of the pageant, the sexist agenda of publicly displaying and judging young women's bodies is disavowed, masked, and legitimated by cultural practice. The ao dai is a form-fitting dress, often made with transparent fabrics, that requires custom tailoring. For a flattering fit, a woman must have a thin, slender, yet curvaceous body. The shape of the female body is accentuated but hidden as the dress clings tightly to it. The ao dai, in essence, produces a certain type of sexual body. This sexualized image, however, is contained within the bounds of respectability and curbed under the sign of the "cultural." No contestant who flaunts her body would be awarded the crown. Even so, the overt expression of female sexuality surfaced frequently throughout the Long Beach beauty contest. Though most beauty pageants allow contestants to introduce themselves and say their own names, the contestants in the ao dai pageant were introduced to the judges and audience in this first round. Dressed in compulsory white or sometimes pastel colored ao dai, young Vietnamese women in the pageant marched out onto the stage, representing the timeless image of adolescent schoolgirls. The second round of the competition featured the contestants in ao dai that each had selected to reflect her personal style. In the third round, the women were clothed in Western evening gowns, a segment of the competition that is borrowed from other mainstream pageants and that reveals the Vietnamese aspiration to enter the American bourgeois. Evening gowns are accoutrements of elite American women.[27] Requiring Vietnamese American beauty queens to wear them in pageants conveys a desire to become part of the elite class in the United States. Moreover, the Western evening gown is the perfect modern American counterpart to the traditional Vietnamese ao dai because both are fashionably middle class. After modeling in three rounds of competition, three of the twenty-one contestants were selected for the final round. In the final round, the young women were asked to speak for the first time during the pageant to demonstrate their ability to speak and perform well under pressure. More importantly, they were also required to answer questions in Vietnamese.

Realizing that they would not be given the opportunity to express themselves through speech unless they made it to the final round of competition, many contestants used their bodies to win the attention of the audience. This was done most blatantly during the Western evening gown competition in which the young women showed off their bodies in sexy, backless, body-flattering, and tight-fitting evening gowns. The contestants with the

Singer Thai Thanh along with the contestants of the *Hoa Hau Ao Dai* Long Beach Pageant of 1995 performing "Hoi Trung Duong" in the opening act. Used with permission from Diem Xua Productions.

skimpiest dresses gained loud applause, uproarious cheers, and catcalls from members of the audience. Those displaying hyperfemininity by swaying their hips and gliding across the stage also received similar ovations. One contestant even wore a tiara on her head and took off the cape of her flashy metallic gown as if she were a model strutting on the catwalk. Since they could only represent themselves through their bodies, some contestants in the ao dai pageant took their chances and transgressed the boundaries of respectability by asserting themselves individually despite the consequences. While the audience mainly consisted of young college students who were cheering for their friends on stage, the judges were often leaders of the community such as lawyers, doctors, business people, and even former beauty queens. Consequently, transgressors met with audience approval but judge disapproval, and although transgressors were never disqualified from the competition, losing the contest could have been the result of their actions.

With a tiara on her head, contestant Vo Thi Ngoc Loan removes the matching high-collar cape that wrapped around her metallic silver gown as she takes her walk for the Western evening wear competition. Used with permission from Diem Xua Productions.

Miss Nguyen Thuy Diem Chau is crowned *Hoa Hau Ao Dai* Long Beach 1995.
Used with permission from Diem Xua Productions.

AO DAI QUEEN AS FEMALE CITIZEN

Although many contestants seemed empowered to challenge the bounds of
respectability in some aspects of the pageant, the ao dai contest could also
be interpreted as an attempt to regulate women's sexuality to the extent that
it imposed a moral code of sexual conduct on young Vietnamese American
women who are considered in danger of becoming "too American." With
the influence of mainstream American media and popular culture, the older
generation invariably fears the loss of "culture" among the youth. Ao dai
pageants provide a safe venue for young people to learn about and preserve
Vietnamese culture while engaging in the Western practice of pageants. The
pageants not only provide young people, such as the college students at
the California State University, Long Beach, the opportunity to organize
a major "cultural" event; they also designate young Vietnamese American
women a cultural role in the Vietnamese immigrant community. Anthro-

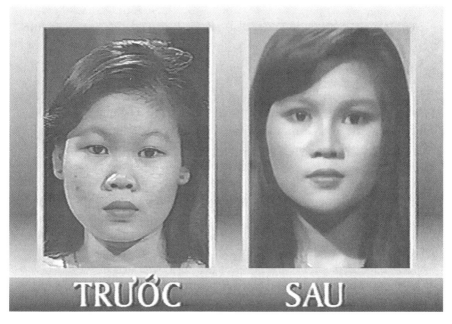

The before and after cosmetic surgery images of Le Chi in the ad for Dr. Vu Ban and Tham My Vien Bich Ngoc, the major sponsor of the pageant. Used with permission from Diem Xua Productions.

pologist Jesse W. Nash observes that, though the community values old men, "the young women represented the links to the future, the hope of [the] community."[28] When asked what the beauty pageant meant to her, one 1996 contestant stated, "This pageant, *Hoa Hau Ao Dai,* is not about one beautiful person wearing *ao dai,* rather it is about the collective group of people coming together to profess their love for the Vietnamese culture and people."[29] Along with this declaration of "love for the Vietnamese culture and people" is a declaration of cultural citizenship. All the contenders for the Long Beach crown demonstrated civic pride and commitment to social responsibilities by endorsing social platforms that worked to either help Vietnamese refugees or end poverty in Vietnam. Many of the women who participated in the pageant claimed to have done so because they believed it was a good way to raise funds to help Southeast Asian refugees.[30] Taking part in Vietnamese cultural events such as the ao dai beauty pageant thus steered young women away from the corrupting forces of American culture and kept them "pure" and "Vietnamese."

Although ao dai pageants give young Vietnamese American women the
chance to "give back" to the Vietnamese community, the sine qua non of the
ao dai queen is her feminine beauty. In his study "Vietnamese Values," Nash
notes that "the loveliest girls in the community participate in the religious
ceremonies, the handsomest women are called to positions of authority,
and the prettiest girls adorn every procession or parade."[31] Though Nash
never clearly defines Vietnamese beauty per se, he further observes that
the Vietnamese appreciation for beauty is not purely aesthetic but must be
accompanied by "a delicate walk," "a good posture," and "a soft voice."[32]
Chi Nguyen, Miss Tet Vietnam of northern California in 1992, provides
an ao dai queen's perspective. She explains that "the Vietnamese standard
of beauty is based on *cong* (domestic skills), *dung* (physical beauty), *ngon*
(speaking skills), and *hanh* (pose and modesty)."[33] Aside from performing
these essentialized forms of ethnic femininity, the contestants also need to
show grace, elegance, poise, and innocence. The queen is meant to embody
idealized forms of femininity as well as project a particular image of beauty
– an image with multiple valences that simultaneously evoke nostalgia and
the "natural" beauty of the "motherland," as well as a beauty connected
to the "modern" that negotiates living in the context of the West. To win,
a contestant must be able to balance delicately the values associated with
the Vietnamese immigrant community as well as ethics associated with an
American upbringing. One Long Beach contestant stated, for instance, that
her ambition is simply to "always be happy." This overly "American" aspiration, which idealizes pleasure and self-fulfillment, does not correspond
with the appropriate "Vietnamese" code of femininity, which values devo-
tion to the family over the self. Maturity, intelligence, and hard work were
also valued attributes the judges favored. The winner was a poised young
woman who aspired to become a doctor and practice in a Vietnamese community in southern California. She not only demonstrated commitment
to Vietnamese culture and community, but she also possessed the ability
to negotiate both Vietnamese and American cultural values by showing
gracefulness and professionalism.

AUTHENTICATING "INAUTHENTIC" ETHNIC IDENTITIES

The stated goal of every Vietnamese American beauty contest is to extol
the virtues of Vietnamese culture through the ao dai. With the absence of
both talent and swimsuit competitions, notions of liberal individualism are
suppressed and downplayed by pageant organizers. Nonetheless, the indi-

vidual identities and subjectivities of the Long Beach contestants constantly emerged throughout the pageant despite the repeated use of the contestants and their bodies as symbols of Vietnamese regional and national culture. By virtue of her presence in the pageant, each young woman demanded individual consideration in the competition for the crown. Though not permitted to introduce herself, each contestant's name, the city from which she came, and a list of hobbies, goals, and aspirations were announced by the masters of ceremony. Each was also allowed to select one ao dai and one evening gown of her choice to wear for the pageant. The pageant's location in southern California and the contestants' upbringing in the United States often interfered with the nationalist and nostalgic myth-making performances.

One of these points of "interference" concerns language. Besides highlighting gender and sexuality, the ao dai contests encourage young women to articulate an "ethnic" identity through the preservation of Vietnamese "cultural traditions" and the upholding of "Vietnamese values." The search for an "authentic" past is, however, a fruitless one because of Vietnam's complex history of colonialism. What becomes most salient to Vietnamese cultural identity, as defined by the Vietnamese community and its cultural elites, is the ability to retain the "mother tongue." Linguistic knowledge therefore is viewed as emblematic of cultural knowledge. One's lack of knowledge of the Vietnamese language can potentially cut one off from the community. Hence, the Long Beach pageant required that the queen be able to speak Vietnamese with fluency so that she would be able to adequately represent her community.

Growing up in the United States, however, has made it increasingly difficult for Vietnamese American youths to retain the Vietnamese language. The demands made by the community and by dominant American culture have compelled many Vietnamese Americans to construct new hyphenated ethnic identities.[34] Participation in the Long Beach ao dai contest permitted young contestants to perform the doubleness of their "ethnic" identity and even subvert notions of cultural authenticity that the community expected each contestant to possess. This subversion was revealed during the most shocking moments in the pageant when one of the three finalists was interviewed in the final round. When asked a question about Vietnamese American youths, the young woman could not find the words to utter back. Betraying what was considered to be authentic, she simply said, "I'm sorry, *em quen* [I forget]." While the contestant's "forgetfulness" may have reflected either her inability to speak Vietnamese or her inability to remember her lines, the young woman had to endure public embarrassment as the audience laughed at her blunder. Nonetheless, the audience could very well be laughing at the judges for selecting the "wrong" contestant to be one of the three finalists because she was able to fool everyone (by appearing Vietnamese without "really" being so) almost through the entire competition.

PROFESSIONAL PERFORMERS OF CULTURAL WORK

Though social responsibilities are expected of the ao dai queen, her main duty is to safeguard and represent Vietnamese ethnicity in cultural events inside and outside of the community. Unlike contestants in the Miss America pageant, the ao dai contestants do not have to demonstrate talent beyond performing an idealized femininity. Instead, pageant organizers hire hosts and hostesses as well as a cast of professional performers to do the cultural work of entertaining the audience. The contestants are left to invoke the beauty of the ao dai and embody ideal Vietnamese American womanhood.

Vietnamese American–produced variety shows have grown into huge capital-generating industries worldwide. Produced in the United States, these variety shows consist of musical and dance numbers, comedic and historical skits, and even fashion shows exhibiting Vietnamese women dressed in high fashion ao dai. Though Vietnamese is the primary spoken language in the shows, it is common for performances to be in English, French, and Chinese and to contain hybrid cultural elements. The shows are generally organized around themes commemorating historical events such as the fall of Saigon or celebrating special events in Vietnamese culture such as the lunar new year, the midautumn festival, or an anniversary. In some instances, the shows pay special tribute to the lifetime contributions of a notable songwriter or to a theme specific to Vietnamese culture. The variety shows within the ao dai pageant can be regarded as a microcosm of the Vietnamese American community because they provide the cultural terrain on which men and women, the young and the old, and Vietnam and America struggle for meaning. Entertainers of the older generation express their concerns about the future while they mourn over the lost nation, singing songs about exile and patriotism. The younger generation, on the other hand, typically perform pop songs and remixes of American oldies, rap, and hip-hop.

Just as entertainers were chosen to draw in the audience, the host and hostess for the Long Beach pageant were also carefully chosen to be the voice of at least two important groups in the community – older men and young women. In this pageant, two distinguished and familiar members of the community served as the host and hostess of the pageant. A public personality, Nam Loc is a middle-aged male songwriter who also works in refugee resettlement and immigrant assistance for the U.S. Catholic Conference. His female counterpart, Thuy Trinh, is a former ao dai queen turned television personality who comes into the homes of southern Californians daily on a Vietnamese entertainment program that introduces contemporary and classic Vietnamese music videos. With opposing points of view, the host and hostess presented the pageant rules, told jokes, stirred up emotions, invoked memories, exchanged commentary about gender, generation, and society, and introduced both beauty contestants and entertainment stars to the audience. The back and forth banter between the two provided comic relief to the audience. More importantly, Thuy Trinh identified with the women, the contestants, and younger members of the audience; Nam Loc, on the other hand, provided the link to the older generation and the cultural elites running the show. As representatives of two groups differentiated by gender and generation, the host and hostess used their identities as points of departure to debate and highlight tensions within the community without attempting to resolve them.

Thus the variety show not only supplemented the pageantry of the ao dai contest, but it also made the contradictions surrounding issues of gender and sexuality in the pageant more explicit. As a rule, the Vietnamese American beauty queen cannot be identified with entertainers because young women performers in the variety shows often openly display their sexuality by mimicking popular American media stars such as Madonna. The Vietnamese community believes that an ao dai queen must not be overly influenced by the American mass media, as it can potentially contaminate her "ethnic" self. The queen is expected to exhibit a Western style of beauty but must remain "Vietnamese" enough to represent the traditions of the imagined nation. In contrast, the variety show typically allows professional performers, who have more flexibility to navigate between cultures, to act out the realities of the young contestants.

SPONSORS AND THE BUSINESS OF MAKING AO DAI BEAUTY QUEENS

It comes as no surprise that the major sponsors of the Long Beach beauty pageant were ethnic businesses: food companies, photography studios, sewing companies, as well as wealthy professional men and women of the community. A Vietnamese ao dai tailoring company dressed the contestants and provided them discounts on their ao dai. The hair and makeup were done by Vietnamese-owned L. A. Cosmetics, another big sponsor. The largest contributor, however, was *Tham My Vien Bich Ngoc* (Bich Ngoc Cosmetic Surgery Center), which donated a total of ten thousand dollars to the ao dai pageant, five thousand of which was awarded to the queen. In return for their financial support, representatives of companies and businesses got the chance to crown the queens and runners-up as well as advertise on the final videotaped product. Though there was never any explicit connection made between cosmetic surgery and the contestants, the Bich Ngoc Cosmetic Surgery Center received a five-minute spot on the Long Beach pageant video, right at the beginning of the second videotape. The video ad profiled the "before" and "after" plastic surgery experience of an adolescent Vietnamese woman. A close-up image of her "before" face was scrutinized and criticized by plastic surgeon Dr. Vu Ban, who stated that Asian women are born with imperfect features: an angular face, a flat nose, no folds on the eyelids, an indistinct chin, and acne. The experienced doctor then introduced his "inexpensive" method of making a more "natural-looking, beautiful" face that he boasted Asian clientele prefer. The young woman's glowing "after" picture with alterations to the eyes, nose, and chin was shown, and she was interviewed. When asked why she decided to have plastic surgery, she explained that many of her friends had done it and they were pleased with the results. She stated that the doctor's inexpensive procedure had made her "beautiful" and increased her self-esteem.

Though definitions of beauty change over time and vary according to context, Western standards of beauty have clearly been imposed upon women of color.[35] The attainment of Western beauty seems to suggest some form of progress to the Vietnamese. In other words, if the goal of Vietnamese nationalism is to modernize and progress, plastic surgery performed on the national body can be seen as a means of improvement. In recent years, plastic surgery has literally transformed the faces and identities of many Vietnamese Americans. Nevertheless, as David Palumbo-Liu has observed, the desire to have plastic surgery to alter the Asian body is "not undertaken necessarily to 'be white,' but to partake of whiteness in a selective fashion."[36] Vietnamese American identities are embodied in ways that are complicated by cultural processes and rooted in a history of terror that begs for the reformation of the body. The strategy to racially transform the Vietnamese body and construct hybrid forms is intricately linked to the process of recuperating from a war-torn past and to becoming middle-class ethnic Americans in the United States.

The partnership forged between the cosmetic surgery industry and the beauty pageant industry indicates that ethnic beauty in the Vietnamese community is becoming more and more hybridized through science and medical technology. While beauty ideals remain highly contested in the Vietnamese community, most agree that in the pageants a hybrid look has become most desirable. Moreover, possession of Western beauty alone would not suffice for the ao dai queen. In order for her to represent the nation and wear the crown, she must embody a number of characteristics including civic virtue, intelligence, and a physical beauty that is reminiscent of the "homeland." Her beauty, however, like that of the young woman whose face was completely transformed by plastic surgery, must be a hybrid beauty. It is not necessarily "Western" because it is still "Vietnamese." This hybrid beauty, mapped onto her body, allows her to represent the hybridity of the imagined diasporic Vietnamese nation.

The theatrical performances of history, culture, gender, and identity displayed by organizers, contestants, and professional performers in the beauty pageant illustrate the magnitude of the cultural and social work being done in the Vietnamese American community. As a cultural practice, Vietnamese American pageants exhibit tensions between tradition and modernity, grapple to define meanings of sexuality and ethnic femininity, and reveal struggles over the control of the Vietnamese female body. They generate capital and unite different groups of people. However, while ao dai pageants have created cultural roles for young women and spaces for them to perform public service, they have also created problems. For example, the notion of a Vietnamese American beauty queen imposes certain idealized and unrealistic beauty standards on young Vietnamese American women. As a result, many Vietnamese are turning to cosmetic surgery and relying on it as the acceptable quick-fix solution to obtaining these beauty ideals.[37] And even though pageant organizers disavow the practice of cosmetic surgery, the sponsorship of plastic surgeons reveals that competing notions of beauty exist within the community. Another example concerns the primary function of ao dai. As in any beauty pageant, the clothing worn is meant to showcase young women's bodies on public stages. What is more troubling about this practice is that it is achieved under the guise of cultural preservation and ethnic and national celebration. The glorification of Vietnamese culture naturalizes gender relations as it inscribes young women's bodies, literally and figuratively, to represent male endeavors. This tendency to make women's bodies a spectacle "to be looked at" reinforces male dominance and maintains unequal sex and gender roles for Vietnamese Americans.[38] However, as long as the ao dai maintains a central role in signifying the nation, and as long as it depends on a woman's body to perform it, young women will play a significant role in determining the rules of gender politics in this cultural nationalist arena.

NOTES

I would like to thank my mom, Nhung Truong, for introducing me to the wonderful world of ao dai pageants, and David Scobey for encouraging me to analyze and write about them. Susan Douglas, Catherine Benamou, George Sanchez, Carroll Smith-Rosenberg, Linda Võ, Marian Sciachitano, and Toan Leung offered insightful comments and suggestions as well as enduring support for my work. Son Lieu worked wonders to get me the photos. Thank you all, I would not have been able to do this without you.

1. All translations are my own.

2. Sarah Banet-Weiser, *The Most Beautiful Girl in the World: Beauty Pageants and National Identity* (Berkeley: University of California Press, 1999), and "Crowning Identities: Performing Nationalism, Femininity, and Race in the United States Beauty Pageants" (Ph.D. diss., University of California, San Diego, 1995); Natasha B. Barnes, "Representing the Nation: Gender, Culture, and the State in Anglophone Caribbean Society" (Ph.D. diss., University of Michigan, 1995); and Beverly Stoeltje, et al., *Beauty Queens on the Global Stage: Gender, Contests, and Power* (New York: Routledge, 1996).

3. Among the few is Judy Wu's examination of a Chinese American beauty pageant, "'Loveliest Daughter of Our Ancient Cathay!': Representations of Ethnic and Gender Identity in the Miss Chinatown U.S.A. Beauty Pageant," *Journal of Social History* 31 (fall 1997): 5–31.

4. Banet-Weiser, *The Most Beautiful Girl in the World*, 125.

5. Lisa Lowe argues that in the case of Asian Americans, their history in the United States "produces cultural forms that are materially and aesthetically at odds with the resolution of the citizen to the nation" (*Immigrant Acts: On Asian American Cultural Politics* [Durham: Duke University Press, 1996], 31).

6. Though my main focus is on Vietnamese Americans, I wish to note that they are not alone in using beauty pageants to reaffirm their ethnic American identity. Other immigrant groups also engage in these ritualized practices, but they are specific to their communities.

7. Most pageants have three rounds of competition where the contestants must wear one compulsory ao dai, one ao dai of her choice, and one Western evening gown. The compulsory ao dai is usually made for the contestants by a sewing company that sponsors the pageant, and the ao dai of choice must be purchased by

the contestants. According to an *Orange County Register* article, the cost of an ao dai ranges from $300 to $530 (Hieu Tran Pham, "Eastern Tradition with a Western Twist," *Orange County Register,* January 19, 1997, E:1).

8. E-mail correspondence with Nguyen Hoang Nam, September 11, 1999.

9. Eric Hobsbawm, "Introduction: Inventing Traditions," in *The Invention of Tradition,* ed. Eric Hobsbawm (Cambridge MA: Cambridge University Press, 1983), 4–5.

10. "Greetings from Organizing Committee," *The 1997 Miss Vietnam Tet Pageant of Northern California,* Huyen Tran Coproducer (VEN Productions, 1997). Website: *http//www.vietet.com/hoahau97.*

11. Benedict Anderson, *Imagined Communities: Reflections on the Origin and Spread of Nationalism* (London: Verso, 1993). What is interesting about the pageants' "imagined community" is that it does not have a state. Vietnamese nationalism is based on a politics of exile that is extremely anticommunist and prodemocracy.

12. The first group to leave mainly consisted of members of the elite and middle class. Having worked closely with the United States government, many of these refugees were airlifted out of Vietnam along with other American evacuees. Between the late 1970s and early 1980s, thousands of others followed, and the world witnessed a mass exodus of "boat people" out of Vietnam. Although the second wave came from more diverse regional, class, and ethnic backgrounds, the exile politics continue to be dominated by the first group of immigrants. For more details about the refugee exodus and the social and political conditions under which Vietnamese people migrated, see Sucheng Chan, *Asian Americans: An Interpretive History* (Boston: Twayne Publishers, 1991); and Gail Kelly, *From Vietnam to America: A Chronicle of Vietnamese Immigration to the United States* (Boulder CO: Westview Press, 1977).

13. Aaron Segal, *Atlas of International Migration* (London: Hans Zell Publishers, 1993); and Bureau of the Census, *1990 Census of Population: Asians and Pacific Islanders in the United States* (Washington DC: Government Printing Office, 1993).

14. The largest anticommunist rally that marked the Vietnamese American community's emergence into the American media spotlight was the Hi-Tek Video protest, where the Vietnamese community of Little Saigon, California, demonstrated against a video store owner who posted a picture of Ho Chi Minh and hung the flag of the Socialist Republic of Vietnam in public view.

15. Van Ngan, "Traditional Vietnamese Male Attire," *Vietnamese Culture – A 1970's Perspective, Vietnam Bulletin* 6 (February 8, 1971), located online at *http://www.things asian.com/destination/vietnam/tranthong.htm.* When President Diem was overthrown in 1963, the national dress was so closely identified with his administration that it sank with him into oblivion.

16. Lan Vu, "The *Ao Dai* Evolution," *Vietnow* (May/June 1996): 51.

17. Ngan, "Traditional Vietnamese Male Attire." Using the ao dai as cultural political resistance against the Communists has become more complicated because the ao dai has made a resurgence in the Socialist Republic of Vietnam. By the late 1980s, the ao dai had regained popularity among young women in Vietnam. It is mainly seen worn by young women in the business sector. It regained its permanent role as the national dress of Vietnam after Vietnam Airlines flight attendant Truong Quynh Mai won the prize for "Best Traditional Costume" at the Miss World Pageant in Toyko in 1995.

18. *Http://www.vietet.com/hoahau97.*

19. *Http://www.vietet.com/hoahau97.*

20. Ngan, International Miss Vietnam Pageant Website, "IMVP Philosophy," emphasis added.

21. In 1995 AT&T donated five hundred dollars to the Hoa Hau Ao Dai Pageant in Long Beach. Because American corporate sponsorship brings funds and prestige to pageants, Vietnamese Americans also benefit. Nevertheless, they cannot always depend on sponsorship from mainstream America because the funds are much more difficult to obtain and require advanced planning, sometimes even up to a year. Some community events, including the ao dai pageant, are planned between four to eight months in advance.

22. Arjun Appadurai, *Modernity at Large: Cultural Dimensions of Globalization* (Minneapolis: University of Minnesota Press, 1996). See also Roger Rouse, "Thinking through Transnationalism: Notes on the Cultural Politics of Class Relations in the Contemporary United States," *Public Culture* 7 (1995): 353–402.

23. Some production companies now also market the videos through the Internet. Though the marketing of these videos in Vietnam is prohibited by the Communist government, they still circulate through the black market. For a more detailed discussion on the Vietnamese American entertainment and variety show video industries, see Nhi Lieu, "Fashioning Identities through Performance: Memory, Nostalgia, and the Hegemony of *Paris by Night* Videos," unpublished paper, 1998.

24. Rita Felski explains that "nostalgia emerges as a recurring and guiding theme in the self-constitution of the modern; the redemptive maternal body constitutes the ahistorical other and the other of history against which modern identity is defined" (*The Gender of Modernity* [Cambridge MA: Harvard University, 1995], 38).

25. It was impossible to know, using visual evidence alone, which region the contestants actually came from or most identified with. Moreover, historical records indicate that it is numerically impossible for all the regions to be equally represented because an overwhelming majority of immigrants migrated from the south. Only a small number of immigrants in the United States were from the north or middle regions. See Sucheng Chan, *Asian Americans: An Interpretive History* (Boston: Twayne

Publishers, 1991), 145–65. Finally, regional identities are never fixed. For example, it is very possible for a northerner to migrate to the South as a child, be raised in the South by parents who speak the northern dialect, and as a result speak both dialects.

26. Among the scholarly works that address the female body and nationalism are Partha Chatterjee, *The Nation and Its Fragments: Colonial and Postcolonial Histories* (Princeton: Princeton University Press, 1993); and Lydia Liu, "The Female Body and Nationalist Discourse: The Field of Life and Death Revisited," in *Scattered Hegemonies: Postmodernity and Transnational Feminist Practices,* ed. Caren Kaplan and Inderpal Grewal (Minneapolis: University of Minnesota Press, 1994).

27. I wish to thank Carroll Smith-Rosenberg for her keen observation here.

28. Jesse W. Nash, "Vietnamese Values: Confucian, Catholic, American" (Ph.D. diss., Tulane University, 1987), 252.

29. Diem Trang, contestant, *The 1996 Miss TET Vietnam Northern California Pageant*, VEN Entertainment. Vietscape website: *http://www.vietet.com/hoahau96.*

30. Extra funds left over from the pageants are meant to be donated to charity organizations. This pageant focused on refugee orphans, but others assist at-risk youths and cultural preservation projects such as Vietnamese language schools.

31. Nash, "Vietnamese Values," 255.

32. Nash, "Vietnames Values," 255–56.

33. Chi Nguyen, quoted in De Tran, "Miss Saigon: Vietnam is miles and years away, but its tradition hasn't been lost on a beauty queen in San Jose," *San Jose Mercury News,* May 30, 1992, 1:8.

34. R. [Rajagopalan] Radhakrishnan, *Diasporic Mediations: Between Home and Location* (Minneapolis: University of Minnesota Press, 1996). What I mean by "hyphenated identity" is that both sides of the "hyphen" are emphasized rather than just privileging one over another. Beauty contestants are expected to negotiate their identity so that they retain both the Vietnamese and the American sides of their identity.

35. See Wendy Chapkis, *Beauty Secrets: Women and the Politics of Appearance* (Boston: South End Press, 1986); and Kathy Peiss, "Making Faces: The Cosmetics Industry and the Cultural Construction of Gender, 1890–1930," *Genders* 7 (spring 1990): 143–69. Peiss's discussion of race and color as it was historically projected by the cosmetics industry and beauty culturalists was most useful to me. I am inclined to think that in the case of the Vietnamese community, plastic surgeons have become the new "beauty culturalists."

36. David Palumbo-Liu, *Asian/American: Historical Crossings of a Racial Frontier* (Stanford: Stanford University Press, 1999), 98.

37. The pressure to look "beautiful" has forced many Vietnamese immigrant women, rich and poor, to go to any length to have plastic surgery done on their

bodies. This includes filing fraudulent medical claims for cosmetic surgeries that do not qualify as medically necessary. According to David R. Olmos, "It has been reported that investigators believe that several hundred patients have been involved in these fraudulent schemes and that 'nearly all are women and roughly 70 percent are Vietnamese Americans undergoing cosmetic surgery'" ("Plastic Insurance Fraud Scheme Alleged," *Los Angeles Times,* October 26, 1997, A1).

38. Laura Mulvey, "Visual Pleasure and Narrative Cinema," *Screen* 16:3 (1975): 22.

Frontiers 21:1/2 (2000): 127–51.

Fence Sitters, Switch Hitters, and Bi-Bi Girls

An Exploration of Hapa *and Bisexual Identities*

BEVERLY YUEN THOMPSON

I had been wondering about taking part in a student theatre project about being Asian American, and I said to Tommy, "The thing is, I don't feel as though I've really lived the . . . Asian American experience." (Whatever I thought that was.)

Tommy kind of looked at me. And he said, "But, Claire, *you are* Asian American. So whatever experience you have lived, *that is* the Asian American experience."

I have never forgotten that.

> *Claire Huang Kinsley, "Questions People Have Asked Me. Questions I Have Asked Myself"*

Claire Huang Kinsley articulates a common sentiment among multiracial Asian Americans regarding their racial and ethnic identity. She describes the reaction that her mixed heritage has provoked from Asians and Anglos, both of whom frequently view her as the "other." In response to these reactions, her faith in her racial identity has been shaken, and she feels unable to identify herself – fearful of being alienated for choosing either her Chinese or Anglo heritage, or both. Although she knows that she is mixed race, the question that still plagues her is whether or not she is included in the term "Asian American."[1]

When I first read Kinsley's article, I was elated to find recognition of a biracial Asian American experience that resembled my own. I have a Chinese mother and an Anglo American father, as does she, and I am constantly confronted with questions about my ethnic background from curious individuals. Like Kinsley, I also question my ability to call myself Asian American because of my mixed heritage. However, in addition to my mixed heritage, I am also bisexual, which brings with it additional complications and permutations around my identity formation and self-understanding. The process of identity formation, especially of multiple identities, is complex and life-long, and my experiences have been no exception.

Though I have always understood that I was mixed race, a true understanding of what this meant in terms of my self-understanding and my relation to the dominant culture and Asian American communities did not develop until I was much older. My first exposure to the political side of identity politics came at the ages of fourteen and fifteen, when I began to develop a feminist understanding of the world around me. Then, at seventeen, I first began to call myself bisexual after two years of questioning my sexuality and believing that the only options that were available were either a lesbian or straight identity. Finally, at the age of nineteen I began to uncover the history of Asians in America through my college course work and developed a newfound understanding of my racial identity and its political implications. Yet, as is usually the case, this process was never as linear as it may sound.

Growing up, I was very aware that I was both Chinese and white – but I did not possess a term or racial category that recognized my position. Instead of creating or claiming a category that would accommodate me, I was left in confusion. How was it possible that I existed outside of the racial order of the census forms in my grade school, and what would I have to do in order to correctly fill in the answer to my racial puzzle? This confusion led to great discussions with my father about how I should identify myself. Well-meaning as he was, the only answer that he could arrive at was to choose between the two. This answer did not satisfy me because it would imply that I would be choosing between my parents – a choice I could not make.

Multiracials of Asian descent have a variety of choices available for self-identification; however, this "choice" may become obscured by others who may be quick to categorize based upon their own monoracial template of racial understanding. Physical traits are frequently scrutinized as ethnic signifiers, and one's mixed-race identity may not be accepted by outsiders. Maria P. P. Root elaborates: "To assume that the biracial person will racially identify with how they look is presumptive, but pervasive. Besides, the biracial person is perceived differently by different people. *Many persons make the mistake of thinking the biracial person is fortunate to have a choice; however, the reality is that the biracial person has to fight very hard to exercise choices that are not congruent with how they may be visually or emotionally perceived.*[2] Biracials and multiracials, then, develop a racial identity that risks criticism or denial from others; this influences the ways in which they self-identify, which may change in different contexts. When faced with the "What are you?" question, multiracials may try and consider what the person is really asking and respond accordingly. Racial fluidity is difficult to "see" in a world constructed by mutually exclusive categories based on a black – white dichotomy.

When I was growing up in white-dominated Spokane, Washington, I spent most of my childhood, like most children, trying to fit in. My racial identity would raise its head occasionally, but most of the time I did not consider race. However, I did spend a great deal of energy rejecting my Chinese heritage, which I thought would certainly differentiate me from my white classmates. I would not allow my mother to teach me Chinese, which she attempted to do; I made fun of the Chinese food in the restaurants where she would take us; and I identified more and more with my father, whose side I would take when he belittled my mother's culture and "superstitions." I thought that if I did not speak Chinese then I could use that as proof that I really was white like everyone else. However, when we did end up in Seattle's Chinatown on vacation, I was secretly proud and impressed that my mother could speak in Chinese to the waitresses and would beg her to do so.

When my racial identity was used against me by my peers in school, it was an upsetting experience. One day in my grade school the other children began teasing me and a classmate, Michael, who was Chinese. Based on our racial similarities, they joked that we were dating. I was horrified to have my classmates group me with this Chinese boy. I took offense, and from that moment on I tried to distance myself from Michael. I thought that if I were friends with him then the Chinese in me would be brought to the surface – made more obvious – and that would be *the* reason we were friends. There were only three Asians in my grade school, and we were two of them; the only other was my best friend, Cassie, who was also *hapa,* or of mixed Asian/Pacific Islander descent.[3] Cassie had a white mother and a Japanese father, who owned a Japanese restaurant downtown, and was therefore never around her house at the same time as any of her friends. She passed as white, and without her father around to connote her Japanese ancestry, her identity was never at issue. Curiously, never once in my eight-year friendship with her did we ever discuss our similar racial identities.

When a few years later I began reading feminist books, I developed a feminist consciousness that consumed all aspects of my life. It fundamentally changed the way I understood myself and the world around me. I was ignited and passionate, seeking out feminist organizations where I could take part in concrete actions around my political philosophy. Yet the literature I read lacked a racial analysis, and this carried over into my developing consciousness. I had moved to Seattle to attend college, and I became active with the National Organization of Women (NOW), Clinic Defense Project, a youth socialist organization, and a queer youth group based in Spokane. I traveled between Seattle and Spokane a great deal and was politically active in both cities. I began to meet many people whose politics and sexual orientation were diverse, and I questioned my own long-held beliefs. My new roommate came out as a lesbian, and we learned a great deal about each other through that experience. She was also a hapa – mixed Hawaiian, Filipina, and white – and she would attempt to engage in racial identity conversations, but that topic did not hold me as much as discussions of politics and sexuality. I had begun to question my sexual orientation: I no longer proclaimed myself heterosexual, yet neither did I adopt a lesbian identity.

As I had years earlier agonized between the choice of seeing myself as Chinese or white, I now agonized between the choice of lesbian or straight. I knew that neither choice represented my feelings, yet I could not comprehend another option. The messages that I received from both the lesbian community and dominant straight society was the same: choose. When I was in college, at around the age of seventeen, I realized that bisexuality existed as an option, and immediately I knew that was the identity that most accurately described who I felt I was. But I also knew that claiming a bisexual identity would be a hardship because others would analyze me through their monosexual template of understanding. Indeed I ran across many people who demanded to know, "Which do you *really* like better, boys or girls?" This question reminded me of how my ethnic identity had often elicited the query, "What are you?" People were again confused. Now both my racial and sexual identity crossed lines of demarcation, enacting border-crossings that people have assumed are unnatural and problematic.

Root suggests that the "racially mixed woman may be more open to exploring sexual orientation" because of their lived experience of understanding racial identity as complex. Therefore, this understanding of racial identity may "transfer over to viewing sexual orientation as flexible and sexual identity as *mutable*."[4] Throughout my life I have had to explain my racial identity instead of having an easy and ready-made label like most monoracials. Yet, besides the occasional difficulty of explaining my race, I also enjoyed being more than one, having more options, and enjoying the benefit of traveling in more than one group. Now with my emerging sexuality, bisexuality seemed the natural conclusion. Already I was racially mixed and therefore I could understand the meaning of a bisexual identity in my own life. Somehow it all came together in a complementary fashion.

After I had come out as bisexual I began to embrace my Asian heritage and accept it back into my life. I was in my senior year at Eastern Washington University, and I began to focus my research on Asian American women and their history. Yet it was not until I went to graduate school in women's studies at San Diego State University that I gained greater exposure to Asian American culture and history. It was an awakening that I compare to the development of my feminist consciousness. I was both excited to find the material and angered that it had taken so long to discover Asian American history. I wrote on the Japanese internment, studied Chinese American history, and read every Asian American studies book I could find.

Slowly I discovered that, although I could relate to some of the issues and material, my reality as a young bisexual hapa woman was not being addressed. I began to question the place of the multiracial Asian in the academic fields of ethnic studies and women's studies. Ethnic studies seemed to focus overwhelmingly on families that fit a specific model – namely, a heterosexual family made up of two immigrant parents of the same ethnicity and the conflicts their children face negotiating between their Asian parents and Anglo society. In women's studies, there was an awareness and commentary on race and difference among women, but that usually focused on the black – white racial dichotomy; Asian American women were rarely mentioned. Where was I to find myself represented in academic theory that claimed to represent women and racial minorities? As I studied further, however, I became aware that I was not the only one grappling with these issues: there were hapa groups forming around the country as well as magazines and books that were addressing this issue and demanding acceptance within the Asian American community and academy.[5]

My challenge in graduate school, as I saw it, was to explore where I could find myself reflected, with all my complexity, in the literature of ethnic studies and women's studies. As Dana Y. Takagi suggests, it is crucial to recognize "different sexual practices and identities that also claim the label Asian American" in order to begin to challenge notions of identity that have, in the past, been accepted "unproblematically and uncritically in Asian American Studies."[6] Within the "Asian American experience" there is a great deal of diversity that has thus far remained underexplored. Issues of interracial relationships, transracial adoption, biracial identity, and queer identity have remained marginalized and considered exceptions to an unspoken norm of Asian American identity. David Eng and Alice Hom believe it is imperative "to recognize that Asian Americans are never purely, or merely, racial subjects" and to dissolve any rigid or monolithic definitions.[7] Once monolithic norms are instituted, diversity and complexity are shut out and remain excluded.

I have seen these norms instituted in a variety of ways within identity base groups in my experiences. Organizations and literature on identity deemphasize aspects that are not considered directly related to the main unifying force they address. I have found myself continuing this silence when in group situations because of the offhanded manner in which comments regarding these other aspects are received. For example, I have usually found myself to be the only Asian American in queer organizations; therefore I feel uncomfortable bringing attention to racial issues because this would presumably turn me into both an object of curiosity and an educator. I prefer to discuss racial issues with others who have similar experiences so that we can share on an equal basis and validate each other in respectful and mutual ways. At the same time, when I am in organizations that focus on racial identity, I also feel silence around sexual identity because, again, I do not want to position myself as an object or educator. In other words, I do not want to detract from my connection with others. Unfortunately, connection is usually based on one issue, with other aspects of identity being minimized instead of validated.[8]

Segregating multiple identities in theories of race and gender results in fracturing self-understanding – separating one's gender from race and sexuality. This segregation is also an impossibility: at any moment we inhabit all of our identities and may face discrimination on any or all levels. It is a painful experience to seek out a community based on race, gender, or sexuality only to have other identities denied and rejected. As Karen Maeda Allman reasons, "Mixed-race lesbians may be suspicious of any kind of identity politics based on single-group membership, whether based on race, gender, or sexual orientation. Too many opportunities exist to exclude us, to declare us as suspect *others*."[9] When people of color come out as queer, race is an important consideration. Rejection from one's racial/ethnic community based on homophobia, and from the queer community based on racism, is a very real consequence that may bar individuals from true acceptance in any specific community. As a hapa bisexual, I am constantly seeking out inclusion and acceptance of my sexuality in the Asian American community as well as acceptance of my racial identity in the bisexual and queer community.

Paula C. Rust comments that "a positive integration of one's racial, ethnic, or class identity with one's sexual identity is greatly facilitated by support from others who share an individual's particular constellation of identities."[10] The first time I experienced being around others with my "constellation of identities" was when I attended the second national conference of the Asian and Pacific-Islander Lesbian and Bisexual Women's Network at UCLA in July of 1998. One of the workshops at this conference was titled "Mixed Girls in the Mix: Hapas, Mixed Breeds, and Other Racial Misfits." Attending this session was a homecoming for me. Never before had I sat in a room filled with hapas who were both bisexual and lesbian. Of the twenty-plus attendees at the workshop, there was a vast array of racial and ethnic diversity. Half of the women were Asian and white, while the other half of the room represented a great diversity of mixed-race hapa women. We explored and discussed numerous issues, and for many of us it was an amazing and eye-opening experience merely to be around other women with whom we had so much in common – and yet still so much in difference. The workshop went overtime, making it very evident that this group needed more time together. Therefore the group decided to create a hapa caucus. Later that evening when the caucuses met, some of the women chose to go to the caucus groups of their ethnicities and some returned to the hapa caucus; we again had to choose between identifying as hapa over our monoethnic options.

I met several women in this newly formed caucus who also identified as both biracial and bisexual. When I mentioned that I was doing research on biracial and bisexual Asian women, one of the women exclaimed, "The bi-bi girls!" and went on to explain that she herself was a "bi-bi girl" as were some of her friends. I was overflowing with excitement to meet someone who shared my same "constellation of identities" and had even coined a term for this identity.

Rust speaks to this topic of the "bi-bi" identity: "Many bisexuals of mixed race or ethnicity feel a comfortable resonance between their mixed heritage and their bisexuality. In a society where both racial-ethnic and sexual categories are highly elaborated, individuals of mixed heritage or who are bisexual find themselves straddling categories that are socially constructed as distinct from one another."[11] Rust captures the ideological and theoretical similarities of bisexual and multiracial identities in this passage, echoing my own experiences of these two identities. Because of the exclusion bisexuals and biracials experience in monoracial and monosexual communities, different responses result when these mixed identities come together in the same individual. For some, this combination brings a sense of familiarity, of being once again outside of the box, of confusing people. Others, however, may be disappointed that they are again marginalized, unwilling to deal with further oppression.

When I think that I must choose between another set of boxes – straight or lesbian – I feel the same pressure and the same inability as I felt choosing between white and Chinese, between my mother and my father. My choice was made for me. It was written on my skin; my face and gestures reflect both parents who made me. And the choice of who I love is decided for me: I love both my mother and my father and will never deny love and acceptance for someone based on their gender or race. Marian M. Sciachitano believes that "taking up a bicultural and biracial politics of difference" means accepting "the contradictions, the uneasiness, and the ambiguity" of such an identity, which may also apply to a bisexual label and the interaction of the two.[12] Yet the contradictions, uneasiness, and ambiguity are imposed from the outside and arise when I must fit myself into the established mutually exclusive order. For myself, I find comfort in the middle ground, in the ability to transgress and question lines of demarcation and challenge systematic segregation.

I am hapa because I am the descendent of two cultures, two languages, and two people who came together across these boundaries. I am firmly located in the late twentieth century in the United States, where interracial marriages have only been legal for a generation. I am one of many people who are hapa, Amerasian, mixed breeds, and mutts. I am constantly called Japanese, Korean, Chinese, Oriental. I am comfortable in other people's discomfort. I am hurt that I denied my mother a proper place in my life. She has divorced my father and has gone to live with Chinese female friends from her childhood, her other life within which I will never be truly included. When I visit her I am left out of the conversation, but the sound of Cantonese soothes me. Sometimes when I pay attention I realize that I am able to follow their body language and remember some Chinese words, but it is the English phrases that are a part of their Chinese American vocabulary that always give me the final gist. I am loyal to my Chinese heritage, I am loyal to my white heritage, and I am loyal to my antiracist beliefs.

I am bisexual because I recognize that both women and men have contributed to my life and I want the freedom to choose a partner based on a person's integrity rather than on genitalia. I am firmly located not only in a time when queer people are oppressed but also in a time when a vital queer community has developed that gives me the ability to understand what that identity means. I am one of many people who are bisexual, queer, fence sitters, and switch hitters. I am called queer, dyke, straight. I am comfortable in other people's discomfort. I am loyal to my love for women, I am loyal to my love for men, and I am loyal to my beliefs in feminism and antiheterosexism.

The question that still lingers in my mind is who will be loyal to me? Which group/community/movement(s) will claim me as their member and comrade? I want to see a movement against oppression that does not trivialize or deny me any aspect of my identity, that recognizes the interconnectedness of my sexuality, race, gender, and politics. I am one of many people whose fight against oppression does not end with their gender, race, or sexuality alone. I am reminded of the words of Teresa Kay Williams: "One day, the debate on passing will become obsolete (will pass), when Asian-descent multiracials can express the full range of their humanity in which boundaries of race, ethnicity, nation, class, gender, sexuality, body, and language can be crossed and transgressed without judgement, without scorn, and without detriment."[13] I find a great deal of comfort reading these words by authors whose identities are similar to my own. I know that I am not alone in this world that consistently tries to deny the existence of multiracials and bisexuals. Merely by existing I am challenging stereotypes and the status quo. This battle against racism, sexism, and bi/homophobia is being fought on many fronts by people who are like me, people who have my back.

NOTES

1. Claire Huang Kinsley, "Questions People Have Asked Me. Questions I Have Asked Myself," in *Miscegenation Blues: Voices of Mixed Race Women,* ed. Carol Camper (Toronto: Sister Vision Press, 1994), 113–32.

2. Maria P. P. Root, "Resolving 'Other' Status: Identity Development of Biracial Individuals," in *Diversity and Complexity in Feminist Therapy,* ed. Laura S. Brown and Maria P. P. Root (New York: Harrington Park Press, 1990), 197, original emphasis.

3. A term of Hawaiian origin, *hapa haole* literally means "half outsider," or half white. Although it was originally used as an insult, it is currently being used on the mainland by Asian/Pacific Islanders as a positive term designating those who are mixed race of Asian/Pacific Islander descent.

4. Root, "Resolving 'Other' Status," 185, original emphasis.

5. Overwhelmingly I find that Asian American literature does not mention non-heterosexual identities, which continues to promote invisibility for queer Asians. A few notable exceptions are Russel Leong, ed., *Asian American Sexualities: Dimensions of the Gay and Lesbian Experience* (New York: Routledge, 1996); Sharon Lim-Hing, ed., *The Very Inside: An Anthology of Writings by Asian and Pacific Islander Lesbian and Bisexual Women* (Toronto: Sister Vision Press, 1994); and David L. Eng and Alice Y. Hom, eds., *Q&A: Queer in Asian America* (Philadelphia: Temple University Press, 1998).

6. Dana Y. Takagi, "Maiden Voyage: Excursion into Sexuality and Identity Politics in Asian America," *Amerasia Journal* 20:1 (1994): 2.

7. David L. Eng and Alice Y. Hom, "Introduction: Q & A: Notes on a Queer Asian America," in Eng and Hom, *Q&A*, 3.

8. I did discover, however, an emerging discussion on multiple identities and their necessary inclusion in feminist research. Through such books as Gloria Anzaldúa, ed., *Making Face, Making Soul/Haciendo Caras: Creative and Critical Perspectives by Feminists of Color* (San Francisco: Aunt Lute, 1990); Gloria Anzaldúa and Cherríe Moraga, *This Bridge Called My Back: Writings by Radical Women of Color* (Watertown MA: Persephone Press, 1981); and Asian Women United of California, ed., *Making Waves: An Anthology of Writings by and about Asian American Women* (Boston: Beacon Press, 1989), the voices of women of color and lesbians are emerging. Indeed, the postmodern phase we are in has pushed the concept of difference to buzz word status. Yet, although frequently mentioned, difference is yet to be completely integrated.

9. Karen Maeda Allman, "(Un)Natural Boundaries: Mixed Race, Gender, and Sexuality," in *The Multiracial Experience: Racial Borders as the New Frontier*, ed. Maria P. P. Root (Thousand Oaks CA: Sage, 1996), 287, emphasis original.

10. Paula C. Rust, "Managing Multiple Identities: Diversity Among Bisexual Women and Men," in *Bisexuality: The Psychology and Politics of an Invisible Minority*, ed. Beth A. Firestein (Thousand Oaks CA: Sage, 1996), 254.

11. Rust, "Managing Multiple Identities," 69–70.

12. Marian M. Sciachitano, "Claiming a Politics of Biracial Asian American Difference," in *A Gathering of Voices on the Asian American Experience*, ed. Annette White-Parks, et al. (Fort Atkinson WI: Highsmith Press, 1994), 52.

13. Teresa Kay Williams, "Race-ing and Being Raced: The Critical Interrogation of 'Passing,'" *Amerasia Journal* 23:1 (1997): 64.

Frontiers 21:1/2 (2000): 171–80.

Contributors

PIYA CHATTERJEE is a social anthropologist and associate professor of women's studies at the University of California, Riverside. Her first book, *A Time for Tea: Women, Labor and Post/Colonial Politics on an Indian Plantation,* was published by Duke University Press in 2001. She writes on feminist ethnography, radical pedagogy, and women's labor and organizing in South Asia. More recently, she has worked on Third World women's politics within the United States.

JUDY CHU was elected to the California State Assembly on May 15, 2001. She represents a southern California district that includes Alhambra City Terrace, parts of East Los Angeles, El Sereno, Monterey Park, Rosemead, and San Gabriel. In addition, she has been active in numerous social service organizations. She is a founder and past president of the Asian Youth Center, a San Gabriel Valley agency helping potentially at-risk immigrant youth adjust to life in America. Chu is also a founding board member of the Greater San Gabriel Valley Community Development Corporation, which helps "nearly bankable" businesses and the "Christmas in April – Monterey Park," a program that provides housing rehabilitation for low-income families. She received the Outstanding Founders Award for her work in founding the Asian Youth Center.

SHELLI B. FOWLER is an associate professor of English and comparative American cultures at Washington State University. Her research is interdisciplinary, and she teaches and publishes in the areas of African American literature and critical pedagogy. She has been the recipient of numerous teaching awards, including the Sahlin Faculty Award in Instruction and the William F. Mullen Excellence in Teaching Award. She was named the Lewis F. and Stella G. Buchanan Scholar in English at Washington State University from 1998 to 2001.

LESLIE A. ITO received her undergraduate degree in American studies at Mount Holyoke College and her master's degree in Asian American studies from University of California, Los Angeles. She is the author of *Japanese American during World War II: A Selected, Annotated Bibliography of Materials Available at UCLA* and "Nisei Students Relocation Commemorative Fund," an afterword to *Storied Lives: Japanese American Students and World War II* by Gary Y. Okihiro. From 1998 to 2000, Ito was a program associate in the Education, Media, Arts, and Culture Division of the Ford Foundation in New York. She has also worked in several Asian Pacific American arts and cultural organizations in Los Angelesand is now the director of program development at Visual Communications in Los Angeles, the nation's first Asian American media arts organization.

NHI T. LIEU graduated from the University of California, San Diego, with an undergraduate degree in history and women's studies. She is a Ph.D. candidate in the Program in American Culture at the University of Michigan. She lives in Chicago, where she is completing a doctoral dissertation that explores multiple sites of diasporic Vietnamese niche media and cultural production and their relationship to the formation of contemporary Vietnamese American identities.

TIFFANY ANA LÓPEZ is an associate professor of English at the University of California, Riverside, and director of Chicano Arts & Social Action (CASA). Her publications include *Growing Up Chicana/o* and the forthcoming *Alchemy of Blood: Critical Witnessing in U.S. Latina Drama.* Her articles include "Violent Inscriptions: Writing the Body and Making Community in Four Plays by Migdalia Cruz," in *Theater Journal,* and "A New Mestiza Primer: Borderlands Philosophy in the Children's Books of Gloria Anzaldúa," in *Such News of the Land: American Women Nature Writers.* She is editorial advisor to *American Theater Journal,* an editorial board member for *Aztlan: A Journal of Chicano Studies,* and cochair of the Latina/o literature affiliate for the American Literature Association.

VALERIE MATSUMOTO teaches history and Asian American studies at the

University of California, Los Angeles. She is the author of *Farming the Home Place: A Japanese American Community in California, 1919–1982*, and coeditor of *Over the Edge: Remapping the American West*. She is presently writing a book on Nisei women and the creation of urban youth culture in Los Angeles during the Jazz Age and the Great Depression.

MARIAN SCIACHITANO teaches courses on contemporary Asian American women writers and filmmakers, feminist theory, global feminism, and "Third World" women and film for the Department of Women's Studies at Washington State University. She has been a member of the *Frontiers: A Journal of Women Studies* collective since 1994. Her research interests include the mail-order bride industry on the Internet, transnational feminist theory, and the politics of representation by women of color filmmakers.

KATHRYN W. SHANLEY is an enrolled Assiniboine from the Fort Peck Reservation in Montana. She earned a Ph.D. in English literature and language from the University of Michigan in 1987, with a focus on the study of American Indian and Third World literatures. She has published widely in the field of American Indian literary criticism, writing about such authors as James Welch, Maria Campbell, Leslie Silko, N. Scott Momaday, Linda Hogan, and Thomas King. Most recently, Shanley edited a special edition of *Paradoxa Journal of World Literary Genres* titled "Native American Literature: Boundaries and Sovereignties." Shanley serves as chair of the Native American Studies Department at the University of Montana.

CAROLINE CHUNG SIMPSON is the author of *An Absent Presence: Japanese Americans in the Making of Postwar American Culture, 1945–1961*. She is an associate professor at the University of Washington in Seattle.

DEBBIE STORRS is a faculty member in the Department of Sociology and Anthropology at the University of Idaho. She teaches courses on race and ethnic relations, gender and sexuality, and social stratification. Her research interest is the construction, maintenance, and performance of identities. Her research has focused on mixed race, contemporary white, and Asian identities.

PAMELA THOMA teaches Asian American studies, women's cultural studies and literature, and feminist theory at Colby College. She is at work on a project exploring a transnational feminist politics of consumption in Asian American women's cultural production.

BEVERLY YUEN THOMPSON is a Ph.D. student in sociology at the New School University, focusing her research on anticorporate activism. She is working on a book on the U.S. anticorporate globalization movement and on the use of direct action within jails and courts. She also works as a project manager at City University of New York Graduate Center for the Scholar-Practitioner Project, which studies the impact of welfare reform on communities of color in the Lower East Side of Manhattan and in Harlem. She resides in New York.

SUZAN RUTH TRAVIS-ROBYNS is a charter schools specialist at Northern Michigan University in Marquette, Michigan, where she teaches labor history. She specializes in working with Native American and African American schools. She is a photojournalist specializing in taking pictures of girls.

CHARLENE TUNG is an assistant professor in the Women's and Gender Studies Department at Sonoma State University. She teaches feminist theories, gender and globalization, and race, class and gender courses. She is currently working on a book manuscript on Filipina migrant careworkers in California. Her current research looks at "border transgressions" within Asian Pacific America, including an oral history project on Taiwanese women's migration through the Americas and an analysis of gender and race in popular culture.

AKI UCHIDA received her Ph.D. in speech communication from the University of Illinois at Urbana-Champaign in 1997. She has lectured in the communication department at the University of California, San Diego, and provides Japanese-English and English-Japanese translations for law firms, corporations, and universities. She has published articles in *Language in Society; The Howard Journal of Communications; Women and Language;* and *Women's Studies International Forum.*

LINDA TRINH VÕ received her Ph.D. in sociology from the University of California, San Diego, and is an assistant professor in the Department of Asian American Studies at the University of California, Irvine. She was a recipient of the UC Humanities Research Institute Fellowship and the UC Berkeley Chancellor's Postdoctoral Fellowship. She has published essays in *Asian and Latino Immigrants in a Restructuring Economy: The Metamorphosis of*

Southern California; *Gender Mosaics: Social Perspectives*; *Asian American Studies: A Reader*; and *Cultural Compass: Ethnographic Explorations of Asian America*. She is working on a book manuscript, "Constructing Asian America: Identity, Community, and Organization," a special issue for *Amerasia Journal*, and a new research project on Asian American communities in Orange County. She is a board member of the Orange County Asian and Pacific Islander Community Alliance, a nonprofit organization that works on education, youth, healthcare, and public policy issues.

TRAISE YAMAMOTO is an associate professor of English at the University of California, Riverside. She is the author of *Masking Selves, Making Subjects: Japanese American Women, Identity, and the Body* and has written articles that have appeared in *positions: east asia cultures critique*; *Signs*; and *The Journal of Asian American Studies*. Her fiction and poetry have appeared in numerous small magazines and journals, and she is one of the poets featured in a forthcoming documentary, *Between the Lines: Asian American Women Poets*. She is at work on a book of essays on Asian American feminisms.

JUDY YUNG is chair and professor of American studies at the University of California, Santa Cruz. She is the coauthor of *Island: Poetry and History of Chinese Immigrants at Angel Island, 1910–1940*, and the author of *Unbound Feet: A Social History of Chinese Women in San Francisco* and *Unbound Voices: A Documentary History of Chinese Women in San Francisco*, in which Flora Belle Jan's writings appear. A revised version of "A Bowlful of Tears" will appear in a forthcoming anthology edited by Shirley Hune and Gail Nomura.

Index